A Woman's War Too

U.S. Women in the Military in World War II

Edited by
Paula Nassen Poulos

National Archives and Records Administration

Washington, DC

Published for the
National Archives and Records Administration
By the National Archives Trust Fund Board
1996

Library of Congress Cataloging-in-Publication Data
A woman's war too : U.S. women in the military in World War II / edited by Paula
Nassen Poulos.
    p. cm.
    Papers presented at a conference entitled "A Woman's War Too: U.S. Women in the
Military in World War II," held in Mar. 1995.
    Includes bibliographical references and index.
    ISBN 1-880875-09-8
    1. World War, 1939–1945—Women—United States—Congresses.
2. United States—Armed Forces—Women—Congresses. I. Poulos,
Paula Nassen.
D810.W7W65 1996
940.54'0973'082—dc20   95-50372
                                                 CIP

The paper used in this publication meets the minimum requirements of the American
National Standard for Permanence of Paper for Printed Library Materials Z39.48-1984.

Cover: "For your country's sake today . . ." Poster by Steele Savage, 1944. Records of the
Office of Government Reports (44-PA-820)

CONTENTS

LIST OF ILLUSTRATIONS

PREFACE

In times of war and conflict, Americans seem to exhibit a heightened sense of patriotism and duty. Our nation's focus and response never seem to be sharper than when we, as citizens, are called upon to protect and defend the ideals that we value. On March 3-4, 1995, a diverse audience gathered at the National Archives and Records Administration for a conference, "A Woman's War Too: U.S. Women in the Military in World War II," to commemorate the actions of the servicewomen who volunteered more than 50 years ago, at the risk of their lives, to help safeguard the principles of democracy that we all treasure.

It is vital for us as a nation to remember, to carefully and deliberately recall the courage, sacrifices, triumphs, and losses of the women who served in the war. We do this best through the records we keep.

This conference served as a reminder of how important it is to maintain a meaningful historical record of persons and events to document and teach us about our national experience. Saving the documentary evidence of the American past means preserving the stories of ordinary individuals as well as of generals and admirals and other officials. We at the National Archives and Records Administration work to ensure that the evidence of American participation in the war, and the record of the American experience in general, are preserved and readily accessible.

Much of the essential documentation of the military service of women in World War II can be found in the holdings of the National Archives. I hope you will examine for yourselves the record of the wartime activities of these citizens as they interacted with the federal government. Perhaps you will investigate Record Group 52 (Records of the Bureau of Medicine and Surgery), where you will find the three-page roster of Army and Navy nurses who lost their lives in service—a roster in which the small print of the names, addresses, and next of kin stand in stark contrast with the largeness of its impact.

You might go to another folder in that same record group where, in a one-paragraph biography, you will note significant events that took place between 1913 and 1946 in the life of a young lieutenant in the Navy Nurse Corps. You will see first one official photograph, then another, then another, together with a memorandum requesting that the photographs be forwarded to the Nurse Corps Office. But what will most likely hold your attention will be the three unidentified newspaper clippings, probably dated March 1945. One headline reads "Nurse Home from Los Baños Anxious to Resume Duties," and under the picture as she steps from the plane, the words "[she] surprises mother." A second article is entitled "Bronze Star Medal Awarded Nurse Who Had Duty Here," while the third announces "Navy Nurse Patient Spent Three Years as Jap Prisoner." You will read about her day-to-day camp life, food, clothes, and the dramatic rescue from the camp by the rangers she describes as "those Americans [who] looked so big and so fat and so good," while she herself had lost 25 pounds. I will not continue her story here; Mary Harrington Nelson will tell you herself in the pages that follow.

Other records are more impersonal in nature and reflect complex administrative issues that each of the women's service branches faced as they struggled to find their organizational niche and carry out their mission—first outside, then within the male military establishment. Here you might turn to Record Group 165 (Records of the War Department General and Special Staffs) to review "A National Study of Attitudes Toward the Women's Army Corps" prepared for the corps in October 1943 by the Research Department of the Young & Rubicam advertising company. In it, you will read the responses of the two groups that were interviewed—first, women considered eligible for the WAC, and second, parents of daughters considered to be possible recruits.

Or you might examine a 63-page green binder in Record Group 24 (Records of the Bureau of Naval Personnel) with the imposing title, "Policies for the Administration of the Women's Reserve, United States Naval Reserve," that governed the organization's operation as of November 1, 1945. Penciled across the top of the cover page are these words, "Captain Mildred McAfee in charge of WAVES."

There is, of course, so much more. The conference speakers have taken the lead in searching for these and other documents—in whatever form they exist—at the National Archives and in military historical centers and numerous manuscript repositories across the country. But there are more stories to be found, especially in the multitude of unpublished veterans' experiences not yet recorded for us to see and to hear.

By coming together for this conference, we highlighted the achievements of World War II servicewomen and focused attention on the evidence that documented their experiences. Through publication of the conference proceedings, we provide even greater access to the record of their contributions. This volume constitutes but one piece of a lasting tribute to all of the brave women who served the United States in the Second World War.

John W. Carlin
Archivist of the United States

INTRODUCTION

In 1967 the National Archives launched a series of conferences for the greater research community to discuss significant historical events and themes depicted in the nation's records. In this tradition, veterans, historians, documentary researchers, educators, and students of American history came together from across the country in March 1995 to participate in a major conference, "A Woman's War Too: U.S. Women in the Military in World War II."

This conference was part of the National Archives' 4-year nationwide observance of the 50th anniversary of U.S. participation in the war. Throughout the commemorative period, the National Archives employed exhibits, films, dramatic and musical performances, publications, lectures, and scholarly programs to educate the public about its extensive wartime holdings, further knowledge of the war through documentary sources, and honor those who served in this global conflict.

Although 50 years have passed since World War II, the story of the more than 350,000 women who volunteered to serve in the Armed Forces of the United States has not been widely told. Existing accounts reveal a compelling and complex story with intricate plots, subplots, and some very memorable characters. High drama is evident in the women's efforts to create units of their own in each of the service branches and integrate them into the traditional military. And inextricably woven through the storyline are the unrelenting realities and emotions of war. The fuller story of this watershed event, however, remains to be explored; its information, interest, and historical nuances, to be mined and made known.

Recognizing this need, the National Archives sought to provide a forum in which conferees could examine U.S. women's military service in the Allied war effort from its different perspectives. The program was designed to include a broad range of topics and speakers representative of the military service branches. Leading figures in women's and military studies, social and military historians, document specialists, and women veterans were invited to lead the discussion.

Drawing upon their rich diversity of experience and knowledge, speakers identified and analyzed published and unpublished sources documenting governmental policy affecting the role and status of servicewomen both during the war and after; the countless contributions and sacrifices made by women in providing medical, training, and support services in all branches of the military and in all theaters of operation; and the personal experiences of women both within the ranks and as veterans. Special emphasis was placed on the means used to collect, preserve, and publish the women's record of their service and the wide variety of primary sources available for research and education. The Honorable Sheila E. Widnall, Secretary of the Air Force and first woman to head that branch of the U.S. Armed Forces, delivered the keynote address and provided a broad context for the conference topic. Sessions concluded with a lively exchange of information and ideas between the panels of presenters and the audience.

It has been encouraging to veterans and scholars alike to witness the increased interest and research in women's military history sparked by the events commemorating the 50th anniversary of the war. The challenge remains to sustain this interest and continue this work beyond the conferences, observances, and lifetimes of those who served. If the challenge goes unmet, the history of these servicewomen's contributions in the conflict will fade from public memory as surely as such history in previous wars.

The key to our remembering is the creation and retention of documentary evidence. But complicating factors stand in the way. Although many veterans have published their memoirs and given oral history interviews, thousands of others have never recorded their stories. Although scholarly research has been pursued, scores of subjects have yet to be investigated. Unless and until narrated accounts, primary source collections, artifacts, and publications are preserved by trained archivists, curators, librarians, and historians—in usable form—and then tapped through research, they will not have an enduring place in history.

This volume of conference papers is being published by the National Archives as both a permanent record of the proceedings and a select guide to resources. It is divided into seven sections consisting of the keynote address and papers based on presentations in six sessions. The section titles convey the major themes: "Setting the Stage," "Making History: Women, the Military, and Society," "Contributing to the War Effort," "Confronting the Realities of

Service Life," "Documenting Women's Service: Memoirs, Museums, Historical Collections," "Documenting Women's Service: National Archives and Records Administration," and "Leading the Way." Each section is prefaced by an introductory statement. These papers are intended to enrich historical scholarship and invigorate the interdisciplinary study of topics in military, women's, and social history.

The length and style of these papers were determined by the speakers as their topics warranted. Military service acronyms have been treated in accordance with the *Government Printing Office Style Manual*. For example, a distinction in capitalization has been made between the acronym referring to a military unit for women (all capital letters, *e.g.,* WAC [Women's Army Corps], WAVES [Women Accepted for Volunteer Emergency Service], WASP [Women Airforce Service Pilots]) and the acronym referring to members of a particular unit (initial capital letter, *e.g.,* a Wac, 15 Spars, a Wave, 6 Wasps on duty). While the acronym for the Marine Corps Women's Reserve is appropriately MCWR, the popular name for individual members during the war was women Marines, which had no associated acronym. A list of frequently used acronyms appears toward the end of the volume.

In conjunction with the conference, the National Archives put on display a small photographic exhibit, "For Her Country," in honor of the women who served in the U.S. Armed Forces during the war. It represented a significant sample of the thousands of images of servicewomen making contributions to the war effort that are available for research in the holdings of the National Archives Still Picture Branch. The curator was Marilyn Paul, and the designer was Michael Jackson, both staff members of the Office of Public Programs. Captioned photographs from this exhibit appear interspersed throughout the text and on the cover of the volume.

The pictures in this publication, with a few exceptions noted in the captions, are from the holdings of the National Archives. To the best of our knowledge, they are in the public domain and have no restrictions on their use. Black-and-white photographic reproductions of the pictures may be obtained for a fee from commercial photographers participating in the National Archives' vendor reproduction program. Color photographic reproductions of the posters are also available. Prints, negatives, and slides of all of the pictures may be ordered in various sizes for differing fees depending on the medium and the vendor. For further information on using photographs obtained from the National Archives and for ordering instructions and price lists, please write to the Reference Staff, Still Picture Branch (NNSP), National Archives and Records Administration, 8601 Adelphi Road, College Park, MD 20740-6001.

The bulk of Army Air Forces photography for World War II, including that of the Women Airforce Service Pilots (WASP), is presently on loan to the Smithsonian Institution's Air and Space Museum. Photographs of Wasps may be ordered by writing to the Archives Division, National Air and Space Museum, Smithsonian Institution, Washington, DC 20560. It will be necessary to obtain permission from that office before photographs may be used.

The National Archives gratefully acknowledges Somerset House Publishing, in association with Sandra Kuck, and The Foundation for the National Archives for their support of this conference. Ms. Kuck, artist and Navy Wave (1966–67), designated a portion of the royalties from her five-print series, *Special Moments: Memories of the American Woman,* for this conference.

Appreciation is also extended to the dedicated staff members and volunteers of the National Archives who worked to ensure a productive conference and presentation of papers in this volume. The efforts of Linda N. Brown, now retired Assistant Archivist for Public Programs and leading advocate for the conference, are especially recognized.

As readers join the conference dialogue through the pages of this publication, the tribute to the courageous servicewomen, and men, of World War II continues. Through this studied effort we remember. We pledge not to forget.

Paula Nassen Poulos
Conference Director and Editor

SETTING THE STAGE

WOMEN IN THE MILITARY
A Perspective From the
Air Force

The Honorable Sheila E. Widnall
Secretary of the Air Force

It is truly an honor to be part of this conference. As I see it, I stand here because of the contributions of the women we are honoring at the conference. Their dedication in defending our country blazed the way for later generations to take more active roles in government, in business, and in the military.

In February 1995, at the Air Force Association Meeting in Florida, I saw firsthand how far we had come. I shared the stage with Jeanne Flynn, our first F-15 fighter pilot; Jackie Parker, our first Air National Guard F-16 fighter pilot; and Sue Helms, our first Air Force astronaut. They represented the dedication and commitment of military women today and the promise of increased choices for tomorrow.

So it is easy for me to start off your discussions of military women in World War II by talking about the current role and status of women in the military. In fact, I am happy to help recount this marvelous success story and give you an up-to-the-minute reading, based on what I see in the Air Force.

In a sentence, the role of military women is to serve their country in whatever capacity they can, without artificial barriers based solely on gender. And I am pleased to say that women are widely accepted and respected as capable members of the force. As former Defense Secretary Dick Cheney said at the end of the war in the Persian Gulf, we could not have won the war without women. And we are not just talking about participation from the sidelines. By 1990 women were so integrated into our armed forces that their involvement in combat was inevitable and unavoidable.

Women in the military have made important gains over the past 50 years. Their story is one of persistence and courage, despite numerous frustrations. I have an affinity for this group since my story is similar, only on a smaller scale.

When I arrived as a freshman at the Massachusetts Institute of Technology, I was one of 20 women in a class of 900. In those days women constituted less than 1 percent of the engineering profession. Only half the women in my class actually graduated. Only a couple of us went on to graduate school. Now 35 percent of undergraduates at MIT are women. We've come a long way, *but we could always go further.*

I have been passionately involved in encouraging women and minorities to participate in the scientific and technical fields. And I have worked hard to reshape academic programs to allow women and men to work together. My goal was the establishment of a professional and human climate built on mutual respect. So I was elated to be appointed as head of the Air Force and to bring my experiences to the strongly maintained traditions of the military.

I assumed my position in 1993, a year when the Air Force opened combat cockpits to women and the first woman missile squadron commander assumed command. Among other duties, my job is to recruit and retain the highest quality people available to perform military missions. That boils down to tapping the best talents from a shrinking pool of young recruits. And they must be able to handle the jobs required by a military that grows smaller but more technologically demanding each day. Having almost all positions open to women makes our recruiting job much easier. For as most of you know, gender is rarely, if ever, the best criterion to determine who fills those jobs.

In the Air Force, we place a premium on using the range of our women members not because they are women but because they are 16 percent of the force and pivotal to readiness. Our record is outstanding. Over 99 percent of all Air Force career fields and positions are now open to women. The few positions that exclude women are connected to units that could be involved with direct ground combat.

Although the military services have had some bad examples of discrimination and harassment, we are dedicated to eliminating these problems. Over the past several months I have co-chaired a task force for the Department of Defense (DOD) to evaluate our existing practices and establish some basic principles for handling complaints. Obviously our ideal is an organization in which all members are valued, respected, and treated fairly.

This is extremely important because the number of women in uniform is growing. In 1994, 24 percent of all Air Force recruits were women. Eighteen percent of our junior officer corps is women. We cannot hope to move into the 21st century with confidence in our abilities if we fail to support such a large portion of our force. As we speak, women are walking through doors previously closed to them and proving their ability to contribute.

Since 1989 the percentage of women pilot trainees in the Air Force has nearly doubled. We now have 300 pilots, 100 navigators, and almost 600 enlisted aircrew members. In 1993 women were allowed for the first time to compete for combat cockpits. We already have 10 women pilots flying combat aircraft, with another 3 in training. And in February 1995, Lt. Col. Eileen Collins lifted off in STS63 as the first woman pilot of the space shuttle. These up-and-coming superstars-in-training build on the achievements of military women who have flown noncombat aircraft for some time.

We have come full circle since the days of Jackie Cochran and Nancy Love. But the circle has widened, and opportunities for women have increased with the changes in society, so I suppose the movement has been more like a spiral.

How did we get here? I would like to spend a few minutes touching on some of the key factors that led to this development.

I will not belabor the significant contributions women made during World War II. The conference papers discuss this in depth. Suffice it to say, women served long hours, in a wide variety of jobs, to help the military. All together, more than 350,000 women served in the military during the war, first in administrative or clerical fields, then in more nontraditional roles. Although the combat exclusion law was in effect, they were shot at, killed or wounded, and taken as prisoners of war.

Yet, as most of you know, at the war's end, only a handful were allowed to remain. In effect, the Pentagon and Congress told them to go home and do the dishes—which may have been fine for some, but certainly not for all. To keep them at home, Congress passed the Women's Armed Services Integration Act in 1948, which restricted the number of women to 2 percent of the total force and capped their rank at colonel, one per service.

During the Korean war, there was a small surge initially in the number of women in the military. But the Pentagon did not attempt to recruit many women since there was a large pool of draft-eligible males. So the increase in numbers was neither significant nor long term.

It was the Vietnam war that finally brought big changes in this situation. Women volunteered in larger numbers. As the war progressed, they were assigned to wartime operational commands and served in nontraditional fields such as intelligence, communications, and transportation.

In 1967 Congress finally removed the 2-percent ceiling on numbers and the grade limitations that previously applied to women. In 1969 the Air Force opened the first ROTC detachments to women cadets on a test basis. Two years later, after initial popularity and success, we opened all 154 detachments to women students. These days, 23 percent of our ROTC cadets are women.

Removing grade limitations also had its effect. In 1971 Col. Jeanne Holm was selected as the first Air Force woman general officer.

The end of the draft in 1973 created a climate of opportunity for women. Without a steady influx of young men, the services had to look elsewhere to recruit enough qualified, enthusiastic young people to fill their positions. Faced with the reality of numbers, gender took a back seat in determining qualification, and the percentage of women began to rise. The women's rights movement of the 1970s also had an impact. As women strove for equality, including the full rights and responsibilities of citizenship, many young women were encouraged to sign up.

We also saw a number of changes in Air Force policy during that decade, allowing for more equitable treatment between men and women. For example, women were no longer automatically discharged if they became pregnant or had adopted children or stepchildren. They also received benefits for their husbands that were in line with those received by Air Force wives.

In 1976 the service academies began admitting women. In another first, 10 young female lieutenants entered pilot training at Williams Air Force Base in Arizona. By the 1980s there were enough Air Force women flying to permit all-female crews. And as the Air Force realized that performance, not gender, is what counts when you put together an all-volunteer force, more and more positions opened up to women.

A lot of that change had to do with taking advantage of all the talent in our work force. Some of it had to do with the blurring of traditional front lines. The front line may be in the sea, air, or wherever a SCUD missile hits. No place is completely safe; bullets and missiles do not discriminate by gender. Women are often close to enemy fire. Primary targets in any war are the opposing side's supply and refueling capability as well as all military bases.

The contributions of our women were key to resolving the military crises of the 1980s. During the Grenada operation, women crewed airlifters and tankers. Seven women crewed the KC-135s that refueled the F-111s that raided Libya. Air Force women flew troops and supplies to Panama for Operation Just Cause.

Then came Desert Storm: 12,500 Air Force women deployed. They served in tanker, transport, and medical evacuation aircraft. They worked as munitions specialists and in aircraft maintenance. No Air Force woman saw direct combat, though 5 Army women were killed in action and 21 wounded—all the result of SCUD attacks, helicopter crashes, or mines. Two women were taken as prisoners of war. All the women in the Gulf endured the same hardships as men, served for the same principles, and played pivotal roles in the outcome. Since the Gulf war, the question of women in actual combat roles has come up again for serious soulsearching. As the saying goes, history might not repeat itself, but sometimes it rhymes.

Since Congress repealed the combat exclusion law in 1991 and left the policies up to DOD, we are guided by Secretary of Defense William Perry's decisions. In January 1994, he established a definition of direct ground combat and directed that only those positions involved in such combat could be closed to women. For the Air Force, that amounts to a bare handful of jobs, including air liaison officer, combat controller, and pararescue.

So the spiral grows ever wider. We are seeing a revolution in the military services because of increased competition in the range of jobs and specialties women may hold. This change will allow women to gain vital experience. It will also enable women to effectively compete for promotions and to be contenders for future three- and four-star combat commands and higher. We are seeing a shattering of the military glass ceiling, or glass canopy, as we say in the Air Force, that limited women of earlier generations. Across DOD, President Clinton's administration has made historic progress in bringing women into senior positions.

As women move into these leadership positions, they provide role models and encouragement for others to follow. And that brings me to what I see as as the biggest challenge for military women of the future: securing and succeeding in leadership positions.

That is, women will still have the personal challenges of juggling professional life, marriage, and family. They will have the cultural challenges of combining strength and sensitivity, projecting an image of confidence and competence. Their supervisors will still have the cultural challenge of recognizing women as soldiers, with the full range of capabilities and responsibilities expected of soldiers in their units. We have come a long way, but as I am sure you are aware, *we can and will go further.*

The opportunities that have been created by this widening spiral of career fields now lead to the challenge of career development and enhancement. In the Air Force, that means being selected for and successfully filling leadership positions. It also means training for and participating in combat positions, since many military leaders still view the crucible of combat as the true test of one's mettle.

In closing, I am encouraged by the young women I see day in and day out, eager to be judged as individuals by the same standards as men in any job for which they can qualify. I am encouraged by the changing attitudes of a new generation of leaders—including men who have daughters, wives, or sisters in the military and see no reason why they should not be able to go as far as their talents and hard work will take them.

Women have proven that they are ready, willing, and able to accept the risks and responsibilities of military service. Today they are building on the gains and successes of the dedicated, courageous women who made such important contributions during World War II. I am excited to be involved as this spiral continues to grow, changing our attitudes and perspectives, and ensuring that we have the best people available to support and defend our country in the 21st century.

MAKING HISTORY
Women, the Military, and Society

Women have played an important part in the American military since the War of Independence. Over the years they performed a wide variety of unofficial and unorthodox duties until eventually being incorporated into the formal military establishment.

This long tradition of military service was captured by D'Ann Campbell in the first paper of the session in an overview of wartime roles played by American women from the Revolutionary War through World War II. The various women's units reached their greatest strength during the Second World War and had more of an impact on the armed services and the women themselves than had previous military roles afforded to women. The contributions of servicewomen to a global conflict that required the complete commitment of U.S. resources were essential to the nation's achieving victory in this total war.

The focus of the remainder of the session was on governmental efforts after the attack on Pearl Harbor to organize individual women's units within the services, supply and train enlistees, and shape public opinion to be supportive of women's participation in the military. Leisa D. Meyer, in her paper on the Women's Army Corps (WAC) and its predecessor Women's Army Auxiliary Corps (WAAC), discussed the threat posed by women's military service to traditional gender and race norms and the steps taken by the WAAC/WAC to construct an image of female soldiers that countered public fear and reinforced, rather than challenged, the conventional system of power relations between men and women and whites and blacks.

Judy Barrett Litoff and David C. Smith drew upon their extensive collection of 30,000 women's wartime letters in presenting the wartime history of the Navy's WAVES (Women Accepted for Volunteer Emergency Service), Coast Guard's SPAR (acronym formed from the organization's *"Semper Paratus*—Always Ready" motto), Marine Corps Women's Reserve, Army and Navy Nurse Corps, and the WASP (Women Airforce Service Pilots). Poignantly captured in the servicewomen's own words were the essence and complexity of the broad-ranging, exciting, intensely personal, and grippingly real war experiences that changed these women and their country forever.

The session was chaired by Col. Bettie J. Morden, World War II veteran, scholar, and author of a prize-winning book on the history of the WAC after World War II.

SERVICEWOMEN AND THE AMERICAN MILITARY EXPERIENCE

D'Ann Campbell

Fifty years ago in March 1945, Germany was collapsing under Allied hammering; in the Pacific, American servicemen and servicewomen were preparing for the invasion of Iwo Jima and had the most difficult island battle, Okinawa, yet to fight. Fifty years ago, 88 percent of Americans alive today were not yet born. For the 70 percent of Americans who were in their twenties, thirties, and forties during World War II and who are still alive today, it seems like "Only Yesterday."[1]

Twenty years ago seems like "Only Yesterday" to me. I was busy at work in the National Archives on the roles women had played during World War II and was beginning my research of American nurses, which led me to the military, which soon led me to the WAC, WAVES, women Marines, SPAR, and WASP.[2] I began reading, researching, and then going to reunions and to conferences. I have met some of the finest people, servicewomen who are veterans of World War II.[3] The National Archives and other military history archives have now organized their records and provide excellent finding aids. The National Archives recently published a reference book, its guide *American Women and the U.S. Armed Forces*, which is an excellent aid to researchers.[4]

Nineteen years ago, historian Susan Hartmann gave a paper at another pioneering National Archives conference on women's history. Hartmann focused on the administrative history of the establishment of the WAC and the WAVES. Hartmann's piece was published in a 1980 collection of these National Archives papers, edited by Mabel Deutrich and Virginia Purdy, entitled *Clio Was a Woman*.[5] It remains the single best description of the early World War II history of these servicewomen.

When 2 years ago *Choice* asked me to write a bibliographic essay on servicewomen during World War II, the editor requested that I limit my references to the top 100 books and a handful of key articles in the field.[6] It was not an easy job, and more quality work is coming out each month.

Just look at the first section of this volume. Leisa Meyer represents the new historians of women. She recently completed the first book on the WAC since Mattie Treadwell's pioneering volume in the 1950s.[7] Judy Barrett Litoff and David C. Smith have been on their own mission, with fantastic results, for the past 10 years.[8] Col. Bettie Morden, the session's chair, has written a prize-winning book on the WAC after World War II and, most important, is a veteran and a scholar who represents our quintessential partnership—she keeps all of us working together.[9]

The conference participants examine why women joined the American military, where they served, how they served, and what difference the war made in their lives. Almost all servicewomen made lifelong friends; reunions serve as "friendship fixes." Some met their future husbands; others used the GI bill to start or complete college or a postgraduate program.[10]

I have jumped ahead of the story, and it is time to go back in history almost 220 years to the American Revolution and introduce our first theme: Servicewomen have always served in the military during American wars. As our keynote speaker, Dr. Sheila E. Widnall, Secretary of the Air Force, so clearly pointed out, as women's roles in American society have grown over the years, so too have they grown in the military.

To begin with the American Revolution we must turn to the work of historian Linda Grant De Pauw. De Pauw has documented a wide range of roles women played in the American Army and in the seafaring new country. She is also the editor of the most important journal and news bulletin in our field, *MINERVA: A Journal of Women in the Military.*

Professor De Pauw estimates that about 20,000 women served during the American Revolution in the semiofficial auxiliary called "Women in the Army." They were subject to military discipline, received half the pay of men, and were allowed half the rations. They did not wear uniforms—but they did make and repair the men's uniforms, as well as cook and nurse.[11] Their chief combat role was to carry water to the artillery (the cannon had to be swabbed out after every shot to prevent sparks and cool the barrel). One such "Molly Pitcher" was Margaret Corbin, who once took command of the battery in action when her husband was killed. She was wounded and after the war received a pension in recognition of her valuable and faithful service.[12]

In the Civil War some women dressed up in men's clothes to join the fight. Women served on both sides as sutlers, saboteurs, and spies.[13] Most women, however, especially in the South, tried to learn how to do their husband's peacetime jobs as they continued to do their own. They had to do so in order to keep the family alive while the men of the house were off defending the Confederacy. Scholarship by historians such as Drew Faust and George Rable has suggested that the key to defeating the Confederacy was to break the will of the Southern women on the homefront. When women began writing to their husbands to come home because their houses were being burned, their food was being destroyed, and death was hovering over their families, the men went AWOL in large numbers.[14]

Women served the Federal and Confederate military primarily as nurses and hospital administrators. The casualty numbers on both sides were staggering (higher than in all other American wars combined until Vietnam), and in numerous battles several thousand wounded men needed immediate medical and nursing attention. Dorothea Dix, working through the U.S. Sanitation Commission, helped provide nurses for the U.S. Army. Clara Barton was a prominent volunteer nurse who later founded the American Red Cross.[15]

After the Spanish-American War demonstrated the need for a permanent, professional nurse corps, women became a part of the Regular Army and Navy establishment (though without any command authority over men). During World War I over 5,000 American nurses served on the western front, giving special attention to gas victims, who needed round-the-clock nursing. The Navy found a loophole in its enabling legislation and accepted 11,500 women to serve as clerk/typist administrators, yeoman (F), for the Navy and Marine Corps. After the Great War, the loophole was plugged. I was lucky enough to attend a meeting of women Marine veterans a dozen years ago and to meet some World War I as well as World War II veterans. Jean Ebbert and Marie-Beth Hall's book *Crossed Currents* has the fullest discussion of the yeoman (F) personnel category to date. Historian Sue Godson's articles, and now book, on women in the Navy promises to add to our knowledge of the women who served in the Navy in each war.[16]

Gen. John J. "Black Jack" Pershing brought 350 American women to France to serve as bilingual communications specialists.

Although they wore uniforms and were under military discipline, they remained technically civilians. These "Hello Girls" of World War I and the Wasps of World War II both received military status retroactively in the late 1970s.[17]

World War II proved to be the watershed event. The United States entered the war 2 years after Britain, and Gen. George C. Marshall and Gen. Dwight D. Eisenhower closely monitored the British experience. They were impressed to see that Britain drafted women, assigning some to munitions factories and others to the Auxiliary Territorial Service (A.T.S.). Princess (now Queen) Elizabeth spent the war in uniform repairing trucks. Mary Churchill, daughter of the Prime Minister, was also drafted into the A.T.S., where she served in a combat role as part of a mixed battery antiaircraft artillery unit (AA then, AAA today).[18]

At the request of General Marshall and the urging of Eleanor Roosevelt and other women leaders like Margaret Chase Smith, Congress created the Women's Army Auxiliary Corps (WAAC) in May 1942. In July, the Navy bypassed the auxiliary stage and created the Women Accepted for Volunteer Emergency Service (WAVES), whose members had the same status as male reservists. By November the Coast Guard had created its women's reserve (SPAR), and finally, the Marine Corps followed in February 1943, establishing the Marine Corps Women's Reserve (MCWR). After President Roosevelt signed new legislation on July 1, the WAAC dropped the auxiliary status and began the 3-month transition to become the WAC (Women's Army Corps). In all, over 350,000 women served in uniform during World War II with a peak strength of 271,000.[19]

Once the legislation was passed, how did the American military entice the "right and proper" kinds of women to join such a masculine organization? Two motivating factors for 99 percent of the servicewomen were patriotism and religion. After these factors, a second reason was often a chance for adventure, and the branch of service might be determined by the cut of the uniform. The Navy may have had the sharpest uniform, designed by a New York designer, Mainbocher.[20]

Women did NOT join the military for rank and hierarchy. In fact, young women recruits were seen saluting airline pilots, postmen, and almost any other person who wore a uniform and bars. Much to the amazement of the drill sergeants, women volunteers loved to drill. Drilling was often used as a punishment for men, but women found that drilling gave them a sense of belonging to something exciting and patriotic.[21]

I began this paper with the theme that servicewomen have always been a part of our American military experience and have participated in all American wars. I would like to develop a second theme that complements and supplements the conference theme, "A Woman's War Too": The nature of Total War in this century necessarily involves women both directly and indirectly in the war effort.

When America and its Allies first entered World War II, women worked in factories and served in the military. To win a war on the scale of the two World Wars of the twentieth century, every man, woman, and child of a nation must be involved, and large bureaucracies must plan, organize, and administer the war effort. The Germans and Japanese held a very different philosophy about their women. Those of you who have read the book or seen the movie *Schindler's List* can remember that the Germans used POWs to staff their factories. Even single women did not work in factories but stayed at home preparing to bear and raise "the Aryan race." Not until Albert Speer became economic czar in 1943 did the Germans begin to use women.[22] The German leaders discovered, as had the Allied Powers, that women exhibited very high morale, quite in contrast to the motivation of the prisoners of war in German

WAVES (Women Accepted for Volunteer Emergency Service) units march in precise formations during a rally at the Washington Monument grounds celebrating the second anniversary of the establishment of the corps, Washington, DC, July 31, 1944.

National Archives, General Records of the Department of the Navy, 1798–1947 (80-G-46257)

factories or civilian slave labor taken from the conquered nations. The German policy makers went full cycle as Germany's case became more desperate. By the end of the war, Hitler had agreed to women serving in the military, even in antiaircraft artillery units, and before the war's end (but too late to implement), he signed the papers to create an all-female infantry unit.[23] The Japanese began training their women when they realized that an invasion of the home islands was very possible. Bands of women, poorly armed and poorly trained, were wiped out with male Japanese soldiers in the battle of Okinawa.[24] The Germans and the Japanese learned how vital women were to the war effort too late to change the fate of their countries.

The majority of American women in the military, about 70 percent, served in jobs that on the homefront were typically seen as female, for example, administrative work as clerks, typists, teletypists, and mail sorters.[25] These jobs were all-important roles in the effort to win a bureaucratic, total war. For every frontline soldier, sailor, or airman, there were seven to nine support staff needed to assist with transportation or supplies and "manpower," pay, mail, and other administrative matters. However, women also served in some new positions such as Link trainers. These schoolteachers could teach men to fly even if the teachers were not pilots themselves. In addition, over 1,000 women served as Women Airforce Service Pilots (Wasps); 39 were killed while towing targets or ferrying and testing planes.[26]

Besides these women's corps, there were the Army and Navy Nurse Corps. More nurses than women of any other profession served in World War II, and nursing came of age during the war. Nurses, with the aid of the wonder drug penicillin, were busy saving lives. Nurses supervised the loading of hospital ships, worked as the first airline stewardesses in unpressurized cabins, and served in the South Pacific, in some areas with a ratio of 1 woman to 10,000 men in a compound. Nurses were at Normandy on D-plus-4-day. Eighty-one nurses were prisoners of war; all survived, and one who is participating in this conference will describe her experience. By 1944 nurses no longer had relative rank, but the same rank, pay, and benefits as did the men.[27]

The role of African-American nurses and African-American Wacs and later Waves will be the focus of subsequent conference papers. Pioneering and ongoing work by Regina Akers, RitaVictoria Gomez, Martha Putney, Darlene Clark Hine, Charity Adams Earley, Brenda

Moore, Janet Sims-Wood, and others with an interest in women's history has benefited all of us.[28]

Now I am not saying that women won the war. What I do say is that in a total war every man, woman, and child must contribute directly or indirectly and that complex bureaucracies supporting vast armies far from home must be team efforts. The side that produces the most and succeeds in sending the most to the fighting forces and in resupplying them most often will win. It was "A Woman's War Too," and women performed heroically in a team effort.

As the war wound down, some of the male governmental policy leaders started to worry that women might like their civilian or

Sp (G) 3/c Florence Johnson and Sp (G) 3/c Rosamund Small, the first Waves to qualify as instructors on electrically operated 50-caliber machine-gun turrets, walk to the target range, Naval Air Gunners School, Hollywood, FL, April 11, 1944.

National Archives, General Records of the Department of the Navy, 1798–1947 (80-G-045240)

military jobs and want to stay. They started sending women some not-so-subtle messages, for example, "You can't have a career and be a good wife," and "Back for Keeps"—which was a picture of a man in uniform returning to his wife and embracing her to remind her that he would now be the breadwinner *if* she kept a good home for him.[29]

The military jobs were only supposed to be "for the duration (and 6 months)," and yet some military leaders who had worked with servicewomen in the field, like Dwight Eisenhower and Omar Bradley, lobbied to create a permanent but small cadre of women, a nucleus of leaders, who could be used as the basis of a major fighting force should the United States ever again engage in a world war, a total war. Col. Mary Hallaren and the late Capt. Joy Bright Hancock worked for the 1948 legislation to establish a permanent women's corps.[30]

Having raised the two broad themes of women's historical participation in all our wars and the nature of total war, we should now commemorate and celebrate, analyze and assess, educate and enjoy the discussions that follow. I have attended over 100 reunions and conferences during this series of 50-year anniversaries and have found this conference, without a doubt, the most professional, the most pioneering of all. We all owe the National Archives staff our sincere appreciation for their hard work and successful efforts.

NOTES

© 1996 by D'Ann Campbell
1. This reference is to Frederick Allen's famous book on the Great Depression, *Only Yesterday* (New York, 1957).
2. The WAAC and WAC were the Army's women's corps; the WAVES was the Navy's women's corps; the SPAR was the Coast Guard's; the WASP was the Women Airforce Service Pilots, originally a civilian organization; and the women Marines had no nickname, and their acronym (MCWR) was not widely used outside of the military.
3. Four hundred eighty-five women veterans in 1984–86 filled out a 140-item questionnaire for me when I attended national reunions of Wacs, Waves, women Marines, and Spars. The results of this survey are detailed in D'Ann Campbell, "Servicewomen of World War II," *Armed Forces and Society* 16 (Winter 1990): 251–270.
4. Charlotte Palmer Seeley, comp., *American Women and the U.S. Armed Forces: A Guide to the Records of Military Agencies in the National Archives Relating to American Women,* rev. by Virginia C. Purdy and Robert Gruber (Washington, DC, 1992).

5. Susan M. Hartmann, "Women in the Military Service," in Mabel E. Deutrich and Virginia C. Purdy, eds., *Clio Was a Woman: Studies in the History of American Women* (Washington, DC, 1980).

6. Campbell, "Women in the Military: A Bibliographic Essay," *Choice* 31 (September 1993): 63-70.

7. Leisa Meyer, *Creating G.I. Jane: The Women's Army Corps During World War II* (New York, 1996); Mattie E. Treadwell, *The Women's Army Corps*, The United States Army in World War II, Special Studies, U.S. Army Center of Military History Pub. 11-8 (Washington, DC, 1954).

8. Judy Barrett Litoff and David C. Smith now have written four books and dozens of articles based on women's letters written during World War II. Their most recent book focuses on letters written by servicewomen. See Judy Barrett Litoff and David C. Smith, eds., *We're in This War Too: World War II Letters from American Women in Uniform* (New York, 1994). Their other works include *Since You Went Away: World War II Letters from American Women on the Home Front* (New York, 1991); *Miss You: The World War II Letters of Barbara Wooddall Taylor and Charles E. Taylor* (Athens, GA, 1990); and *Dear Boys: World War II Letters from a Woman Back Home* (Jackson, MS, 1991)

9. Bettie J. Morden, *The Women's Army Corps, 1945-1978* (Washington, DC, 1990).

10. See Campbell, "Servicewomen," for details.

11. Linda Grant De Pauw, "Women in Combat: The Revolutionary War Experience," *Armed Forces and Society* 7 (Winter 1981): 209-226. For additional information on women in this period, see De Pauw, *Founding Mothers: Women of America in the Revolutionary Era* (Boston, 1975).

12. On her tombstone at the U.S. Military Academy, West Point, there is information about Margaret Corbin. In addition see "Margaret Corbin" file, Special Collections Division, U.S. Military Academy Library, USMA, West Point, NY.

13. The study of women's participation in the Civil War is resulting in a growing field with new publications each year: Mary Massey, *Bonnet Brigades: American Women and the Civil War* (New York, 1966); Bell Irvin Wiley, *Confederate Women* (New York, 1975); DeAnne Blanton, "Women Soldiers of the Civil War," *Prologue: Quarterly of the National Archives* 25 (Spring 1993): 27-33; Lauren Cook Burgess, ed., *An Uncommon Soldier: The Civil War Letters of Sarah Rosetta Wakeman, alias Pvt. Lyons Wakeman, 153d Regiment, New York State Volunteers, 1862-1864* (Pasadena, MD, 1994); Thomas P. Lowry, *The Story the Soldiers Wouldn't Tell: Sex in the Civil War* (Mechanicsburg, PA, 1994); Isabel Quattlebaum, "Twelve Women in the First Days of the Confederacy," *Civil War History* 7 (December 1961): 382; Jane E. Schultz, "Mute Fury: Southern Women's Diaries of Sherman's March to the Sea, 1864-1865," in Helen Cooper, Adrienne Auslander Munich, and Susan Merrill Squier, eds., *Arms and the Woman: War, Gender, and Literary Representation* (Chapel Hill, NC, 1989), pp. 58-79; Nancy Grey Osterud, "Rural Women During the Civil War: New York's Nanticoke Valley, 1861-1865," *New York History* 71 (October 1990): 367-369.

14. Drew Gilpin Faust, "'Altars of Sacrifice: Confederate Women and the Narratives of War," *Journal of American History* 76 (March 1990): 1200-1228; George

C. Rable, *Civil Wars: Women and the Crisis of Southern Nationalism* (Urbana, IL, 1989).

15. See Leni Hamilton, *Clara Barton* (New York, 1988); Stephen B. Oates, *A Woman of Valor: Clara Barton and the Civil War* (New York, 1994); Charles Schlaifer, *Heart's Work: Civil War Heroine and Champion of the Mentally Ill, Dorothea Lynde Dix* (New York, 1991); Dorothy Clarke Wilson, *Stranger and Traveler: The Story of Dorothea Dix, American Reformer* (Boston, 1975).

16. Jean Ebbert and Marie-Beth Hall, *Crossed Currents: Navy Women from WWI to Tailhook* (Washington, DC, 1994); Susan H. Godson, "The Waves in World War II," *United States Naval Institute Proceedings* 111 (December 1984): 46–48; Godson, "Womenpower in World War II," *United States Naval Institute Proceedings* 110 (December 1984): 60–64; and Godson, "Captain Joy Bright Hancock and the Role of Women in the U.S. Navy," *New Jersey History* 105 (Summer 1987): 1–17.

17. For more information on the roles women played overseas in World War I, see Dorothy Schneider and Carl J. Schneider, *Into the Breach: American Women Overseas in World War I* (New York, 1991). Chapter 7 is on the "Hello Girls."

18. For information on the A.T.S. and the roles of Princess Elizabeth and Mary Churchill, see Gen. Sir Frederick Arthur Pile, *Ack-Ack* (London, 1949), and Shelford Bidwell, *The Women's Royal Army Corps* (London, 1977).

19. See Hartmann, "Women in the Military Service," and Campbell, *Women at War with America: Private Lives in a Patriotic Era* (Cambridge, MA, 1984), chap. 1.

20. Ruth Cheney Streeter, "History of the Marine Corps Women's Reserve: A Critical Analysis of Its Development and Operation, 1943–1945," Dec. 5, 1945, Schlesinger Library, Radcliffe College, Cambridge, MA; Campbell, "Servicewomen," pp. 254–256.

21. See Campbell, "Fighting with the Navy: Women's Experiences in World War II," in Jack Sweetman, ed., *Tenth Naval History Symposium Proceedings* (Annapolis, MD, 1993), pp. 343–360; Campbell, "The Regimented Women of World War II," in Jean Elshtain and Sheila Tobias, eds., *Women, Militarism, and War* (Lanham, MD, 1990), pp. 107–122.

22. For a discussion on the German division of gender roles and its effects on the mobilization of German women during World War II, see Jill Stephenson, *The Nazi Organization of Women* (London, 1981); Claudia Koonz, *Mothers in the Fatherland* (New York, 1987); Leila Rupp, *Mobilizing Women for War* (Princeton, NJ, 1981); and the bibliography listed in Campbell, "Women in Combat: The World War II Experience in the United States, Great Britain, Germany, and the Soviet Union," *Journal of Military History* 57 (April 1993): 314, n. 40.

23. Ibid., pp. 316–317.

24. Women soldiers did in fact die in hand-to-hand combat on Okinawa. The saga of the all-female "Lilly Brigade" is now part of Japanese folklore. See Thomas R. H. Havens, *Valley of Darkness: The Japanese People and World War Two* (New York, 1978), pp. 188–190.

25. See Campbell, *Private Lives,* for a discussion of traditional roles of servicewomen. There are now dozens of autobiographies and biographies of service-

women. Excellent starting points include, for Waves, Marie Bennett Alsmeyer, *The Way of the Waves: Women in the Navy* (Conway, AK, 1981); for Wacs, Anne Bosanko Green, *One Woman's War: Letters Home from the Women's Army Corps, 1944-46* (St. Paul, MN, 1989), and Georgia Watson, *World War II in a Khaki Skirt* (Moore Haven, FL, 1985); for women Marines, Peter A. Soderbergh, *Women Marines: The World War II Era* (Westport, CT, 1992); and for Spars, Mary Lyne and Kay Arthur, *Three Years Behind the Mast: The Story of the United States Coast Guard SPARS* (Washington, DC, 1946).

26. For an introduction to the WASP, see Byrd Howell Granger, *On Final Approach: The Women Airforce Service Pilots of World War II* (Scottsboro, AZ, 1991); Jean Cole, *Women Pilots of World War II* (Salt Lake City, UT, 1992); Marianne Verges, *On Silver Wings: The Women Airforce Service Pilots of World War II, 1942-1944* (New York, 1991).

27. For information on the nurse POWs, see Elizabeth M. Norman and Sharon Eifried, "How Did They All Survive? An Analysis of American Nurses' Experiences in Japanese Prisoner-of-War Camps," *Nursing History Review* (1995): 105-127. G. Alan Knight, San Antonio College, is currently writing a biography of Capt. Leora B. Stroup, Army Nurse Corps, a World War II pioneer in aeromedical evaluation of the sick and wounded. The U.S. Army Nurse Corps is having a registered nurse with a Ph.D. in history write a history of the Army Nurse Corps during World War II. For the earlier period, see Elizabeth Shield, "A History of the United States Army Nurse Corps (Female): 1901-1937" (Ph.D. diss., Columbia University, 1980), and Julia Catherine Stimson, *Finding Themselves: The Letters of an American Army Chief Nurse in a British Hospital in France* (New York, 1918). To understand the developing role of military nurses, it is essential to review the history of American nursing. Valuable background appears in Mary M. Roberts, *American Nursing: History and Interpretation* (New York, 1954); Philip Kalisch and Beatrice Kalisch, *The Advance of American Nursing* (Boston, 1978); Susan Reverby, *Ordered to Care: The Dilemma of American Nursing, 1850-1945* (New York, 1987); and Barbara Melosh, *"The Physician's Hand": Work, Culture, and Conflict in American Nursing* (Philadelphia, 1982).

28. Martha Putney, *When the Nation Was in Need* (Metucken, NJ, 1992); Charity Adams Earley, *One Woman's Army: A Black Officer Remembers the WAC* (College Station, TX, 1989); Darlene Clark Hine, *Black Women in White: Racial Conflict and Cooperation in the Nursing Profession, 1890-1950* (Bloomington, IN, 1989).

29. Illustrations in *Ladies Home Journal* (January 1944).

30. Maj. Gen. Jeanne Holm's *Women in the Military: An Unfinished Revolution* and the aforementioned book by Col. Bettie Morden do a first-rate job of providing us with the knowledge and perspectives of women in the postwar military. See Jeanne Holm, *Women in the Military: An Unfinished Revolution*, rev. ed. (Novato, CA, 1992); Morden, *The WAC;* Joy Bright Hancock, *Lady in the Navy: A Personal Reminiscence* (Annapolis, MD, 1972); Janann Sherman, " 'They Either Need These Women or They Do Not': Margaret Chase Smith and the Fight for Regular Status for Women in the Military," *Journal of Military History* 54 (January 1990): 47; M. C. Devilbiss, *Women and Military Service: A History, Analysis, and Overview of Key Issues* (Maxwell Air Force Base, AL, 1990).

CREATING A WOMEN'S CORPS
Public Response to the WAAC/WAC and Questions of Citizenship

Leisa D. Meyer

In this paper I examine racial and gendered constructions of citizenship through the lens of women's service in the Army during World War II. In particular, I analyze the potential challenge presented to these constructs by Euro-American and African-American women's military service and the ways in which this threat was contained by the ideological frameworks used to both support and oppose the women's corps. I address these issues in two major ways: by examining the fears and concerns articulated in the media and in Congress over the adverse effect women's military service would have on gender and racial hierarchies and by analyzing the military response to these fears, a response that constructed the "female soldier" in ways to counter public anxieties and reinforce conventional gender and racial norms.

Under the banner of expediency, male Army leaders accepted the entrance of women into the Army in 1942. Supporting the formation of a women's corps seemed a reasonable solution to the expected increase in the numbers of "women's jobs" involving tasks such as clerking, typing, and communications—and such support also enabled the Army to maintain control over this type of labor and those employed to do it. Moreover, sponsoring the creation of such a corps allowed the Army, not civilian legislators, to dictate the terms of female military participation.

In the civilian sector, those who believed that women's rights and duties as citizens should not be limited strongly advocated women's entrance into the Army. Yet those who opposed women's participation argued that it must be tolerated and encouraged only to the degree that it did not disrupt systems of male dominance and power. Supporters of the WAC* constructed the "female soldier" as a symbol of American women's patriotism, self-sacrifice, and courage. Some, like Representative Edith Nourse Rogers, saw the corps as a long-awaited symbol of recognition for all the women who had worked with the military in previous American war efforts, an important step toward women's status as full citizens, deserving of the rights and benefits long enjoyed by men. Others constructed the "female soldier" as a modern Molly Pitcher, who, in response to a national emergency, temporarily left her home and family to "lend a hand." In contrast, opponents characterized the "female soldier" as not a heroine but a dire threat to the home and family and to the privatized gender relationships within them, especially the husband's status as breadwinner and head of household. To these commentators, the "female soldier" epitomized the wartime anti-heroine, a figure whose potential sexual and economic independence from men subverted the "natural order" and whose position as a female protector usurped men's status and power, both within and outside of the home.

Representative Edith Nourse Rogers of Massachusetts authored the bill to create a Women's Army Auxiliary Corps. In defending the proposed legislation to her congressional colleagues, Rogers invoked her experience from the previous world war, noting, "So far back as the first World War, when I was in England and France, I saw the need for such an adjunct to our military forces."[1] Rogers argued that because most women who served with the military during World War I were civilians, they were not eligible for the

---

*The Women's Army Auxiliary Corps (WAAC) existed from May 14, 1942, to September 30, 1943, when it was replaced by the Women's Army Corps (WAC). WAAC recruiting closed on August 8, 1943, and WAC recruiting opened the following day. However, it was not until September 1, 1943, that the process of swearing in WAAC officers and enlisted women who chose to continue with the new organization began. This process continued throughout the month of September. On September 30, 1943, the WAAC was officially disbanded (or as Treadwell puts it, "ceased to exist.") Throughout this article, I use the acronym WAC to refer to the organization and Wac (lowercase) to refer to individual enlisted women within the corps. In addition, to avoid repetition, I use the terms "corps" and "women's corps" interchangeably with WAC. To avoid confusing terminology, I use the acronym WAC in most discussions of the women's corps throughout World War II. When I discuss material that is specific to the early auxiliary years of the corps, I will specifically note this by referring to the corps as the WAAC.

same benefits as the men in uniform with whom they worked. She contended that women's service with the military must be recognized and that as patriots they must be entitled to similar rewards from the state for the faithful discharge of their duties. In locating her argument for women's treatment as full and equal citizens within the arena of military service, Rogers acknowledged the degree to which military service was critical to any definition of citizenship within the United States. She supported her position by discussing the problems faced by women who served in the previous war:

> They received no compensation of any kind, in the event they were sick or injured—and many were. It was a most unsatisfactory arrangement and has been the cause of much dissatisfaction ever since the Armistice. Many Members of Congress have felt as I do, that these women who gave of their service, unselfishly, and tragically, and under conditions comparable to that of men, should have received pay and privileges for that service. The knowledge of these heart-breaking cases, the bitterness which some of these loyal, patriotic women felt, was one of the prime factors in my plan for a WAAC.[2]

The debate on the floor of the House and Senate over the WAAC bill indicated the degree to which some Members of Congress viewed women's military service, and the rights and privileges such service was assumed to accord women, as profoundly threatening. Some legislators questioned whether military service was the most effective mode of mobilizing women in support of the war effort. Others focused their concerns on the possible problems arising from the "masculine" environment that would be the Waacs' new home. In particular, they discussed the implications of women's military service for American "manhood" and "womanhood." One Congressman opposing the bill declared,

> I think it is a reflection upon the courageous manhood of the country to pass a law inviting women to join the armed forces in order to win a battle. Take the women into the armed service, who then will do the cooking, the washing, the mending, the humble homey tasks to which every woman has devoted herself? Think of the humiliation. What has become of the manhood of America?[3]

The opposition of "soldier" and "woman," homefront and battlefront, posited by this author framed most of the discussion of women's presence in the U.S. military throughout World War II. For the most part, the congressional debate focused on gender issues and did not delineate between different racial or ethnic groups of women. Yet the persistent oppositional positioning of "male soldier" versus "woman" more clearly reflected the gendered tensions of the white community. These oppositions rested upon the clearly delineated and distinct wartime duties ascribed to the female and male citizen: Men were expected to bear arms in order to protect and defend their country and "their" women; women were expected to support and sustain this effort by keeping the "homefires burning," bearing children, and filling the role of the "girl back home," the symbol for which the "boys in uniform" were fighting.[4] These reciprocal obligations of citizenship rested upon the privatized gender relationships between women and men in the "home" and the particular asymmetrical relationship between the male protector and the female protectee.[5]

The WAAC bill, passed by Congress on May 14, 1942, threatened to upset these gender relationships and the construction of citizenship they represented. As Kathleen Jones has argued in her essay on female citizenship, "Women cannot become active in their own defense without either calling into question their identity as women or threatening the sexual iconography upon which the discourse [of citizenship] is based."[6] In particular, the public debate during World War II focused on concerns that the creation of a corps of "female soldiers" would lead women to abdicate their responsibilities within the home and usurp the male duty of protecting and defending home and country.

On the one hand, the WAAC was depicted as an "unnatural" organization and soundly criticized for demanding that women "give up" motherhood for the duration of the war. As one editorial queried:

> Is it advisable, long before the supply of manpower shows any sign of running short, to take a lot of young, vigorous women into a vaguely defined noncombatant branch of the Army; and is it advisable then to tell them they must not have children? Wouldn't it be wiser just to leave them out of the armed forces, and encourage them to marry, produce children, and thus contribute in the old, natural way to the war effort?[7]

On the other hand, military women's usurpation of men's duties as "protectors" was symbolic of a potential shift in women's relationships to and power over men in the Army and within the home. The consequences of such a shift were starkly addressed in a series of nationally syndicated cartoons caricaturing the new "female protector." In visual illustrations of the potential results of women's presence within the Army, large "manly" Waacs towered over diminutive servicemen. These men were not only smaller and shorter than their female counterparts, but they were always of lower rank than the Waacs with whom they interacted. These cartoons implied the emasculation of men at the hands of empowered women; the men were not only diminished in physical stature but also made to appear less masculine in contemporary terms by the servicewomen's assumption of the obligations previously assigned only to male citizens. In one popular series, *Private Berger Abroad,* for instance, a tiny GI with glasses sits at a desk typing a report as a WAAC sergeant strides out of the office. Another male soldier in the office turns to him and says: "Stop Griping! SOMEBODY had to be chosen to release her for combat!"[8] By inverting the early WAAC recruiting slogan that urged women to join the corps in order to "release a man for combat," this cartoon exemplified concerns that women's military service would turn gender norms and relationships upside down, leaving men protected by and subordinate to women.

The popular media also depicted the emasculation of men by portending the subversion of men's role as head of the household and women's role as supporter and helpmeet to men. Other nationally syndicated cartoons, for instance, depicted men sitting at home knitting sweaters for their Wac wives, as well as frail-looking, bespectacled husbands, wearing aprons and wielding brooms, asking their Wac wives for their monthly allowance.[9] In these examples, women assumed the male position of breadwinner and the male obligation of military service while men were relegated to the domain of the home. Another cartoon addressed the possible postwar changes in men's and women's circumstances by showing three Wacs watching a male soldier on kitchen police (K.P.) duty peeling potatoes; the women were saying, "after the war some lucky girl will come home from a day at the office, to be met by Him in a cute little bungalow—apron—and all the potatoes peeled."[10]

The concern that women's service with the Army would drastically change gender norms within the family was underscored by the structural relationship between the military and individual women that often superseded women's relationships to their husbands. The military, in many ways, usurped the patriarchal rights of servicewomen's husbands. WAC Headquarters and the War Department (WD) received numerous applications from husbands who asked that their Wac wives be transferred or discharged so they could be closer to them. Many of these requests were generated by men who were recently discharged and wanted their wives to begin "creating homes for them." These letters from servicemen were often supported by Army chaplains who urged WAC Director Col. Oveta Culp Hobby to use her authority to "return" these women to their husbands. Implicit in many of these applications was the belief that men had a vested interest in and right to control their wives and that whenever possible Hobby and the WD should try to restore women to the keeping of their husbands. As one civilian husband lamented, "I cannot understand how a married woman can enlist in the WAC without the consent of her husband."[11] Most of the men had not previously contacted their wives about their petitions, and many asked that WAC Headquarters and the War Department not inform the women of their requests. Clearly, however, these actions were representative of some men's attempts to reassert their rights as husbands to have some control over their wives' choices and options, a prerogative with which women's service in the WAC was interfering and that their letters implied the state should protect, not threaten.

All women's presence within the military was shaped by the gendered constructions of citizenship and the gendered nature of the benefits they could expect in exchange for their military service. African-American women's position as soldiers, however, was framed not only by gender ideologies that questioned women's right to trespass on a male domain but also by racial ideologies that challenged the right of African Americans to enter a bastion of Euro-American power and authority. Entrenched racial hierarchies depicting African Americans as inferior to Euro-Americans influenced, and were reinforced by, Army policies and public attitudes toward all black military personnel. Army Jim Crow policies, for example, segregating all African-American military personnel from their Euro-American counterparts, were clear indicators of the lesser status and authority afforded black men and women in the Army during World War II.

During the war, black Americans were extremely aware of discrimination at home, and most no longer believed that service within the U.S. military could be exchanged for civil and political rights. African-American community leaders and the black press encouraged men and women to serve with the armed forces but characterized this service as part of a larger "Double V" campaign: Victory overseas *and* victory at home against the domestic enemies of racial discrimination and unequal opportunity and access. As historian Bernard Nalty has argued, "Instead of assuming good will on the part of white authority, they sought to trade military service for measurable progress toward full citizenship."[12] Within this campaign, the black press became one of the main forums for criticism of Army treatment of African-American personnel. These articles echoed the arguments of the National Association for the Advancement of Colored People (NAACP) and national black leaders who asserted that the future status of African Americans as citizens in the United States depended upon their service as *equals* in the armed forces.[13] African-American women's service was situated within this larger framework, which characterized the military during World War II as one of the major arenas in which the fight for racial equality must take place.

Like its white counterparts, the black press demonstrated concern with the impact female military service might have on postwar relations between the sexes.[14] In the black press, articles addressing women's military service, however, also lauded their efforts as akin to those of black men in improving the position of the race and bolstering the status of African Americans as citizens within the United States. As one editorial observed, "Negro women serving in the WAC are winning a respect and admiration throughout the nation that will reflect in greater race equality after the war."[15] Others reported critically on the derogatory attitudes and poor conditions African-American women encountered at various posts. In one article, the top-ranking African-American WAC Officer, Maj. Harriet West, related her own frustrating experiences with segregated transportation and the lack of respect demonstrated by both white officers and noncommissioned officers. When she was scheduled to speak at a recruiting rally in Columbus, OH, for instance, she asked: "How . . . could [I] induce other women to wear the uniform that drew such flagrant disrespect whenever it was worn by a colored soldier?"[16]

National African-American women's organizations, especially the National Council of Negro Women (NCNW) and black sororities like Alpha Kappa Alpha (AKA), provided support and sympathy for African-American servicewomen. Many African-American Wacs wrote of their struggles to NCNW president Mary McLeod Bethune, asking her to take action on their behalf. The NCNW supported the WAC as an "opportunity for . . . women of the race." Bethune simultaneously cautioned, however, that their endorsement of the organization should not be interpreted as an endorsement of segregation, remarking, "This . . . is the other half of our battle. [But] it must not, in any way, lessen our support or participation in our country's victory effort." Bethune, like the African-American press, framed the battle against segregation and prejudice within a larger support of the war effort.[17]

The experiences of racial discrimination reported by black Wacs, and in particular Wac officers, were the product of a system of race relations that excluded African Americans from most positions of authority and power and punished those who sought to change or improve their status. Some Euro-Americans' fears of the disastrous consequences resulting from any alteration of this system were very much a part of responses to the presence of black women in the military. Thus, while the African-American press criticized the Army's Jim Crow policies, some Euro-Americans felt that the Army was not segregated enough. WAC Headquarters and the War Department received numerous letters from white people complaining about the adverse impact black Wacs had on various communities. In several letters, Euro-American male community leaders and Members of Congress passed on and seconded their constituents' concerns about the lack of strict segregation reported at some Army posts.[18] Other complaints emanated from segregated white communities when black Waacs were stationed in their vicinity. Euro-American leaders in a segregated suburb of Chicago, for instance, protested the presence of African-American Wacs stationed at Gardner General Hospital. Apparently, members of the white community felt the position of the black WAC barracks in a restricted Euro-American residential and park area, and close to a "white only" bathing beach, could lead to potential violence and racial antagonism.[19]

The concerns represented by these protests and complaints were that the presence of African-American Wacs would challenge the carefully constructed system of race relations and hierarchies in place and undercut the assumptions of white status and authority on which they were based. Thus, African-American Wacs were forced to confront both the gender and racial ideologies circumscribing their military participation. Simultaneously, their presence and role as black women within the military called into question the gendered and racial constructions of citizenship and the relations of power and privilege upon which these ideologies rested. The NCNW, which depicted the role of black women in the WAC as important not only for African Americans in general, but for black women in particular, articulated the potential meanings of this service. In one statement, the NCNW placed African-American women's military service within the context of advances toward status as full citizens occurring for all women during the war:

> The role of the Negro woman . . . is immediately connected to the strategic gains made by all women in the present world situation. These general gains must be expanded and consolidated. There must be no recession from the encouraging advances already made by women . . . . Sex must never again be a determinant affecting broad opportunities for women. Prejudice based on sex has no place in the present scheme of social activity—where it is accentuated by the factor of color, affirmative steps must be taken to eliminate both.[20]

The response of the Army and WAC administrations to public concerns about the threat women's military service represented to gender and racial hierarchies constructed "female soldiers" in ways that reinforced the existing systems of power relations. The Army's efforts to accomplish this took three major forms: First, the Army and WAC Bureaus of Public Relations (BPRs) depicted the women's corps as an organization that nurtured and supported women's love of home and desire to return to it at the close of hostilities. Second, the WAC implemented policies and procedures that privileged the position and status of Euro-American women, and thus undercut the threat to white power and prerogatives represented by African-American women in uniform. Third, the military reformulated the categories of combatant and noncombatant in order to preserve distinctions between male and female soldiers and maintain white male soldiers' positions as "protectors."

The WAC and Army BPRs created propaganda to offset initial public antagonism and used it continuously during the war to counter public fears of both the disruptive impact women's military service could have on gender roles and relationships, and the corresponding consequences women's independence from men might have on the "American family." One of the foundations of the framework the Army developed was the portrayal of Wacs' service as based upon their familial relationships—as daughters, mothers, sisters, wives, and sweethearts of the fighting men. The Army, for instance, eagerly seized on and fed to the press various stories of Wacs who joined because of their connections to men who had been killed, were prisoners of war, or were fighting overseas. One writer who visited a WAC post reported, "The reason behind most enlistments is a man in the armed forces." He went on to observe that like male GIs, women kept pictures of the opposite sex in their lockers, but in contrast to the men, "There are no movie stars. Every picture is there by right of kinship—either blood or heart."[21] Thus, Wacs were depicted as enlisting not for personal gain but in order to hasten the war's end, and public acceptance of Wacs was made conditional on their giving first priority to the men in their lives.[22]

To repeatedly emphasize that military service did not rob women of their desire to return to the home, the WAC and Army Bureaus of Public Relations sent articles to the press, for example, detailing the "homelike" environments women had created at their posts. These articles depicted servicewomen planting flowers, painting their barracks a "soft green," and adding pretty matching curtains as well as "sprucing up" the unglamorous Army foot lockers and field tables by transforming them with chintz skirts into "smart dressing tables." The press also reported that the materials that Wacs used to "feminize" their surroundings were supplied by male GIs in exchange for women's sewing and ironing, thus replicating familiar, gendered patterns of labor and exchange.[23] Other articles described normal Army routines, such as inspections, as servicewomen's opportunities to show off their skills at keeping their kitchens and rooms "clean and sparkling . . . . just like any Army wife."[24]

Although WAC publicity stressed that Army life did not inhibit women's desire to create a "home," it also made it clear that most servicewomen wanted nothing more than to return to the "real thing" once the war ended. Several supporters of the WAC suggested that military service would actually make women better wives, especially to male GIs returning after the conflict. After visiting WAC training centers, for instance, church leaders reported to the press that servicewomen

> are sincerely looking forward to the time when they may take up again those time-honored joys which surround home life and children, which still stand as women's historic contribution to the society of which they are a part.[25]

Several letters from civilians supported this argument, asserting that the Army taught young women valuable lessons in discipline, budgeting resources, and behavior and that this would result in "these girls making a fine bunch of mothers when they come back." For a short time, moreover, the War Department used the slogan "The Wac who shares your Army life will make a better postwar wife!" to promote women's military service.[26] Thus, the efforts of the WAC administration and the various WAC publicity agencies throughout the war were pointed toward creating a framework of reassurance, which portrayed military service as supporting, not

Mrs. Franklin D. Roosevelt, an early supporter of women in the military, and Col. Oveta Culp Hobby, first Director of the Women's Army Corps, tour the first Women's Training Center, Fort Des Moines, IA, February 14, 1943.

National Archives, Records of the Office of the Chief Signal Officer (111-SC-163772)

inhibiting, women's femininity, and as teaching women valuable lessons that would make them better wives and mothers, all of which were consistent with prescribed gender norms.

Although Colonel Hobby repeatedly argued that the WAC was a democratic organization within which all women were treated equally, the racially segregated housing, recreational facilities, and occupational structure of the WAC contradicted this assertion. These Jim Crow policies combined with the WAC's 10-percent quota for black women were the subject of protests throughout the war.[27] The WAC response to these complaints was framed by the War Department and claimed that the women's corps was simply following the "lines laid down by our present social order" and that racial segregation would be handled in accordance with "accepted social customs." In particular, Col. Oveta Hobby argued that while the WAC did not discriminate on the grounds of race, religion, or creed, it was not the correct arena for "settling racial problems."[28]

Despite Colonel Hobby's claims of equal treatment for all women within the corps, WAC administrators, including Hobby, were not always supportive of efforts aimed at recruiting African-American women into the organization. In fact, WAC Headquarters received numerous reports from African-American women and Bethune concerning misinformation given black women at recruiting stations. Several African-American women, for instance, complained of being turned away by recruiters who told them that the corps was not accepting "colored applicants."[29]

WAC leaders were also careful to remove publicity on the recruitment of African-American women if such publicity threatened to jeopardize their major recruiting efforts among white women. The most telling illustration of this unstated WAAC policy occurred when the corps removed African-American recruiting officers from the field in 1943. One result of this action was that from April through July of 1943 Hobby and the War Department received numerous letters from the black press and African-American leaders asking why "Negro recruiting officers" were being removed from their communities. A telegram from Walter White of the NAACP as well as a memorandum from John J. McCloy of the Negro Newspaper Publishers Association reported:

We have noted the closing down of recruiting offices in many or all of our urban communities for the enlistment of Negro

Wacs. We would like to know if it is the policy of the War Department to discontinue further recruiting of Negro women?[30]

In response to these queries, Colonel Hobby claimed that a shortage of instructors and administrative personnel for training work had caused a "general reassignment of Negro officers to training centers from other assignments." She went on to state that this was necessary in order to get black WAAC units out into the field but that "everything possible" would be done to return the recruiting officers to their posts as soon as the shortage was over.[31]

Internal WAAC memorandums provided a telling contrast to Hobby's public explanation. Maj. Harold Edlund, Chief of WAAC Recruiting, stated that the reason behind the removal of black WAAC recruiting officers was that "because of adverse public opinion two service commands requested the withdrawal of Negro recruiting officers in early April [1943]." Accordingly, from April 14 to June 14, the WAAC arranged for all black female recruiting officers to be gradually withdrawn from the field. Edlund expected "no serious repercussions" as a result of what he saw as a "necessary" action, reporting that the "use of Negro recruiting officers in some sections of the country is a retardant to recruiting which more than offsets the advantages of their use in the country as a whole." He recommended not returning African-American recruiters to the field but recognized that the "public policy question involved may dictate that we put them back."[32] Overall, recruitment efforts directed at African-American women were abandoned by the WAC if they were thought to inhibit the recruitment of white women to the corps.

In dealing with racial issues, Colonel Hobby played both sides of the fence, guaranteeing to black leaders that African-American Wacs were treated equally despite segregation and arguing that although she was sympathetic to their contentions, she had no control over the War Department's segregation policy and could not change it. At the same time she assured white men and women who wanted segregation maintained that she understood their concerns and that "every effort" was made to ensure that black women were housed and messed separately from their white counterparts. In response to Texas Representative George Mahon's concern over the "breakdown" of segregation at Fort Des Moines, the Director explained that contact between African-American and white Waacs was kept at a minimum, though some contact was "temporary and practically unavoidable."[33] Hobby attempted to straddle a number of different racial discourses, distilling the opposition of African-American male and female leaders and white liberals with sympathetic replies and visits to NCNW meetings, while also reassuring white men and women who supported segregation and more rigid racial policies that the WAC was upholding entrenched racial hierarchies.[34]

Military distinctions between combatants and noncombatants worked to circumscribe the position of *all* servicewomen and African-American servicemen and marginalized their contributions as soldiers. Combat status was integral to the idea of the soldier and crucial to defining the male citizen's rights and obligations as protector. By publicly acknowledging its reluctance to utilize black men in combat roles—a reluctance based largely on racial stereotypes—the War Department and the Army denied African-American men access to the status of protector and further reinforced black women's position as unprotected.[35]

The distinction between the noncombat service of women and the potential and real combat service of men was established in part by the legislation creating the WAC, which prohibited the employment of women as combatants within the Army and was supported by succeeding Army regulations that prohibited the use of weapons or arms of any kind by members of the women's corps.[36] This differentiation between women's and men's service broke down on several occasions during the war, occasions that demonstrated both the practical flexibility of the line drawn between combat and noncombat service as well as the Army's desire to keep such flexibility concealed.

In the United States, the first breakdown occurred in the formation of an experimental antiaircraft (AAC) unit in the Washington, DC, area staffed by white female and male personnel. The creation of this unit was prompted by fears early in the war that the United States might be subjected to air raids and was modeled after the British government's successful use of women in fixed AAC gun installations in the British Isles. Within a construct of "total war," employing women in an antiaircraft "combat" unit within the United States was deemed acceptable by the Army because it involved a passive defense of the homefront, not an aggressive attack on an enemy in areas outside the United States. Despite women's training, however, abstract gendered labels persisted, and men were designated as combatants and the women serving alongside them as noncombatants.[37]

The contradictions in the Army's practice designating servicewomen as noncombatants became most apparent overseas. In combat theaters, the differentiation between male soldiers as combatants and female soldiers as noncombatants took account of neither the risk nor danger their respective duties entailed and was undermined by the general blurring of combat and noncombat areas. The distinctions between front and rear areas deteriorated as advances in air warfare and longer range artillery made them less meaningful. Thus, despite the presumed greater danger on the front, Wacs overseas found themselves in rear areas under fire in the same manner as their male counterparts and the civilian noncombatants around them.[38] Wacs, for example, sought shelter during V-2 rocket attacks in Britain and from air raids in France,[39] and in the Southwest Pacific they served in forward areas, coming under attack from Japanese snipers and planes.[40]

I do not mean to suggest that Wac noncombatants had experiences exactly like male GIs fighting on the fronts. On the other hand, the major structural differences in men's and women's military service were, first, that some men were stationed much closer to the area designated as the front, and second, that women had no weapons or weapons training and could not shoot back if fired upon. As such, combat personnel were defined neither by the designation of the area in which they were stationed nor by whether or not they were subject to hostile fire but by whether or not they had the right and ability to shoot back. The right to fire a weapon and to kill in defense of country were "privileges" accorded without question only to Euro-American men. Yet only 12 percent of male soldiers faced combat during the war, thereby necessitating the Army's maintenance of rigid ideological distinctions between men as combatants or potential combatants and women as noncombatants in order to clarify gender hierarchy in the military and larger society.[41] As one writer protested to WAC Headquarters, "I have always resented the thought of a man being kept by a woman, but I never thought that we in America would come to the point where women would be placed in war theaters while our young, able-bodied men are kept home."[42]

Women's presence in combat theaters when male GIs remained on the homefront suggested a crumbling of gender norms, particularly as they concerned men's and women's respective obligations during wartime. Thus, the paradox of women's military service during World War II and today is that by utilizing women and designating them as noncombatants, the Army could preserve the roles of men as protectors/defenders and women as the protected/defended at the same time that women's very presence within the military threatened to undermine these absolutes.

All women's military service during World War II had the potential to explode gender norms and hierarchies based on the male protector/female protected paradigm. In addition, African-American women's military service challenged racial norms and hierarchies that had traditionally excluded black women from positions of power and status. During the Second World War, these broader implications of women's military service were in constant tension with efforts of both supporters and opponents of the women's corps to control and contain this potential and to present the Women's Army Corps and its members in the least threatening way possible. As a result, women's military service did not ensure them greater access to nor fuller appreciation of the rights and benefits of full citizenship, and contemporary constructions of citizenship remained intact. Thus, one small piece of the WAC story is the tale of the many competing visions of who and what a female soldier or officer was or could be, a competition in which the American public, the press, Congress, and the Army and WAC administrations participated and a competition entered by the thousands of women who served in the corps who offered their own interpretations as to the meanings of their service.

NOTES

© 1996 by Leisa D. Meyer
1. *Congressional Record,* 77th Cong., Appendix, Women's Army Auxiliary Corps, 88, pt. 56 (Mar. 17, 1942), pp. 2658-2659, Folder: Congressional Record, box 217, series 55, Records of the War Department General and Special Staffs, RG 165, National Archives and Record Administration, Washington, DC (hereinafter cited as RG 165, NA).
2. Ibid.
3. Mattie E. Treadwell, *The Women's Army Corps,* The United States Army in World War II, Special Studies, U.S. Army Center of Military History Pub. 11-8 (Washington, DC, 1954), p. 25. See also *Congressional Record,* 77th Cong., 88, pt. 55 (1942).
4. Robert Westbrook, " 'I Want a Girl Just Like the Girl That Married Harry James': American Women and the Problem of Political Obligation in World War II," *American Quarterly,* December 1990, pp. 603-606.

5. Judith Stiehm, "Women, Men, and Military Service: Is Protection Necessarily a Racket?" in Ellen Boneparth, ed., *Women, Power, and Policy* (New York, 1982), pp. 287–291. See also Judith Hicks Stiehm, *Arms and the Enlisted Woman* (Philadelphia, 1989), pp. 224–230. I am indebted to Robert Westbrook's article, " 'I Want a Girl Just Like the Girl That Married Harry James' . . ." for clarifying my thinking on the concept of reciprocity as a means of analyzing the gendered obligations of citizenship during World War II.

6. Kathleen Jones, "Citizenship in a Woman-Friendly Polity," *Signs* (Summer 1990): 786.

7. "No Babies for the WAACs?" Folder: Clippings, WAAC 1942, box 3, Oveta Culp Hobby Papers, Library of Congress (LC), Washington, DC.

8. Dave Berger, *Private Berger Abroad,* and Phillips [*sic*], "Glory Hallelujah," both in Folder: Cartoons/Humor, WAC Reference Files, WAC Museum, Fort McClellan, Anniston, AL. See also *Philadelphia Afro-American,* Apr. 22, 1944, p. 5. In this cartoon a man is being interviewed by a woman for a job. She is sitting in her own office at her desk, in the background there are only women in the outer office. The caption reads, "Your references are fine, but we women have taken over, and I'm not sure we'll be using men after the war."

9. Folder: Cartoons/Humor, WAC Reference Files, WAC Museum.

10. "Tin Hats," Folder: Cartoons/Humor, WAC Reference Files, WAC Museum. See also "Who Said Army Rates Over Home? Don't Worry Gals; Men Would Give a Million to be With You Now; What They Did in the Army They Can Do at Home; No More Lords and Masters," *Philadelphia Afro-American,* Jan. 29, 1944, p. 17. In this article the author notes, "I've never seen an army camp, but there surely must be someone to empty ash trays, pick up cigarette butts, fold the papers, lay out his shirt, tie and socks, find his gloves. What man doesn't expect those things done for him? It will be a fine thing to initiate him to these duties upon his return home." "Tin Hats" was a comic strip.

11. Chaplain (Maj.) Alwyn E. Butcher for Sgt. Max F. Blum, USMC, to Colonel Hobby, WAC Director, Nov. 7, 1944, box 17 095 A to B. Maj. Patricia Chance, Executive WAC Director, to Lt. Col. Mary Hallaren, WAC Staff Director, ETO, Oct. 29, 1945, box 19 095 F to K. Marlin E. Smythe to Lt. Col. Jessie Rice, Feb. 16, 1945, box 29. Jack White to Maj. Gen. Stephen G. Henry, Army Personnel Chief, Oct. 5, 1945; Harry J. Wurster to Hon. Robert A. Taft, Dec. 27, 1944, Folder: W, box 30. All in series 54, RG 165, NA.

12. Bernard Nalty, *Strength for the Fight: A History of Black Americans in the Military* (New York, 1986), p. 141.

13. Lee Finkle, *Forum For Protest: The Black Press During World War II* (Rutherford, NJ, 1975), pp. 61–66, 82, 84, 88–89.

14. For example, see "Who Said the Army Rates over Home?. . . ,"*Philadelphia Afro-American,* Jan. 29, 1944, p. 17. See also the cartoon described in note 8, *Philadelphia Afro-American,* Apr. 22, 1944, p. 5.

15. "Women Honored at WAC Rally," *Toledo Blade,* Mar. 27, 1944, Dovey Johnson Roundtree Papers, Bethune Museum and Archives, Washington, DC. See also Mrs. Edwina T. Glascor, assistant director, Youth Department, Columbus Urban League, to Gen. Don C. Faith, Dec. 20, 1943, concerning the positive impact black servicewomen have on the pride and morale of the African-American community, box 12, series 54, RG 165, NA.

16. Pvt. Joan Willis, "Diary of a WAC Private—Army Rule is No Excuses Accepted; WAC's Must Salute Colonel's Car, Whether He is in it or Not; Clothes Must Be Buttoned When Hanging Up," *Philadelphia Afro-American,* Oct. 2, 1943, p. 5. Lula Jones Garrett, "Jim Crow Irks WAC Recruiter," *Philadelphia Afro-American,* Feb. 5, 1944, pp. 1, 16. See also Charity Adams Earley, *One Woman's Army: A Black Officer Remembers the WAC* (College Station, TX, 1989), pp. 126–127, 206.

17. "Mrs. Bethune Endorses WAACs," Folder: 535, box 38. See also Nov. 10, 1942, Mary McLeod Bethune to Mrs. Harriet B. Hall, Boston, MA, Dec. 20, 1943, concerning her opinion on segregation at Fort Des Moines, Folder: 237, box 14; Jeanetta Welch Brown, executive secretary, National Council of Negro Women (NCNW), to Mr. Charles P. Howard, general manager, The Howard News Syndicate, Sept. 29, 1943, concerning segregation at Fort Des Moines, Folder: 230, box 14; Maj. Gen. J. A. Ulio, adjutant general to Mary McLeod Bethune, Sept. 21, 1944, concerning the Army's general practice of segregation, Folder: 67, box 4. All in series 5, NCNW Papers, Bethune Museum and Archives. See also National Non-Partisan Council of Public Affairs of AKA Sorority to Secretary of War Henry Stimson, May 17, 1942, concerning planned segregation of the WAAC organization, box 10, series 54, RG 165, NA.

18. Mr. John G. McCormack, general manager, KWKH.KTBS Radio Stations, Shreveport, LA, to John Ewing, president of these radio stations, Apr. 17, 1943, concerning the fact that in Des Moines both white and black Waacs were stationed at the Chamberlain Hotel while attending the Cooks and Bakers Schools. Though they slept on separate floors, they shared the same eating facilities as well as K.P. and other duties. The women who wrote him indicated that this created a great deal of anxiety for them and was in general distasteful. This letter was passed on to Hobby. Representative George Mahon of Texas to Col. Howard Clark, Chief Operations Services, Army Service Forces (ASF), Apr. 22, 1943, concerning reports he had received from white people in his district about the plight of white Wacs forced to share their quarters and other facilities with black women, Folder: 291.21, box 50, series 54, RG 165, NA. Most of these writers felt that the Army and the WAAC were "deceiving" young white women by putting them in situations where they were "forced" to associate with African-American women, thereby creating a great deal of stress and hardship for the Euro-American women.

19. Memorandum for Director of Personnel, ASF, Apr. 6, 1945, "Report of Protest on Assignment of Negro Wacs to Gardner General Hospital, Chicago, Illinois, Folder: 291.2, box 49, series 54, RG 165, NA.

20. Jeanetta Welch Brown, executive secretary, NCNW, brief statement on "The Role of the Negro Woman in the Post-war World," Folder: 239, box 14, series 5, NCNW Papers, Bethune Museum and Archives.

21. "A WAC Talks Back," T5g. Bernice Brown of the New York Port of Embarkation, box 1, series 54, RG 165, NA; "Idea Sheet for WAC Allocation 20 Feb 1944," Feb. 11, 1944, Folder: 330.13, box 90, series 54, RG 165, NA. See also Blake Clark, "Ladies of the Army," *Readers Digest,* May 1943, pp. 85–88, condensed from *This Week Magazine, New York Herald Tribune,* Apr. 14, 1943. S.Sgt. Blanche A. Bordeaux, "What the WAC has Meant to Me," *Christian Science Monitor,* May 11, 1946, p. 10. See also D'Ann Campbell, "Service-

women of World War II," *Armed Forces and Society* 16 (Winter 1990): 254. Campbell argues that "patriotic" statements concerning women joining the WAAC/WAC because of male family members and friends and a desire to hasten the end of the war were much used by Army and WAAC/WAC publicists.

22. Joyce Melva Baker, *Images of Women in Film: The War Years, 1941-45* (New York, 1981). Baker argues that the real heroine during World War II was not "Rosie the Riveter" or a servicewoman but the "housewife/mother" who sacrificed her own needs to engage in temporary employment to aid the war effort. She further discusses military women specifically by noting that films dealing with women in uniform focused predominantly on nurses and that their public acceptance was conditional on their giving first priority to the men they loved.

23. "Off the Waac's Record," *Waac News,* May 15-22, 1943, p. 6, box 212, series 55, RG 165, NA. See also "Wac's Wiles Are Womanly," *Recreation,* June 1945, p. 108. See also "Homemaking Instinct Outs: WAAC Barracks Grow Fully," *Philadelphia Afro-American,* June 5, 1943, p. 16.

24. Mrs. Ruth Massey, "From an Army Wife," *Dallas News,* Mar. 15, 1945, Folder: Clippings, WAAC 1942, box 3, Hobby Papers, LC. See also transcript of Larry Lesueur interviewing Hobby in London, Folder: Colonel Hobby Overseas, box 188, series 55, RG 165, NA.

25. Press Release, June 11, 1943, "Statement from Nine Church Leaders," box 21, series 54, RG 165, NA. See also Ernest O. Houser, "Those Wonderful GI Janes," *Saturday Evening Post,* Sept. 9, 1944, pp. 26-28, 60, 63. He noted that "soldiering hasn't transformed these Wacs into Amazons—far from it. They have retained their femininity, and if you ask them what they want to do after the war, the majority will reply, 'Have a home and babies . . . ' "

26. Mrs. A. Guttentag to Mr. Stimson Secretary of War (SW), June 17, 1943, box 90, series 54, RG 165, NA. See also *WAC Newsletter,* September 1944, box 218, series 55, RG 165, NA; Folder: SPWA 080 USO, box 15, series 54, RG 165, NA; and "Statements by Members of the Advisory Council" at the conclusion of their trip to Fort Des Moines and Camp Crowder, Apr. 16-18, 1943, Folder: 536 WAC 1945-47, box 38, series 5, NCNW Papers, Bethune Museum and Archives.

27. Bethune to Mrs. Harriet B. Hall, Nov. 10, 1942, concerning segregation at Fort Des Moines. Bethune writes, "There is only one thing I can say regarding segregation there—that I never have and never will give my consent to segregation at Des Moines or any where else. . . . Nobody is more grieved than I at the growing tendency toward any segregated set-up at Des Moines." See also Jeanetta Welch Brown, executive secretary, NCNW, Sept. 29, 1943, to Mr. Charles P. Howard, general manager, The Howard News Syndicate, where she writes, "We feel that any move which will make permanent the policy of segregation is not in keeping with our present day idea of full integration." Folder: 237 Correspondence H, box 14, series 5, NCNW Papers, Bethune Museum and Archives. See also Bethune for NCNW to Hobby, ca. November 1943, Folder 291.2, box 49, series 54, RG 165, NA.

28. Personnel Division WAAC Intra-Office Memorandum, Hobby to Executive Officer, Aug. 31, 1942; Adj. Gen. J. A. Ulio to Mr. George M. Johnson, Assistant Executive Secretary, Office for Emergency Management, War Manpower Com-

mission, Aug. 22, 1942. The adjutant general also made the argument that black Waacs were actually given preferential treatment over white Waacs because of the 10-percent quota that reserved space for them within the women's organization, Folder: SPWA 291.21 (8-10-42), box 49, series 54, RG 165, NA. See also Statement of WAAC re: Negro Personnel, Nov. 18, 1943, Folder 291.2, box 49, series 54, RG 165, NA; and the Washington Bureau Fraternal Council of Negro Churches in America booklet "GI Bill of Rights," August 1944; Ulio to Bethune, Sept. 21, 1944, Folder 329 Military Training 1943–45, box 21, series 5, NCNW Papers, Bethune Museum and Archives.

29. Hobby to Bethune, June 19, 1942; Major Grant, recruiting officer to Sergeant Stephenson, recruiter, May 27, 1942; Mary Elnora White to War Department, July 1, 1943, box 50, series 54, RG 165, NA. On the unequal treatment of black inductees, see Horace Claying, Director of Housing for Recruits to the Armed Forces, Induction Station 1, 639th Service Unit, Chicago, IL, July 8, 1944, Folder: 535-WAC 1942–45, box 38, series 5, NCNW Papers, Bethune Museum and Archives.

30. Telegram, Walter White to Hobby, July 12, 1943, Folder: NAACP, SPWA 291.2; Memorandum to Assistant Secretary of War from John J. McCloy, Executive Committee of the Negro Newspaper Publishers Association, July 16, 1943; L. Virgil Williams, Dallas Negro Chamber of Commerce, to Hobby, July 2, 1943, Folder: 291.2, box 49, series 54, RG 165, NA; June 10, 1943, ARL 543, WD HG WAAC Sixth Service Command, Chicago, IL, re: Lt. Ruth L. Freeman's removal as WAC recruiting officer (Negro) in Chicago, Folder: Assignment, WAAC Officers to All Training Centers, June 1, 1943, box 37, series 54, RG 165, NA.

31. Hobby to White, July 12, 1943, Folder: NAACP, SPWA 291.2; First Officer Elizabeth C. Strayhorn, WAAC, to Mr. L. Virgil Williams, executive secretary, Dallas Negro Chamber of Commerce, July 17, 1943, Folder: 291.2, box 49, series 54, RG 165, NA; June 20, 1943, ARL 543 WD HG WAAC Sixth Service Command, Chicago, IL, Folder: Assignment, WAAC Officers to all Training Centers, June 1, 1943, box 37, series 54, RG 165, NA.

32. WAAC Memorandum Maj. Harold Edlund to Colonel Catron, Subject: Negro Recruiting, Folder: Untitled, box 39, series 54, RG 165, NA; Internal Memorandum Edlund to Hobby, July 14, 1943, Folder: 291.2, box 48-9, series 54, RG 165, NA.

33. Representative George Mahon of Texas to Col. Howard Clark, Chief, Operational Services, Apr. 22, 1943; Hobby to Mahon, May 5, 1943; Rev. Palfrey Perkins, president, and Seaton W. Manning, executive secretary, Boston Urban League, to Hobby, Nov. 17, 1942, and Hobby's response, Dec. 2, 1942, box 50, series 54, RG 165, NA.

34. Hobby Speech to United Daughters of the Confederacy, National Convention, Columbus, OH, Nov. 19, 1943. In this speech Hobby lauds the "heroes of the great Confederacy" who fought in a "noble losing cause, but who had so much honor" and characterizes the WAC as made up of their women descendants. Obviously, she is not including African-American women in her list of "descendants," box 15, series 54, RG 165, NA.

35. For a discussion of the ways that the Army denigrated African-American servicemen's participation during World War I and World War II, see Nalty, *Strength for the Fight*, pp. 107–124, 168–177.

36. Memorandum No. W635-19-43, Sept. 1, 1943, "Prohibition of the Use of Weapons or Arms by Members of the WAAC/WAC," Folder: WAAC Circulars, Bulletins, Regulations, box 215, series 55, RG 165, NA.

37. Study reported by Hobby to Chief of Staff, Nov. 16, 1942, re: Use of British women in fixed AAC gun installations in British Isles; Conference held on suggestion to use Waacs in fixed AAC installations, Nov. 18, 1942; 150th and 151st WAAC AAAC Companies constituted, Jan. 1, 1943; Draft of Amendment to WAAC Act of May 14, 1942, Folder: WAAC, SPWA 320.2, series 55, RG 165, NA. Treadwell, *The Women's Army Corps*, pp. 302–303.

38. Oral History Questionnaires, Olive C_____ (#9), Supplement, p. 3. Wacs served in every overseas theater during World War II, with the largest numbers serving in the European Theater (8,316), the Southwest Pacific Area (5,500), and the Mediterranean and North African Theaters (over 2,000). Treadwell, *The Women's Army Corps*, pp. 380, 410, and appendix A, table 7, "Strength of Women's Army Corps in Overseas Theaters: 1943–46," pp. 772–773.

39. "Housing," p. 7, Folder: June 1944–August 1945, European Division ATC Historical Record Report, WACs in the European Division ATC June 1944–August 1945, box 308.04-1 (Jan. 31, 1945)–308.072 (June 1944–August 1945), Air Force Center for Historical Research, Maxwell AFB, Montgomery, AL. See also Edith Davis, WAAC and ETO Experiences, Oral History #1, May 16, 1986, Fifth WAC Reunion, Fort McClellan WAC Museum Oral Histories, Fort McClellan, AL. "We Also Can Serve," June 1943–June 1945, Yearbook from the 6,070th Post Headquarters Company, box 11, Hobby Papers, LC.

40. Folder: WDWAC 314.7 Military Histories, Historical Data and Notes on SWPA Wacs, box 55, series 54, RG 165, NA. See also Treadwell, *The Women's Army Corps*, pp. 418–450.

41. Susan Hartmann, *The Homefront and Beyond: American Women in the 1940s* (New York, 1982), pp. 47–48.

42. John J. McManus, president, Rolls-Royce, to Hobby, Feb. 8, 1945, box 19, series 54, RG 165, NA. See also "History AAF, Eastern Flying Training Command (EFTC), p. 59 "Training," Folder: V.1 January–June 1944, box 222.01 (January–December 1943)–222.01 (January–June 1944), Air Force Center for Historical Research.

THE WARTIME HISTORY OF THE WAVES, SPARS, WOMEN MARINES, ARMY AND NAVY NURSES, AND WASPS

Judy Barrett Litoff and David C. Smith

You asked if I'd like to go home. More than anything on earth, but I couldn't leave now. Our work is just beginning.

Lt. Aileen Hogan, Army Nurse Corps, to Dear Family
Somewhere in France—Christmas Day, 1944[1]

For the past decade, we have been involved in a nationwide search to locate letters written by United States women during World War II. In the early 1980s, when we began this search, many of our colleagues and friends discouraged us from taking on this challenge because of the received wisdom that few, if any, letters written by American women had survived the vicissitudes of the war and the postwar years. Today, some 30,000 letters and 10 years later, we can state unequivocally that the received wisdom was wrong.[2]

Our search for women's wartime correspondence has led us down many circuitous paths and avenues. We have traveled to 23 states and Washington, DC, submitted authors' queries to all of the daily newspapers in the United States, aired appeals on radio and television stations, conducted research at scores of libraries and archives, targeted minority groups, and written more than 2,500 letters of inquiry.

Many of the women in uniform who have donated letters to our archive have included the caveat that they doubt that there is anything of value in their missives because they were careful to follow the dictates of strict wartime censorship regulations. Others have apologized for the cheery, upbeat quality of their letters, noting that they did not want to cause the recipients, who were often family members, undue worry and stress. These same letter collections, however, contain telling accounts of the courage of African-American women in uniform as they combatted racism at home and fascism abroad, glimpses of the stress and strain that lesbians in the military encountered, and the blossoming of hetero-sexual love in the face of battle. They speak of dodging "buzz bombs" in England and helping to perform emergency surgery in evacuation hospitals at the front, providing aid and comfort for returning prisoners of war who had been incarcerated at Japanese internment camps, caring for the survivors of Dachau, and coping with the tragedies of war's carnage, as well as sharing intense camaraderie with other women in uniform as they assumed new and challenging responsibilities on behalf of the war effort. Clearly, censorship regulations were not nearly so strict as many have believed. In fact, what is most extraordinary about the letters in our archive is how much—rather than how little—frank and detailed commentary they contain. Our reading of these letters has con-vinced us that women's wartime correspondence captures the com-plexity and essence of women's experience of World War II better than any available source.

When the United States entered the war in December 1941, the opportunities for women to serve in the military were limited to registered nurses who qualified for membership in the Army or Navy Nurse Corps.[3] At the time of Pearl Harbor, the Army Nurse Corps numbered 5,433 members, while 823 women were members of the Navy Nurse Corps. By the end of World War II, with the help of American Red Cross recruitment campaigns, the number of military nurses had increased tenfold. All told, 76,000 women, representing 31.3 percent of all active professional nurses, served in the armed forces during World War II.[4]

Following the devastating events of December 7, 1941, the 119 Army and Navy nurses stationed in Hawaii faced exhausting workloads. Navy nurses aboard the hospital ship, the U.S.S. *Solace*, anchored at Pearl Harbor at the time of the attack, attended to injured military personnel who were rescued from the waters of the lagoon. Although these women sent hastily composed cable-grams and brief letters of assurance to relatives and friends in the States, it was often several weeks before they found the time to write letters that included detailed accounts of the events of December 7.

Lt. Monica Conter of Apalachicola, FL, was one of two Army nurses on duty at the Station Hospital, Hickam Field, HI, at the time of the Japanese attack. She described the chaotic events of December 7 in a December 22 letter to her parents:

> The wounded started coming in 10 minutes after the 1st attack. We called Tripler [Hospital] for more ambulances—they wanted to know if we were having "Maneuvers." Imagine! Well, the sight in our hospital I'll never forget. No arms, no legs, intestines hanging out. . . . In the meantime, hangars all around us were burning—and that awful "noise." Then comes the second attack—We all fell face down . . . in the halls, O.R., and everywhere and heard the bombers directly over us. We . . . had no helmets nor gas masks—and it really was a *"helpless"* feeling. . . . [T]he bombs were dropping all around us and when a 500 lb. bomb dropped, . . . it felt like it had hit us. . . . You know, I [have] always loved activity and excitement—[But] for once, I had "enough."[5]

The events of December 7 were also the subject of a letter that Monica Conter wrote to Maj. (later Col.) Julia O. Flikke, Superintendent of the Army Nurse Corps. Acknowledging that "there were parts of that day I can hardly account for," Conter concluded her letter with the comment, "There are days like December 7 when a nurse can fully appreciate her profession as never before, and deep inside there is a feeling of satisfaction and thankfulness that she was able to do her bit to help 'Keep 'em flying.' "[6]

In the months before the Pearl Harbor attack, as the nation stepped up its preparedness efforts, a campaign to establish official women's branches in the various military services was initiated. Representatives Edith Nourse Rogers of Massachusetts and Margaret Chase Smith of Maine, as well as First Lady Eleanor Roosevelt, were strong proponents of women in the military.

Following the establishment of the Women's Army Auxiliary Corps (WAAC) on May 15, 1942, the women's branch of the Navy, the WAVES (the acronym for Women Accepted for Volunteer Emergency Service), was created on July 30, 1942. By the end of the war, approximately 100,000 women had served in the WAVES. The women's reserve of the U.S. Coast Guard, SPAR (the acronym formed from the Coast Guard motto, *"Semper Paratus*—Always Ready"), was established on November 23, 1942, and 13,000 women eventually joined the Coast Guard. The Marine Corps Women's Reserve was founded on February 13, 1943, and some 23,000 women served in the Marines during the war years. All told, approximately 350,000 women served in the military during World War II.[7]

The establishment of women's branches within the military services generated considerable debate. Both inside and outside the military, significant objections to women's performing "men's jobs" were voiced. Moreover, neither young men in the military nor their loved ones were necessarily enthusiastic about women's joining the armed services in order to release men for combat. During the latter months of 1943, these types of concerns were expressed in a series of letters written by coast guardsmen who were disdainful of women in the military. The letters were printed in the *U.S. Coast Guard Magazine* and promoted strong replies from Spars, which were also published. One respondent, Yeoman Mary B. Coolen, countered, "None of us joined the U.S. Guard because we thought it was glamorous, or because we had a mercenary idea in mind. . . . Don't you think that we would make quite a lot more money in civilian life, right now? . . . Personally, I joined the Coast Guard because a Coast Guardsman (a true Coast Guardsman) rescued my father during the last war. Somewhere today that same man is fighting for all of us. At the time of my enlistment I remember his words in a letter: 'God bless the women of America, and may God especially bless you. You've chosen a top-notch outfit—be as proud of it as I am of you.' "[8]

Almost without fail, women who entered military service during World War II expressed great excitement and immense pride in their new status. Recruits wrote enthusiastic letters to family members and friends about life in the military and the camaraderie they shared with other women in uniform.

Twenty-one-year-old Eunice McConnell of Brooklyn, NY, who enlisted in the WAVES in February 1943, wrote to her parents from the Naval Training Station at Indiana University in Bloomington and exclaimed, "First of all I love it. I thought I loved it before I got here, I *knew* it when I got here, and I'm *more sure* of it every minute that I stay!" The camaraderie she shared with other Waves, her satisfaction in knowing that she was making an important contribution to the winning of the war, and her growing sense of self are recurring themes in the letters she wrote to her parents.[9]

In June 1943, following McConnell's assignment to the Naval Air Station in Alameda, CA, where she worked as a storekeeper, she reported, "Oh, Mom and Dad, I'm so happy. I'd be happy no matter where the Navy should send me. I'm happy because I know

I'm doing my share to help our side win and at the same time making such unusual acquaintances and having such wonderful experiences." Two months later, she commented, "Honestly, living here at the barracks with all these girls is really the most wonderful thing that ever happened to me. You'll probably find I've changed. It certainly teaches a person tolerance, and consideration for others and so many worth-while things."[10]

Pearl Gullickson of Donnelly, MN, was equally enthusiastic about her life as a Spar. Writing in December 1943 from the Coast Guard Training Station in Palm Beach, FL, she proudly informed her sweetheart that her storekeeper school class had been chosen to serve as the honor company during a visit by Capt. Dorothy Stratton, Director of SPAR, and Congresswoman Margaret Chase Smith, a strong proponent of women in the maritime branches of the military. Following the regimental review for the visiting dignitaries, Gullickson reported that "we did ourselves up proud like. Comments were that the Honor Company marched as one person, like a machine. Do we feel good!" A few months later, writing from her new duty station at the District Coast Guard Office in New York City, she described a trip to the Polo Grounds to see an "exciting" baseball game between the Giants and the Dodgers. She related how she and three other Spars "cockily" approached the gate designated as "free to men in service" and were "bowed through" by the ticket takers who said "This way for servicemen *and women*."[11]

The Marines were the last of the service branches to admit women. Indeed, Marine antipathy toward women in the military was quite strong, and according to the standard work on the history of the Marines, "there was considerable unhappiness about making the Corps anything but a club for white men."[12] Yet following the admittance of women into the Marines early in 1943, Commandant of the Marines Gen. Thomas Holcomb remarked, "There's hardly any work at our Marine stations that women can't do as well as men. They do some work far better than men. . . . What is more, they're real *Marines*. They don't have a nickname, and they don't need one. They get their basic training in a Marine atmosphere, at a Marine Post. They inherit the traditions of the Marines. They are Marines."[13]

In recognition of the important work of the women in the corps, Maj. Ruth Cheney Streeter, Director of the Marine Corps Women's Reserve, sent an open letter to her "girls" at boot camp in October 1943 and stated, "It is not easy to 'free a Marine to

Women Marines take charge of water transportation and consolidation of freight at Camp Lejeune, the huge Marine Corps training center in North Carolina, n.d.

National Archives, Records of the U.S. Marine Corps (127-N-6801)

fight.' It takes courage—the courage to embark on a new and alien way of life. . . . Your spirit is a source of constant inspiration to all who work with you. Your performance is a promise not only of a victory in the grim struggle in which we are engaged, but . . . of a better world than we have ever known before."[14]

In a January 1945 letter, written to her sister from boot camp at Camp Lejeune, NC, Pvt. Mary Cugini of Brighton, MA, accentuated the special esprit of women Marines: "We had our Captain's Inspection this morning. . . . She looked at my feet and read me off because my feet were not at a 45 degree angle. So you see, that's what the Marine Corps is—a very highly disciplined organization. That's why a Marine is so proud and full of pride—with a training like this, who wouldn't be." Two weeks later she remarked that Marine training "makes fine men and women out of us, and no kidding, . . . I feel like a woman of the world and I'm not afraid of anything or anyone (Rugged, huh?)." Reflecting on her experiences as a woman Marine from the perspective of almost 50 years, Mary Cugini Necko recently remarked, "My life changed forever when I stepped off the train at Camp Lejeune."[15]

Entrance into the military provided many new job opportunities for women. Although a large percentage of women in uniform performed administrative and clerical work, many other employment possibilities existed, especially in the field of aviation, where women served as metalsmiths, aircraft mechanics, parachute-riggers, air traffic controllers, flight orderlies, and Link trainer instructors. (A Link trainer was an on-ground flight simulator invented by Edwin A. Link.)

After completing basic training at the Hunter College Naval Training Station in The Bronx, NY, Mary Louise Wilkerson excitedly reported to her mother that she was among the "1% of all Waves" who were selected for "Litis," the acronym for Link Trainer Instructor's School. Following a rigorous Link training course at the Naval Air Station near Atlanta, GA, she confessed that "the last week . . . was simply hell. Everyday someone would come in to report they had been washed out. . . . In the final count over 25% of the class were washed out." Although her work as a Link instructor usually involved training naval cadets, Wilkerson was sometimes called upon to train officers. She acknowledged that the officers were not "unkind or anything," but she did admit that, as an enlisted woman, it was "something of a strain to be teaching the big-shots." While Wilkerson occasionally groused about the long hours of work demanded of Link trainer instructors, she took great pride in her duties, especially when one of her "boys" was "awarded a Silver Star for a direct hit on an enemy craft."[16]

Wave Betty Ann Farris of Detroit, MI, wrote animated letters to her parents about her work as a flight orderly. Despite occasional bouts with air sickness, she commemorated her first 6 months in the WAVES by exclaiming: "My 1/2 yr. anniversary in the Navy! Six whole months? It doesn't seem possible. I've loved every minute of it and have never once regretted joining. . . . It has been the most wonderful experience of my life."[17]

Yet the work required of flight orderlies could be quite daunting, especially for those women who were assigned to aircraft carrying sick and wounded servicemen evacuated from overseas. WAVE flight orderly June Kintzel, based at the Naval Air Station in Olathe, KS, accompanied many injured service personnel on flights across the United States. In an August 8, 1945, letter to her parents, she described the serious condition of patients, recently evacuated from Okinawa, that she assisted during one cross-country trip: "Eleven litter and four ambulatory cases made up the load and some of the litters were really bad off. Four of them looked like skeletons—being nothing but skin and bones, and having awful colors. One of them was dying of blood poisoning. Some of the others had both legs in casts, while another Marine was paralyzed from the chest down."[18]

One of the most unusual and exciting of the new jobs available for wartime women was that of ferrying aircraft throughout the United States for the Women Airforce Service Pilots (WASP), a quasi-military organization affiliated with the Army Air Forces. From September 1942 until December 1944, when the WASP was disbanded after it was not accorded full military status, approximately 1,000 women had the distinction of flying aircraft of all types throughout the United States.[19] The Wasps gloried in their work, and their wartime letters are filled with details of their love of flying. In an April 24, 1943, letter to her mother, Wasp Marion Stegeman of Athens, GA, recounted her joy of flying:

> The gods must envy me! This is just too, *too* to be true. (By now you realize I had a good day as regards flying. Nothing is such a gauge to the spirits as how well or how poorly one has flown.) . . . I'm far too happy. The law of compensation must be waiting to catch up with me somewhere. Oh, god, how I love it! Honestly, Mother, you haven't *lived* until you get way *up* there—all alone—just you and that big, beautiful plane humming under your control.[20]

When they were not on duty, women in uniform often led active social lives. They spent weekend leaves visiting nearby towns and cities, went to United Service Organizations (USO) shows, danced to wartime swing music at local nightclubs, saw scores of movies, ate restaurant meals away from their duty stations, and enjoyed a variety of other activities, such as roller skating, swimming, bowling, and playing tennis. From reading the letters of women who were stationed at stateside postings, one almost gets the sense that social activities were available every night of the week. One young Wave wrote to her parents and assured them that even though she might "talk about seeing so many different fellows and having dates with so many," she was not "fickle." Later, she wrote, "I have met hundreds of fellows since I've been in service. Some older, some younger, some richer, some just like ourselves, some with high-school educations, some with college degrees, some handsome, some ordinary." But she reassured her parents, "I choose my companions very carefully."[21]

As one might expect, some of these military romances resulted in marriage. Despite the widespread misconception that women in the military could not be married, marriage did not disqualify women from enlisting, nor was it grounds for discharge. Certain restrictions against marrying did apply, however, and commanding officers at local bases sometimes exercised their discretionary judgments.

Ens. Janet Murray of Johnstown, PA, a member of the Navy Nurse Corps, met her future husband, Lt. Robert Wooddall of Fairburn, GA, while they were both on active duty. As with many war marriages, Janet Murray introduced herself to her future parents-in-law by letter. In a May 2, 1944, letter to "Dear Mr. and Mrs. Wooddall," she frankly admitted that "this is a pretty difficult letter to write but I have wanted to do it for a long time." With unpretentious honesty, she continued,

> I realize how you both must feel about [your son] marrying a girl whom you have never met. My own parents feel the very same way. Golly, I'm not doing so well in writing this, am I? But, it all boils down to just this.—I love Bob, very much and always will, and I know that with God's help we will have a very happy married life.[22]

Service in the military brought people together from many different ethnic, religious, geographic, and socioeconomic walks of life. Bernice Sains Freid of St. Paul, MN, who served in the WAVES during the war, recently observed, "I had never been to a museum, seen an ocean, a mountain or a waterfall. Therefore, when I entered the Navy, I was like a WAVE in Wonderland."[23] In letters to her friends back home, Freid wrote with awe about her travels throughout the United States. Yet, as the only Jewish servicewoman in Yeoman School at the Naval Training Station in Stillwater, OK, she sometimes felt very alone and isolated. In a December 1944 letter to a friend, she confided that about two weeks after she arrived in Stillwater "a real melancholy swept over" her when she realized that she was "the only Jew on the campus." Fortunately, her sense of isolation was eventually eased when the USO at Oklahoma City put her in contact with a Jewish family that entertained Jewish servicemen and women each Saturday night.[24]

Military service provided African Americans with the opportunity to travel to distant places, meet new people, take on new jobs, and confront new challenges. For both black women and men in the military, however, this almost always occurred within segregated units.

Coping with prejudice and discrimination was a regular part of the experience of black women in the Army Nurse Corps. Letters written by African-American Army nurses to Mabel K. Staupers, executive secretary of the National Association of Colored Graduate Nurses and the unofficial watchdog of highly placed government and military officials during the war years, provided details about the deleterious conditions they regularly encountered. Letter writers told of being required to perform menial jobs, such as "scrubbing and cleaning of quarters," in place of and in addition to their nursing assignments, and they denounced the practice of routinely assigning black nurses to care for prisoners of war.[25] African-American nurses who were sent to England in the summer of 1944 and assigned to care for German prisoners at the 168th Station Hospital complained that they felt "pretty much let down to learn they travelled all that distance to take care of German prisoners" and that this was "really a 'bitter pill' to have to swallow."[26]

At the end of the war, approximately 500 black nurses were serving in the Army Nurse Corps (ANC). More black nurses would have enrolled in the ANC had it not been for the implementation of a quota system during the early years of the war. Not until January 1945 were black nurses admitted to the Navy Nurse Corps (NNC). Only four black women served in the Navy Nurse Corps, and they were fully integrated into the Navy.[27]

Black women were not accepted into the WAVES and SPAR until November 1944, a change that only occurred after substantial effort and protest by progressive organizations. Near the end of the war, in July 1945, the Navy reported that there were 2 black officers and 72 black enlisted women in the WAVES. The Coast Guard reported that four black women had been accepted into the SPAR. Both black Waves and Spars were fully integrated into their service branches. However, neither the Marines nor WASP accepted African Americans.[28]

Clementine Forsyth, an African-American apprentice seaman in training at the Hunter College Naval Training Station in The Bronx, NY, wrote to Walter White, the executive secretary of the National Association for the Advancement of Colored People, and informed him that "we mingle as freely with each other as though we were all of the same race. Everyone has the same opportunities and we may go up as far as we like. . . . To hear it from a person who is experiencing it is not only cause for gratitude, it's an authentic report of what is really going on."[29]

While uniformed women from the United States did not participate in organized combat during World War II, they were regularly assigned to postings that brought them up to or near the front lines of battle. Dressed in battle fatigues, 60 Army nurses waded ashore in North Africa on November 8, 1942, the day of the North African invasion. Army nurses went ashore on the Anzio beachhead in Italy on January 27, 1944, 5 days after the troop landings. On D-plus-4-day, June 10, 1944, Army nurses arrived in Normandy to set up field and evacuation hospitals for the troops.[30]

Army nurse June Wandrey served in North Africa, Sicily, Italy, France, and Germany, where her work as a combat surgical nurse

Army nurse 2d Lt. Mary V. Foger and patient Pfc. Everett C. Newburg, an infantry soldier, at a hospital in Normandy, France, January 25, 1945.

National Archives, Records of the Office of the Chief Signal Officer (111-SC-199813)

brought her close to the front lines of action.[31] Writing from "Poor Sicily" in August 1943, she bluntly informed her parents:

> We were so close to the [front] lines we could see our artillery fire and also that of the Germans. . . . Working in the shock wards, giving transfusions, was a rewarding, but sad experience. Many wounded soldiers' faces still haunt my memory. I recall one eighteen year old who had just been brought in from the ambulance to the shock ward. I went to him immediately. He looked up at me trustingly, sighed and asked, "How am I doing, Nurse?" I was standing at the head of the litter. I put my hands around his face, kissed his forehead and said, "You are doing just fine soldier." He smiled sweetly and said, "I was just checking up." Then he died. Many of us shed tears in private. Otherwise, we try to be cheerful and reassuring.[32]

Helen K. McKee, an Army nurse anesthetist with the 300th General Hospital in Naples, Italy, was assigned to evacuation hospitals during the Anzio landing and Cassino drive. Writing to her family in San Antonio, TX, about those difficult days, she confided that "our patients came to us with only first aid care. We debrided their wounds, did the amputations, took slugs out of the livers and removed their shell fragments from all vital organs. We cleaned them up—killed the maggots in their wounds, and *put them to bed between clean sheets."*[33]

Army nurse Ruth Hess arrived in France in late June 1944. In a long retrospective letter, written on August 8, 1944, to friends and colleagues at the Louisville (KY) General Hospital, Hess described her first days as a combat nurse in Europe:

> We embarked by way of a small landing craft with our pants rolled up—wading onto the beach a short distance. . . . We marched up those high cliffs . . . about a mile and a half under full packs, hot as "blue blazes"—till finally a jeep . . . picked us up and took us to our area. . . . Next afternoon we joined our unit in an enormous convoy and started toward the place we were supposed to set up our hospital. . . . For nine days we never stopped [working]. 880 patients operated; small debridement of gun shot and shrapnel wounds, numerous amputations, fractures galore, perforated guts, livers, spleens, kidneys, lungs, . . . everything imaginable. . . . It's really been an experience.

. . . At nite—those d—d German planes make rounds and tuck us all into a fox hole—ack ack in the field right beside us, machine guns all around—whiz—there goes a bullet—It really doesn't scare you—you're too busy—but these patients need a rest from that sort of stuff.[34]

During the summer of 1944, Army nurse Marjorie LaPalme served in England where she helped care for wounded soldiers who had been evacuated from the European battlefields. Disappointed that her assignment placed her far from the enemy lines, she wrote a letter to her parents in July, protesting that "everything is happening across the channel." Following a transfer to the 41st Evacuation Hospital in Belgium in October 1944, however, her morale significantly improved.[35]

Two months later, Marjorie LaPalme found herself caught up in the throes of the Battle of the Bulge. Her New Year's letter to her family provided further evidence that the work of Army nurses often occurred close to the battlefront:

Just before midnight . . . all Hell broke loose around here. Enemy planes strafing and bombing. . . . We are really scared—these explosions are so close. . . . The number of amputations is appalling. We get some terrible cases in. I can honestly say one lad with a horrible chest wound turned (his hair) white over night he was in such horrible pain.[36]

In a January 10, 1945, letter, marking the end of the Battle of the Bulge, LaPalme expressed both gratitude and relief that

our boys have pushed the Germans back to their original lines. They certainly put up a great stand—great fighters—such heroism. We have seen these kids, tired, dirty, sad, seeing their buddies mown down, but they always have a smile for the U.S. Army nurses, always willing to help us—wanting to talk to us about home and families. Grand kids. I love them all! like my own brothers! When I came over here I was just 21—among the youngest—Now here these kids are coming in at eighteen.[37]

The war against Japan encompassed a huge geographic area in which horrendous fighting took place. The story of the courage and fortitude of the more than 100 Army and Navy nurses who served in the Philippines in December 1941 and the early months of 1942 as they carried out their work in woefully overcrowded, makeshift hospitals at Bataan and Corregidor is well known.[38] When Corregidor fell on May 6, 1942, 67 Army nurses serving in the Philippines were captured and imprisoned at the Santo Tomas internment camp, where they remained until their liberation on February 3, 1945. In addition, 11 Navy nurses were captured and incarcerated at the Los Baños internment camp until their rescue on February 23, 1945.[39]

With the collapse of the U.S.-Filipino military effort in the Philippines in the spring of 1942, large numbers of American personnel, including military nurses, were evacuated to Australia, where Gen. Douglas A. MacArthur, former commander in chief of the Philippines and Supreme Commander of the Southwest Pacific Theater, established his headquarters. As General MacArthur planned for the Japanese campaign, troops and supplies from the United States were directed to the Southwest Pacific. Mary Mixsell, an Army nurse stationed in Australia in 1943 and 1944, wrote a letter to the *American Journal of Nursing* that included a description of her tent hospital "with [its] wooden floors, which never looked any cleaner after scrubbing." After discussing how she had learned "to improvise and economize with whatever was on hand," Mixsell concluded,

> Although I might have chosen to stay at home and help the war effort there, I wouldn't trade my present job with anyone else on earth and I hope that they don't send me home until the war is over for good. I like to be in the thick of it, have my information first-hand, and hear another American say, "Gee, it's good to talk to an American girl."[40]

Among the many military personnel to arrive in Australia during 1943 and 1944 were 15 African-American Army nurses who were assigned to the 268th Station Hospital, the only all-black hospital in the U.S. Army. Arriving in Sidney in early November 1943, the nurses of the 268th traveled to a staging area in Brisbane, where they trained for the difficult conditions they would soon encounter. In May 1944 they were transferred to the newly constructed 268th Station Hospital in Milne Bay, New Guinea, where they cared for hundreds of black troops. A year later, in May 1945, the 268th Station Hospital was reassigned to Manila to provide medical support for the impending invasion of Japan. The nurses of the 268th remained in Manila until October 1945, when they returned to the United States for discharge.[41]

Because of the fierceness of the jungle warfare in the Pacific, military commanders prohibited Army nurses from entering combat areas until they were declared "secured." This policy represented a sharp departure from the European and Mediterranean theaters where Army nurses often worked in field and evacuation hospitals close to the front lines of battle. From their hospital stations in Australia, New Zealand, the Fiji Islands, New Caledonia, the New Hebrides, New Guinea, and other "secured" areas, Army nurses received war casualties evacuated to these noncombat areas. Not until the invasion of the Philippines in October 1944 did Army nurses have the opportunity to care for battle casualties near the front lines. Arriving in Leyte on October 29, 1944, 9 days after the initial invasion, Army nurses began caring for the wounded within 3 hours of their landing.[42]

Throughout the war, Navy nurses were stationed on hospital ships sailing the waters of the Pacific, where they cared for the sick and the wounded. Writing from the U.S.S. *Bountiful* in January 1945, Navy nurse Georgia Reynolds observed, "Presented in terms of a civilian hospital, the task of the Navy hospital ship would be an impossibility. Imagine receiving approximately five hundred fresh casualties within the space of a few hours! . . . The wonders of plasma, the sulfa drugs, and penicillin could never be better demonstrated than on a hospital ship caring for fresh casualties."[43] During the early months of 1945, specially trained Navy flight nurses were assigned to hospital-equipped aircraft that evacuated critically wounded patients from captured airfields on Iwo Jima and Okinawa. The patients were then transported to hospitals in Guam, Pearl Harbor, and the continental United States.[44]

Originally, Waves, Spars, and women Marines were not permitted to serve outside the continental United States. In 1944, however, Representative Margaret Chase Smith introduced legislation in Congress allowing Navy women to serve in Alaska, Hawaii, and the Caribbean. When a contentious Congressman suggested that these women would find hardships that no American woman should endure, Smith tersely replied, "In that case, we'd better bring all the nurses home." The bill was approved, and early in 1945, a few Waves, Spars, and women Marines were assigned to duty in Hawaii and Alaska.[45]

Pvt. Lorraine Turnbull was assigned to the Marine Corps Air Station at Ewa, HI, where her skills as a flight mechanic were put to good use. She was one of just a thousand women Marines who were selected for overseas duty in Hawaii. In an April 5, 1945, letter to her mother, Turnbull provided an enthusiastic account of her first days at work as the "crew chief on an S.N.J. Texan" (a single-engine monoplane). She informed her mother that "I take care of it; inspect it each day, rev it up, gas and oil it, and keep it in 'going' condition always. When a pilot takes my plane, I have to guide the plane out and then bring it in. It's what I've dreamed about ever since I joined the M.C."[46]

President Harry S. Truman's proclamation of the cessation of hostilities on August 14, 1945, called for a nationwide holiday and a period of thanksgiving. Throughout the United States, millions of Americans triumphantly celebrated the end of the Second World War. Yet for many uniformed personnel, victory was celebrated with restraint; for they, more than most civilians, understood the difficult tasks that lay ahead.

In her "victory" letter to her parents, Wave Annabel Goode of Virden, IL, a Link trainer instructor stationed in Hawaii, responded to the news of the end of the war with thankful reserve:

> This is the day the whole world has been living for. Pau! (the end). I consider it a privilege to have received the news of peace here on the very island where our nation's part in the war began. I was at my Link desk giving a hop when the official message came over the radio this afternoon. . . . A silent surge of happiness seemed to possess each one of us. Our thoughts raced backward to December 7, 1941 and then forward to the civilian future we have hardly dared to contemplate seriously until today. Then, tying our four years of memories into one package with a prayer, each went on with his own occupation and plan for celebration.[47]

On the other side of the world in Germany, an Army nurse reported: "The war isn't over for us. . . . Everyone is thrilled, but it has been very quiet. Just like any other day."[48]

Combat and killing may have come to an end, but a multitude of tasks still faced uniformed personnel, especially those who were overseas. Released prisoners of war needed to be restored to health and reunited with loved ones. The survivors of the concentration camp "hell-holes" were in desperate need of food, medicine, and civilized human treatment. The "Displaced Persons" who poured into Western Europe with the end of the Nazi empire also needed the succor that could only be provided by the victors. Indeed, nurses and doctors began the work of rehabilitation even as the war was still raging.

On February 25, 1945, just 2 days after the liberation of the Los Baños internment camp, Navy nurse Mary Rose Harrington wrote a "short and how sweet you'll never know" letter to her mother in which she described the "spectacular rescue" of the internees by "fast and amphibious tank." She assured her mother that she and the other Navy nurses who had been incarcerated were "all in pretty good shape and with a bit of good chow for a few days we'll be raring to go again."[49]

In early June 1945, Army nurse June Wandrey wrote a heartrending letter to her family that recounted her arduous efforts to care for hospitalized victims from Dachau. Describing the patients as "corpse-like" with "macerated skin drawn over their bones, eyes sunken in wide sockets, hair shaved off," she noted that their bodies were "riddled with diseases" and that "you have to gently shake some of the patients to see if they are still alive."[50]

In a September 12, 1945, letter to her parents, Navy nurse Beatrice Rivers, stationed aboard the hospital ship U.S.S. *Relief,* off the coast of China, reported that the arrival of 800 recently liberated prisoners of war who had been incarcerated in Japanese internment camps "was an experience I'll never forget." She wrote that the "grateful" prisoners "came running down the dock waving their meager luggage" and were "sprayed . . . with DDT powder" as they boarded the ship. Although the *Relief* normally carried 621 passengers, Rivers explained that the ship made room for the 800 former prisoners by using makeshift cots and stretchers. Remarking that she had "heard atrocity stories which make your blood run cold," she revealed that "one group of 1290 men had only three hundred survivors."[51]

Most women who donned uniforms in World War II agreed then, and recall now, that they were significantly changed by their wartime experiences. For many, World War II was the defining event of their lives.[52] The challenges presented by their years at war enabled them to become stronger, more capable, and more tolerant individuals with a clearer sense of themselves and their capabilities. Writing to her parents from Germany in late August 1945, Army nurse Marjorie LaPalme spoke for many women in the military when she explained how the exigencies of war had dramatically transformed her life:

One thing is sure—we will never be the naive innocents we were at home—none of us. . . . It was a wonderful experience—no doubt the greatest of my entire life. I am sure nothing can surpass the comradeship and friendship we shared with so many wonderful men and women from all over our country—the good and the bad, suffering death and destruction falling from the skies, but perhaps most of all I will remember the quiet courage of common, ordinary people.[53]

Yet the postwar world that loomed before U.S. women presented a picture that was dim and unclear. The incredible devastation of the Second World War—capped with the horrors of Iwo Jima, Okinawa, Dachau, Belsen, Hiroshima, and Nagasaki during the last 6 months of the fighting—was such as to give serious persons much pause for thought. The future was not known, and the prospects were sobering for many. But what was generally understood was that U.S. women, drawing upon their myriad wartime experiences, *could* and *would* play a much stronger role than ever before in determining what the future would bring.

NOTES

© 1996 by Judy Barret Litoff and David C. Smith

1. Aileen Hogan to Dear Family, Dec. 25, 1944, in the World War II Letters of United States Women Archive, Bryant College, Smithfield, RI. A selection of the letters of Aileen Hogan appears in Judy Barrett Litoff and David C. Smith, *We're In This War, Too: World War II Letters From American Women In Uniform* (New York, 1994), pp. 163-168.

2. For additional information on how we located the letters, see Litoff and Smith, *We're in This War, Too,* "Introduction: The Case of the Missing Letters," pp. 3-9, and Judy Barrett Litoff and David C. Smith, *Since You Went Away: World War II Letters From American Women On The Home Front* (New York, 1991), pp. vii-x. A 70-reel microfilm edition of all 30,000 letters, to be published by Scholarly Resources, Inc., is in preparation.

3. No book-length study of the history of women in uniform during World War II has been published. The best introduction to this topic is D'Ann Campbell, *Women at War with America: Private Lives in a Patriotic Era* (Cambridge, MA, 1984), chapters 1 and 2. Campbell has published several excellent articles on servicewomen and World War II. Of special interest is "Women in Combat: The World War II Experience in the United States, Great Britain, Germany, and the Soviet Union," *Journal of Military History* 57 (April 1993): 301-323. Another good general account of uniformed women during the Second World War is Susan M. Hartmann, *The Home Front and Beyond: American Women in the 1940s* (Boston, 1982), chapter 3. Also useful is Susan M. Hartmann, "Women in the Military Service," in *Clio Was a Woman: Studies in the History of American Women,* Mabel E. Deutrich and Virginia C. Purdy, eds., (Washington, DC, 1980).

4. Philip A. Kalisch and Beatrice J. Kalisch, *The Advance of American Nursing* (Boston, 1978), p. 485, and "The Nurses' Contribution to American Victory," *American Journal of Nursing* 45 (September 1945): 683-686. A useful introduction to the history of the Army Nurse Corps during World War II is Judith Bellafaire, *The Army Nurse Corps in World War II* (Washington, DC, 1993). See also Susanne Teepe Gaskins, "G.I. Nurses at War: Gender and Professionalism in the Army Nurse Corps during World War II" (Ph.D. diss., University of California, Riverside, 1995). On the history of the Navy Nurse Corps, see the Bureau of Medicine and Surgery, U.S. Navy, *White Task Force: History of the Nurse Corps, United States Navy* (Washington, DC, 1946).

5. Litoff and Smith, *We're in This War, Too,* pp. 18-19.

6. Ibid., p. 19. The letter to Major Flikke originally appeared in the *American Journal of Nursing* 42 (April 1942): 425-426.

7. The standard work on the history of the Women's Army Corps is Mattie E. Treadwell's pioneering study, *The Women's Army Corps,* The United States Army in World War II, Special Studies, U.S. Army Center of Military History Pub. 11-8 (Washington, DC, 1954). Also valuable is Leisa Meyer, *Creating G.I. Jane: The Women's Army Corps During World War II,* (New York, 1996). On the history of African-American Wacs, see Martha S. Putney, *When the Nation Was In Need: Blacks in the Women's Army Corps During World War II* (Metuchen, NJ, 1992), and Janet Sims-Wood, "We Served America Too: Recollections of African Americans in the Women's Army Corps during World War II" (Ph.D. diss., Union Institute, 1994). There is no book-length study of the WAVES, either the organization or its members. An overview of the World War II experiences of Waves is contained in Susan H. Godson, "The Waves in World War II," *Naval Institute Proceedings,* December 1981, pp. 46-51. Godson is currently working on a book about the WAVES. Good information on the WAVES during World War II is included in Jean Ebbert and Marie-Beth Hall, *Crossed Currents: Navy Women from WWI to Tailhook* (Washington, DC, 1993). A useful review of the literature about the WAVES is Regina T. Akers, "Female Naval Reservists During World War II: A Historiographical Essay," *MINERVA* 8 (Summer 1990): 55-61. Very little has been published about SPAR. A recent pamphlet, produced by the Coast Guard, is *The Coast Guard & the Women's Reserve in World War II* (Washington, DC, 1992). An unpublished official history is "The Coast Guard at War, Women's Reserve" (Washington, DC, 1945). Two recently published, well-researched histories of the Marine Corps Women's Reserve are Mary V. Stremlow, *Free A Marine To Fight: Women Marines in World War II* (Washington, DC, 1994), and Peter A. Soderbergh, *Women Marines: The World War II Era* (Westport, CT, 1992). An unpublished, official history is Pat Meid, "Marine Corps Women's Reserve in World War II" (Washington, DC, 1968). Two other groups of women who served in uniform were dietitians and physical therapists. In 1943 both civilian dietitians and physical therapists who worked in Army hospitals, who could pass the physical examination, and who had no children under 14 years of age were "requested" to join the Army. Qualified women were granted blanket commissions and then assigned to duty with the Medical Department of the Army. At the end of the war, 1,600 dietitians and 1,100 physical therapists were serving in the Army. U.S. Department of Commerce,

Bureau of the Census, *Statistical Abstract of the United States, 1946* (Washington, DC, June 1946), p. 221.

8. "The Mail Buoy," *U.S. Coast Guard Magazine*, January 1944, p. 7.

9. Litoff and Smith, *We're in This War, Too*, p. 94.

10. Ibid., pp. 96–97.

11. Ibid., pp. 104, 107.

12. Allan R. Millett, *Semper Fidelis: The History of the United States Marine Corps* (New York, 1980), p. 374.

13. Pat Meid, "Marine Corps Women's Reserve in World War II," p. 64.

14. The Streeter letter is quoted in Soderbergh, *Women Marines*, p. 53.

15. Litoff and Smith, *We're in This War, Too*, pp. 109–110. Mary Cugini Necko to the authors, Oct. 8, 1992.

16. Mary Louise Wilkerson to her mother, Aug. 11, Oct. 23, 1943; Mar. 29, 1944; Jan. 27, May 20, 1945, in the World War II Letters of United States Women Archive.

17. Litoff and Smith, *We're in This War, Too*, p. 52.

18. Ibid., p. 246.

19. On the history of the Women Airforce Service Pilots, see Marianne Verges, *On Silver Wings: The Women Airforce Service Pilots of World War II* (New York, 1991).

20. Litoff and Smith, *We're in This War, Too*, p. 115.

21. Eunice G. McConnell to her parents, June 27, July 7, 27, 1943, in the World War II Letters of United States Women Archive.

22. Litoff and Smith, *We're in This War, Too*, p. 62.

23. Bernice Sains Freid to the authors, n.d. [received September 1992].

24. Litoff and Smith, *We're in This War, Too*, pp. 64–65.

25. See, for example, ibid., pp. 68–71.

26. Ibid., p. 70.

27. Jesse J. Johnson, *Black Women in the Army Forces, 1941–1974* (Hampton, VA, 1974), p. 48.

28. Ibid., p. 33. *The Coast Guard & the Women's Reserve in World War II*, p. 5. Regina Akers is working on a history of black Waves during World War II.

29. Litoff and Smith, *We're In This War, Too*, p. 79.

30. Robert V. Piemonte and Cindy Gurney, eds., *Highlights in the History of the Army Nurse Corps* (Washington, DC, 1987), pp. 14–18.

31. For an excellent account of Wandrey's World War II experiences, see June Wandrey, *Bedpan Commando: The Story of a Combat Nurse During World War II* (Elmore, OH, 1989).

32. Litoff and Smith, *We're in This War, Too*, p. 128. This letter originally appeared in Wandrey, *Bedpan Commando*.

33. Ibid., pp. 133–134.

34. Ibid., p. 159.

35. Ibid., p. 171.

36. Marjorie LaPalme to Dear Family, Jan. 1, 1945, in the World War II Letters of United States Women Archive.

37. Litoff and Smith, *We're in This War, Too*, p. 175.

38. An especially good article, with an extensive bibliography, is Philip A. Kalisch and Beatrice J. Kalisch, "Nurses under Fire: The World War II Experience of

Nurses on Bataan and Corregidor," *Nursing Research,* November–December 1976, pp. 409–429. Also useful is Elizabeth M. Norman and Sharon Eifried, "How Did They All Survive? An Analysis of American Nurses' Experiences in Japanese Prisoner-of-War Camps," *Nursing History Review* 3 (1995): 105–127. The story of these nurses has been poignantly depicted in the Department of Defense documentary film, *We All Came Home—Army & Navy Nurse POWS.* Two feature-length movies, *So Proudly We Hail* (1943) and *Cry Havoc* (1943), also depict the experiences of the nurses at Bataan and Corregidor.

39. *White Task Force,* [p. 5]. Piemonte and Gurney, eds., *Highlights in the History of the Army Nurse Corps,* p. 14.

40. *American Journal of Nursing* 44 (March 1944): 290. Quoted in Litoff and Smith, *We're in This War, Too,* pp. 180–181.

41. We would like to thank Prudence Burns Burrell, one of the 15 African-American Army nurses to serve with the 268th Station Hospital, for providing us with this information.

42. The following April, six Army nurses assigned to the hospital ship U.S.S. *Comfort* off the coast of Leyte were killed in an attack by a Japanese suicide plane. A total of 16 Army nurses died as a result of enemy action. All told, 201 Army nurses died during World War II. For additional information on Army nurses in the Pacific during World War II, see Bellafaire, *The Army Nurse Corps,* pp. 24–29, 31.

43. Litoff and Smith, *We're in This War, Too,* p. 200. The letter of Georgia Reynolds originally appeared in the *American Journal of Nursing* 45 (March 1945): 234–235.

44. *White Task Force,* [pp. 10–11].

45. Frank Graham, Jr., *Margaret Chase Smith: Woman of Courage* (New York, 1964), p. 41.

46. Litoff and Smith, *We're in This War, Too,* p. 219.

47. Ibid., pp. 222–223.

48. Ibid., p. 227.

49. Mary Rose Harrington to Mrs. Petra Harrington, Feb. 25, 1945, in the World War II Letters of United States Women Archive. We would like to offer a special thank-you to Mary Rose Harrington Nelson for making this letter available to us. For a good account of the last days at Los Baños, see Anthony Arthur, *Deliverance at Los Baños* (New York, 1985).

50. Litoff and Smith, *We're in This War, Too,* p. 225. This letter originally appeared in Wandrey, *Bedpan Commando.*

51. Litoff and Smith, *We're in This War, Too,* p. 234.

52. An excellent discussion of this topic, using wartime and contemporary surveys, is D'Ann Campbell, "Servicewomen of World War II," *Armed Forces and Society* 16 (Winter 1990): 251–270. After surveying the opinions of more than 700 women who served in the military during World War II, Campbell concluded that "the war was one of the best experiences of their lives. . . . It was a moment in their lives when patriotism and personal opportunity came together and shaped their future," pp. 262, 266.

53. Marjorie LaPalme to Dearest Mom, Dad, and Kids, Aug. 25, 1945, in the World War II Letters of United States Women Archive.

CONTRIBUTING TO THE WAR EFFORT

When Pearl Harbor was attacked in 1941, the only women serving in the U.S. military were members of the Army and Navy Nurse Corps. With America's entry into the war, more than 350,000 women volunteered to serve in the various branches of the Armed Forces to help ease the shortage of resources. Servicewomen performed a wide variety of noncombat military jobs, ranging from clerical tasks considered well-suited to the skills of women to occupations traditionally held by men. Their contributions were important to the war effort in every theater of operation.

In the first paper of the session, Col. Mary T. Sarnecky highlighted the work of women in the medical professions during the war. She portrayed the nurses, physicians, dentists, dietitians, physical and occupational therapists, and enlisted medical technicians as patriotic, selfless, caring, and innovative women who exerted power in eminently powerless roles under often perilous conditions.

Mary B. Johnston was stationed in New Guinea and the Philippines during the war as a cryptanalyst in the Women's Army Corps (WAC). In her paper she gave a descriptive account of her cryptographic training and role in deciphering Japanese military codes as well as the satisfaction that she felt upon making a difference in the war in more personal and unexpected ways. The social, political, and environmental factors that framed her experiences were woven into the narrative.

RitaVictoria Gomez drew upon richly detailed primary sources in presenting the history of women pilots in World War II. She recounted the efforts of Nancy Harkness Love and Jacqueline Cochran to create experimental units of women pilots for noncombat duty, establish flight procedures, train cadet pilots, shape military and public opinion in support of women pilots, and seek recognition through military status. Although merger of the Women's Auxiliary Ferrying Squadron (WAFS) and the Women's Flying Training

Detachment (WFTD) produced only a short-lived Women Airforce Service Pilots (WASP) program, its contributions were notable.

The session was chaired by Maj. Constance J. Moore, Army Nurse Corps historian at the U.S. Center of Military History in Washington, DC, and author of studies on nursing history, research, and practice.

WOMEN, MEDICINE, AND WAR

Mary T. Sarnecky

The epoch of World War II serves as a watershed in the history of women in the military. Although the Army and Navy Nurse Corps had served as integral elements of the force since 1901 and 1908 respectively, no other women, medical or otherwise, had been allowed within the portals of the male-dominated military establishment for many years. The dire conditions and voracious demands of that global conflict, World War II, provided the opportunity for a host of women in the medical professions to gain entrée. The women's participation and their contributions subsequently represented a giant step toward military equal opportunity, which began in 1901 and which will someday culminate in absolute gender parity within our country's armed forces.

Although Army and Navy nurses were among the first women to contribute to the U.S. military effort in World War II, a number of other patriotic health professionals soon joined their ranks. These women were physicians, dentists, dietitians, physical therapists, occupational therapists, and enlisted technicians.

Dietitians and reconstruction aides (later called physical therapists) served as civilian employees of the Army during and after World War I.[1] The status of dietitians and physical therapists as civil servants continued until 1943, when these professionals gained the status of relative rank. Occupational therapists, however, were not granted relative rank at that time. Their conspicuous lack of rank resulted in recruitment difficulties, and their civilian status precluded overseas service during World War II. In 1944 regular rank followed for dietitians and physical therapists.[2]

The dietitians and physical therapists of World War II served in all theaters of action. Three dietitians and one physical therapist not only served but also became prisoners of the Japanese in the Philippines early in 1942. They remained imprisoned there until 1945.[3]

Prevalent shortages, even absences, of supplies and equipment quickly transformed the women physical therapists and dietitians into masters of improvisation during World War II. Mary Motley was a dietitian who was captured and sequestered in the Santo Tomas internment camp in Manila. Motley's comments demonstrate the versatility of these professionals. Not only did she prepare and serve meals, but she also grew the provisions for her fellow prisoners and fashioned cooking equipment from very basic raw materials:

> We had to dig pits in which to build a fire . . . the equipment we used most was a 50 gallon oil can with the top cut off; this was placed over the fire pit, and in it we cooked the rice, which was our main food.
>
> In our camp we had a small garden, so we had to do most of the planting on a mass production basis. It takes a lot of vegetables to feed 4,000 people! We found a plant called talinum which grew very rapidly, a green vegetable similar to spinach except that it is rather slick when cooked. We found that we fared much better if we had this green vegetable along with the rice. Many didn't like it, but they ate it and were glad to get it.

Motley concluded by saying:

> I have seen many horrible things, but I have also seen many acts of bravery, courage and sacrifice that make me proud to think I am an American. I know I never realized before what it meant to be a free American, and I am happy just to be alive and to be back with you again.[4]

Although Motley's experiences paint a picture of resourcefulness in unusual circumstances, they were not unique. Another dietitian, 2d Lt. Helen F. Boswell, who was stationed in Tunisia, traded among the local tribesmen in an effort to procure eggs—a rare commodity! Boswell and her mess sergeant offered to exchange readily available Army tea for more scarce eggs in Bizerte in North Africa. An afternoon's bartering could yield perhaps 15 dozen eggs.[5]

Physical therapists in other areas also improvised. When there were no treatment tables available, they used mess tables padded with blankets.[6] Some used a clothing iron to apply therapeutic heat. The physical therapist insulated the body part with several blankets and a sheet and then cleverly ironed it as if it were a piece of clothing.[7] Paraffin also served as a modality to apply heat to a specific body part. However, it was impossible to procure this material through normal supply channels. Instead, the resourceful physical therapists of World War II procured paraffin by melting candles, raiding the laboratory for histologic paraffin, or visiting a nearby oil refinery.[8] All of these dedicated women demonstrated ingenuity and creativity in a myriad of ways in order to provide care for our boys.

By the end of the war in September 1945, 1,580 dietitians and 1,300 physical therapists were on duty.[9] Occupational therapists serving in the Zone of the Interior (the continental United States) numbered 899.[10] The contributions of these World War II women veterans paved the way for the establishment of a permanent corps. In the aftermath of the war, leaders in these professions focused significant energy and attention on efforts to establish the Women's Medical Specialist Corps, a branch of the Regular Army exclusively consisting of dietitians, physical therapists, and occupational therapists. They achieved their objective in 1947.[11]

Before World War II, women physicians who sought to serve in the armed services met with failure. The military adamantly prohibited women from joining the medical corps. This prohibition motivated the American Women's Medical Association to form a legislative committee in 1939. The committee's purpose was to foster legislation authorizing commissions for women physicians. The group met with success in April 1943, when Congress acted to appoint female physicians in the Army and Navy Medical Corps for the duration of the war plus 6 months.[12] As a result of their efforts, 75 women served as medical officers in the Army, and 35 served with the Navy during the war.[13] But even before these determined women became officers in the medical department, a few managed to serve their country by joining the Navy's WAVES (Women Accepted for Volunteer Emergency Service) and the Army's WAAC (Women's Army Auxiliary Corps).[14]

Dr. Margaret Craighill was the first woman officer in the Army's medical corps. The dean of Philadelphia's Woman's Medical College, she served in the surgeon general's office as the WAC (Women's Army Corps) liaison.[15] One of Major Craighill's most significant contributions was her development of standards governing the screening of women applicants and the medical care of Wacs in the areas of gynecology, psychiatry, and other medical conditions.[16]

Many military hospital units claimed a woman physician on their staff. One such unit, the Army's 239th General Hospital serving in

France, had four women medical officers on its roster. Capt. Jessie Reid of New Jersey served as Chief of General Surgery although her training was in obstetrics and gynecology. Capt. Bronislava Reznik of Chicago served as an otolaryngologist (ear, nose, and throat specialist). Captain Seno of Wisconsin did general ward duty, and Capt. Clara Raven from Detroit was Chief of the Laboratory Service.[17] Another medical officer, Maj. Margaret Janeaway of New Jersey, also made notable contributions. She attended the first contingent of Wacs to deploy overseas, serving in Africa. Janeaway investigated and made recommendations for health standards governing women soldiers overseas.[18]

Cornelia Gaskill was one of the first woman doctors to serve as a reserve officer in the Navy. A 1937 graduate of Cornell University School of Medicine, Gaskill left a busy New York City practice in 1942 to serve her country. Lieutenant (jg.) Gaskill's initial assignment was at the National Naval Medical Center in Bethesda, MD. Her husband served as well but as an Army doctor.[19] Hulda Thelander was another pioneer woman physician in the Naval Reserve. On April 19, 1944, she assumed her duties in San Francisco at the Headquarters of the Marine Corps, Pacific. Like the women doctors in the Army, Gaskill's and Thelander's commissions were for the duration of the emergency plus 6 months.[20] It was not until 1948 that the Navy appointed Dr. Frances L. Willoughby as a lieutenant commander with a regular commission in the Navy Medical Corps. Willoughby was a native of Pitman, NJ.[21]

The Navy blazed the trail in the ranks of women dentists. Sara G. Krout was the first woman dentist to serve in World War II. A native of Latvia, Krout earned dental degrees both in her homeland and at the University of Illinois. Because women were prohibited from joining the Navy Dental Corps at that time, she accepted a commission in the WAVES in 1944. Krout served for 2 years at Great Lakes Naval Training Station providing routine dental services, teaching denture construction, and taking part in research. Following the war, she remained active in the Naval Reserve. Like Krout, Alice Tweed also served in the Navy from 1944 until 1946. Originally from Arizona, Tweed made her contributions in general operative dentistry at the San Diego Naval Hospital. A third woman dentist and oral surgeon was pioneer Helen Myers. Myers earned her dental degree from Temple University in Philadelphia. She attempted to join the Army in 1941. Her initial efforts met with defeat. It was not until 1951 that Myers was accepted into the Army Dental Corps as the first woman dental officer in that branch of the military.[22]

At its peak the strength of the Navy Nurse Corps during World War II totaled 11,086. Of those, five Navy nurses became prisoners of the Japanese on Guam. They subsequently were shipped to Japan and imprisoned for almost a year.[23] Eleven Navy nurses became Japanese prisoners in Manila in 1942. They remained as prisoners of war for 37 months in the Los Baños internment camp.[24] Navy nurses within the United States served in 40 hospitals, 176 dispensaries, and 6 schools for hospital corpsmen. Outside the United States, they could be found providing nursing care in seagoing vessels, in land-based units, and in air-evacuation craft.[25]

A number of Navy nurses were assigned to the hospital ship *Relief*, which operated in the Pacific theater during World War II. The vessel's mission was to transport casualties from ever-changing rendezvous points to shore hospitals, usually in Guam, Saipan, and Tinian. As all nurses do in combat, the *Relief*'s contingent of nurses became proficient operating under nightly conditions of blackout. They participated in ship's drills to insure speedy and efficient evacuation in case of enemy attack. At one point, while under the double threat of both a typhoon and an enemy attack, the nurses assisted in taking on 691 patients in little more than an hour. The ship's crew used derricks and gangplanks to load the wounded, "shooting them into wards for their wounds and into surgery when they needed it." After the invasion of Okinawa, the *Relief* census included many burn patients. The wise, proficient Navy nurses lifted these patients' morale by assigning more able-bodied patients to feed and provide routine care for their more helpless shipmates. Another labor-saving and morale-enhancing ploy involved assigning one convalescent patient as "water boy," making him responsible for providing and recording fluid intake to every patient every hour.[26]

Land-based Navy nurses served in hospitals in the Aleutian Islands, Alaska, New Zealand, Australia, the New Hebrides Islands, New Caledonia, Russell Island, the Solomon Islands, the Admiralty Islands, the Mariana Islands, Hawaii, England, Africa, Italy, Newfoundland, Bermuda, the Canal Zone, Puerto Rico, Cuba, and Trinidad.[27] One member of the Navy Nurse Corps serving in a hospital in Portsmouth, VA, was instrumental in catching a spy. Evelyn Hope George worked in a fever therapy program. Sailors with venereal disease were placed in "fever cabinets" used to elevate their body temperature and thus treat their condition. George recalled that the suspected spy, a physician, would

> question the boys that were delirious and ask them questions about boats and ship movement and things. I thought it was irregular.... I asked another doctor . . . who I could trust, . . . if he thought that that was proper procedure. He said he didn't think so but that I had better not discuss it with anyone. The following day two men came in the department and questioned me.... They were in civilian clothes and they went into the main office and got [the "therapy"] doctor . . . they ushered him out and he left his cap with his scrambled eggs on it. We didn't see him again.[28]

The Navy Nurse Corps had a flight nurse program as well. In 1943, two Navy nurses attended the Army's flight nurse training program at Bowman Field, KY. Following graduation they were detailed to Rio de Janeiro, where they helped to establish an air-evacuation program for Brazilian Air Force nurses.[29] In early 1945, flight nurses based in Guam cared for air-evacuation patients who were casualties from operations on Iwo Jima and Okinawa.[30]

Army nurses also served around the globe in World War II, sometimes side by side with Navy nurses. They too became prisoners of the Japanese in the Philippines. Eighty-eight Army Nurse Corps (ANC) officers were assigned to the Philippines when the Japanese bombed those islands on December 8, 1941. Extensive bombings forced the nurses and their patients to retreat to the Bataan Peninsula and later to a tunnel built under the Malinta hill on Corregidor. Although some of the nurses escaped by aircraft or submarine, 66 were ultimately taken prisoner by the Japanese and courageously endured deprivation, primitive jungle conditions, and internment at prison camps at Santo Tomas University in Manila and remained there for 37 months until 1945.[31]

The first step in winning the war in Europe was securing the Atlantic approaches to Europe. From 1942 until 1945, Army nurses served in the bridging areas of Iceland, Greenland, Newfoundland, Canada, Bermuda, the Caribbean, Panama, Egypt, Africa, and the Persian Gulf.[32] Army nurses came ashore in Algeria with the troops in November 1942. They were the vanguard of the 5,000 nurses who tended the wounded and sick in North Africa, Sicily, Naples, Anzio, and the Alps of northern Italy. Army nurses also landed with the troops on the Anzio beachhead in January 1944. Enemy fire quickly turned the landing force into a blood bath of several months duration before the armies could begin their journey north to the Alps.[33]

Nurses served in units in the communications zone in North Africa from 1942 until well after Victory in Europe (V-E) Day. There, as everywhere, they were called upon to improvise in urgent situations. One nurse in Oran described how nurses in her unit employed tin cans as field expedients:

> Tin cans—we almost came to blows over them! The mess sergeant had to put special guards over them. One day one female thief picked up a bright shiny can and backed away with it behind her, talking loudly and laughing all the while. She fell backwards over a fence . . . on her nice new G.I. can. The kind sergeant said she could keep it. These cans were used for everything. The men cut them down and made covers so that we used them for soiled and salvage dressings. . . they were bath basins; they were used for a long time to carry food from the messhall. Everyone was so tin can conscious that we even put our initials on them. We were on British rations for a few weeks. The only good thing about that was that tea and cigarettes came in small flat tin boxes which were ideal for vaseline gauze. If we were fortunate enough, white enamel cans could be obtained from Medical Supply for dressings. Those who did not get them improvised with cans and others used wrappers. Cigar boxes covered with white paper or paint, and peanut jars made very nice thermometer trays. All bottles, such as shampoo, were requested urgently by the pharmacy.[34]

Any potential container was a valuable commodity.

Nurses destined for the European theater of operations (ETO) gathered in the staging areas of Britain in 1942. They spent 2 years preparing, training, and forming their units under conditions of nightly blackouts and frequent enemy bombings. By D-day, June 6, 1944, the theater had 10,000 Army nurses assigned to 88 different units. Nurses of two field hospitals and two evacuation hospitals came ashore at Utah Beach in Normandy on June 10, 1944. The Army nurses of another field hospital arrived at Omaha Beach on June 11, 1944. The hospital units kept pace with the advance of the combat lines.[35]

The campaign against the European Axis took first priority over the war in the Pacific. However, while war raged in Europe, Army nurses served in the south and central Pacific in Australia, New Guinea, New Zealand, New Hebrides, Tonga, Fiji, New Caledonia, Guadalcanal, Saipan, Guam, and Kwajalein. As the Allies island-hopped throughout the Pacific driving the Japanese forces out, the nurses closely followed.[36]

In 1943 Army nurses arrived in the China-Burma-India (CBI) theater. Two years later, over 1,300 nurses welcomed Victory over Japan (V-J) Day in duty stations in India, Ceylon, Burma, and China.[37] A description of the CBI context tells of one Army nurse's experiences while facing primitive conditions. Her story involved overcoming almost insurmountable communication and cultural barriers as well. Second Lt. Margaret G. Petrikin of the 20th General Hospital confronted an unusual sight on her first day of duty at the hospital on Mile 31 of the Ledo Road, where no American nurses had thus far served:

> Looking down the ward, nearly afraid to move, all I could think of was, what can I do with this place. Thirty-six Chinese, practically all bed patients, chattering away, happy as could be. Orange peels, eggshells, chicken feathers, and vegetable peelings piled high beside each bed. . . . I just stood there with a grin on my face, not knowing what to say. . . . I turned my head to what I supposed was the office. An eight by eight space with . . . table already stained with red and blue ink, a couple of chairs . . . a packing box for medicines . . . with a lock . . . nailed to the bamboo wall. I sat down and the corpsman tried to tell me what he was doing. Charts were pinned together . . . loose leaf pages for orders and the available drugs listed on a huge sheet of stiff cardboard. . . . I knew I was sent here to have Chinese wards function like any American ward, but I felt . . . I had . . . an assignment I couldn't fulfill. I . . . left the remaining desk work until later. I went down the ward nodding and smiling to this sea of strange faces, taking two steps forward and sliding one backwards, like in a bad dream, wanting to get it over and yet knowing this was where I was to work for maybe months to come.[38]

Later, Petrikin "had a vague idea" that she "might enjoy the work." She discovered that the Chinese were "naturally friendly, smiling, happy and ha[d] a marvelous sense of humor."[39]

Army nurses pioneered the flight nurse role. Over 1,000 budding flight nurses attended the School of Air Evacuation at Bowman

Field, KY, from June 1943 to October 1944.[40] They subsequently moved on to other assignments in every theater of action and took part in many dangerous and wearying missions. Flight nurses endured plane crashes and hostile fire from enemy aircraft. A number were injured, some died, others were missing in action, still another became a POW.[41]

On September 2, 1945, V-J Day was proclaimed. More than 57,000 Army nurses served worldwide in the war. Sadly, 201 nurses died. Sixteen of the 201 were lost as a result of enemy action.[42]

Many American women also served as enlisted medical technicians in the WAVES and WAC during the war. Unfortunately, the constraints of time preclude any in-depth discussion of their contributions.

Throughout World War II, female medical personnel coped with extremes of climactic conditions in deserts, jungles, and the Arctic. They lived with driving rain, overwhelming dampness, gooey mud that would envelope their knees, frigid cold, blizzards of snow, slippery ice, oppressive heat, blowing sand, and swarms of flies and mosquitoes. They cared for badly wounded and severely ill soldiers as a matter of course. They suffered illness and sustained combat injuries with some dying from a plethora of causes. These women exerted power in eminently powerless roles. They endured rudimentary housing and inadequate food, complaining but never faltering on the front lines with the soldiers in every theater. They were patriotic, selfless, caring, and innovative. It is an honor to have known some of these women and to have heard their stories. It is a pleasure to be able to chronicle their messages and to count them among our predecessors as women of the medical professions during World War II.

NOTES

1. Harriet S. Lee and Myra L. McDaniel, *Army Medical Specialist Corps*, Office of the Surgeon General, Department of the Army (Washington, DC, 1986), pp. 18–21; Ann M. Hartwick, *The Army Medical Specialist Corps, the 45th Anniversary,* Center of Military History, United States Army (Washington, DC, 1993), p. 13.

2. Lee and McDaniel, *Army Medical Specialist Corps,* pp. 7–8; Hartwick, *45th Anniversary,* p. 18.

3. Lee and McDaniel, *Army Medical Specialist Corps,* p. 120.

4. Ruby Motley, "Impromptu Address," *Journal of the American Dietetic Association* 22 (1945): 201–205. Talinum also was referred to as talinum kan kong or water lily greens. The Navy also had a dietitian in Los Baños prison, Miss

Evans, who was similarly creative. See C. Edwina Todd, "Nursing Under Fire," *The Military Surgeon* 100 (April 1947): 335-341.

5. Lee and McDaniel, *Army Medical Specialist Corps,* p. 221.

6. Ibid., pp. 264-265.

7. Ibid., p. 267.

8. Ibid., pp. 269, 272.

9. Ibid., p. 127.

10. Hartwick, *45th Anniversary,* p. 22.

11. Lee and McDaniel, *Army Medical Specialist Corps,* pp. 341-358; Hartwick, *45th Anniversary,* p. 24.

12. "Commissioning of Female Doctors, U.S. Army," *Army Medical Bulletin* 68 (July 1943): 217.

13. Clara Raven, "Achievements of Women in Medicine, Past and Present— Women in the Medical Corps of the Army," *Military Medicine* 125 (February 1960): 105-111; "Strength of the Army," July 1, 1945, p. 26, U.S. Army Center of Military History, Washington, DC.

14. Raven, "Achievements of Women," p. 109; Esther P. Lovejoy, *Women Doctors of the World* (New York, 1957), p. 366.

15. Lovejoy, *Women Doctors,* p. 366; "First Woman in Medical Corps," *The Military Surgeon* 91 (July 1943): 99.

16. Mattie E. Treadwell, *The Women's Army Corps,* The United States Army in World War II, Special Studies, U.S. Army Center of Military History Pub. 11-8 (Washington, DC, 1954), pp. 178, 602-612.

17. Raven, "Achievements of Women," p. 109.

18. Ibid., p. 109.

19. Navy Department, "Women Reservists at National Naval Medical Center," Press and Radio Release, Nov. 13, 1942, Bureau of Medicine and Surgery Archives, Washington, DC.

20. Joseph N. Kane, *Famous First Facts,* 3d ed. (New York, 1964), p. 407

21. Ibid.

22. Henry Cimring, "Something Different in Uniforms," *The Journal of the American Dental Association* 63 (July 1961): 95-97; "GI Molars Get Feminine Touch," *Arkansas Dental Journal* 24 (1953): 50-52.

23. Doris M. Sterner, "A Few Historical Facts—The Navy Nurse Corps," *NNCA News* 7 (November 1993): 8-9.

24. Todd, "Nursing Under Fire," pp. 335-341; Dorothy Still Danner, "Reminiscences of a Nurse POW," *Navy Medicine* 83 (May-June 1992): 36-40.

25. Edna S. Popiel, "The Navy Nurse Corps, Try to Remember Our Heritage," *The Colorado Nurse* 67 (May-June 1967): 5-7; Bureau of Medicine and Surgery, "History of the Nurse Corps, U.S. Navy," unpublished document, Army Nurse Corps Archives, U.S. Army Center of Military History, Washington, DC.

26. Christine Curto, "Nurse Pioneers and the Hospital Ship *Relief,*" *Navy Medicine* 83 (May-June 1992): 20-25.

27. Popiel, "The Navy Nurse Corps," p. 6; Bureau of Medicine and Surgery, "History of the Nurse Corps," p. 5.

28. Sterner, "The History of the U.S. Navy Nurse Corps," *NNCA News* 8 (November 1994): 16-18.

29. "Navy Nurses Train Flight Nurses for Brazil," *American Journal of Nursing* 44 (November 1944): 1086-1087.

30. Popiel, "The Navy Nurse Corps," p. 6; Bureau of Medicine and Surgery, "History of the Nurse Corps," p. 4.

31. Josephine M. Nesbit, "History of the Army Nurse Corps in the Philippine Islands, September 1940-February 1945," unpublished manuscript; Ruby Grace Bradley, 1st Lt., ANC, "Victory Loan Drive Speech," n.d., unpublished manuscript; Ruby G. Bradley, "Factual Notes," Mar. 6, 1945, unpublished manuscript; all in Army Nurse Corps Archives, U.S. Army Center of Military History, Washington, DC.

32. Stetson Conn, Rose C. Engelman, and Byron Fairchild, *Guarding the United States and Its Outposts,* U.S. Army Center of Military History (Washington, DC, 1964).

33. Charles M. Wiltse, *The Medical Department: Medical Service in the Mediterranean and Minor Theaters,* U.S. Army Center of Military History (Washington, DC, 1965); Ruth Y. White "At Anzio Beachhead," *American Journal of Nursing* 44 (April 1944): 370-371; Margaret Bourke-White, *They Called It "Purple Heart Valley"* (New York, 1944).

34. Katherine E. Baltz, "Report of Activities," Dec. 10, 1943, unpublished ms., Army Nurse Corps Archives, U.S. Army Center of Military History, Washington, DC.

35. "Annual Report, Nursing Division, Office of the Chief Surgeon, European Theater of Operations, U.S. Army, 1944," Army Nurse Corps Archives, U.S. Army Center of Military History, Washington, DC.

36. Eileen W. Brady and Nola G. Forrest, "The Pacific Theater in World War II," 1961, unpublished manuscript, Army Nurse Corps Archives, U.S. Army Center of Military History, Washington, DC.

37. "Strength of the Army," Sept. 1, 1945, pp. 2, 6; "History of the Medical Department, Services of Supply, India-Burma Theater, Oct. 24, 1944-May 20, 1945," pp. 37-39; both in U.S. Army Center of Military History, Washington, DC.

38. "Informal Report, Experience in Organizing Chinese Wards at the 20th General Hospital," n.d., Army Nurse Corps Archives, U.S. Army Center of Military History, Washington, DC.

39. Ibid.

40. Evelyn Page, ed., *The Story of Air Evacuation, 1942-1989* (Dallas, TX, 1989), p. 4.

41. "Crash Sends Air Nurse Home With 3 Medals," *New York Herald Tribune,* Aug. 6, 1944, newsclipping in Leora Stroup Collection, Army Medical Department Museum, Fort Sam Houston, TX; Charles M. Ertell, "Service Women Casualties," Feb. 16, 1963, unpublished report, Army Nurse Corps Archives, U.S. Army Center of Military History, Washington, DC; "Flight Nurse Tells of Life in German Prison," *New York Herald Tribune,* Mar. 4, 1945, newsclipping in Leora Stroup Collection, Army Medical Department Museum, Fort Sam Houston, TX.

42. Robert V. Piemonte and Cindy Gurney, *Highlights in the History of the Army Nurse Corps,* U.S. Army Center of Military History (Washington, DC, 1987), p. 18.

THE WAC AS CRYPTOGRAPHER

Mary B. Johnston

On December 7, 1941, we in the United States were completely taken aback when the Japanese bombed Pearl Harbor because we had been so focused on the happenings in Europe. As the Japanese proceeded to conquer the Philippines, where we had many servicemen and civilians, accounts of Japanese atrocities against prisoners became the subject of daily conversations of the American people. We did not hear much about the torture and abuse of prisoners taken by the Germans, so the stories coming from the Far East were most upsetting.

By December 1942, when my story begins, the war with Germany was full blown, Allied forces in the European theater of operations were facing great obstacles to stem the tide of Nazi aggression all over Europe, and the Japanese had been expanding across the Pacific and Southeast Asia. Because of the threat these dictatorships posed and the atrocities, there was a great stirring of people to do what they could for our country. Most fellows I knew were drafted or volunteered for one of the services. The college girls wanted to do something. We felt we could complete our education later, but just now our country needed us.

When my father suggested I join the Army in their newly formed Women's Army Auxiliary Corps (WAAC), I was ready to launch out. My father had evidently explored the possibility of enlistment for himself and found that he was not eligible because of age. He was a World War I veteran and remembered the trouble the Allies had stopping the Germans. He did not want his country to be overrun as was happening to so many other nations. His sons were preteens, and his only child eligible to serve in the armed forces was his oldest daughter . . . me. I was within one quarter of graduating from college, but that did not deter either one of us.

My father marched (he always marched) me down to the local recruiting office. There I was given a physical and a written test. I did not pass the physical because I was underweight. Dad figured we could overcome that, so he took me out for dinner that evening and ordered a big thick steak and six bananas, all of which I had to eat that night. The next day I weighed just enough to pass. The test I had taken placed me second from the top, which was disappointing to my father because he thought I should have come in first. My results were good enough to get into the WAAC, though. Later we found out that the person who received the top grade had wandered in from the insane asylum, and Dad was taken aback. In addition, Dad had convinced the recruiter to wave the age regulation of 21 years old. I was to be 21 in January 1943, so 1 month would not make that much difference. Maybe they were anxious to make their quota because, to top it off, I had flat feet. Be that as it may, I was sworn in on December 8, 1942.

As I left my family, we were all struck by the seriousness of the situation. I had signed up "for the duration," whatever time that would mean. We knew that I would be away from home for a long time. Our family ties were very strong. My parents had bound us together with prayer and daily devotions. We committed ourselves to God to protect all of us.

Immediately, Army life became a learning experience. Far from my sheltered life at home, I learned K.P. (kitchen police), guard duty, "latrine Queen" duty, marching, and group physical exercise. Discipline was not new to me since I was raised by an Army dad. The WAAC was made up of women from all walks of life; some I understood, and some were rather strange. Take the way I got my nickname. In my squad was a rough woman whose name was also Mary. After she had answered a few times to someone calling me, she planted herself in front of me and said, "What do you want to be called? My name is Mary, and I've had it longer than you. So let's change yours." Oh, well. I did not want to get into a confrontation with her, so I shrugged my shoulders. "O.K. Since you are from Virginia, we'll call you 'Ginny.' " A new life and a new name . . . I wondered what else was coming in these unfamiliar times.

In the Army one is told to go here or there, and one has to go here or there without knowing any reasons or having any warning as to what one would find when one got there. After basic training we were sent all over the country to camps where we were needed according to our Military Occupational Specialty (MOS). According to the Army system of classifying each individual, I was given three MOS ratings: interpreter, special services, and concrete mixer operator. In respect to my abilities and experience, the first two were quite accurate, but where the evaluators got the last classification has always been a puzzle. At least, it has been a subject of conversation, but the Army was to be neither understood nor questioned.

My first duty base was Norfolk Army Base, where I was indeed employed as an interpreter. The war in North Africa was drawing to a close. The wily General Rommel's troops were being beaten back by the Allies, and many prisoners were being sent to America for internment. As they came off of the ship, they were deloused and sent to a tent area for identification: name, rank, serial number, home address, and identifying characteristics. A good many were arrogant even though we took care to be polite and explicit. Sometimes we had to call the MPs for assistance. The hatred in their eyes, especially those of the officers, was hard to take. As soon as the whole shipload was processed, we staggered back onto the ferry to go to camp for much-needed rest until the next shipload came in.

For a year and a half, stateside duties were spent in different camps that were all preparing me for duty in the Southwest Pacific Area (SWPA). Some of the rules and regulations of the Army irked me because I thought they were unnecessary, especially when they insisted upon strict adherence to the letter of the law. They tended to depersonalize and make automatons of the troops. Of course, that is exactly what they were intended to do; yet after a year and a half, many of us had become half-spirited about obeying our orders to the letter. We found ways to get around them without getting caught. For instance, I heard the sergeant coming in the front door of our barracks and perceived that she wanted someone for K.P. I quickly headed out the back door because my name was near the top of the alphabet; I knew I was a top candidate. As a group, a lot of our habits had to change, and change we did, grumbling all the way. However, if the Army had not stuck to the rules, we would not have been fittingly trained to survive the rigors of a war. The overall picture was of a unit moving together for one purpose: to win the war against the aggressors.

Most of us wanted to go overseas, where we felt we could take the place of a soldier who was needed on the front lines. Because of my proficiency in French and German, little did I suspect that instead of Europe, the SWPA would be my destination. One day I was called into the captain's office. (I wondered what I had been caught doing.) She asked me if I would consider going overseas.

"Yes, ma'am." (What else had I been thinking of ever since I had enlisted?) Her next question startled me. "Would you be willing, then, to be frozen in rank to go overseas?" By this time, I had been promoted to corporal and rather liked the feeling. On the other hand, I had joined the Army to go where I could best serve my country, and if not getting another stripe would get me overseas, then so be it. At that time, I was not told what I would be doing. I was to pack immediately and leave on a train for Washington, DC. The training I was to receive was to be the end of my duties here in the States.

I joined a special group of 20 Wacs selected from the 10 service commands all over the country and assembled in Washington, DC, in June 1944. We were taken by bus to Vint Hill Farms (VHF), VA, near Warrenton, VA. It was a real-looking farm with barns and a bean field that came up to the door of the barracks. I think one of the group fell by the wayside at the beginning, leaving 19 to take the group of classes. Still, we were not told what we would be studying until we had been thoroughly examined physically, had our background credentials checked and rechecked, and signed forms that impressed upon us the seriousness of our mission. We learned that four organizations were involved in our clearance: the Federal Bureau of Investigation, Military Intelligence (G-2), Post Finance, and a private detective agency. That was enough to make us forget pettiness and get down to business. We could not figure out why we had to have all that extra clearance because we had been cleared already in order to serve in the Army in the first place. Shortly, we found out that we were to do top-secret work, and all the pieces fell into place. None of us was qualified to be a cryptanalyst. In fact, cryptography was only a word to be looked up in the dictionary until we started our classes. We learned the art of cryptography, which involves the enciphering and deciphering of messages in code and cipher. We learned to master a number of systems but went even further. We had to learn how to analyze the messages because we were being trained as cryptanalysts. We worked with the M-209 encipher-decipher machine,[1] which we never saw again after leaving Vint Hill Farms.

Not only did we have classes in cryptology but also in Hepburn Kana, the system for converting Japanese characters into syllables. We learned a lot of Japanese military and naval (water transport) vocabulary and the grammatical structures we would likely find in their messages. There was no longer any doubt as to where we

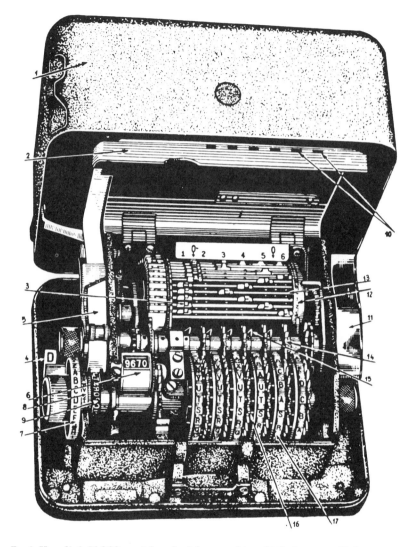

Boris Hagelin's M-209 encipher-decipher machine. 1) Outer cover 2) Inner cover 3) A lug 4) Encipher-decipher knob, set at D for decipher 5) Paper tape 6) Letter counter 7) Indicating disk, on which input letters are set 8) Reproducing disk, on which output letters are shown 9) Typewheel, which prints output letters 10) Windows to display keyletters on keywheels 11) Power handle 12) Cage disk, numbered for each slide-bar 13) A slide-bar, which moves left to become a tooth of the variable gear 14) Keywheel advance gear 15) Upper part of angled face of guide arm of keywheel 4; lugs in column 4 will strike it as cage rotates forward, driving slide-bars to the left 16) Pin for S on keywheel 4, in ineffective position 17) Keywheel 5.

Reproduced from The Codebreakers: The Story of Secret Writing, *with permission from the author, David Kahn.*

would be going. We focused on learning as much about the language as we could and how to read words in the Japanese codes. It was an intense time. We looked forward to going, even though we had no idea what to expect about the places to which we would be going, nor did we care where they might be. We did have second thoughts about leaving the good 'ole U.S.A., but not enough to make any of us back out. We knew we could make a difference.

Another MOS was added to our list: cryptanalysis technician-MOS #808. The qualifications and duties were described officially in Army regulations at that time:

> Decodes and deciphers coded messages and cryptograms without the aid of the device and key used in preparing them.
> Must be thoroughly familiar with the technique of using all known types of coding and cipher devices and systems and their common variations employed by modern armies; must be an extremely patient worker who understands all methods employed in breaking down coded messages and cryptograms; must be able to use deductive reasoning. Must have a knowledge of the pertinent foreign language.[2]

Our little group of 19 members was made up of librarians, teachers, linguists, and lab technicians. We became a close-knit group, realizing that we were to do a special job that our sister Wacs were not privy to, and so we worked through our individual differences. Our life at Vint Hill Farms was not unpleasant, though none of us could figure out why we had to stand K.P. when its rigor knocked us out for a day afterwards. It just took precious time away from the class time we needed. The post staff could have been more efficient in running the duty roster, but they did not ask us, and we had to suffer. We were granted passes to go into Washington, and some of us did. Mostly we stayed on the post, absorbing the peacefulness of the countryside and taking an occasional side trip away. The highlight of our VHF experience was forming an honor guard for one of our members, Pfc. Mary Jane Ford, when she was presented the Soldier's Medal for rescuing a drowning soldier at Fort McCoy, WI. We were so proud of her since she was one of only 10 Wacs to receive the medal.

Once our classes were over, and we were declared well instructed to proceed to the SWPA, the rest of the plan was put into motion. We were sent to Fort Oglethorpe, GA, for overseas training. This training was the same as for the fellows, including scaling a huge net to get on and off a ship, hugging the ground while real bullets zinged over us, and marching miles with a pack on our backs—not as heavy packs as the men had to carry but heavy for us at any rate. We concentrated on survival skills and returned to the barracks dirty and tired. Somehow or another we were bonded together into a unit that would keep us intact until we could come home again. Behind all the physical rigor, none of us talked about the things we had learned at VHF. We took seriously our pledge not to have "loose lips." The hard part was not telling our relatives who came to visit us. I knew my mother knew intuitively that I would be going overseas. My father had gotten into the Allied Military Government (AMG) and was in the European theater. Mother was left at home to care for the five other children without a father around. Sometimes the war was harder on those left behind than for those of us who went abroad.

We traveled across the country by train to Camp Stoneman, CA, where we were to embark on our trip overseas. During this time, we felt as if we were in limbo. We had nothing to do, nowhere to go, nothing to talk about, and all we heard were rumors. Finally, we were told to get our duffel bags down to a truck and be ready to move out. After a wait (hurry up, and wait) of about 2 hours, we put our knapsacks on our backs and moved out in columns down a road. It was hot, and the bags were heavy. We moved close together so the one behind could lift the knapsack a little and help the girl in front. I had packed my knapsack full of things that I thought I could not do without in case my duffel bag got lost: a change of clothes and a bottle of Emeraud perfume. I was not about to lose my femininity!

We were a month on the high seas in a converted luxury liner, the *Lureline*. Converted was right. In a state room for two, there were six bunks reaching up to the ceiling. They were so close together that one had to slide horizontally into bed. Our duffel bags took up any other space available. We were allowed one helmet full of fresh water daily for our bathing and washing. We could use salt water in the showers, but it was unsatisfactory for washing our hair. After trying all sorts of shampoos, we found that shaving cream worked. Since we had a lot of men aboard, we managed well. Most of the GIs lounged up on the deck, as we did, too. The staterooms were hot and cramped, and so was the deck, but it was more interesting. We were just off the coast of Hawaii when orders came for the ship to proceed to the South Pacific. We thought we were going to Alaska because our duffel bags were packed with cold-weather clothes. These were gathered up and, hopefully, sent to troops in colder climes and not to Davy Jones's locker, as rumor had it.

We passed close to some of the South Pacific islands—so close that we could smell the dampness and see the battle scars inflicted by a horrible battle. It was a sobering forecast of things to come for our men. We arrived in Ora Bay, New Guinea, on November 3, 1944, where the Wacs disembarked to make room for some Australian soldiers. Ora Bay was located at the southern tip of New Guinea and during the summer had been occupied by Japanese soldiers until they were driven north. The sky and sea were travel-brochure beautiful, but there were signs everywhere of the battle. We stuck close to camp and were within call of our fellows if we needed them. We were not allowed to go to the latrine unless a soldier accompanied us. We did fashion bathing suits out of our khaki skirts and handkerchiefs so we could go swimming in the beautiful, clear water, but at all times, except when swimming, we had to wear helmets because the coconuts were ripe and falling. The natives were large, 6-foot-tall black men who had orange hair. Quite a sight. They had dyed their hair with moist paper they had gotten from the orange wrappings around the Navy's oranges. We women were a novelty and were greeted by shouts of "Hubba-hubba."

Immediately, we had to take daily doses of Atabrine and spray our tent area every night as protection against malaria and mosquitoes. We had to stand guard duty in our tent area along with the GIs. There were still a few Japanese snipers left around, and some had infiltrated the area thinking their troops still occupied it.

We did not have any incidents, but there was always the possibility. Soon a C-47 came to take us on up to Hollandia, where our camp was to be. The fly-boys flew right up the coast high enough to be out of the range of the flak we saw from Japanese installations at Wewak, where General MacArthur had bypassed the garrison and isolated it as part of the strategy to speed our advance, rather than fight for *every* island. We realized that we were in a war zone and prayed a little harder.

Hollandia was a very busy place when we arrived. The harbor was a mass of ships arriving for the push north to the Philippines. The Seabees were building airstrips and roads. Jeeps and trucks plowed up a winding, twisty road to the top of the big hill that overlooked the harbor where General MacArthur had his headquarters and where the WAC camp was located. All sorts of installations were being set up. Everyone was busy. We unloaded our duffel bags into our tent area, which had a perimeter of canvas strung around it. We set up our own cots, made our beds with two blankets, used a bathrobe for a pillow, strung the mosquito netting snug and tight, and took our mess kits to the mess hall for lunch. After lunch we washed the kits in a big soapy drum, rinsed them, and hung them outside the tent to dry. We were warned to keep our sleeves down, wear our wool socks, take Atabrine daily, and watch out for wallabies (small rodent-like kangaroos that bumped under our cots at night), tarantulas (dump boots every morning), and snakes. A boa constrictor was found somewhat later twined around the tent pole in one of the tents. Our tents seemed large after the crowded ship: six cots around the perimeter and space to walk to each cot. We had electricity displayed in one 25-watt bulb in the center of the tent. The tents were hot during the day and cold at night because we were sitting right on the Equator. We had cold showers, mail call, regular meals, and dust everywhere. I cannot remember that all of this bothered us to any great extent. The boredom after work did. So each one of us found ways to amuse ourselves.

The GIs were so glad to see American women. Some had not seen a girl since leaving home months ago. They planned many ways to entice us to date them or to go to a meal or movie or to the rec room just so they could talk with us. We always accepted a meal offer and sometimes put on a Ping-Pong tournament in our rec room. The chaplain needed someone to play the organ for services, and I was glad to oblige. It turned out to be my way of spending profitable time outside of work. I had a little Estey organ that had to be pumped and sometimes squeaked, but with the two of us, the services had music. We organized a choir and scheduled fellows who sang. Sometimes our schedules were interrupted by the fellows moving on, and one time our soloist was killed in a plane accident. It was always a time of flux, a time of making do, and a time of deep prayer for our fellows.

Not all of my time was spent in the chapel. There was a swimming hole made from a mountain stream, which was clear and cool. Some fellows and girls went there, and so did I . . . just once. After swimming I came out to dry and sat on a rock to watch the others. There was a group of natives over to one side, whom we generally ignored. As I rested, I noticed several natives gathering around me. The spokesman was a wizened little man. I knew they were headhunters, a fact that did not give me any comfort, but I was polite and tried not to show my concern. He said, "You woman?" I nodded. "You married?" How he knew these words beat me. "You marry me?" I saw him looking at my ditty bag, which had a big safety pin on the outside. I had three options: take him up on the offer just to see what would happen (but I thought better of it because I did not want my head to end up shrunken on his shelf); give him the safety pin (which I did); or get out of there, making tracks as fast as my GI escort could get himself together.

One of my dates was with a medic who told me about the hospital down off of GHQ (general headquarters) hill. He took me down and introduced me to a nurse who told me all they could do was to dress the bandages of the wounded, and I would be welcome to help where I could. I gathered some of the Wacs, and we went down to the 51st Base Hospital not having any idea of what or how we could help. Each of us took a ward, just walking through, stopping here and there to speak to the patients. Those boys had all sorts of terrible wounds and were, for the most part, swathed in bandages. They were dirty; blood and dirt were caked all through their hair and on their hands. One asked if I could just sponge him off. That led to my getting a basin of water and a towel and washing even his hair; I washed as many others as I could. We tried to think up things that would help take their minds off of their wounds: writing letters, reading the Bible, smoking cigarettes (they had only a few, and the Wacs gave as many as they could out of their own carton-a-month ration), singing Christmas carols (we had quite a group of GIs and Wacs who participated), and making Valentines (we made a silly head of a donkey, colored it, wrote a verse, and gave one to each fellow). It was quite a trauma to see our wounded fellows, to know who was terminal, and to miss that one or two the next time we went down. I made up my mind to be as cheerful as I could be, and yet I came away feeling uplifted myself from the upbeat attitude of the fellows. Great Americans!

Our work was centered in Quonset huts down the hill. Our group of 19 from the States was joined by Wacs from Brisbane, Australia, who had been trained on the job there. Our 19 were the only group trained in a class. We worked with pencil, paper that was in large squares, and our codebook of Japanese words. Our group worked on the water transport codes sent to Japanese garrisons alerting them to the arrival of certain convoys, their points of departure and destination, the number of ships in the convoy, and the number of men and quantity of matériel. There were many messages.

Evidently, the Japanese did not know we had broken some of their codes because day after day they followed the same pattern of changing codes three times a day. They encoded their messages using numbers in four digits. The first set indicated the code system in use. The second set of four numbers indicated the key register, specifying the exact page, column, and row. Then came the message.

The American interceptor recorded the dots and dashes on a prescribed form. The form was sent to Arlington Hall near Washington, DC, for decryption and analysis. The decrypter had to use two codebooks to decode: one of Japanese characters, and one in digits and numbers. Later the messages intercepted in Brisbane and other SWPA places were sent to us in Hollandia. The Signal Security Agency had transliterated the Japanese ideographs into Roman letters. We received the messages in letters from which we searched for key words that made sense.[3] The letters were put into the squares like a crossword puzzle and filled in as we assumed values and tested for validity.

Little by little, through long days and nights (we worked three shifts around the clock), through perseverance and intuition, we broke the codes. It took all of us working together as a team to make a difference in the war. We alerted General MacArthur to troop movements so that he was able to plan his campaign to get the war over with as soon as possible.

We Wacs must have been doing something right because we became a pain in the neck to the Japanese in Tokyo. They might have thought that we were out there enduring the uncomfortable conditions just to provide moral support for our troops. I do not think they were aware that we were breaking their codes. At any rate, they thought if they destroyed us, they would demoralize our troops, making them easy targets. Their plan was diabolical. First, they would frighten us so we would go home. If that did not work, they would simply bomb us. They selected "Tokyo Rose" to broadcast in English that we surely would want to go back to the plush life we had at home. Why would we continue to be so miserable when great food and good times were waiting for us? We thought, "What a stupid woman!" She and the brass behind her grossly underestimated the American woman. It was not long before she broadcast that she simply had to bomb the Wacs off of GHQ hill . . . "So solly, pweeze." She even gave the time. The night came. Some of the girls thought they would be safer in the ravine. Others took a more fatalistic viewpoint and stayed in the tent area. As for me, I went to bed, tucking my netting around as usual. Then I sang a hymn, "Be not dismayed whatever betide. God will take care of you." Believing, I slept well. Our planes did intercept the Japanese planes and turned them back. The ravine Wacs came up bedraggled, dirty, and tired but just as safe as the rest of us. I can tell you that there are no atheists in fox holes or in ravines.

Most of my time outside of work was spent in the chapel, helping the chaplain organize the Sunday service and other activities, such as choir, and playing the little organ. One Sunday service went especially well. After the service an officer spoke to the chaplain, who then came to me and asked if I would play privately for General Alexander. What could I say but "of course"? The general came in the afternoon and sat off to one side. I played as many pieces as I had music for and then played variations of them. Finally, I ran out of music. The general shook my hand and that was that, I thought. Not so. It was Christmas time. One day the general's driver delivered to me in our work place a big box full of American chocolates! His note thanked me again and said I had given him a brief respite from the war. That was a difference I wanted to make. I gave each person a chocolate and had enough left to give one to each of the fellows on my ward at the hospital. Thus our days and nights were spent doing all we could to break those codes, share home with all, and try not to let our own homesickness get the better of us. The war ground on. It was hard not to wonder if it would ever end. V-E Day came, and we knew it would not be long before the troops from Europe would join us for the push to the Philippines. Sure enough, some very pale soldiers appeared on the scene. We, with our yellow-Atabrined skin, must have looked as funny to them as they looked to us. General MacArthur accelerated his drive for the Philippines. We had no sense of his timing until Hollandia harbor emptied of all the ships, and the personnel left—all except the Wacs and some of the headquarters group.

After General MacArthur established his headquarters in Manila and the land had been mostly cleared of Japanese soldiers—except up in the hills where our men fought on—the WAC cryptanalysis group finally left New Guinea in June 1945 and moved to San

Miguel, north of Manila, above Clark Field at the site of a former sugar mill. The mill had a very tall skinny smokestack with a Japanese flag painted at the top. We were much too busy to shimmy up that stack to repaint it, so the flag stayed, becoming a beacon to Japanese soldiers straggling in from the hills. They came, one at a time, and were quite surprised to encounter women soldiers, plus American soldiers, who took them away to detention.

It was hot and dusty in the Philippines. We had better accommodations than in New Guinea, but they were still quite primitive. We did have Filipinos to wash and iron our clothes and to perch on the fence around the compound to watch us. Our showers were warm only because the tank was up on the roof of the shower house, an example of future solar heat. We soaped with one hand and pulled a chain with the other to rinse. We became quite good at "moonlighting" (getting what you need without authorization). For example, I swapped my beer ration for a chest of drawers and sheets and a pillow, no doubt pilfered from some hapless officer. True to the Army style, I asked no questions.

We worked our shifts as before and supplied headquarters with messages they needed to get ready to conquer Japan. My off-duty hours were spent in the chapel. The chaplain and I went down to the south of Manila to contract for nipa stalks for the roof of the chapel. We had to work through the Roman Catholic priest who lived in the barrio. He supplied us with as much as we needed and then invited us to see the church. I was astonished at the beautiful hand-carved teak pews and the glitter of gold on the statues. How could this be when the people just outside the church building lived in abject poverty? The contrast seemed all out of proportion. I did not voice my concern for the people as we headed back, but I never forgot it. Once back at San Miguel, the nipa was put on the roof, where it kept out the rain and provided a home for the little lizards that sometimes fell on people coming into church. At the services I played the Estey organ, which I had brought from New Guinea. Once I played for the wedding of a Wac who had been in Brisbane and her Australian sergeant. It was just as beautiful and meaningful as any here in the States.

About September, the jungle rot I had gotten on my foot in New Guinea got much worse, and I was sent to the hospital at Clark Field. I never did return to San Miguel because they wanted to send me home. First, though, they did try to cure it but to no avail. While in the hospital, I had a visitor, my first cousin who was with the 33d Infantry up in the hills where they were still fighting. Somehow he got leave and came down to find me. He had made arrangements for me to get leave and meet him at San Estaban, where there was a rest center. I was not able to go until I had been transferred to Manila to await transportation home. Since none was available, I was granted leave. As far as I knew, there was no transportation up to San Estaban, so I simply stood on the side of a thoroughfare out of town and thumbed. A big 10-ton truck pulled over, and a GI asked where I wanted to go. It turned out that he was taking some GIs up to the rest center and would give me a ride. I rode in the cab with him all the way and even went to sleep leaning on him. On the way up, we saw a little train puffing along over the rice paddies loaded with Japanese soldiers in open boxcars headed for detention near Manila. By this time Baguio, the summer capital of the Philippines, was conquered, and a mop-up operation was in progress. While waiting for my cousin to come, I went swimming in the South China Sea. The water was clear and warm. We explored a Japanese ship that had gone aground and saw the gaping holes in its hull. A few days later I noticed that the salt sea had cured the jungle rot on my foot, something the medics had not been able to do. Soon my cousin came down the mountain to take me to see Baguio. As we rode in his jeep, we would pass men with 10 or more skinny dogs on leashes. Evidently, they would go down to the barrios, grab the dogs, and take them back to their villages for food. We stopped at a big Roman Catholic church just at the entrance to Baguio. The nuns there made beautiful filigree jewelry. I selected some pieces and paid for them, trusting the nuns to send them to me. Almost a year later, they arrived at my home.

Back in Manila, I had to wait with all the others for our trip home. The war was declared over on October 22, 1945. Finally, in November, we boarded the *Lureline* for the trip home. We were just as crowded as we had been going out, but we did not mind . . . we were going home. There were not many cheers as we sailed under the Golden Gate Bridge because we remembered those who did not come back. Also, each of us had fears of what our lives would be. We were changed, and our concern was whether we would be acceptable to our folks. Though the Golden Gate Bridge was in need of paint, it was just beautiful. America seemed so prosperous; people had cars, gasoline, clothes, and plenty of food. We were given a meal at Camp Stoneman that was scrumptious.

We could order anything we wanted. I had a steak, a whole head of lettuce, and a huge chocolate milk shake. Shortly, we were put on a train for Fort Des Moines, IA, where I was issued out on December 7, 1945, 3 years after I had volunteered. We had been warned not to mention the work we did to anyone. Only recently did we begin to recapture mental pictures of our service, people, places, and what we did as cryptanalysts. And we know this: The Wacs contributed much to the war effort; we did make a difference.

LIST OF WAC SPECIAL GROUP

1. Harriott Bell (Moebius-DeBrahe)
2. Mary "Ginny" Blakemore (Johnston)
3. Marion Bowman (Redfield)
4. Irene J. Brion
5. Margery L. Cady
6. Maxine Clopine (Hinshaw)
7. Sue Cross (Santa Maria)
8. Mary Jane Ford (Wolter)
9. Violet Flower (Horton)
10. Helen Ginkins (Kost)
11. Jaunita Howell
12. Beatrice Hart
13. Ruth J. Hamilton
14. Margie Morris
15. Edith McMann
16. Betty McBeath
17. Gladys Trask
18. Mary Somerhalter (Rothman)
19. Marjorie Wilhelm (Hart)

As far as I know, we were the only Wacs to be frozen in rank for all the years that we served.

ACKNOWLEDGMENTS

Irene J. Brion, "The Lady G.I." (unpublished manuscript, 1993)

Joseph E. Richard

> With Colonel Sinkov, Sgt. Joseph Richard found the connection that facilitated the breaking of the Japanese water transport codes in 1943.

Evelyn M. Haddican

Wac, Staff sergeant, Headquarters Group in Hollandia. Evelyn Haddican came up from Brisbane in 1944 to work with the company commander to keep the Wacs as comfortable and safe as they could. She knew all of us and has been invaluable in helping me to remember.

Sue Cross Santa Maria (letters)

Private first class. One of the 20 Wacs trained at Vint Hill Farms for cryptanalysis, Sue Cross Santa Maria was quick to recognize the codes and was a dedicated worker. Her bubbly personality enlivened the group, sometimes getting us into trouble, but Sergeant Haddican was there to smooth things out. Forty years after the war, Sue made a great effort to find all 19 of us and organized a reunion, prodding all of us to go. Sue Cross Santa Maria died in 1994.

My mother, Mrs. John A. Blakemore, who saved all my wartime letters.

My husband, Dr. William C. Johnston, and our children, William C. Jr., Margaret Johnston Sibley, Robert Buchanan, and John McLean, who prodded and encouraged me to write my memories of the war.

NOTES

1. David Kahn, *The Codebreakers: The Story of Secret Writing* (New York, 1967), pp. 427-429.
2. War Department, Army Regulations, no. 615-26, para. 17 (Washington, DC, Sept. 15, 1942), p. 512.
3. Edward J. Drea, *MacArthur's ULTRA: Codebreaking and the War Against Japan, 1942-1945* (Lawrence, KS, 1992), pp. 6-7.

"ANGELS CALLING FROM THE SKY"
The Women Pilots of
World War II

RitaVictoria Gomez

The day was clear and still. In the peaceful skies over the United States a pilot could forget the European war. Suddenly, a control tower broke silence, reporting, "Listen Joe, angels calling from the sky. Now I've heard everything."[1] These "angels" were women civil service pilots flying for the Ferrying Division of the Air Transport Command (ATC). Their chance to fly for the Army Air Forces (AAF) began shortly before World War II.

American aviators, among them Nancy Harkness Love, had been thinking of ways to aid their country in the event the war spread to U.S. shores. In a letter of May 2, 1940, Love advised Lt. Col. Robert Olds, then in the Plans Division of the Office of the Chief of the Army Air Corps, that one source of additional pilots might well lie in the ranks of qualified women fliers. She wrote: "I've been able to find forty-nine I can rate as excellent material. . . . There are probably at least fifteen more of these whom I don't know about. . . . This list is up to handling some pretty complicated stuff. Most of them have in the neighborhood of 1,000 hours or more, mostly more, and have flown a great many types of ships."[2]

Love's letter coincided with Olds's work in developing contingency plans to meet any possible pilot shortage. Olds agreed that if 100 women pilots were obtained to work for the Army Air Corps as copilots in transport squadrons and for ferrying single-engine aircraft, an equal number of male pilots might be made available for combat duty.[3] Olds wanted the women commissioned as second lieutenants in the Reserve. After a short refresher training course, they would be qualified for transport and ferrying duties.[4] Olds's proposal went to the Chief of the Army Air Corps, Gen. Henry H. (Hap) Arnold, who rejected his plan. Arnold believed that there existed more than enough male pilots among the Reserve and commercial ranks. He felt women could better support their country by replacing commercial aviation pilots.[5]

Love persisted. She correctly forecast the Ferrying Division's pilot shortage as American factories increased airplane production. By June 18, 1942, she was reproposing her idea of recruiting a group of highly qualified women pilots. This time Love got the support of Headquarters, Ferrying Command.[6]

By 1942 the Ferrying Command was interested in the idea of using women pilots for domestic deliveries of primary and liaison aircraft but only if the women had a great deal of flying experience. In a July 1942 memorandum to General Arnold, Gen. H. L. George, Commander of the Ferrying Command, argued for a chance to hire women pilots on an experimental basis. He stressed to Arnold that this might serve as a means for "determining the suitability of utilizing women pilots in the delivery of military aircraft."[7] Nonetheless, the military's emphasis remained on viewing women pilots only as experimental. This reaction was natural in view of the novelty of the idea, and the use of women pilots was the subject of much conjecture by the military, the general public, and even among the women themselves.[8]

General George argued that a cadre of 50 women pilots was an adequate basis to judge women's overall flying potential with no additional hiring necessary until the capabilities of this experimental group were thoroughly tested.[9] This *experimental* unit of women pilots would ferry smaller Army aircraft (training and liaison airplanes) from factories in the United States to domestic airfields. George wanted only 40 active pilots and 10 to handle administrative duties. Their actual administration would be delegated to a woman director. In order to tailor the job for Nancy H. Love, George ordered that the director be a qualified female commercial pilot with over 1,200 hours accumulated over 12 years and experienced in ATC operations in various administrative capacities. She would work directly for the group commander.

In order to be hired, the women needed to have credentials comparable to those required of male civilian pilots. A woman pilot had to be 21 to 35 years of age, possess a high school education, and hold a commercial pilot's license with a 200-horsepower rating. In addition, she needed no fewer than 500 logged hours of certified flying time, including cross-country flying experience. She also needed a letter of recommendation from a previous employer or someone of substance in her community. Once the AAF (in June of 1941 the air arm of the U.S. Army had become a separate force, the Army Air Forces) received a woman's application, her records would be checked, and if found suitable, the woman might then go to Wilmington, DE, at her own expense for an interview and a thorough flight check in one of the Army's training planes, given by a qualified military instructor pilot. The check would include general flying techniques, such as takeoffs, landings, and stalls. If the prospective applicant successfully completed her flight check, she would meet a board of three officers who would once again review her credentials and the outcome of her flight check. Absolutely *no* exceptions to any of the above qualifications would be allowed. A final condition for employment was to successfully pass the flight surgeon's physical exam. These requirements were so rigid that only a few women could meet them.

If accepted as a pilot, the woman would next undergo a course of instruction lasting from 4 to 6 weeks. Ground school would be conducted in the mornings, while afternoons would be for flying. The course would cover standard operating procedures for military aircraft, technical orders for delivery of the aircraft, military organization and procedures, forms and formats needed for ferrying, data contained in the Pilot Information Files, ferrying routes, and other related subjects. A woman who successfully completed all of the above was employed on a 3-month conditional status. If she proved herself useful to the AAF, she would remain on duty for automatic 3-month extensions until the exigencies of war subsided.[10]

On July 14, 1942, General George forwarded these proposals, amended to include U.S. citizenship, to Arnold. George requested that this proposed Women's Auxiliary Ferry Troop (WAFT) be hired as civil service employees until their capabilities and usefulness to the Ferry Command were determined. General George also wanted the Director of Women Pilots to take charge of these new pilots and, during the hiring and schooling phase, supervise living arrangements and sit on selection boards. As planned, Nancy Harkness Love was the only woman meeting George's requisites for a director.

Arnold's reply urged George to forestall hiring women if there were any possibility of obtaining male pilots from the Civil Aeronautics Administration (CAA) or Civil Air Patrol (CAP). Arnold remained opposed to using women as pilots and informed George that he would give his permission for a woman's unit only after "exhausting" the supply of male pilots.[11]

Aircraft production increased further in September 1942, marking the beginning of severe male pilot shortages. On September 3, George sent Arnold a memorandum requesting reconsideration of the experimental women's ferrying troop and approval to bring the women on as officers within the framework of the Women's Army Auxiliary Corps (WAAC). Love would be commissioned a first lieutenant and assigned as operations officer overseeing all the women pilots. Arnold conceded, directing George to take "immediate action." By September 5, 1942, the Air Staff advised Arnold that the Director of the Women's Pilot Group had been appointed.[12]

That same day, Love sent telegrams to 83 prospective applicants whose CAA files showed they met the prerequisite qualifications. Since WAAC legislation did not authorize women flying officers, or flight pay, the idea of commissioning the women was temporarily postponed in order to hire them quickly.[13]

On the morning of September 10, 1942, the Secretary of War announced the formation of the Women's Auxiliary Ferrying Squadron (WAFS).[14] The WAFS was to be based with Col. Robert H. Baker's Second Ferrying Group, New Castle Army Air Base, Wilmington, DE. This base was close to both the eastern aircraft producers and Washington, DC, which allowed for careful scrutiny by Air Forces Headquarters.[15]

In keeping with George's proposals, prospective applicants had to have flown 50 hours in 200-horsepower aircraft within the preceding 12 months and pass both the flight surgeon's physical exam and a flight test. Since transportation costs to Wilmington were at the expense of the applicant, many unqualified candidates were eliminated before making the trip. Despite these stiff prerequisites, the War Department, the AAF, Baker, and Love were still deluged by requests for information and jobs, mostly from newspaper reporters, women pilots, and some cranks. Form letters stating qualification requirements were sent in response to all inquiries. Some women applied to add excitement to their lives; others, because of the chance to work in close proximity to relatives. Nevertheless, the majority of applicants were seriously interested in flying and making a contribution to their country.[16]

Colonel Baker's orders were to hire as many women as needed, under civil service regulations and at minimum salaries of $3,000 a year ($250 a month). He had complete hiring and firing authority, the women were subject to military rules and regulations, and they could be discharged "in exactly the same manner as male civilian pilots."[17]

No women's squadron was formally activated. The Women's Auxiliary Ferrying Squadron (WAFS) was nothing more than a convenient yet unofficial designation for the women. In reality, the women were "Civil Pilots" (the official designation for the male civilian pilots already in Army employ). However, in recognition of their sex, they were organized into a separate and distinct organization of 50 women under their assigned group commander. Love was in charge of this first squadron and designated Chief Woman Pilot. Other women squadron leaders were to be selected as more women were recruited. Ferrying Division's leadership believed this system the best method of meeting all present and future contingencies.[18]

Although civilians, the women pilots received all the privileges accorded to officers, including use of clubs and messes. There was to be no distinction between male and female civilian pilots, and women followed the same mixture of AAF regulations, CAA rules, and the AAF's Ferry Instructions as male pilots. Women stood formation and started their day with 8 A.M. roll calls.[19] Military uniforms were recommended but not mandatory.[20] The standardized uniform for women was a tailored jacket, shirt, and skirt. The women substituted slacks for the skirt when they were on flying duty.[21]

By September 17, 1942, Colonel Baker had hired the desired complement of 25 women civilian pilots to ferry AAF planes. They included some of the more prominent women aviators of the day. Professionally, the great majority of original squadron members (21 out of 25) had superior qualifications. The first 13 women assigned had flying times that ranged from 532 to 2,627 hours. The average was 1,162 hours.[22]

Five owned their own planes and had flown them all over the United States. One had even done a great deal of flying in England and France before the war. All had been instructors at one time or another, and five had made instructing their principal job for the preceding 2 to 3 years; one had run her own airport.[23]

Many in the military and among the public asked if the women would indeed be able to serve in the military as pilots. No one could speak with any certainty on whether women had the necessary stamina to handle the jobs assigned or on the effect of women's physiology on their usefulness.[24]

Pilot Elizabeth L. Gardner is about to take off from Harlingen Army Air Field, TX. Photograph released March 20, 1944.

National Air and Space Museum, Smithsonian Institution (photograph #29183AC)

Worried about their endurance capabilities for long ferrying trips, the military hierarchy at first restricted them to flights of 1,800 miles. Greater distances, it was felt, might weaken the women and cause fatal accidents. Air Force doctors braced themselves for an onslaught of operational or flying fatigue complaints from women. It was soon discovered, however, that not only did their complaints number far fewer than those of male pilots, but they flew far more trips, relatively, than their male coworkers. Flying for the male pilots was nothing more than a job; for the women, it was adventure personified. Soon, long-distance trips were not unusual, with the Wafs flying from the southeastern states to Alberta, Canada—a distance of over 2,500 miles.[25]

Public curiosity was intense. No matter how routine the flight, the women simply were not allowed the anonymity of ordinary ferry pilots. Newspapers and magazines wanted to capitalize on the public interest in women pilots, and the women's flying duties provided a rich source of interesting material. Typical of the incidents reported was one WAFS flight that landed at Winder, GA; although the field had a radio station for weather, there were no facilities for obtaining either gas or services. Resourcefully, the Wafs hitchhiked into town and soon were able to obtain both a gasoline truck and gas from a local dealer.[26]

Another area of concern dealt with menstruation's effect on dependability and flying capabilities. The generally held belief was that women were incapacitated for several days each month and that they were accident-prone prior to and during the menses.[27] Since 1940 the CAA had obtained gynecological histories on women applying for their flying licenses and advised women flyers that fainting was a definite possibility if they flew 3 days prior to or 3 days after menstruation. Obviously, any instance of fainting while flying aloft boosted the chances of a plane crash. Pregnancy was also an absolutely disqualifying condition.[28]

On March 29, 1943, the Ferrying Division more closely aligned its policies closer to those of the CAA. A letter was sent to all group commanders directing that the women ferry pilots be grounded 1 day before, during, and 2 days after menstruation. This restriction meant an average of 6 to 8 days of lost flying time per month. In addition, pregnancy resulted in an automatic grounding. The women protested that this policy was unsound, and the ATC surgeon wrote to the Air Surgeon for a ruling. The Air Surgeon ruled that each woman could make the decision on whether or not she wished to be grounded. If the woman had a truly incapacitating condition but refused to acknowledge it, the senior Waf at her station was responsible for making the condition known to the group flight surgeon, who then took the necessary steps for a mandatory monthly grounding. Additionally, no woman was to be disciplined for failure to meet schedules during her menstrual cycle. Both the ATC Surgeon and his Air Staff colleague, however, remained firm on grounding pregnant women, citing the possibility of spontaneous miscarriage or excessive vomiting. The amended policy, while far more realistic in terms of application, still remained largely unenforceable without the full concurrence of the women themselves. Those women grounded during their menstruation, generally used the days to fulfill their ground school requirements or attend to necessary paperwork or equipment. Although the ban against flying while pregnant remained in force, many women, through ignorance of their condition, continued to fly through the early months of pregnancy.[29]

The large amounts of lost time anticipated as a result of menstruation never materialized, and overall, male pilots lost more flying time than did female pilots for any reason. When accidents—both fatal and nonfatal—occurred, menstruation was never found to be a contributing nor even an extenuating cause.[30]

The areas of difficulty that did arise came from the sometimes excessive weight of the women's parachutes, difficulty with ill-fitting oxygen masks, and problems with urinary relief while flying. The women's relative shortness in comparison to male pilots was not a problem because the females' leg length in a sitting position was usually equal to that of male pilots; therefore the women encountered no difficulty in reaching the controls.[31]

These new women pilots in uniform quite confused the American public. Some thought they were Girl Scouts; others, pilots of ferry boats. On one occasion, a woman bustled up importantly to two Wafs and said, "That is the first time I have ever seen a uniform of the Mexican Army. How do you like it here?" Nonplussed, one of the women murmured, "No comprende," and both turned away.[32]

Throughout 1942 the women ferried only Primary Trainers (PT 19As) and Liaison planes (L4-Bs). But soon their services were required for the more advanced aircraft. The WAFS quickly took over the ferrying of high-performance pursuit planes such as the P-41 and P-47. They also ferried the larger C-47s, A-36s, and B-25s.[33]

By April 1943 the Women's Auxiliary Ferrying Squadron at New Castle had proved its worth. The unit was split and reassigned to three additional bases located near aircraft production facilities. These were Romulus, MI, Dallas, TX, and Long Beach, CA.[34] The WAFS organization had women squadron leaders for each group, and Love was the Senior Squadron Leader. Otherwise, there was very little administrative or organizational difference between the women and their male pilot peers.

The Wafs were not the only women flying for the Army Air Forces. Almost simultaneously with Love's decision to approach the military with the idea of using women pilots came a similar proposal from Jacqueline Cochran. Cochran was the complete antithesis to Nancy Love. Born in rural Florida, Cochran did not even know her own birthdate (1905 or 1908), and Cochran was a name she had picked out of a telephone book. Her childhood had been one of unrelieved poverty and fending for herself from an early age.[35]

Cochran dragged herself up from poverty and finally succeeded in escaping her bleak childhood. In 1929 she arrived in New York City and began working as a beautician in a society salon.[36] There she met Floyd Odlum, the wealthy husband of one of her clients. Odlum had a gift for making money and a decided interest in Cochran. They were soon an item, and Odlum divorced his first wife and married Jackie in 1936.[37] Cochran quit work as a beautician and became the owner of a successful cosmetics firm.[38] In order to cover more sales territory for her line, Cochran took Odlum's suggestion that she become a pilot.[39] After only 3 weeks of training, Cochran got her pilot's license.[40]

A license was just the beginning for Cochran. With Odlum's backing and her own determination, Cochran took up competitive flying and won almost every trophy she went after.[41] Both Odlums knew that the war was coming, and Cochran was interested in organizing a group of women pilots with herself as director. Since Odlum had given Franklin Delano Roosevelt's 1936 Presidential campaign a $100,000 donation, Cochran was welcome at the White House. So were her ideas for women pilots to help out the war effort. In the summer of 1941, Roosevelt told Cochran to take her ideas to the War Department, and the department in turn listened and referred her to General Arnold.[42]

Unwilling to commit himself to the use of women pilots, but equally unwilling to ruffle any political feathers, Arnold told Cochran that she could best serve her interests by helping out the British war effort. The British were already using women for noncombat flying, and Cochran could show her administrative capabilities as well as the feasibility of women as military fliers by organizing recruits for Britain. Cochran agreed but managed to get Arnold to commit himself to promising her that any women's pilot group organized by the military would have Cochran as director. Cochran took off for England with her recruits.[43]

With America's entrance into the war in December 1941, Cochran came back to the United States. Much to her chagrin and annoyance, her arrival coincided with the news that Love's group of women pilots had been organized. She quickly arranged an appointment to see Arnold and reminded him of his promise. Arnold was caught off guard, but he quickly regrouped. Cochran would be the director of a new women's pilot group. This one would teach only those women who were just a few hours short of the Ferrying Command's required flight hours to fly. This would not only mollify Cochran but also get more women into ferrying military planes. Cochran agreed to this proposal, which led to the establishment of the Women's Flying Training Detachment (WFTD) in September 1942.[44]

Over the next year, Cochran slowly and inexorably widened her program. She changed it from one that taught women who had quite a good deal of flying experience to one for women with minimal flying qualifications and made them qualified pilots. Fortunately for Cochran and her women pilot students, the high pilot fatality rates resulting from combat meant an ever-increasing demand for pilots, male or female.

Since 1942, Arnold had radically altered his stance on the use of women pilots. Faced with increasing wartime demands for manpower, he ordered that women pilots perform practically all the noncombat flying jobs in the continental United States. This decision meant greater numbers of women needed to be recruited for flying duties. The excellent job that the WAFS had been doing, combined with an ever-increasing need to free military pilots from stateside flying duties, forced the AAF to take the idea of women pilots seriously. In order to obtain even more women, Jackie Cochran's schools at Houston and Sweetwater, TX, were recognized as being the key to providing the AAF with increasing numbers of women pilots. In July 1943, again at Arnold's direction, these two organizations merged. Both groups of women aviators were now one, and their new name was the Women Airforce Service Pilots (WASP).[45]

Cochran's success was to be short lived. The WASP program was doomed. By spring 1944 air superiority in the combat theaters seemed to point toward a reduced need for pilots. Combat losses were at an all-time low, and more veteran pilots were returning home. Cochran canvassed more than 50 WASP bases. Commanders agreed that there would be a decreasing need for the women flyers. There were persistent indications that by mid-December 1944 there would be ample male pilots to fill both stateside and overseas flying assignments. These indicators convinced Cochran that deactivation was inevitable. On October 3, 1944, the Army Air Forces announced that "unless there are unexpected and much higher combat losses in the air war over Germany," the WASP would be deactivated on December 20, 1944.

The last class graduated December 7, 1944. Graduates were assigned as close to home as possible. The public relations people urged a small closed ceremony to mark the end of WASP training. They cautioned against giving the press any chance to question the inception, continuance, or deactivation of the program. The press would be given handouts describing the program's history and successes, as well as copies of the farewell addresses by Cochran, Gen. Barton K. Yount (commanding general of the AAF Training Command), and General Arnold. Newsreels and radio coverage would use only Air Force-approved pictures and text.

A certificate similar to that granted to AAF officers was issued to Wasps for honorable service and discharge. A Wasp was in good standing if she had faithfully performed her assigned duties and had been on active duty until deactivation. If she had resigned prior to that, she needed to have her commanding officer's approval or proof that her resignation was not detrimental to the organization. Those still in training would be separated upon graduation. Each Wasp would be given a final physical 72 hours prior to departure. All Wasps would be allowed to ride home in military aircraft. Certificates would also be issued to survivors of Wasps killed while serving.

Coupled with this certificate would be AAF letter 40–41, Eligibility for CAA Civil Pilot Certificate. Based on WASP training, flying, and operational experience, the women were designated military aircraft pilots, each with an aircraft horsepower rating. The required solo flying status of 6 consecutive months was to be counted from the date of each woman's first solo in WASP training. The CAA also allowed Wasps to take their flight tests for instrument rating prior to passing the written exam. In order to pass the flying portion, military aircraft would be made available to them whenever practicable. This certificate, combined with successful completion of the air commerce rules and regulation exams, would grant each Wasp a CAA commercial license.

All AAF stations were informed that after December 20 no women were to be employed by the AAF in any flying capacity. They would, however, be considered for any available civilian clerical, professional, or technical ground positions.

Even without individual awards, the women could well be proud of their achievements. Although there had never been an official recruiting campaign organized for the WASP, more than 33,000 women had applied to join. Of those selected, 1,074 graduated. These women, throughout the length of their service, met the highest aviation standards. In the 2 years and 18 classes of WASP trainees, the elimination rates for Wasps closely paralleled that of the male flying cadets.

Most of the women had higher than Class I pilot status. For example, Nancy Harkness Love qualified to pilot a four-engine C-54 after only 3 hours of instruction and then made three deliveries flying coast to coast. During the program there were 402 airplane accidents—about 1 fatality for every 16,000 hours of flight. Every heavy bomber and cargo plane ferried by a woman was safely delivered to its destination without a single mishap. Wasps averaged at least as many flying hours per month as male pilots working similar jobs. They were more effective in most duties and reportedly were more eager, willing, and self-disciplined than their male counterparts. The planes used by the WASP included light and low-powered training planes (BT-13, AT-7, AT-10, AT-11), cargo (C-47, C-64, C-78), light bombers (RA-24, RA-25), and medium bombers (B-34, B-25, TB-26). At least one Wasp checked out on the P-63 and B-24. In the course of their AAF flying, Wasps flew more than 75 million miles (the equivalent of six times around the earth, counting every day of training and flying operations). This mileage averaged 5 million miles per month overall, and each Wasp averaged over 14 flying hours per month.[46]

With the WASP deactivation, the "angels of the sky" were grounded for more than 20 years. During these years, the exploits and achievements that marked the women's association with the Army Air Forces lay forgotten.

NOTES

© 1996 by RitaVictoria Gomez
  1. Cochran, "Comments . . . With Respect to the Historical Report of the Ferrying Division of the Air Transport Command Concerning Women Airforce Service

Pilots in Said Division," Air Transport Command, roll A2253, frame 1808, 220.0721-6 (6/45, vol. 1) thru 220.0721-12 (12/42-1/45, vol. 4), Center for Air Force History, Bolling AFB, Washington, DC (hereinafter cited as CAFH).

2. History of the Air Transport Command, Women Pilots in the Air Transport Command, roll A3003, frame 1335, 300.07-1 (10/44-12/47) thru 300.0721-2 (10/42-12/44), CAFH.

3. Ibid.

4. History of the Women Airforce Service Pilots Program and Activities in the AAF Training Command, roll A2252, frame 1470, 220.0721-1 (11/42-12/44), CAFH.

5. Ibid., frame 1418.

6. Ibid., frames 1429-1434.

7. Ibid., frames 1436, 1438, 1439.

8. Ibid., frames 1486, 1488, 1489.

9. Ibid., frame 1349.

10. Ibid., roll A2253, frames 370, 1721.

11. Ibid., roll A2252, frames 1484, 1487.

12. Ibid., frames 1338, 1488.

13. Ibid., roll A2253, frame 1741.

14. Ibid., roll A2252, frames 1355, 1490; roll A2253, frame 1739.

15. History of the Air Transport Command, Women Pilots in the Air Transport Command, roll A3003, frame 1335, 300.0721-1 (10/42-12/44), p. 64, CAFH.

16. History of the Women Airforce Service Pilots Program and Activities in the AAF Training Command, roll A2253, frames 1733-1734, 1724, 220.0721-1 (11/42-12/44), CAFH.

17. History of the Air Transport Command, Women Pilots in the Air Transport Command, pp. 32, 65, roll A2253, frame 54, CAFH.

18. Ibid., pp. 40, 47, roll A2252, frame 1494.

19. Ibid., roll A3003, frame 1573.

20. Ibid., roll A2253, frame 165.

21. Ibid., roll A3003, frames 1554-1555.

22. Ibid., roll A2252, frame 1004; roll A2253, frames 631, 1733-1734, 1724.

23. Ibid., roll A2254, pp. 17, 75, 132.

24. Ibid., roll A2252, frames 976, 1005-1006, 1406; roll A2253, frames 636-639.

25. Ibid., p. 241, roll A2252, frame 1859.

26. The Origins of the Ferry Division, roll A3011, frame 1164, CAFH.

27. History of the Women Airforce Service Pilots Program and Activities in the AAF Training Command, roll A2254, frames 1006, 1857, 1164, 636-639, and Report of Women Pilot Program, draft copy with comments, frame 1857; Nels O. Monserud, Medical Considerations of the WASPs, n.d., 220.0721-14 (Revision), Aug. 21, 1945, vol. 1, Women Pilot Program, Material on Wasps, Files of Director of Women Pilots, World War II, CAFH.

28. History of the Air Transport Command, Women Pilots in the Air Transport Command, p. 103, roll A2254, frame 1171, CAFH.

29. Ibid., pp. 102-105, 110, 130, roll A2254, frame 1174.

30. Ibid., roll A2254, frames 1192, 1007-1008, 1013, 1857, 1160, 1164, 1166, 1167.

31. Ibid., roll A2254, frames 178-179, 1010-1012, 1861-1862.

32. Ibid., roll A2252, frames 1733-1734.

33. The Origins of the Ferry Division, roll A3011, frame 1164, CAFH.

34. General Arnold's Material, roll A1763, frame 684, CAFH.

35. Jacqueline Cochran and Maryann Bucknum Brinley, *Jackie Cochran: An Autobiography* (Toronto, 1987), pp. 7-11, 15.

36. Ibid., pp. 54-55.

37. Ibid., p. 126.

38. Ibid., pp. 118-119.

39. Ibid., p. 57.

40. Ibid., p. 75.

41. Ibid., pp. 133, 144, 150, 157, 166.

42. History of the Air Transport Command, Women Pilots in the Air Transport Command, roll A2252, p. 62, CAFH.

43. Ibid., roll A2253, frame 1413.

44. Ibid., roll A2252, frames 1804-1808.

45. Ibid., frames 991-992, 1017; pp. 122-123, 125. "Women Pilots in the Air Transport Command," roll A2252; roll A2253, frames 1176-1777, 1795, 1787-1789; roll A2252, frame 1805; roll A2253, frames 1987-1990, 43, CAFH.

46. Ibid., roll A2253, frame 43.

CONFRONTING THE
REALITIES OF SERVICE LIFE

A fter the United States was drawn into the war, an unprecedented number of women volunteered to serve in the military's newly organized women's units and the more established Army and Navy Nurse Corps. Their reasons for enlisting were as personal and varied as the ways they responded to the other realities of service life they encountered.

Dorothy Jeanne Gleason enlisted in the U.S. Coast Guard's Women's Reserve in 1943. In the first paper of the session, she offered an engaging look at the pleasures and pitfalls of being assimilated into military life as a Spar (an acronym derived from the organization's "*Semper Paratus*" motto) through such experiences as boot camp, duty assignments, personal rewards and challenges, V-J Day, and closeout activities. She concluded her account with an acknowledgment of notable Spars and a brief history of the SPAR after World War II. Captain Gleason retired from the ready reserve program in 1978.

Janet Sims-Wood employed excerpts from oral history interviews and a conference panel discussion in her paper to recount the personal experiences of black women who served in the Women's Army Corps (WAC) and its predecessor Women's Army Auxiliary Corps (WAAC). The women's comments revealed an uneasy association with a military system that reflected society's racially discriminatory practices against which black Wacs, the black press, and black leaders protested. Their statements also conveyed their sense of pride in knowing that they had served their country in spite of the many disappointing hardships.

When the Japanese occupied Manila in the Philippines on January 2, 1942, Lt. Mary Harrington Nelson was serving in the Navy Nurse Corps in Cañacao. During the next 37 months, she and 10 other Navy nurses were held as prisoners of war in civilian internment camps in Manila and Los Baños. Her paper examined the interplay between the ordinary and extraordinary acts and emotions that characterized POW life as well as the factors that helped them survive the terrible ordeal.

The session was chaired by Regina T. Akers, an archivist with the Naval Historical Center in Washington, DC, and author of historical studies on the role and experiences of women in the military during World War II.

MY EXPERIENCES AS A SPAR DURING WORLD WAR II
(February 1943-June 1946)

Dorothy Jeanne Gleason

I appreciate the opportunity to discuss the Spars who served in the Coast Guard Women's Reserve in World War II. I was asked to relate my personal experiences, but as any service person knows, we were each part of a group and shared many similar experiences. I hope these comments will be taken in part as a "We" account rather than an "I" account.

I must start by expressing affection and admiration for our first director, Capt. Dorothy Stratton, former dean of women at Purdue University, who saved us from a disaster. She coined our name— SPAR—from the Coast Guard motto: *Semper Paratus*—Always Ready. (The Coast Guard men were considering calling us Worcogs [Women's Reserve of the Coast Guard]!) So to our gallant lady, our respect and appreciation for giving us a very appropriate name. She was 96 in March 1995 and still active and much interested in what was going on.

At one time after the war there was so little known about the SPAR that those of us still active referred to ourselves as the "endangered species." Then came the approach of the significant 50th anniversaries: our anniversary, D-day, and then V-E and V-J Days, which generated both press and public interest. I have given many interviews, and they usually start with one question:

"Why did you go into the service? The draft was not concerned about you."

The first answer is that it was the patriotic thing to do; one certainly did not join for money. As a civilian, I was a civil service employee, a clerk in the U.S. Post Office, living at home with my parents in a small Kansas town. The princely sum of $50 a month for military service was only a fraction of what I was already earning!

A second answer is adventure—a chance to be a part of something affecting all our lives and an occasion to leave home and see some of the rest of the country. Finally, I would have to say that joining the service was a chance to change a career pattern and perhaps learn a new skill; it was also a personal challenge to see if I could "hack" it.

The next question commonly is: "How did you select the Coast Guard? Certainly it was not well known in your part of the country. The Army or Navy would have been more familiar to you."

The Army and Navy recruiters had office space in the post office where I was working. When the WAAC (Women's Army Auxiliary Corps) was established, the Army sergeant talked to me about enlisting. I said no (in the presence of the Navy chief) but added, "If the Navy decides to take women, let me know; I look better in blue than khaki!" The chief followed up on that remark in the late fall and talked to me about coming into the WAVES (Women Accepted for Volunteer Emergency Service). It sounded really exciting. Because the postmaster asked me to stay through the holiday rush, it was early February 1943 before I went to Kansas City, MO, to the Navy recruiting office. Field recruiters were not permitted to actually enlist women.

The Wave ensign who talked to a group of about 20 women that morning said that the area quota for WAVES was filled for 5 months, but the Coast Guard was enlisting women for the SPAR (thank heavens that name was used; I doubt if WORCOGS would have been very inspiring). Recruiting was under way for the second class because the first class was already formed. We sat there until finally someone asked, "What is the Coast Guard?" The answer was classic: "It is the same as the Navy—you will wear the same uniform, train in the same schools, and might even be assigned to a Navy station. However, to distinguish you from the Waves, you will wear a shield instead of a star," as she pointed to her sleeve. (That was a little inaccurate since the enlisted Wave did not wear a star.) I could not see why I should wait 5 months to wear a star, so I requested consideration for the Coast Guard. I enlisted that day, February 6, 1943, as an apprentice seaman, United States Coast Guard Women's Reserve.

Recruiters told you very little, and from their remarks, I left with the mistaken impression that I was going to Hunter College, The Bronx, NY, for a month of "orientation" on how to become a Spar. I was told I would live off campus in apartment houses taken over by the Navy but eat and attend classes on campus. In my mind it was like taking a course; I assumed I would be part of a group going to eat and to classes, and when the day was over, there would be free time. I even envisioned weekend sightseeing in New York City!

I went home to await my orders and try to placate a completely baffled family, co-workers, and friends. What is the Coast Guard? Why didn't you join the Navy? Although I was the only woman in the entire county to serve in the armed forces, very few people ever realized that I was Coast Guard. I would be met with such questions as "How are the Wacs?" or "What do you do in the Navy?" When I was commissioned, my hometown newspaper modified the official Coast Guard release to state that I had been commissioned in the Coast Artillery. Not even the shield helped!

Shortly after enlistment I received more forms to complete, so I missed the second class, which was to start the first of March. In due time I received orders to depart on March 24 for the third class at Hunter College. In addition to a train ticket and meal vouchers came instructions on what to bring. The first item was for civilian clothes to last only 1 week. The uniform would consist of a blouse, shirt, skirt, raincoat, hat (with havelock), and purse. I had to furnish all other articles: low heels, tie oxfords (black leather), stockings (flesh colored), underwear (white), and night wear. I was to bring only luggage that I could carry because each enlistee would be responsible for her own things.

On the train I met two other women who were going to Hunter College as Spars. We teamed up, and it gave the three of us a feeling of confidence as it was a fact that not one of us had any idea of where we were going.

A uniformed Red Cross volunteer was to be at Grand Central Station when I arrived to escort me to Hunter College. It all sounded fairly simple and well planned. Famous last words! First and probably most crucial was that we did not get our uniforms for 34 days (just prior to shipping out). You can imagine the condition of our civilian clothes when we shipped them home.

We arrived at Grand Central Station in the late afternoon, and the Red Cross volunteers were there with big signs—"Hunter College—Lines form here." About 10 of us were assigned to one Red Cross woman, and we took off for our first contact with the New York subway—and during the evening rush hours! We stood all the way—jostled and jerked about—obviously first timers, finally reached the Hunter station, and walked quite a few blocks to report to our living quarters.

The Navy had taken over several large apartment houses on the fringe of the campus, and my group drew one that had just opened and had never been lived in. In the lobby we checked in, picked up our orders, and got room assignments. The three of us were put together in one bedroom of a two-bedroom apartment with one bath. We were allowed to take the elevator to the sixth floor and admonished that we would never use it again until we shipped out. We were shown the way to the stairs. The three occupants of the other bedroom had arrived earlier, but there was little time for conversation.

I learned my first lesson in the service that night—*Do not volunteer!* When we were issued bedding, we were asked if we knew how to make a bed with square corners. I held up my hand as I had just completed a home nursing course with the Red Cross and immediately heard, "Seaman Gleason, you will show the women on this floor how to make up a bed." Of course the women were delighted to have me take over and watched while I made up beds. Finally, on my way back to my room to make up my own, we heard "Lights out in 5 minutes." I protested to the woman who had accompanied me and said that I did not have my own bed made, and she said to do the best I could in the next 5 minutes, but lights out will be observed. I never volunteered again!

0530: "*Hit the deck!* You have 30 minutes to dress, make up your beds, straighten your room, walk down 5 floors and muster in front of the building at 0600. *Do not be late!*" This was our first brush with shared living with mature women. One of the women in the other bedroom had gone into the bathroom, locked the door, and refused to come out. We pounded and threatened, but she only came out when the word came, "5 minutes to muster." It never happened again after we all agreed to limit our time in consideration of the others in the apartment. It was a long walk, about four blocks at least, in the cold Bronx March weather to the cafeteria on the campus. Food was not the first order of the day though; the long lines for the restrooms demonstrated that apparently our experience was shared in other areas.

The day was filled with completing more forms, orientation classes, exercises, and our first drill. By the time we got back to the room in the late afternoon we were exhausted. We looked forward to an evening to get adjusted or to get to know each other, but instead we heard, *"Report to the lounge room on the fifth floor."* We had a beautiful Coast Guard ensign from Texas who loved to sing, and we sang with her until it was time to report to our rooms for lights out at 2130.

The days melted into one another. Coast Guard instructors taught us about the service. We drew duty assignments: cleaning the officers' quarters, KP, policing our own rooms, and, yes, swabbing beautiful, highly waxed parquet floors! The drilling, shots, medical exams, and a session with a psychiatrist kept us busy. Classes covered Coast Guard history and information from the Bluejackets Manual (the Navy primer for all new enlisted personnel).

We were given tests of all kinds; the final aptitude test was to determine the first assignment after boot camp: either to a school or as a striker (a position indicating that you had experience equivalent to the training the school could give). Students and strikers

Ens. Mary S. Hacker plots an air course while on duty at the Coast Guard Air Station at Dinner Key, Coconut Grove, FL, n.d.

National Archives, Records of the U.S. Coast Guard (26-G-05-04- 44(12))

would then be classed as yeomen or storekeepers (the ratings the Coast Guard was looking for at the time). One followed a progression from striker to seaman (apprentice, SN2, SN1) to petty officer (Storekeeper 3, 2, 1; Yeoman 3, 2, 1) to chief. I apparently satisfied all requirements as I was sent out as a striker qualified to advance to either yeoman or storekeeper. In civilian life, the yeoman would be equivalent to a secretary, and a storekeeper to a bookkeeper. What it meant to be a striker never really registered with many of us—it just seemed like a place-holder until you found your niche!

One incident stands out during the training. Eleanor Roosevelt came to a WAVES graduation, and we were assembled so she could review the troops. The Waves were in full uniform, and some distance behind, in the last row, was a collection of Spars and women Marines still in civilian clothes and much the worse for wear. I will always remember the gracious gesture of the First Lady—after trooping the lines of immaculate Waves, she came back to the "urchins" and said that she understood that our uniforms had not arrived and she regretted not seeing us in uniform but wished us well.

I must say a few words about drilling. We had on shore duty from the South Pacific a Marine sergeant who obviously hated every minute of it. He took a dim view of duty with women, and he was merciless in teaching us how to march. I never did decipher his cadence calls; drill sergeants have a language all their own.

The day finally came to graduate from boot camp. We went through the line to draw our uniforms: cap, havelock, blouse, skirt, two shirts, topcoat, and shoulder purse. We had to go through another line to get Coast Guard insignia for our blouses, ribbon for our hats, and a white shield for our blouse sleeves. We had the rest of the day to get it all together, as this was Saturday. We were to attend Easter service off campus and ship out on Monday.

Sunday found us mustering in uniform for a full uniform check, followed by the announcement, "All Catholics fall out and form at the end of the platoons. The rest of you are Protestants and will attend service at St. John the Divine." Easter Sunday in a "high" Episcopal church was quite an experience for many Protestants. After the service we were dismissed and free to enjoy New York City until 2100! Four of us teamed up and found a nice restaurant on Broadway—I can still remember the steak! Then we went sightseeing, and since we had no idea if any of us would ever return to New York, we wanted to see as much as we could—Grant's

Tomb, Coney Island, the Statue of Liberty, Rockefeller Center, the Empire State Building, Madison Square Garden—and we made it back in time!

I have spent a lot of time on the boot camp portion of my service, but that is the most critical phase of women's preparation for fitting successfully into the service. We were to have 10,000 enlisted women in the SPAR, from all walks of life, ethnic backgrounds, and religious affiliations—women who were not school children but adults, many of whom had been in the work force for years and had formed opinions of what life was all about and what they wanted from it. We were given a month to establish an esprit de corps and pride in being in the Coast Guard and to become disciplined to receive and execute orders without a long conversational bout. These results could not be brought about without a drastic change in most of the routines of our lives. Boot camp determined whether we would make or break the system.

On Monday morning we shipped out to our first assignments. My orders were to go to Cleveland, the 9th Coast Guard District Headquarters, along with seven other Spars. The first class of women Marines had started with our class, and two of the women were on the train with us. We went by troop train, via Canada, and it took until the afternoon of the following day to get to Cleveland. There we were greeted by Coast Guard enlisted men who had been sent to pick up luggage and show us how to get to the Hollanden Hotel, which was only a short way from the train station. The Navy had taken over much of it, and the Spars were given one wing of one floor because there were so few of us. Two to a room; imagine only two to a bathroom! We were told to get settled and to report the following morning to the District building, also within walking distance of the hotel. We would be given an allowance for meals since no mess facility was available.

There were only eight enlisted and two SPAR officers assigned to the 9th Coast Guard District when we arrived. Upon reporting, our "screening" for assignment was almost like eeny, meeny—one side for striker yeoman, the other for striker storekeeper. My resume showed that I had been a postal clerk, so I was to be a striker yeoman and report to the mail room. Running interoffice memorandums around the building was a far cry from what I had done, and I really did not see how this would ever qualify me for petty officer rating as yeoman or storekeeper. I was indeed fortunate on the first payday, when one of the pay officers told me how to sign the payroll, to be able to tell him I had been signing one for 4 years. He asked a few questions: where I had worked, where I was now, and whether I would like to come to the pay office. I said yes. The following day I was called to the Personnel Office and told to report to the Chief of the Pay and Disbursing Office—thus began a very satisfying career in the Coast Guard.

I was advanced to Seaman 2 upon leaving boot camp ($54); after a month on the pay books, I advanced to Seaman 1 ($66). I next advanced to Storekeeper 3, then Storekeeper 2, and by January 1, 1944 (less than 9 months in the Coast Guard), to Storekeeper 1. Others were able to do the same. Because yeomen and store-keeper rates were frozen for men on shore, the ratings were available to the women when their supervisors felt they were ready for it. This was not as "loose" as it sounds, as the men who came in from civilian life were given rates at the beginning, whereas all women were brought in as apprentice seamen. So advancements provided the necessary match between pay and the jobs we were performing.

Some of the women were striving for ratings other than yeoman or storekeeper. One became a gunner's mate; others became pharmacist mates, photographer's mates, and radiomen as well as truck drivers and telephone operators. As the schools turned out more women, they were gradually filling the offices.

Cleveland was a most delightful city, and the Coast Guard was very popular and well known. The city gave service people free transportation, theater tickets, and movie tickets, and the citizens were very generous in picking up meal tabs.

We lived with the Waves until there were too many of us for the space allowed. As a stopgap measure, we were billeted at the Evangeline Home for Women, run by the Salvation Army. Later the Coast Guard negotiated a downtown hotel, and it became the SPAR barracks.

At the turn of the year 1944, I was interviewed, given tests, and selected for Officer Candidate School (OCS) to be a pay and supply officer. There was a great need for such officers as the ships needed them, and there were not enough men to handle both ship and shore assignments. I left with five others to attend the second class of pay and supply training at Palm Beach, FL. The Coast Guard had taken over a resort hotel, the Biltmore at Palm Beach, to provide boot, rating, and pay and supply OCS training. Spars attended OCS at the Coast Guard Academy (the only service academy to train women) in Palm Beach and later at Manhattan Beach, Brooklyn, NY. Communications training (officer and enlisted) was mainly at Atlantic City. On a humorous note, women officers were called "sir" by direction of the Commandant. It took a little doing to respond to "Good Morning, Miss Gleason, Sir!"

Palm Beach meant different things to Spars depending on their reason for being there. Boot camp is just that, regardless of palm trees and ocean beaches. OCS was much the same: lots of studying, with lots of homework, and little liberty (Tuesdays and Thursdays until 2100 and Saturdays until 2300). Permanent detail personnel lived under rules somewhat more relaxed than those for the trainees but in the atmosphere of a training station nevertheless.

However, the fact that this operation was all Coast Guard and was the SPAR's own training made up for much of the required regimentation. I have pleasant memories of Sunday afternoons cycling around the island, going deep sea fishing, and, of course, the beach, although that presented hazards to those of us who were fair skinned, blonde, or red headed. Sunburn was subject to disciplinary action (in addition to the pain!). We were expected to drill at 1600 in the hot sun on the white sand and to pass the obstacle course before graduation. I could take the crawling on my belly under barbed wire, the running on logs across water, the zigzagging through auto tires, but the most terrifying part was to climb up a cargo net strung between two trees and cross over and go down the opposite side. I was simply terrified (and had a lot of company) but more terrified of failing and not being commissioned. It was an ordeal that I will never forget.

We were two to a room with bath, early to bed and early to rise, and stood fire watches at night. Inspections were rigid, and demerits were given; the two "sins" that cost me demerits were "eyes astray" (moving my eyes to follow the inspection party) and "hair adrift" (leaving a strand of hair in my brush). But all in all, it was a survivable experience. A few in our class failed academically. (As an aside—by the time the Spars celebrated their 25th reunion, the Biltmore hotel had been sold and was about to be converted into condominiums. The Coast Guard, however, was able to persuade the hotel to reopen for a week to permit the reunion to take place there. It was quite a homecoming for many of us, and it satisfied the curiosity of those who never went there.)

On graduation day, June 14, 1944, we were asked to give our preferences for assignments. I had selected Cleveland and San Francisco. However, my orders were to report to the Coast Guard Training Station, Manhattan Beach, Brooklyn, NY, along with three other classmates. This was the Coast Guard's largest training station during World War II for boots and some schools. It was also a receiving and shipping-out station for duty afloat. I was assigned as the deputy disbursing officer; one classmate went to the Pay Office; one to Supply; and the fourth to the Clothing Locker.

We had to live off base as there were no officers' quarters, so another officer and I learned about renting sublets in Brooklyn when the owners moved from winter to summer residences. Eventually I moved into Manhattan and became a commuter. As an ensign my pay was $150 plus subsistence and quarters, a sum that did not go very far. We had no food stamps and ate out frequently. I learned a lot about the automat. Though meals were available on the base, the hours were not compatible with commuting.

When I arrived at Manhattan Beach, the training was for men. When Palm Beach closed, training became co-ed. Many women officers from Palm Beach came with the training program. Manhattan Beach was a pleasant place for the permanent staff. The Coast Guard had celebrities on the rolls here. Jack Dempsey was a commander in charge of sports activities. Alan Hale, Jr., was a boatswain mate. We were able to draw some of the USO shows because the Maritime Training Station was adjacent, and the combined audience warranted an evening's entertainment by some of the top stars of the time.

In 1945 Hawaii and Alaska opened up for SPAR volunteers. I made a request, only to be "requested" by the Executive Officer to "withdraw" due to the scarcity of pay and supply officers. I withdrew; so much for "overseas duty."

V-J Day will always remain vivid in my memory. I had stayed late to sign out a shipment, and another Spar and I were going into Manhattan. Then the news arrived: THE WAR IS OVER! Discipline went out like a candle! The recruits climbed over the high fence and were off on foot to Coney Island (adjacent to us) and to Sheepshead Bay, a short walk from the base. When I came out of my office, two male officers of the day (ODs) stopped and asked if my Spar friend and I would accompany them on a round of checking out Coney Island. We were given brassards with an SP (Shore Patrol) and night sticks, and seated in an open Jeep with two male officers in front, off we went to Coney Island. We were only concerned with those who were bound to get into trouble. Many of the boots were not of legal age to drink, but the bartenders could not have cared less! We toured all the bars, and when some of the boots had obviously drunk beyond their limits, we called the patrol to take them back to Manhattan Beach—no names, no charges—just lucky we could take care of them.

The other Spar and I left at midnight and went into Manhattan to join the throngs that were gathered around the Times Square News Building—what crowds—what excitement—what a night!

I was selected as one of the officers to remain to close out the training station in January 1946, and by March the paperwork had been completed. I was assigned to Coast Guard Headquarters as Chief, Ships Service Stores, a policy assignment to close out Ships' stores (equivalent to the Army Post Exchange) of all nonpermanent ships and stations of the Coast Guard. All reserves were to be off the rolls as of June 30, 1946, and so along with many others, I departed the Coast Guard. A war had been won, and I left with a deep feeling of satisfaction that I had played an active part in it, a wealth of longtime friendships, and a lot of confidence gained over the 3 years and 3 months I had served.

I would like to mention some of the women who have been unique to the SPAR. I believe we had the only gold star mother of a Congressional Medal of Honor winner, Lt. Edith Munro, mother of Douglas Munro. I do not think any other service can make that claim. Another was Florence Ebersole Smith, who as a young girl was interned by the Japanese in the Philippine Islands; she later married a Coast Guardsman and joined the SPAR. (I know that other servicewomen were POWs and internees, but this was one for the SPAR.) I also wish to mention women associated with LORAN (Long Range Aid to Navigation). The LORAN communications system, designed to calculate the exact position of ships and planes, was a classified assignment so secret that even those who were assigned to it had no idea what they would be doing. It was most unusual to have a woman designated as commanding officer of a station as well as to have an all-women crew. Lt. (jg.) Vera Hameschlag was the commanding officer of the Chatham, MA, station—the only one in the world manned completely by women.

Many people, including some in the Coast Guard, thought that the SPAR faded out after World War II and that it was never again part of the Coast Guard. This mistaken assumption was carried along for many years. For the record, the wartime legislation that established the Women's Reserve expired in July 1947 and, with it, the authority for the SPAR. Even officers who held a 3-year commission at the time of release in 1946 were affected. The Coast Guard Commandant pressed for legislation that would restore the Women's Reserve, and in November 1949 the bill was passed. Attempts were made to contact as many former members of the SPAR as possible, but since the women had not been required to keep the Coast Guard apprised of changes in their names and addresses, those 3 years made a tremendous difference as to who could be found.

About 200 of us returned to the Women's Reserve. I was sworn into the inactive reserve early in December 1949. In 1950 I entered a reserve unit, which was all volunteer, nonpay, for both men and women. In a public address in the early 1950s, the Commandant was asked when there would be a program to bring in more women. His answer was quite definite: He could not foresee any situation that would require women to be called to active duty. He did allow, however, that should that happen, a few of us would form a cadre to start the process of recruiting, training, and establishing a competent force. Less than a year later, the Korean war caused the Coast Guard to request a voluntary recall of women and men reservists to active duty.

With the close of the Korean war, some of the women elected to stay in order to complete 20 years of active duty. Women officers on active duty could not be promoted beyond commander, but no such restrictions on years of service or promotion applied to male reservists who remained on active duty. There were also no promotion restrictions placed on women in the reserve program and not on continued active duty. Eventually some went from volunteer nonpay units to ready reserve units in pay status. Women not on extended active duty were considered for promotion along with the men. I went from ensign to captain through the ready reserve (not on active duty). During this time the needs of the service permitted a few women to be enlisted and attend Navy schools for needed ratings and to help with unit administrations.

Very little information exists for the years 1950 to 1973, except in the memories of those involved. There were "new firsts" during this period: the first woman warrant officer in the Coast Guard, Elizabeth Splaine; the first woman master chief, Pearl Faurie; and the first woman to be promoted to captain since World War II, Eleanor L'Ecuyer.

In 1973 new legislation was passed that permitted women to choose a career in the regular service or the reserve. The first woman regular in the Coast Guard was a Spar, Alice Jefferson, now a retired warrant officer.

The rest of the story about women in the Coast Guard is well known. The Coast Guard Academy was the first service academy to take women as cadets. Women are assigned to duty afloat and flight training—a whole new world. But the fact remains that the few who held on during the 1950s and 1960s prompted the legislation in the 1970s that led to the expanded programs. It is hard to believe that this great change would have taken place without women being on active duty in the reserve units.

Many interviewers ask a final question: "What did I gain from being in the service?" I answer

1) a true fulfillment of a patriotic action, a deeply satisfying sense of having served my country in a critical time;
2) the adventure of new places and new skills;
3) lifetime friends;
4) the confidence to go forward and to realize aspirations, a belief that I can do it! and
5) a totally unexpected financial gain: the GI bill (or unemployment checks for those who did not have jobs or education to return to); veterans preference placing me in the top category of the civil service; and when I retired from the reserve as a captain, a monthly retirement check.

Let me close with a quotation from Captain Stratton on the occasion of the SPAR 50th reunion in November 1992:

What fun—reliving those days of learning, duty, fear of failure, excitement, and sometimes, boredom. Because it was a strange new world and because we were all in it together, we quickly made new friendships which have lasted half a century. As we relive those days, we grieve for those who are no longer with us. We miss them, not only today, but always. But this is more than a celebration of days passed—it is a rededication to peacetime service to our beloved country. I salute you!

Service Life in the Women's Army Corps and Afro-American WACs

Janet Sims-Wood

After World War II began in Europe in 1939, President Franklin Roosevelt announced the neutrality of the United States. At that time the majority of the people in the United States still felt that we should stay out of the war; yet most wanted an Allied victory. Roosevelt urged all aid "short of war" to nations fighting the Axis. Eventually, Brazil, Canada, Mexico, and the United States sent troops to fight in Europe, and the United States played a key role in the final Allied victory, both in Europe and the Pacific.

Roosevelt initially hoped to defeat the Axis Powers by equipping the Allied nations with ships, tanks, and other war matériel. Japan, not Germany, finally plunged the United States into World War II. The United States opposed Japan's expansion in Southeast Asia. When General Tojo became Premier of Japan in 1941, he and other Japanese military leaders realized that only the U.S. Navy had the power to block Japan's expansion into Asia, and they decided to cripple the U.S. Pacific Fleet.

Without warning on December 7, 1941, Japanese aircraft attacked the U.S. Pacific Fleet at anchor in Pearl Harbor in Hawaii. The bombing was a major success for the Japanese. It disabled much of the Pacific Fleet and destroyed many aircraft, but the Japanese planes missed the U.S. aircraft carriers, which were out at sea.

The United States, Canada, and Great Britain declared war on Japan on December 8, 1941. The next day, China declared war on the Axis. On December 11, Germany and Italy declared war on the United States, the United States reciprocated, and World War II became a global conflict.

In May 1942 Congress established the Women's Army Auxiliary Corps (WAAC). The act called for the recruiting of 25,000 women between the ages of 21 and 45 for noncombat duty with the Army

in order to relieve male soldiers for combat duty. The only requirements for enlistment in the WAAC were good health and character
and a high school education. The WAAC did not have Army status
yet, so its members did not receive the benefits that male soldiers
did (burial benefits, hospitalization, et cetera).

This paper gives a brief overview of the WAAC and the Women's
Army Corps (WAC), established in July 1943, and recounts some
of the personal experiences of a few black women who served in
the military during World War II.

Dovey Johnson Roundtree, one of the first 39 Waacs to enter
the military and graduate from Officer Candidate School, related
how in 1941 she sat with Eleanor Roosevelt, Congresswoman Edith
Nourse Rogers, and Mary McLeod Bethune as they drafted the
WAAC resolution that was presented to Congress. She remembers that

> [w]hen I think back and see Mrs. Bethune sitting in her big
> chair at 1318 Vermont Avenue, NW, Mrs. Roosevelt sitting
> there, and Mrs. Rogers would always come a little late, but
> she would come and join the group. What happened was the
> kindering of a spirit, which would grip you if you stayed around.
> I had no idea that Mrs. Bethune would recommend that I be a
> part of it. . . . The more I heard, the more I was satisfied that
> this was something, if I could, I wanted to do.[1]

Thus on May 28, 1941, Congresswoman Rogers introduced H.R.
4906 in the House of Representatives to establish a Women's Army
Auxiliary Corps for service with the Army of the United States.
After much debate and many recommendations from the War
Department, the Bureau of the Budget, and General of the Army
George Marshall, who was a supporter of the WAAC legislation,
Congresswoman Rogers reintroduced the bill as H.R. 6293 at the
end of 1941. The House of Representatives finally approved the
bill, and on May 14, 1942, the Senate approved it by a 38 to 27 vote.[2]

Oveta Culp Hobby was made Director of the corps, and she
took her oath of office on May 16, 1942. She soon announced that
the first contingent of WAAC recruits would report to Fort Des
Moines, IA, for training as officers. The War Department announced
that the WAAC would follow Army policy and admit black women
with a 10-percent quota. Initially there were to be 440 officer
candidates, of whom 40 would be black. After these 440 finished

their basic 6-week training course, other women would be enrolled and trained as privates and officers.

Dovey Roundtree recounts that the first major hurdle black women faced was getting an application for the WAAC. She recalls that

> the most difficult part of it, the one that black women overcame, was to knock down the doors of the United States Post Office and get the application to apply. That was far harder for me than passing the mental alertness test. I have heard other women recount similarly. One of the reasons we didn't have as many as we might have—women who applied, in Atlanta, in Augusta, in Greensboro, became discouraged and just didn't bother. And when I went to the post office in Charlotte, NC, and they told me that they didn't know anything about it, and I'm sitting there with the very bill still with the ink kind of moist on it. That was really our first battle, which became across this country a campaign; for if they could shut you out and you couldn't get in the door to get the application, that was an easy way to eliminate you.[3]

The first contingent of officer candidates arrived at Fort Des Moines on July 20, 1942. The selection of black officer candidates had been particularly delicate because the black press had attacked the choice of Mrs. Hobby, a southerner, as WAAC Director, and some black organizations had protested her appointment to the position.

When the 39 black women arrived at Fort Des Moines for Officer Candidate School, they were put in one separate company and lodged in separate quarters; they ate at separate dining tables and used separate recreation rooms although they shared classrooms with the white trainees.

In recounting the first trip to the mess hall, Roundtree remembers that

> we marched or walked, and when we got there, the white girls had marched in, for they were all together, and when you march in together as scared as we were, you naturally sit together. And then we looked. There were four long brown tables and a little sign so large and one word, "colored," on the end of it. Some of us sat; some of us ate; some of us got a plate, turned it over, and marched out. We found the post exchange and got

something to eat and went back to the barracks. I contacted Dr. Bethune to let her know that we couldn't eat because with those signs on and the flags outside, something was wrong. . . . In 2 days the signs disappeared, and within a week, Mrs. Bethune came to meet with us.[4]

Charity Adams Earley, who became the company commander and was also one of the first 39 black women to attend Officer Candidate School, related the cultural shock she experienced at Fort Des Moines upon her arrival. She recalled that

the day the group from Ohio arrived at Des Moines—and here we were 18 women strong, with 5 or 6 blacks—they asked us all sitting there in the room that all colored girls move on this side of the room and then proceeded to give us our assignments by name. They could have done this with all of us sitting there, but we had come together, we had slept in the same berth in the sleeping car together and had come to know each other, and it was probably one of the most integrated situations I had ever seen in my life, and then suddenly to get there and they said for you colored girls, move over there. Now that's really a cultural shock. When they did that, we knew from then on what to be looking for.[5]

On August 29, 1942, 36 black women were among the 436 Waacs who graduated at Fort Des Moines with the rank of third officer. They took over positions such as messenger, typist, laboratory technician, chauffeur, public relations officer, and nurse's aide.

It had been hoped that the new women's corps would break the tradition of segregated units long familiar to men. However, the demand that the WAAC place black and white women in the same unit was rejected because the WAAC had to follow Army policy. It was recommended that Mary Bethune and one other black be commissioned as Assistant Directors, but there was a no-direct-appointment policy in the Army. In assessing the negatives that the black women had to face, Mrs. Earley stated that

we were segregated with housing; we were held back in terms of field assignments to other posts because once you had a group trained, there was no commanding officer who requested them. One of the biggest struggles we had was when we first got a company; some recruiting officers only recruited whites so we would have 10 blacks when we needed 200 to get a company started. We would have to hold them until some more women came in. It might take 6 to 8 weeks before we had enough people to get started. So there was some prejudice in the selection process. We received prejudice and discrimination on public facilities and in public restaurants.[6]

It also soon became apparent that not enough qualified black women had presented themselves as applicants for Officer Candidate School, and it was feared that the WAAC failure to fill the 10-percent quota would be viewed by the black press as discrimination. Army officers then had to make hurried trips to college campuses to recruit qualified women. Mrs. Bethune assisted in the selection of these candidates.

As of January 1, 1943, there was still less than the 10-percent quota of black women in the Army. The number would have been higher had there been adequate recruiting efforts and no set quotas. Many black organizations felt that had the WAAC never set a 10-percent quota but instead limited black enlistment to a few women who met the highest standards, it not only might have avoided the burden of unassignable low-grade personnel but also could have successfully abolished segregation. But the WAAC could not achieve these objectives without a change in Army policy on blacks in the military.

One valuable source for information on black Waacs was the black newspapers. Since black women in the military were considered unique, since so many served during World War II, and since many groups were checking for instances of discrimination, there was a lot of coverage in the newspapers. Formation of a press pool by a number of black newspapers in 1943 greatly facilitated the flow of war news on black Waacs. Papers making up this pool were the *Afro-American, Pittsburgh Courier, Chicago Defender, Louisville Defender, Michigan Chronicle, Detroit Tribune, Norfolk Journal & Guide, Kansas City Call, New York Amsterdam News, Houston Informer, Atlanta Daily World, Philadelphia Tribune*, and *Chicago Bee*.

A special news agency staffed by a black reporter and black officers was created to serve as a clearinghouse for reports from black military units. There was also a black correspondent on the staff of *Stars and Stripes*, the Army newspaper for overseas troops.

In relating the value of the press during the war, Charity Adams Earley stressed, "that's how you got things done. Some of the instances when Waacs were sent out and mistreated or given assignments that were not appropriate, if it had not been for the press, it would have never been solved."[7]

As of February 1943, there were 4 black Waacs holding the rank of first officer and 32 holding the rank of second officer. Fifteen of the 36 were acting as recruiting officers in various sections of the country, and 2 officers were on the headquarters staff in Washington, DC.[8]

In July 1943 it was announced that the WAAC would be an integral part of the regular Army. Its members would be classified under the same ranks as soldiers and would abide by all Army regulations. The unit name would be changed to the Women's Army Corps (WAC).

There were black officers serving at WAC headquarters in Washington, at the first training center at Fort Des Moines, and at another training center at Fort Devens, MA. There were black units at 10

Maj. Charity E. Adams inspects the first contingent of African-American Wacs assigned overseas, England, February 15, 1945.

National Archives, Records of the Office of the Chief Signal Officer (111-SC-200791)

Army installations in the field: Camp Atterbury, IN; Fort Bragg, NC; Fort Breckinridge, KY; Fort Clark, TX; Fort Custer, MI; Fort Dix, NJ; Fort Huachuca, AZ; Fort Knox, KY; Fort McClellan, AL; and Walla Walla Air Base, WA.

In August 1943 representatives of the National Council of Negro Women held a conference with Col. Oveta Hobby to discuss recommendations aimed at improvement of the status of black Wacs.[9]

In the fall of 1943, WAC Band #2 (Negro WAC Band) was organized and assigned to the first WAC training command at Fort Des Moines, IA. This original group included 35 women; 80 percent of these were starting from scratch, and most of the remaining 20 percent had only minimal musical experience. The leader had a bachelor's degree in music and teaching music but no band experience. Three of the women had played in bands, one was an accomplished singer, and a few could read music. The progress of WAC Band #2 was outstanding. The women were taught to read music by forming a chorus. They were guided through the intricacies of organization, sectional and group playing, marching and concert band performances, and band drill, plus a host of other details by the musical director of the 400th Army Service Forces (ASF) Band.

Dr. Clementine McConico Skinner joined the WAC in 1943 and, after basic training, was assigned to the WAC Band #2. Almost immediately, the band took to the field and began to master marching maneuvers. After learning to play their first march, the band members practiced marching and playing until they got it right. The band was a very select group and worked very well as a unit. Skinner relates that

> I had the opportunity to learn to play the trumpet and the French horn, a chance to sing as a soloist and as a member of the band chorus. As a member of the trumpet section, I shared the duty of playing bugle calls. Playing taps and watching the lights go out on the post on a star-studded night was an inspiring experience for me. Leonora Hull Brown of Jacksonville, FL, was the director of the chorus. I also participated as a member of the interpretive dance group, which was instructed by Capt. Mildred Davenport Carter of Boston, MA. Captain Carter had the dance group's appearances recorded in the *Congressional Record.*[10]

In July 1944 WAC Band #2 was deactivated and then reactivated in September 1944 as the 404th ASF Band. It continued to improve, presenting musical concerts at service clubs and the National Association for the Advancement of Colored People (NAACP) National Convention in Chicago, IL, and throughout the state of Iowa. The band kicked off the seventh war bond drive in Chicago with actress Ida Lupino. Before the end of the war, the 404th ASF Band became the 404th Army Band. The 404th ASF Band was the first and only all-Negro WAC band in the history of the U.S. Army. The band was deactivated permanently in December 1945.

Complaints ran rampant that black Wacs were not given proper consideration in the matter of promotions and upgrading and that those who resented discrimination were persecuted. According to *The Negro Handbook, 1946-47*, Wacs performed 155 kinds of work, and an official War Department survey of 758 of the approximately 4,000 black Wacs indicated that they filled only 25 percent of these job categories.

Although there were many black Wacs with college and postgraduate educations, it was estimated that more than two-thirds of black Wacs had fourth- or fifth-grade reading levels, while only one-fourth of the whites scored so low. This situation may have accounted for the complaints of lack of training and not having a proportionate number of black Wacs in the more specialized technical and professional courses. Most were being trained in motor equipment, cooking, or administrative work.

The major complaint, however, was that no black Wacs were sent overseas. So strong was the desire of black Wacs to go overseas that it was reported that prospects for overseas duty were used as a lure in some recruiting efforts. Still, the Army admitted that there were no plans to use any black Wacs overseas. The War Department explained that no overseas commanders had asked for black Wacs and that a commander had the right to designate the race or color of units being sent to him.[11] In late November 1944, Eleanor Roosevelt interceded on behalf of the black Wacs and was given that same excuse. However, Colonel Hobby told her there was consideration of sending black Wacs overseas.

Pressure from black groups finally forced the War Department to direct commanders in the European theater to accept black Wacs. The European theater finally submitted a requisition for 800 black women to set up half of a central postal directory. The unit members of the 6888th Central Postal Directory Battalion were selected from both the air and service forces in order to give all black military women a chance at overseas service, but sufficient volunteers to fill the unit could not be found.[12] Nevertheless, on February 12, 1945, this unit arrived in England. Later the detachment was sent to Rouen, France, where it also formed a postal unit.

Myrtle Rhoden, an administrative clerk, received orders to go overseas with the 6888th Central Postal Directory Battalion while stationed at Fort Guber, OK. From there she was sent to Fort Oglethorpe, GA, for overseas warfare training.

Mail had been over in England for many, many months, even years, without delivery, and General Eisenhower wanted it delivered to help the morale of the soldiers. The war had been so intense that mail could not be directed to the men as they moved from war zone to war zone.

Ms. Rhoden recalls,

> I remember going to Fort Oglethorpe, GA, in the middle of the night, in the fog and the dark. They gave us all brand new uniforms and taught us warfare tactics (how to jump into ditches, how to use the gas masks, and how to smell the different gases).[13]

After the training, the Wacs were routed to New York, where they boarded a ship for Scotland. Ms. Rhoden remembers that

> when we got to New York, we boarded a ship, the *Ile de France*, which used to be a luxury ship, and when I woke up the next morning, we were at sea. We landed in Scotland, which took us 9 days to get there. Our commanding officer, Charity Adams [Earley], met us at the gangplank and saluted us, and we received her salute. Also Gen. Benjamin O. Davis saluted us as we came down the gangplank.[14]

The women were welcomed to the area, and Ms. Rhoden fondly remembers that "they took us to a nice place to have dinner, and the Scottish people played American music on bagpipes." She recalls how astonished the people were that they were so brown. She notes that she could hear the Scottish people talking about the women, saying "They're so brown. It must be very warm where they come from; the sun keeps them brown."[15]

The duty of the 6888th was to get the mail rerouted to the right soldier. Rhoden notes that

> we found buildings with mailbags piled up to the ceiling. This mail was almost 3 years old and . . . no one could work on it

because of the fighting. We had to resort mail. We knew where everybody was because we had the central directory from A to Z. We had a certain alphabet, and if we had a Mr. Brown, we took his mail out of the bag. Sometimes we had 10 or 12 letters for the one soldier, which were redirected to him. Then there was another room where there were packages of birthday/ Christmas gifts with grandma's cookies and cakes and things. That was the package room, and some of those rats were big as cats in there. It was a lot of debris in there for the food had rotted and molded. That was not the cleanest job. Girls wore certain types of water-repellant clothes that would protect them from the wetness and stuff. They also wore a certain kind of boot. They repacked anything that was salvageable, such as jewelry, socks, or anything wearable. They repacked them and sent them to the soldiers. We were given 6 months to get the job done, and we did it in 3 months, working three round-the-clock shifts. From there, we were sent to Rouen, France, where we found the same situation, and again we rerouted the mail in record time. General Eisenhower gave us some service awards and ribbons for our work with the postal directory battalion.[16]

Commanding officer Charity Adams Earley praised the women for their outstanding ability to match the right package with the right soldier. She noted that

we did an unbelievable job redirecting those parcels. Three hangars of Christmas packages had to be moved out, and we were working 24 hours a day. It was packed to the ceiling. That's when we developed that great package restoration unit. They could take a box, and they would look at the color of the paper, the indentation of the cans, and sometimes using the newspaper that was stuffed in the package, they could see where the package came from. I was just amazed at how good they were.[17]

Mrs. Earley did note that after the black Wacs went overseas, the black press seemed to turn against them.

We decided that it was because they didn't hear anything about us. We then developed a newsletter because someone had written that they didn't hear anything about the Wacs. We didn't know they weren't hearing about us. We were not responsible for PR. So the press began to write things like "I guess

they're over there disgracing us," although they had no spe-
cifics. The way we knew about the bad press was that we were
a postal unit, and one of the *Pittsburgh Courier* wrappers broke
open, and the ladies became very incensed about this news
report. As a commanding officer, they did me the biggest favor
they ever could because they said "we'll show them," so we
didn't have any bad activity.[18]

When President Harry Truman announced the end of the war
in August 1945, many black soldiers and Wacs began to prepare
for civilian life. The *Chicago Defender* and many other papers noted
the grim job prospects for black veterans and war workers. The
Chicago Defender speculated that

1. Close to 1 million blacks would be jobless by Spring, 1946.
2. The Fair Employment Practices Committee would close shop
   and industry would again be allowed the policy of "last
   hired, first fired."
3. Black veterans would not be able to find jobs.[19]

Even with the grim economic outlook, most black veterans
were proud of their service and looked forward to a promising
future. Dr. Skinner probably best describes the military experience
of many black women. She proudly asserts that

it is important to keep in mind that the experiences of Wacs
differed in numerous ways, from post to post in states across
the country. When I entered the WAC, there were many in my
family, community, et cetera, who were not supportive of the
idea of my going into the Army. Most Wacs had this experience.
Eventually, my family, friends, and the general public had a
change of attitude and began to take pride in the Afro-American
women who were participating in the war effort by serving in
the Women's Army Corps. Those of us in the WAC missed out
on making the big bucks. As a result of the Fair Employment
Practices Act, all companies with government contracts had to
hire Afro-Americans, both men and women, and the wages
were good for the day and time. We in the WAC made the
fabulous salary of $50 per month.
    Those of us who entered the service did so for many reasons.
I entered the service to continue my education and to travel.
I can only say, that while I was a member of the band, it
was my pleasure to see, meet, play, sing, and dance for many

wonderful people of all ages. I was pleased to have had the opportunity to serve my country, for I am truly an American. The extensive traveling I have done outside of the United States (over many years) has convinced me that with all of its faults, I'll take America every time. No doubt about it. My grandfather served in the Civil War, 1863 to 1865. I served in World War II, 1943 to 1945. This gave us the right to demand a share of any and all benefits this nation has to offer all of its citizens, including Afro-Americans. I am proud to know that I played a part in helping the war effort of my country and that I played a role, although minor, in the history of my people, my city, and my country. In a small way, I helped lay the foundation which all women in the military services, who serve today or will serve in the future, have had and will have the opportunity to build upon for those who are destined to follow them.[20]

In the area of women and work during World War II, noted oral historian Sherna Gluck stresses that "the study of women's wartime work experience, specifically their entry into previously male domains, and the impact of that experience on their postwar lives raises substantive and methodological questions for women's history."[21] Gluck further states that "the experience affected women who are participants in a wide variety of ways, ranging from little impact beyond the pleasure derived from having participated in the war effort to major changes in self-concept and self-direction. Sometimes these changes were translated into the public realm, sometimes they were only revealed in the private realm."[22]

Women talking in the 1990s about their experiences during the war some 50 years ago negotiate quite difficult terrain. On the one hand, they acknowledge that they were successful at moving into areas previously defined as "male" and can today talk about how proud they are of doing those jobs. It is less easy for them, though, to talk about their patriotism and about fighting for their country in today's environment in which war is thought of in very negative terms. Thus, memories of the war years can be influenced by a range of factors, all crucial to the understanding of what the experience meant to each woman.

June A. Willenz has noted in her book on women veterans that "to a significant degree the full impact of war upon women has not been totally recognized or documented, perhaps because history has concentrated on the consequences of war from a male perspective. At a time of an awakening consciousness among women of their roles in history, an exploration of what war and its aftermath has meant for them is long overdue."[23]

These black Wacs are unsung heroines in our society. They were among the trailblazers in opening up opportunities for women to enter the previously all-male domain of the military. They returned to their homes and communities with stretched horizons and deepened self-esteem. Their military experience gave them an opportunity to change the quality of their lives; it opened doors for women of all races to enter the military; and it gave the black community pride in knowing that both men and women served their country despite the many prejudices and hardships they encountered.

NOTES

© 1996 by Janet Sims-Wood

1. Panel discussion recording, "Black Women's World War II Military Experiences," Association for the Study of Afro-American Life and History Conference, Washington, DC, Nov. 1, 1991.
2. Mattie E. Treadwell, *The Women's Army Corp*, United States Army in World War II, Special Studies, U.S. Army Center of Military History Pub. 11-8 (Washington, DC, 1954), p. 45.
3. "Black Women's World War II Military Experiences," Nov. 1, 1991.
4. Ibid.
5. Interview of Charity Adams Earley by author, Washington, DC, June 10, 1992.
6. Ibid.
7. Ibid.
8. Florence Murray, ed., *The Negro Handbook, 1944* (New York, 1944), pp. 107-108.
9. Ibid., pp. 108-109.
10. "Black Women's World War II Military Experiences," Nov. 1, 1991.
11. Florence Murray, ed., *The Negro Handbook, 1946-47* (New York, 1947), p. 342.
12. Treadwell, *The Women's Army Corps*, p. 599.
13. Interview of Myrtle Rhoden by author, Charlotte, NC, July 14, 1992.
14. Ibid.
15. Ibid.
16. Ibid.
17. Interview of Charity Adams Earley, June 10, 1992.
18. Ibid.
19. Ben Burns, "400,000 Fired in Cutbacks!," *Chicago Defender* (Aug. 25, 1945): 1, 6.
20. "Black Women's World War II Military Experiences," Nov. 1, 1991.

21. Sherna Berger Gluck, "Interlude or Change: Women and the World War II Work Experience: A Feminist Oral History," *International Journal of Oral History* 3 (June 1982): 92.
22. Ibid., pp. 107–108.
23. June A. Willenz, *Women Veterans: America's Forgotten Heroines* (New York, 1983), p. 4.

World War II Experiences of a POW Navy Nurse[*]

Mary Harrington Nelson

I was working at St Joseph's Mercy Hospital in Sioux City, IA, in 1936. One of my instructors had been a Navy nurse during World War I. She told us it had been the best duty she had ever had. One of the interns at the hospital received some literature from the Navy Bureau of Medicine and Surgery. I wrote to the address, and soon I had an appointment to the Navy Nurse Corps. In January 1937 I went to San Diego; in the summer of 1939 I went to Mare Island; and then in January 1941 I went to the naval hospital at Cañacao, near Manila, in the Philippines.

I remember very well the night World War II started. It was a beautiful moonlit night. I was on night duty. I had just finished my rounds of the sick officers' quarters, which was in a cottage on the bay. It was such a lovely night that I decided to walk outdoors and not go through the administration building to the main hospital building.

I passed other cottages overlooking Manila Bay, where officers' families had lived. As I walked by, I heard the commanding officer and the executive officer talking loudly, and I wondered what they were doing up at that hour. Then I noticed an overhead light on in another cottage. It was the war plans officer's home. Apparently he had become frustrated trying to find materials and codes by flashlight and had turned on the overhead light. (I learned this later.) We had been under "blackout" orders for some time.

---

*See Elizabeth M. Norman and Sharon Eifried, "How Did They All Survive? An Analysis of American Nurses' Experiences in Japanese Prisoner-of-War Camps," *Nursing History Review* 3 (1995): 105–127, for a broad study of the subject, including the experiences of Mary Harrington Nelson as recorded in taped interviews and correspondence.

I went on to the large wards, made rounds, then talked to the corpsmen. The assistant night master-at-arms came in and said, "We just got a message that Honolulu has been bombed." I asked him, "Did you say Honolulu or *the Honolulu*?" There was a heavy cruiser by that name. He said that all he knew was what he told us.

The next day, we cleared the hospital of all the patients we could because we thought we would soon be needing the space. The men filled sandbags and put them around the buildings, most of which were off the ground with space underneath.

The big Army airfields were bombed on Monday and Tuesday. At noon on Wednesday the naval shipyard at Cavite was destroyed, and we had many patients. The operating rooms were very busy until dark.

Many "90-day wonders" (young officers just out of training who had been on torpedo boats) came to the hospital to volunteer their help. One asked me what he could do. I gave him my bandage scissors and told him to get those patients undressed. I thought that he would take off a trouser if there was a leg wound or take off a jacket for an arm wound. He went to work, and in a little while I realized that there was squirming out on the ward. These poor, stark-naked casualties were trying to crawl under the top bedsheet! I got a corpsman and said, "For heaven's sake, cover those poor souls!" and he quickly did.

The next day we evacuated all the patients to Sternberg, the Army hospital in Manila. We went with them and worked there for several days. With supplies from the Army and Navy stores, we set up several satellite hospitals in schools in Manila. When Manila was declared an "Open City" and the Army went to Bataan, we had no orders to leave. We stayed in Manila and gathered the patients into one location at Santa Scholastica School.

On January 2, 1942, the Japanese occupied the city of Manila. In March the Japanese sent the Navy nurses to Santo Tomas, a university in Manila that had been converted to a civilian internment camp. A Japanese officer was in charge of our transfer to Santo Tomas. Our chief nurse, Laura Cobb, asked him if we should take our beds, and he said yes. Some of our officers did not want us to take our beds, but since the Japanese officer said we should, we did. Thanks to him, we had decent beds for the next 3 years. He came into camp several times and took packages and letters to our doctors, who had been moved to Bilibid Prison in Manila. Once he took a picture of the Navy nurses and gave each of us a copy.

All military prisoners from the Manila area were sent to Bilibid; some were later sent to Japan. We could see the Bilibid tower from Santo Tomas. While in Santo Tomas, we worked in the hospital caring for civilian patients. The Army nurses came from Corregidor in July, so there were plenty of nurses at Santo Tomas.

The Japanese decided to get internees out of the city, and the site selected was the agricultural college of the University of Manila, which was at Los Baños, about 50 to 75 miles from Manila. The first group to go consisted of 800 able-bodied men and 11 Navy nurses who volunteered to go along. Missionary and private-practice doctors went too. In Manila there were several missionary hospitals, and all of their doctors were interned with us.

The Japanese took us by truck to the railway station. We were permitted to take all the baggage we wanted, and that followed us by truck to Los Baños. Laura Cobb was determined to take all our Navy records, so she wore them inside her blouse. Some friends made leaf and flower leis for her to wear to disguise the bulges.

Ours was the last truck that left for the station. The public address system at Santo Tomas played "Anchors Aweigh," and I left with tears rolling down my cheeks. As we were the last ones, and the Japanese were anxious to leave, they did not go through our baggage very carefully. They put two or three nurses in each boxcar, probably for security. We could not open the doors until we were out of the city. It was so hot! They put about 60 men in each car. I carried a big Filipino hat with me, and I gave it to the men to use as a windscoop to bring a little air into the back of the boxcar. Finally we arrived at the railway station in Los Baños; a truck took us the remaining 2 miles to the agricultural station.

A Japanese soldier was put on our truck; I believe he felt insulted to have to guard a bunch of women. I think he was really put out, judging from the look on his face. Some of the men got a little worried that we were being shipped off with a Japanese guard, so they hopped on our truck. The soldier seemed to feel a little better now that he had some men to guard.

Once we got settled, we set up the hospital with what we had and started working. People had a lot of skin problems from poor sanitary conditions, athlete's foot (jungle rot), and a kind of prickly heat that would get infected. There were bathing facilities but no hot water, and soap was scarce.

At first the doctors used medicines from their own bags because either the internment camp Central Committee or the hospital staff at Santo Tomas would not give us any of their medical supplies. (Most medicine, bandages, and equipment were Army or Navy supplies that had been salvaged in the early days of the war.) Later some Red Cross supplies were sent to the camps, and Los Baños finally got a fair share.

The construction crew made utensils for the hospital, mostly from sheet-metal roofing. They made wash basins, foot basins, and whatever else was needed. They were our own "sea-bees." A bus made a round trip once a week from Santo Tomas to bring supplies. We acquired enough to do quite a few operations, including three appendectomies on our Japanese guards. We had a good surgeon and they did not.

Every able-bodied person was supposed to work an hour or two a day for camp service. That included picking weevils out of the meal and rice, cleaning vegetables, working in the hospital, in

Wearing new clothes, these Army nurses just released from the Santo Tomas prison in the Philippines board an Air Transport Command bus and head for rest and relaxation in the Hawaiian Islands before returning to the States, January 1945.

National Archives, Records of the Office of the Chief Signal Officer (111-SC-200727)

the kitchen, or cleaning—in fact, anything to make the camp as livable as possible.

Los Baños was out in the country, and it was very pleasant. There were many things with which to occupy the time. We even had entertainment in the evening; we took our folding chairs up to the ball field and listened to music broadcast over an internee-built public address system. I did not know until much later that sometimes they played "live" radio music. We wondered where the new records came from because we were familiar with all the records they had. The answer was always, "Someone brought them from Manila." Somebody brought something from someplace! Because we were definitely not supposed to have a radio, we were always afraid the station might cut in with a news bulletin, an occurrence that could have led to some executions. Variety shows as well as several plays were broadcast as radio shows; we had one "mike," which we shared. An Englishman from Hong Kong was the director.

One of the nurses who was a serious reader had quite a few books, so she started a lending library both in Santo Tomas and Los Baños. People could study many subjects taught by professors from various schools. The Japanese guards enjoyed the softball games in the early evening. Our first death in camp came after a player suffered a heart attack.

At times things were pretty easy. At other times, if the Japanese had had a defeat someplace, they clamped down for a while. So, up and down, you just went with it.

We did get some mail from home, although it was heavily censored. A few times we got postcards to mail home. We were allowed a twenty-five-word message. Some of the letters I received had hardly anything marked out; others were heavily censored. Both Americans and Japanese censored the mail. One letter I received from a Navy friend, who had been so careful how he stated things, had one whole paragraph blacked out. I never figured out a way to learn what had been so offensive.

A few men were shot by the Japanese for going through the fences, but on the whole we kept our distance and they kept theirs. We kept busy working. People kept coming into the camp. First there were the 800 able-bodied men, and in a few months their wives and children were permitted to come. Filipino laborers built barracks. Later, 300 old men came. A barracks was set up as an infirmary for them, and nursing nuns cared for them.

Food supplies kept going down, and we tried to make it on what we had. We were finally issued unthreshed rice, but not many people knew how to thresh and then winnow it in the air as the Filipinos did. We had a Filipino nurse with us whose husband was a naval officer. She helped us so much because she could speak the local dialect and knew the customs and local plants.

There were radios in the camp, and we had news coming in. There were technicians in camp who could make almost anything you could want. One man built a radio receiver. He had enough parts for a transmitter, which he hid under the hospital. The Japanese went a bit easy on the hospital, so men used to hide things there. Behind the hospital was a canyon with a creek and just one line of barbed wire, so it was easy to drop things over and hide stuff under the leaves.

In early 1945 we heard rumors that the Americans were coming. A couple of men went out of the camp to meet with the guerrillas. One was George Grey, a State Department man who was redheaded and very light skinned; the other was Freddy Zervalskas. They sat behind the hospital, waiting for dark, ready to slip down what was getting to be a path going *out of* camp—I am surprised that the Japanese did not see it. Freddy told George to put on long sleeves and long pants: "You're too white—you'll shine in the night." George was quite impressed by his contact with the guerrillas in town, and he had good information that things were about to happen.

A few days later, a P-38 bombed an ammunition dump about 2 miles from camp. The planes were almost overhead and flying very low. We were not supposed to watch, but we could not help but watch our own planes!

The day we were rescued (February 23, 1945), there was a heavy rumbling before daylight. You could feel it and hear it. We got up and dressed as usual. We were to line up for roll call at 7 o'clock. We lined up in front of the hospital. As soon as it was over, Laura ordered us back inside.

I was working in the clinic, and because I feared we would get many casualties, I took all the instruments and started to boil them for sterilization. I will never know why I did not just leave them be as "clean" instruments. When we did need them, we had a mess of hot, wet instruments!

We could still hear that rumbling. Once when we looked out from the balcony, we saw a parachute coming out of a plane that was flying just a little distance from the camp. I thought they were dropping supplies and just missing the camp. Soon the object straightened, and you could tell it was a man. The guerrillas began shooting at the Japanese guardhouses. Soon we could hear the paratroopers coming up the road. Tanks were breaking the bamboo wall that surrounded the area. I thought if those were Japanese tanks, we would be right in the crossfire. The guerrillas had encircled the camp during the night, so we were really in a three-pronged attack with the paratroopers coming up the main road and the amphtracs (amphibious tracked vehicles) of the 672d Amphibious Tractor Battalion on the road through the camp. There was a lot of shooting for a while.

Later the soldiers told us they were scared when they came through the first gate and saw no one. They were afraid they were too late, but they kept on coming. We had been moved from the permanent building to the barracks.

Those GIs looked so big and nice and healthy when they came out of those tanks. One old lady went over and hugged and kissed every one she could get her hands on. Somebody said, "Hey, have those guys got beriberi too?" When you had beriberi, in the morning your face would be nice and full; by night, after standing during the day, your feet and legs would be puffy from the disease. Anyhow, it showed that our humor was still intact.

During the rescue attack, one girl was badly hurt. She had a bullet wound in the pelvis, but soon the Army medics had her bandaged and on an I.V. We dressed a paratrooper's shoulder and a few other cases in the clinic.

We crossed Laguna de Bay in the amphtracs and were trucked to the prison at Muntinlupa. Three days later we went to Manila. Our next stop was Leyte and then the big base at Samar. Then we island-hopped toward home.

Before we left Leyte, which was a staging area, we were issued some Army uniforms. Arriving nurses wore them from the States, and others wore them back. When we got to Guam, no one at first realized who we were; they thought we were another group of Army nurses on their way to the front.

We were interviewed and photographed. Somebody found out that there were two sailors from my home town in South Dakota on Guam. One was on duty someplace, and I could not get in touch with him, but I did talk to the other. He was a bit nervous from the attention and asked "What do I do?" I told him "Oh, just stand there." We had our pictures taken in front of the big relief map of Guam. Soon we nurses were on our way—Kwajalein, Johnston, and then Honolulu.

In Honolulu, we went to Aiea Hospital, which had a dormitory for transients. Nurses had donated all kinds of clothing—uniforms, shirts, shoes, underwear, etc. You just looked around until you found your size. It was good to look like a Navy nurse again.

The nurses had some of the usual camp ailments—dysentery, dengue fever, and malnutrition—but on the whole we did pretty well. We found that people who had kept busy were far better off than those who just sat and waited for MacArthur to return. Having watched people during the real hard times out there, I would say it did not seem to make much difference what your educational background was—it was something in the person, some internal strength. The saying "There are no atheists in foxholes" is probably true, and I know that a lot of the internees prayed.

I think our Navy discipline, nurses' training, and the fact that we worked helped us survive.

DOCUMENTING WOMEN'S SERVICE
Memoirs, Museums, Historical Collections

The women who played pioneering roles in the service branches during World War II wrote bold new chapters in both military and personal history. Their experiences recorded in artifacts and other documentary sources will survive beyond their lifetimes to hold an enduring place in history. The rest will fade regrettably from memory. The papers in this session and in the following session on records of the National Archives and Records Administration focused on published and unpublished sources documenting women's wartime service and steps that veterans, researchers, and overseers of collections could take to enhance the accuracy and completeness of the account.

In the first paper, Linda Grant De Pauw discussed the importance of personal memoirs in telling women's stories and the ways in which memoirs differ from other primary sources. Although many veterans have written and published their memoirs, two challenges remain—to locate and provide general access to materials already in existence and to encourage the production of additional service-women's narratives. De Pauw also identified helpful reference tools as well as practical approaches to writing, publishing, and marketing memoirs; utilizing technology; and selecting locations in which to deposit memoirs.

Eleanor Stoddard's paper was presented as an annotated guide to select archival holdings in U.S. repositories chronicling women's military service during the war. Listings were arranged geographically in order to facilitate planning of research trips. Collections contain mostly textual documents providing both organizational information (e.g., policies, reports, speeches, news releases) and experiences of officers and enlisted women often shared by others (e.g., personal papers, diaries, scrapbooks, letters). Oral history interviews were highlighted for their special value.

Clare M. Cronin featured museum collections, film and graphic archives, and educational resources as unique sources that should not be overlooked by veterans or researchers. She addressed issues central to both donating or loaning possessions and volunteering time to museums and archives; offered a starting point for locating film and photographic archives, museums, and educational resources relating to servicewomen; and described select collections especially useful for research.

The session was chaired by Linda Grant De Pauw, professor of history at The George Washington University in Washington, DC, and director of the only doctoral program in women's military studies. She is also founder and president of The MINERVA Center, Inc., which is sponsoring a bibliographic project to identify women's World War II memoirs not yet part of research collections.

PUBLISHING AND SELF-PUBLISHING MEMOIRS

Linda Grant De Pauw

Shut not your doors to me proud libraries,
For that which was lacking on all your well-fill'd shelves, yet
needed most, I bring,
Forth from the war emerging, a book I have made.

—*Walt Whitman*

Personal memoirs differ from other primary sources in that they bring the perspective of time to an eyewitness account. While letters or diary entries written at the time events occurred have unique value for historians, the vision of a participant looking back on events has a quality no historian can supply. "You had to be there to understand," as veterans often say. Published memoirs also differ from interviews or oral histories. Rather than telling a story spontaneously over the course of a few hours or days, with memories arising partly through the stimulus provided by a questioner, a personal memoir grows slowly as memories are mulled over and the narrative gradually reshaped. Older people taking on such projects often find that writing it all down gives them a fuller understanding of the meaning of their lives.

Many women veterans of World War II have already written and published their memoirs. There are far more of these memoirs than scholars realize. It is common to read in articles on World War II women that there are only a few. In fact, hundreds have been published, and there are probably many times that number of unpublished manuscripts in the hands of family members. For those of us working today to establish the field of women's military history as a permanent academic specialty, there are two challenges.[1] The first and most pressing is to encourage the production and publication of as many memoirs as possible. The second is to locate and make accessible the material that already exists.

Writing Memoirs

Several organizations encourage autobiographical writing by older Americans.[2] Recent technological advances have made writing much less physically demanding than it once was. Prospective writers who overcome their initial apprehension of the "newfangled" apparatus will find a way to continue creative work even despite failing vision or physical disabilities. Stroke victims who can no longer speak clearly and cannot use a pen have become eloquent again on computer bulletin boards.[3] Some children or grandchildren of veterans have collaborated with elderly relatives to produce memoirs. Sometimes older people are ready to share certain memories only when they feel they are facing death.[4]

Many women veterans are quite capable of writing a book on their own and need only a bit of encouragement. Reading others' autobiographies is a good place to start. Seeing how someone else has done it can lead to the insight, "I could do that!" Then there are a great many books directed at potential writers, including books directed specifically at writers interested in autobiographical work.[5] These works include practical advice on how to get started.

Some people write autobiographies at several points during their lives. So if you have done it once, you may still want to do it again. Memory may not be as strong, but wisdom and perspective may be stronger than they were a decade or two ago. Some subjects that used to be untouchable need no longer be deep dark secrets. Today writers freely discuss premarital sex, pregnancy, and lesbian relationships. Some World War II women veterans who were sexually assaulted 50 years ago and suffered in silence for decades are now coming in to Veterans Administration PTSD (Post Traumatic Stress Disorder) clinics to tell their stories and ask for help for the first time. Not everyone had a good war, and accurate history must include painful episodes as well as happy ones.

Publishing Memoirs

Writing an autobiography is a worthwhile activity even if the manuscript is not shared with anyone. But most people who have done the work necessary to write their histories realize that their lives have more than personal value and want to share their experiences. Those wishing to publish a book should know that rising costs for printing, storing, and shipping books and the electronic media revolution are causing rapid and continuous change in the publishing industry. Some books are published in electronic form by downloading from a computer or printing single copies on paper only as the publisher receives orders. Change in the publishing industry is so rapid that books of advice for writers are often outdated by the time they are in print.[6]

Recently, mergers of publishing houses have created half a dozen giant communications conglomerates, each of which releases books under numerous imprints. These conglomerates have taken over most medium-to-large publishers. On the other hand, university presses and small independent presses are growing in number and significance.[7] When they are well promoted, books from small presses are now marketed successfully through large bookstore chains as well as through the more commonly used (and more profitable) mail-order houses.[8]

The only publisher specializing in material relating to women and war is The MINERVA Center. Unfortunately the center is currently too small to publish very much. Since beginning book publication in 1992, the center has released three titles, one of which deals with World War II.[9] Women's World War II memoirs have also appeared in issues of *MINERVA: Quarterly Report on Women and the Military*. Several writers have found publication in *MINERVA* to be a help in causing larger presses to become interested in their work.[10]

New desktop publishing technology has also made self-publishing easier than ever before. The stigma once attached to self-publication has virtually disappeared. And for those who have the energy to do the work necessary to produce and promote bound volumes, self-publishing can be far more profitable than the standard contract offered by large presses.[11]

Preserving and Locating Memoirs

Although an author may be satisfied with having a manuscript to pass on to grandchildren or a few dozen bound books to share with family and friends, the only way to be sure that a book will be useful to historians is to deposit a copy in a research library.

As anyone who has ever searched in vain for an old favorite novel well knows, even bestsellers go out of print and may be impossible to find a few years after publication. Most people believe that the Library of Congress has a copy of every book that is copyrighted. At one time that was true, but so many books are now published every year that no library in the world could hold all of them. Formally registering a copyright for a book still requires completing a two-page form, paying a small fee, and sending two copies to the Library of Congress. But even the library can keep only a fraction of these books. Furthermore, under current law, legally establishing copyright no longer requires going through the formal procedure. Simply placing the copyright notice (©) on the book is sufficient notification of one's claim, but registration with the Library of Congress Copyright Office will expedite others' finding you or your heirs to discuss use of your material.[12]

Books donated to a public library or a small college library may or may not be kept on the shelves. Only research libraries can afford the shelf space for large permanent collections. Most library books will be discarded after a short period of time if no one borrows them. The capability to store books electronically in what is known as hypertext will change this situation in the future, but books that are discarded before the technology is at hand will not be there for processing when libraries are ready to scan them into machine-readable form.[13]

Currently, the largest collections of women's World War II memoirs appear to be in the hands of private individuals. Specialized research centers, such as the U.S. Naval Historical Center and the U.S. Army Center of Military History in Washington, DC, have collections confined to one branch of service. Many of the books were originally issued in small printings and have titles that do not immediately suggest their content, which makes it impractical to seek them out through secondhand book dealers until one has precise publication information.

The MINERVA Center has undertaken a bibliographic project to identify women's World War II memoirs not yet in research collections. I am a professor of history at The George Washington University as well as president of The MINERVA Center, and I offer the only doctoral program anywhere in women's military studies. I have been able to persuade the university library that collecting women's wartime memoirs is a worthy undertaking in support of our established academic program.[14] If you have shelves of books, you can help these efforts by sending a list of authors, titles, and publication data to The MINERVA Center.

NOTES

   1. The MINERVA Center, Inc., of which Dr. De Pauw is the founder and president, is a nonprofit educational foundation dedicated to providing "information

and inspiration" and to promoting women's military studies in the broadest sense. Dr. De Pauw cheerfully answers questions by telephone, letter, or e-mail and assists those who wish to network with others. She can be reached at The MINERVA Center, Inc., 20 Granada Road, Pasadena, MD 21122; telephone 410-437-5379; e-mail: minervacen@aol.com.

2. The person who has done the most work in studying techniques for teaching creative writing to older people is Julie Ward, 43/44 Gladstone Terrace, Sunni-side, Bishop Aukland, County Durham, DL134LS, England. In the United States, the National Council on the Aging, Inc., has sponsored a project funded by the National Endowment for the Humanities called "Remembering World War II." For information, contact Sylvia Riggs Liroff, Senior Program Manager, Older Adult Education, NCOA, 409 Third Street, SW, Washington, DC 20024; telephone 202-479-6990.

3. SeniorNet is a nonprofit organization for older adults interested in using computers. There is a yearly membership fee of $35, which includes unlimited access to the online facilities. The easiest way to join is by typing the keyword "SeniorNet" from the America Online connection. Those preferring to make their first contact in a more familiar way should write to SeniorNet, 399 Arguello Boulevard, San Francisco, CA 94118; telephone 415-750-5030. To join America Online, you need access to a computer with a modem. The price of this equipment is falling all the time. Both the Macintosh and IBM computers (also known as PCs) work equally well. SeniorNet gives advice to prospective computer purchasers and special rates on equipment. In addition to the computer (the "hardware"), you need "software." Free software for America Online will be sent to you if you call 1-800-827-6364. A free software disk is also packaged with Tom Lichty, *The Official America Online Tourguide* (Chapel Hill, NC, 1994), which is available in bookstores.

4. A software salesman told me about a program he used when his father suddenly began to reminisce about the Normandy invasion. The program enabled him to help his father put his random memories into order. It is an interactive CD-ROM computer program developed by Walter E. Wood entitled *How to Write Your Autobiography* that may appeal to some who feel overwhelmed by starting a major project. It requires a computer with a multimedia capability—the kind used to play computer games. It costs $39 and may be ordered from Ellis Enterprises (telephone 1-800-729-9500). In addition to basic tools, be these yellow pads and pencils or ultramodern computers, writers need self-confidence and psychological support. The lack of these is what causes "writer's block." SeniorNet has a special network for writers who wish to share information, experiences, and support in what is always a lonely activity.

5. Books illustrating a variety of approaches to the task are Lois Daniel, *How to Write Your Own Life Story: A Step by Step Guide for the Nonprofessional Writer*, 3d ed. (Chicago, 1991); B. J. Hatley, *Telling Your Story, Exploring Your Faith: Writing Your Life Story for Personal Insight and Spiritual Growth* (St. Louis, MO, 1985); Mary Jane Moffat, *The Times of Our Lives: A Guide to Writing Autobiography and Memoir* (Santa Barbara, CA, 1989): Kirk Polking, *Writing Family Histories and Memoirs* (Cincinnati, OH, 1995); Donna Sinclair, *Worth Remembering* (Winfield, British Columbia, 1984); Dan Wakefield, *The Story of Your Life: Writing a Spiritual Autobiography* (Boston, 1990).

A book written especially for women is Janet Lynn Roseman's *The Way of the Woman Writer* (Binghamton, NY, 1995). Every writer benefits from having a knowledgeable and supportive editor. For the past 15 years, however, the editorial profession has been in decline. A writer who wants a good editorial job may have to hire her own editor and proofreader or trade editorial work with another writer. A recent book is illuminating: Leslie T. Sharpe and Irene Gunther, *Editing Fact and Fiction: A Concise Guide to Book Editing* (New York, 1994).

6. Three books describing the publishing world as it was in the recent past, including discussion of copyright law, agents and production schedules, are Nancy Evans and Judith Appelbaum, *How to Get Happily Published: A Complete and Candid Guide* (New York, 1978); Richard Balkin, *A Writer's Guide to Book Publishing* (New York, 1977); and John P. Dessauer, *Book Publishing: A Basic Introduction* (New York, 1989).

7. For information on publishers in search of manuscripts, consult the *1995 Writer's Market: Where and How to Sell What You Write* (Cincinnati, OH, 1995).

8. Whether self-published, published by a small press, or published with a well-established university press or trade publisher, every author must help promote her own book. Useful to every author is John Kremer, *1001 Ways To Market Your Book* (Fairfield, IA, 1989).

9. C. Kay Larson, *'Til I Come Marching Home: A Brief History of American Women in World War II* (Pasadena, MD, 1995).

10. One of these writers, Josette Dermody Wingo, recently published *Mother Was A Gunner's Mate: World War II in the Waves* (Annapolis, MD, 1994) through the Naval Institute Press. She has volunteered "to serve as Exhibit A" for MINERVA. Contact her at 833 19th Street #A, Santa Monica, CA 90403; telephone 310-453-2104.

11. Useful books on the subject of finding a publisher include Dan Poynter, *The Self-Publishing Manual: How to Write, Print & Sell Your Own Book,* rev. ed. (Santa Barbara, CA, 1986), and Tom Ross and Marilyn Ross, *The Complete Guide to Self-Publishing,* rev. ed. (Cincinnati, OH, 1989). Once a writer has a completed manuscript, a few hundred copies of a book, nicely bound with a dust jacket, can be produced quickly by sending it to a printer. Since 1988 The MINERVA Center has worked with a printing company notable for high-quality and user-friendliness that specializes in short runs of books. Mention *MINERVA* when you contact the Center's customer representative: Linda Skrzypek at Thomson-Shore, Inc., 7300 West Joy Road, Dexter, MI, 48130-9701. Her direct telephone line is 313-426-6205; her e-mail address is lindas@t-shore.com.

12. The form used to register book copyrights is Form TX. To obtain a copy together with instructions for filling it out and filing it, call the Library of Congress Copyright Office Hotline at 202-707-9100.

13. Research libraries increasingly rely on holdings in other institutions to supplement their own collections through interlibrary loans. To search computerized library catalogs for women's memoirs in research libraries worldwide, the most efficient method at present is to use the keywords "Women and Personal Reminiscences and World War." This method will lead you to works by

women of all nations and from both world wars, so you will have to cut out
the unwanted material. Systems currently in use will not accept more than
three keywords in a search.

14. For information about the project to establish a collection of Women's World
War II Memoirs at The George Washington University contact: Dan Barthell,
Reference Librarian, Gelman Library, The George Washington University,
Washington, DC 20052; telephone: 202-994-6049; e-mail: barthell@g-
wuvm.gwu.edu.

A Traveler's Guide to Chronicles of Military Women in World War II

Eleanor Stoddard

Where can one find the chronicles of military women that have been taken from closet shelves and attics and women's memories and placed in boxes in public archives? What route or process would these records have followed to arrive there? I imagined that my search for answers would be much like that of a botanist who, upon looking for a rare species in an ecosystem, might find it growing either in clusters here and there or scattered alone in isolated corners. That turned out to be the right picture.

Forty-seven collections of material relating to American women's participation in the military during World War II were identified for this paper (National Archives materials are discussed separately in the next section of this volume). They are located in established archives and manuscript repositories in 19 states throughout the country as well as in the District of Columbia. Their range could certainly be extended if additional inquiries for materials were to be made of all state historical societies and the dozens of universities and colleges whose facilities were commandeered during the war for military training purposes. But as it stands, the following inventory of sources can offer researchers both a useful place to start and an indication of discoveries yet to be made.

Research Trail

I first became aware of materials available in the Washington, DC, area during the 1980s after conducting a series of oral history interviews with World War II military women. In order to develop background for their stories, I called on archivists in several military repositories, where I received an overview of their resources. I made visits to the U.S. Army Center of Military History, the Naval

Historical Center, the Marine Corps Historical Center, and the Office of the Coast Guard Historian—all in Washington, DC—and the Army Military History Institute in Carlisle, PA.

To prepare this paper, it was necessary for me to revisit these centers for a more complete understanding of their reference systems and an inspection of their collections. Archives that had contained quite limited holdings of papers and oral histories of individual military women several years before were now making efforts to add such histories to their materials. I also paid first-time visits to two repositories. These were the Navy Bureau of Medicine and Surgery, which documents Navy nurses, and the Center for Air Force History at Bolling Air Force Base, which contains microfilmed papers and records relating to Air-Wacs and Women Airforce Service Pilots.

To go further afield, I consulted the *Directory of Archives and Manuscript Repositories in the United States,* compiled by the National Historical Publications and Records Commission (Phoenix, AZ, 2d ed., 1988), and spent a number of hours browsing through the Library of Congress *National Union Catalog of Manuscript Collections* (Washington, DC, 1959-) under headings related to war, women, and the different armed services. I turned up references to the papers of a few military women. These papers were in various archives in Massachusetts, Virginia, Wisconsin, Missouri, and Michigan. Even though outdated, *Women's History Sources: A Guide to Archives and Manuscript Collections in the United States,* edited by Andrea Hinding and Sheldon Bower (New York, 1979), provided a few more leads—enough to start a research trail.

One of my first queries was to the George C. Marshall Research Foundation in Lexington, VA, where I found the papers of a Women's Army Corps (WAC) officer I had interviewed, along with other relevant collections. Another query, to the Mugar Memorial Library of Boston University and its Nursing Archives, unearthed the papers of Florence Blanchfield, Chief of the Army Nurse Corps in World War II, a name mentioned in another of my interviews. Right away, connections were building.

The search then led to other archival centers in Massachusetts, including Smith College in Northampton and the Schlesinger Library at Radcliffe College in Cambridge. My network of sources gradually extended across the country as I made contact with the rest of my original leads as well as with several others that came in over the transom to The MINERVA Center. It was evident that interest in

Lt. Comdr. Mildred McAfee, USNR, Director of the Women's Reserve; Rear Adm. Randall Jacobs, USN, Chief of Naval Personnel; and Mayor Fiorello La Guardia attend commissioning ceremonies at Hunter College, The Bronx, NY, a training school for the WAVES and the SPAR (Coast Guard), February 8, 1943.

National Archives, General Records of the Department of the Navy, 1798-1947 (80-G-23754)

preserving the stories of World War II military women had increased over the last few years.

The Inventory

The outcome of my search is not a comprehensive catalog but an inventory that highlights a variety of institutions and collections that can serve as a starting point or inspiration for a more complete directory. The resource centers are grouped by geographic region (north to south and east to west) and within region, by state (north to south and east to west), except for the District of Columbia. This arrangement was devised, in part, to aid the researcher in making travel plans for research trips.

Collections generally comprise two kinds of information. One consists of organizational background material in the form of military regulations, policy decisions, course outlines, speeches, station records, reports, and news releases and clippings. The other gives evidence of the personal experiences of servicewomen as reflected in diaries, letters, manuscripts, scrapbooks, and oral histories.

The descriptions of papers and oral histories listed in this inventory are based on those provided by the archivists in charge of individual collections. Their descriptions have been edited for brevity, but no reported collection bearing on the participation of women in the World War II military has been omitted.

The Collections

Each archive has its own distinctive character. It may be a military repository; part of a university library; part of a public library; a quasi-governmental establishment, like one of the Presidential libraries; or an adjunct to a museum. It may offer a highly concentrated collection like that of the Women Airforce Service Pilots (WASP) at Texas Woman's University at Denton, TX, or it may offer a smattering of women veterans' papers like those within the large library system of the University of Washington in Seattle. The archives range from Carlisle Barracks, with its vast collection of personal military papers extending back to colonial times, to The University of Iowa Libraries, which have started a collection on Iowa women. Most archives require a personal visit to examine their collections. The reference archivist is the tour guide and, in most cases, prefers that researchers make appointments for their visits so that searching can begin before their arrival.

Most collections cited in this paper contain the memorabilia of only a few women veterans. In some cases only one woman has donated her papers to an archive. This dearth of papers suggests that most people are either unaware of archives and their value or consider their own records of insufficient historical interest to donate to archives. Now is the time for archivists to seek the documents of this unique military group before its surviving members, or their heirs, throw away their testimony.

Not surprisingly, one will probably not find important collections of papers and oral history transcripts in museums, whose chief interest is in artifacts; similarly, artifacts are fairly scarce in archives, whose chief interest is in paper collections. Even so, the reading material in museums should not be overlooked.

Some of the collections in this paper are especially valuable for background, notably those in military repositories and, to some

extent, the Roosevelt, Truman, and Eisenhower Presidential libraries. The military records can include station reports, rosters of
names, unit histories, training manuals, regulations, biographies,
and much more. Documents in the Presidential libraries can shed
light on the way government leaders viewed and acted on military
women's issues. These multiple records can help to place the findings of one's own research in a broader context and provide reference points for a truer perspective.

Other collections cited herein, like those in the Schlesinger
Library or at The State Historical Society of Wisconsin, focus on
the stories of individuals. These collections can consist of letters
by women in the services to friends and relatives, diaries, journals,
discharge papers, scrapbooks, photographs, and oral histories.

Oral Histories

Except for letters or journals written at the time events occurred,
oral history interviews provide the best way to capture personal
experience. An oral history, like a personal letter, deals with impact.
If you learn from an official document that the 149th WAAC Post
Headquarters Company was ordered to North Africa in January
1943, a personal account can tell you how it felt to be seasick on
the trip across the Atlantic in winter. Or if you read that a contingent
of Waves was stationed at Corpus Christi Naval Air Station in Texas
that spring, only a personal memoir will tell you how the tar stuck
to and burned the feet of the specialist (T)(LT) as she stood in the
heat for 1½ hours on a brand-new asphalt road while awaiting
orders to march.

The archival collections detailed in this paper contain approximately 350 oral history interviews of World War II military women
in the form of transcripts, plus a few on tape not yet transcribed.
Outside of archival collections, more than 1,000 interviews have
been reported as captured on tape but not yet transcribed.

Tape recordings are the primary source for oral histories and
are of great value in providing close contact with the narrator. You
can hear voice inflections, hesitations, tonal quality, and emotion
that a transcript cannot convey. Because tapes have a limited life—
perhaps 5 or 6 years before they lose their audibility—it is essential
to the preservation of the historical record that all significant tapes
be transcribed.

A transcript, in most cases, has been carefully reviewed for
fidelity to the speaker's words, which are not always easy to pick

T/4 Jerryellen Phillips, 2664th WAC Postal Company, is one of many Wacs who sorted, readdressed, and forwarded millions of wartime letters and packages, Caserta, Italy, n.d.

National Archives, Records of the Office of the Chief Signal Officer (111-SC-199908)

up when first listening to a tape. A transcript also offers readers an opportunity to compare statements made at different stages of an interview simply by turning pages back and forth. If you wish to study a group of interviews of any size, you will be able to absorb information far more rapidly from a transcript than from a tape— approximately 20 minutes of reading time versus 1½ hours of listening.

The best oral history interviews are conducted under relaxed conditions with enough time allowed to permit the narrator to associate one memory with another until a full account of past events has been obtained. When a servicewoman recalls events at a later period in her life, she has the advantage of speaking from a lifetime perspective as well as the opportunity to reflect on influences that her wartime military experience may have had on the way she changed and developed.

Carefully conducted interviews can reveal the texture of a person's experience. They can show the impetus behind a woman's decision to volunteer for military service, the pressures of adapting to discipline, the shocks, the self-mastery, the discovery of different aspects of human nature, the attainment of skills, and the aftermath of changed attitudes and growth. They can offer a basis for comparison between the experiences of enlisted personnel and officers, blacks and whites, and men and women and between one service and another.

The universe of potential World War II narrators is shrinking rapidly. For this reason researchers would do well to train themselves in oral history techniques and protocols so as to be able to record candid information of lasting value. Interviews need to be conducted in such a way that rapport between the parties is developed, questions elicit as complete a record as possible, the narrator's rights are protected by releases, and copyrights are established. Tapes and transcripts should be placed in archival collections where they can be used by future historians and authors.

The best procedure for preparing to conduct interviews is to enroll in an oral history training class. Two well-known courses are offered by Columbia University and Vermont College each summer. The Columbia University Oral History Research Office holds a 2-week Summer Institute for Advanced Training in Oral History. For information, contact the Oral History Research Office, Box 20, Butler Library, Columbia University, New York, NY 10027. Week-long oral history workshops at Vermont College in Montpelier are

Capt. Frederick L. Rauch accompanies Brig. V. Galway and Maj. L. R. Roberts of the British Signal Office to observe WAAC telephone operators Pfc. Harriette Ryan and T/5 Pearl Freund at the American switchboard tent during the Cairo Conference. Photograph released April 21, 1944.

National Archives, Records of the Office of the Chief Signal Officer (111-SC-183033)

taught by Charles Morrissey twice each summer. For information on course content, call Mr. Morrissey at 713-798-4501. For information on fees, lodging, and meals, contact the Office of Continuing Education at the college. Inquiries to history departments at other colleges or universities may also uncover oral history course offerings.

The Oral History Association is also an important contact. It conducts an annual conference and publishes *Evaluation Guidelines, Oral History and the Law,* and other pamphlets. Write to the Oral History Association, P.O. Box 97234, Baylor University, Waco, TX 76798-7234, for more information. Donald A. Ritchie's book *Doing Oral History* (New York, 1995) is highly recommended. Ritchie, a specialist in the field, discusses all aspects of oral history. His book includes an extensive bibliography and index.

Projects in Process

In the course of this investigation, I learned of a number of projects still in process: oral histories not yet transcribed or donated to an institution, questionnaires still being amassed and not yet compiled, papers being solicited but not yet deeded to repositories, and projects not yet recorded in official catalogs. Papers and oral histories are of no use until they are in a safe place of public access with proper releases signed and delivered. The one exception would be materials belonging to authors for use in their own writing. Authors would serve history further, however, if they were to donate their materials to an archive after publication of their manuscripts.

Acknowledgments

My heartfelt thanks to the willing and helpful archivists and librarians who provided the information for the compiled inventory that follows. Their large number makes it impossible to list them each by name, but they all made enthusiastic efforts to fulfill my requests and educate me on the creative uses of the resources that lay in their domains.

Wave Mary Anne Gasser assembles a generator that has been cleaned and overhauled, Jacksonville, FL, September 1943.

National Archives, General Records of the Department of the Navy, 1798-1947 (80-G-471714)

CONTENTS

The listings of institutions and collections are arranged by geographic region (north to south and east to west) and within region, by state (north to south and east to west), except for the District of Columbia. National Archives facilities are marked by an asterisk and listed in the appropriate geographic region for reference, but descriptions of their holdings relating to military women are in the next section of the volume. Historical materials maintained by individuals are cited in the notes.

1.   New England

    Boston, MA
    1.1   Boston University, Mugar Memorial Library, Nursing Archives

Cambridge, MA
1.2   Radcliffe College, The Arthur and Elizabeth Schlesinger
       Library on the History of Women in America

Northampton, MA
1.3   Smith College, Sophia Smith Collection
1.4   Smith College, College Archives
1.5   Forbes Library

South Hadley, MA
1.6   Mount Holyoke College, College Archives

Smithfield, RI
1.7   Bryant College, World War II Letters of
       United States Women Archive

Newport, RI
1.8   Naval War College

2.   Middle Atlantic

Hyde Park, NY
2.1   Franklin D. Roosevelt Library*

New York, NY
2.2   Columbia University, Oral History Research Office
2.3   Hunter College, Wexler Library
2.4   Lehman College Library

Carlisle, PA
2.5   U.S. Army Military History Institute

Latrobe, PA
2.6   St. Vincent College, Center for Northern
       Appalachian Studies

3.   District of Columbia

3.1   Bethune Museum and Archives, Inc.
3.2   Center for Air Force History
3.3   Library of Congress, Manuscript Division
3.4   National Archives and Records Administration*
3.5   Office of the Coast Guard Historian
3.6   Smithsonian Institution, National Museum of American
       History
3.7   Smithsonian Institution, National Air and Space
       Museum
3.8   U.S. Army Center of Military History

3.9 U.S. Naval Historical Center
3.10 U.S. Navy, Bureau of Medicine and Surgery
3.11 U.S. Marine Corps Historical Center

4. Southeast

Arlington, VA
4.1 Women In Military Service For America Memorial Foundation, Inc. (WIMSA)

Lexington, VA
4.2 George C. Marshall Foundation

Atlanta, GA
4.3 National Association of Women Veterans, Inc.

Anniston, AL
4.4 The Women's Army Corps Museum

Maxwell Air Force Base, AL
4.5 Air Force Historical Research Agency

5. Middle West

Detroit, MI
5.1 Detroit Public Library, Burton Historical Collection

Bowling Green, OH
5.2 Bowling Green State University, Center for Archival Collections

Madison, WI
5.3 The State Historical Society of Wisconsin

Urbana, IL
5.4 University of Illinois at Urbana-Champaign, University Archives

Waterloo, IA
5.5 Grout Museum of History

Iowa City, IA
5.6 The University of Iowa Libraries, Iowa Women's Archives

Columbia, MO
5.7 University of Missouri-Columbia, Western Historical Manuscript Collection

Independence, MO
5.8 Harry S. Truman Library*

Bismarck, ND
5.9   State Historical Society of North Dakota

Abilene, KS
5.10   Dwight D. Eisenhower Library*

Oklahoma City, OK
5.11   The Ninety-Nines, Inc.

6. Southwest

Denton, TX
6.1   Texas Woman's University, Blagg-Huey Library

Nacogdoches, TX
6.2   Stephen F. Austin State University, East Texas
        Research Center

7. West Coast

Seattle, WA
7.1   University of Washington Libraries, Manuscripts and
        University Archives Division

Berkeley, CA
7.2   Judah Magnes Museum

Stanford, CA
7.3   Hoover Institution on War, Revolution, and Peace,
        ATA Archive

Long Beach, CA
7.4   California State University, Long Beach,
        Library Archives

INVENTORY

1. New England[1]

1.1 Boston University
Mugar Memorial Library
Nursing Archives
771 Commonwealth Avenue
Boston, MA 02215

The Nursing Archives was started in the mid-1960s under a federal grant and has now grown to include 44 institutional collections and at least 135 collections of papers of individuals. The archives staff answer countless inquiries by researchers on every aspect of nursing history. Institutional collections include those of the American Nurses Association, the *Journal of Nursing History,* the U.S. Public Health Service Division of Nursing, and many hospitals and associations. The individual collections include 150–175 letters of Florence Nightingale and papers of many other nurses, including the following that are relevant to military nursing in World War II.

Personal Papers

Blanchfield, Florence A., 1884–1972
Papers, 1916–67. 3 boxes.

This collection covers Blanchfield's career in the Army Nurse Corps, including World War I and the World War II period when Colonel Blanchfield was head of the corps. It includes manuscript materials, correspondence, official papers, photographs, and general historical material about the Army Nurse Corps; it also documents the period 1915–51 and includes a transcript of an oral history interview conducted by Mary Ann Garrigan, first curator of the Nursing Archives.

Cavanagh, Mary Frazer
Correspondence, 1942–45.

Mary Frazer entered the Army Nurse Corps in 1942 and was sent overseas with the Sixth General Hospital, Massachusetts General Hospital Unit, in February 1944. The collection consists of 47 letters to family members between May 1942 and October 1945 from Camp Blanding, FL; Camp Kilmer, NJ; Casablanca, Morocco; and various locations in Italy. Frazer's letters provide details of Spartan living and contrast Army wards with civilian nursing in Boston.

Clarke, Alice R.
Papers, ca. 1935–50s. 22 boxes.

Alice Clarke was the editor of *Nursing Forum.* Her collection includes extensive reports and records, including material on mobilization of nurses in World War II. Materials pertaining to nurses in the U.S. Army and Navy Nurse Corps serving in the Southwest Pacific Area in World War II include a diary kept by Clarke while en route to Australia and photographs of nurses in Japanese prisoner-of-war camps and Army field hospitals.

Leone, Lucile Petry, 1902–
Papers, 1940–60s. 19 boxes.

Leone was a leading nursing educator and author. She directed the U.S. Cadet Nurse Corps in World War II; she was the first nurse assistant surgeon general, 1949-66, and the recipient of many awards. Her papers include correspondence with leading military and political figures; research, articles, and speeches covering the World War II period; and many photographs of the U.S. Cadet Nurse Corps. Also included is a transcript of an oral history interview conducted by Teresa E. Christy in August 1969.

Phillips, Elisabeth Cogswell
Papers, ca. 1920s-65. 2 boxes.

These papers and writings include 50 letters to family and friends written by this public health nurse while she was stationed at the American Red Cross Hospital at Salisbury, Wilts, England, in 1941 and 1942.

Slanger, Frances Y., 1914-44
Papers, 1932-48. 5 boxes.

Frances Slanger was a member of the U.S. Army Nurse Corps. She was the first Army nurse killed in Europe in World War II. The collection includes poems, letters, news clippings, photographs, telegrams, and a copy of an article that Slanger wrote for *Stars and Stripes* on the night she was wounded by the shelling of her hospital tent in Belgium. She died 17 days later on October 21, 1944. The article, later published as an editorial, tells of her admiration for the bravery of the wounded American soldiers.

Oral History Interviews

Tully, Margaret; Hale, Doris; McGuigan, Pauline; Scanzani, Priscilla; and others

This item is a videotape of interviews conducted by Maureen Tully Lopez with six Army nurses. They were all members of the 10th Evacuation Unit, which was sent to Australia in April 1942, then assigned to a field hospital in Port Moresby, New Guinea, to treat the wounded from the Buna-Gona campaign.

1.2 Radcliffe College
The Arthur and Elizabeth Schlesinger Library on the
History of Women in America
10 Garden Street
Cambridge, MA 02138

The Schlesinger Library is well known for its extensive collections of papers, oral histories, and other memorabilia of notable American women. The following collections relate to military women in World War II.

Personal Papers

Barton, Jane
Papers, 1938-84. 2.75 linear feet.

Jane Barton trained at Mount Holyoke College WAVES school and was in the first class to receive boot training. She was stationed in Washington, DC, and served in public relations for the Potomac Naval Command. She was editor of *Scuttlebutt,* later renamed *Havelock.* The collection includes scrapbooks, correspondence, press books, clippings, and photographs.

Boehner, Ruth P.
Papers, 1943-58. 1 folder.

Boehner, a teacher, enlisted in the WAC in 1943. A typed letter describes her first months in service; the collection also includes information on her subsequent career.

Clark, Bertha Marie Strittmatter
Typescript, "When WAC Was a Dirty Word," 156 pp.

Corporal Strittmatter enlisted in the WAAC and stayed on in the WAC. She was stationed at Stout Field, Indianapolis, IN, and was a columnist for *Wactivities* and *The Fielder.*

Groover, Mary-Agnes Brown, 1902–
Papers, 1940-85. 1 linear foot.

A lawyer in the Veterans Administration, Mary-Agnes Brown left her job and joined the WAAC. She was on active duty for 4 years and was promoted to lieutenant colonel. She served as executive director to Col. Oveta Culp Hobby and as acting director in her absence. She retired in 1959. The collection includes biographical and family information, correspondence, service records, and speeches.

Lord, Mary Pillsbury, 1904-78
Papers, 1927-72. 1.75 linear feet.

Active in civic affairs, Lord was U.S. Representative to the U.N. General Assembly and U.S. Representative to the Commission on Human Rights, among other influential appointments. She was chair of the National Civilian Advisory Committee of the Women's Army Corps and cochair of Citizens for Eisenhower-Nixon, 1952.

Correspondence, speeches, articles, reports, and photos, including material on her work with the WAC, reflect Lord's career.

Peirce, Ruth Thompsom
Papers, 1902-65. 2 linear feet.

Peirce joined the WAAC in November 1942 and was one of the first women intercept operators for the Boston Intercept Command. She was later stationed at Bangor, ME, as a flight dispatcher. She also worked for a fellow Wac, Catherine Falvey, who was a prosecuting attorney at the Nuremberg trials. The collection includes correspondence, scrapbooks, awards, and clippings.

Peplau, Hildegarde E.
Papers, 1923-84. 49.5 linear feet.

Peplau was a psychiatric nurse, educator, and author who served in the U.S. Army Nurse Corps, 1943-45. In her subsequent career, she was influential in advocating professionalism for nurses and furthering mental health causes. Personal papers are closed to researchers except by written permission of donor or family.

Reynard, Elizabeth, 1898-1962
Papers, 1934-62. 6 linear feet.

Reynard was Assistant Director of the WAVES during World War II. Her papers contain correspondence, articles, reports, newsletters, manuals, and other material. The collection includes materials relating to her assignment to WAVES officer training school and the U.S.S. *Hunter,* and information about WAVES personnel and organization regulations.

Rogers, Edith Nourse, 1881-1960
Papers, 1854-1961. 11 linear feet.

A nurse and Republican Congresswoman from the Fifth District of Massachusetts, Rogers was elected in 1925 and reelected to every successive Congress until she died while in office. She had served as chair of the Veterans Affairs Committee and was a member of the Foreign Affairs Committee. She was the sponsor of the WAAC bill (H.R. 4906) in May 1941 and worked to push subsequent legislation for the WAVES and, later, the postwar Integration Act through Congress.

Streeter, Ruth Cheney, 1895-1990
"History of the Marine Corps Women's Reserve: A Critical Analysis of Its Development and Operation, 1943-1945," 447 pp.

Originally an internal document, this history was written by Streeter, the first Director of the Marine Corps Women's Reserve, and Col. Katherine A. Towle, Assistant Director.

Warren, Dorothy, 1905–
Papers, 1905–83. 0.25 linear feet.

Warren served as Director of Training and records officer for the WAC, 1942–46. She had a later career in vocational training, real estate, and church work. Her collection contains photographs, clippings, manuals, and official documents related to her WAC service.

Records

U.S. Naval Reserve, Women's Reserve
Records, 1954–57. 1 folder.

The collection includes biographies of Capt. Winifred Redden Quick and Capt. Louise K. Wilde, both of whom served in the WAVES; a history of the WAVES; and papers from a conference of women district and air command assistants.

The following collections that are concerned with the postwar period could be of interest to World War II researchers.

Personal Papers—Post-World War II

Riley, Emma Jane, 1912–
Papers, 1957. 1 folder.

Col. Emma Jane Riley was the Staff Director of the Women's Air Corps Air Transport Command, 1946–48; Chief of the Basic Military Training and Officer Candidate School Branch of the U.S. Air Force, 1948–52; Staff Director of the Women in the Air Force (WAF) and Chief of the Career Actions Branch, Military Air Transport Service, 1952–57; and Director of the WAF, 1957. A biographical sketch and photograph are included.

Records—Post-World War II

U.S. Defense Advisory Committee on Women in the Services (DACOWITS)
Records, 1951–59. 1.75 linear feet.

DACOWITS was organized in 1951 to assist the Department of Defense on matters relating to women in the armed services. This collection contains minutes, reports, directives, recommendations, speeches, publications, biographies of commanders, and information on the various services.

Oral History Interviews

Hopper, Grace Brewster Murray, 1906–92
Three interviews for *60 Minutes* television news program, 1983.

Admiral Hopper, who started as a member of the WAVES and went on to a career in the Navy, was the inventor of COBOL, a computer language. She helped program the first large-scale digital computer, Mark I, and also worked with Mark II and Mark III computers.

Streeter, Ruth Cheney, 1895–1990

This interview with Streeter, the first Director of the Marine Corps Women's Reserve, was sponsored by the U.S. Naval Institute.

Towle, Katherine Amelia, 1898–1986

Towle was a university dean and colonel in the Marine Corps Women's Reserve in World War II and later Director of Women Marines. This oral history interview was sponsored by the Regional Oral History Office of the Bancroft Library, University of California, Berkeley, as part of the University History Series.

Women in the American Military Oral History Project
Interviews, 1984–85. 3.5 linear feet.

Dorothy Schneider and Carl J. Schneider interviewed more than 300 women in the mid-1980s from all 5 branches of the military to discover how women functioned in a traditionally male world and how their presence there was changing it. See Dorothy Schneider and Carl J. Schneider, *Sound Off!* (New York, 1988), which is based on these interviews.

1.3 Smith College
Sophia Smith Collection
Northampton, MA 01063

The Sophia Smith Collection at Smith College includes the following papers.

Bragdon, Helen Cushman
Papers, 1943–45. 1 box.
Manuscript group no. 218.

Bragdon joined the WAAC in summer 1942. She trained at Daytona Beach, FL; was assigned to Fort Bliss, TX, where she did newspaper and radio work; and was in the first contingent of Wacs to be sent to the Southwest Pacific Area (SWPA) in spring 1944. Letters to her family in Larchmont, NY, provide a detailed account of the day-to-day routine of a WAC detachment, including overseas tours of duty in Australia, New Guinea (Netherlands East Indies), and the Philippines.

Hermance, Lorena Estelle, 1898–
Papers, 1942–85. 2 boxes.
Manuscript group no. 190.

This material primarily represents Hermance's service in the Signal Corps and overseas in Europe with the WAC during World War II. The collection includes Army memorabilia, 25 photographs, articles about women in the military, and Hermance's letters to her sister, Julia Winslow, 1942–45. Of special interest is Hermance's journal, "As You Were" (1942–45), plus short diary and biographical writings. Hermance was the first grandmother in American history to be formally inducted into the U.S. Armed Forces. The first box also contains a typescript, "Far From Eden," written by Hermance's friend Camilla May Franks about her own war experience.

Rich, Frances, 1910–
Papers. 4 boxes.

Rich is a noted sculptor, and most of the material in the collection relates to her career. During 1941–45, however, she was an officer in the WAVES, and four folders in box 2 relate to that period. They contain photographs and correspondence relating to an oral history of Admiral Nimitz and the WAVES, 1969–70.

Van Voris, Jacqueline
Unpublished typed manuscript.
Catalog card: U.S. History—World War, 1939–45, WAVES

This 157-page unpublished manuscript, "Quiet Victory: the WAVES in World War II," 1969, includes notes and correspondence with people involved in the WAVES.

1.4 Smith College
College Archives
Northampton, MA 01063

Smith College Alumnae Association and Smith College records relating to the WAVES presence on campus, including contracts, timelines, correspondence, clippings, and extensive photographs, are housed here. The following items provide useful background on the Naval Reserve Midshipmen's School at Smith College during World War II.

Box 1—Waves, A–R: Alumnae House Diary, 1942-45; transcripts of broadcasts, August 15, September 3 and 21, 1942, and January 6, 1944; commencements with lists of graduating companies; history of the founding of the midshipmen's school; naval records; information on male officers; photographs; record of Mrs. Roosevelt's March 24, 1943, visit; and other related material.

Box 2—Waves, S–Z: Smith College letter to students; contract with the Navy for use of the Alumnae House as WAVES headquarters; film, *Waves at Smith College,* 1943; instructions governing the school; Smith participants; and Florence Snow, 1944-45, director of the Smith College Alumnae Association, who negotiated the contract with the Navy.

Box 3—Publications: *Guide Right: A Handbook for Waves and Spars* by Mary Virginia Harris; *How To Serve Your Country in the Waves or Spars* by Ens. Jane Leeds and Ens. Ruth Simon; "History of the Naval Reserve Midshipmen's School (WR)" (unpublished); *Marching to Victory* songbook; newsletters, 1945 to 1946; issues of the newspaper *Sounding Off,* March 24, 1943-October 31, 1944; *Angel of the Navy: The Story of a WAVE* by Joan Angel; and *USNR Naval Customs: Traditions and Usage* by Leland P. Lovette.

Box 4—Clippings: News clippings, June 1942-April 30, 1943.

Box 5—Clippings: News clippings, May 1, 1943-1946.

Records of the Alumnae Association of Smith College: One records center box of unprocessed miscellaneous WAVES material, for example, information on Mount Holyoke naval school; WAVES publicity in the *Smith Alumnae Quarterly;* Navy Day 1942; procurement; publicity; individuals (Mildred McAfee, Lt. Elizabeth Reynard, Louise Wilde, Capt. Herbert W. Underwood, and others); teas for Smith Waves and others; financial reports, August 1942-December 1944; the Alumnae House agreement; details on charges, wages, and employees; records of meetings; photographs; and copies of booklets (*The Story of You in Navy Blue* and *Be a Marine . . . Free a Marine to Fight* and *How To Serve Your Country in the Waves or Spars*).

1.5 Forbes Library
Northampton, MA 01060

The World War II scrapbook collection in the Reference Room, prepared by Forbes Library staff, contains all newspaper clippings from the *Daily Hampshire Gazette,* the *Springfield Republican,* and the *Springfield Union* relevant to World War II. The scrapbooks contain much material about the WAVES officer training center at Smith College; these are general articles but include many references to individuals. The clippings also cover local Northampton men and women engaged in the war effort. Both the clippings and pictures are very complete. An article based on the scrapbooks, "The U.S. Naval Reserve Midshipmen School, Northampton, 1942 to 1945: A Personal Account," by Margaret Dwyer, was published in *Historical Journal of Massachusetts* 22 (Winter 1994).

Similar scrapbooks cover World War I.

1.6 Mount Holyoke College
College Archives
50 College Street
South Hadley, MA 01075-6425

Mount Holyoke College War Collection, 1908–
5 linear feet. 12 boxes.

This collection includes "job reports," in which alumnae describe their work experience, including military service, during World War II, as well as correspondence, articles, and photographs relating to training programs for Waves and marines at the college, 1943–44. Of particular interest are issues of *Sounding Off,* a newspaper published by the women in the Naval Reserve Midshipmen's School (WR) at Mount Holyoke College and Smith College from January 1943 to December 1944. The "job reports" are supplemented by questionnaires completed by alumnae who were asked to reflect on their experiences during the war, collected by Lori Laudien, class of 1989, as part of research for her senior honors thesis. 2 linear feet.

Personal Papers

American Red Cross (ARC)
Papers.

This collection includes diaries, letters, and other papers of alumnae who served with the ARC, usually overseas, during the war.

Harlan, Olivia, class of 1922
Typescript, 6 pp.

"A WAC Looks Back," 1944, is an account of Olivia Harlan's experiences as a member of the Women's Army Auxiliary Corps from September 1942 to September 1943.

1.7 Bryant College
World War II Letters of United States Women Archive
Department of History
1150 Douglas Pike
Smithfield, RI 02917

This archive consists of 30,000 letters written by more than 1,500 women, both military and civilian, representing diverse social, economic, ethnic, and geographical circumstances. The archive was created in 1988 by historians Judy Barrett Litoff and David C. Smith in response to an author's request for information about women's wartime correspondence. Litoff and Smith submitted the query to about 1,500 daily newspapers throughout the nation. The archive includes significant letter collections written by women who served with the WAC, WAVES, SPAR, Marine Corps Women's Reserve, Army Nurse Corps, Navy Nurse Corps, and WASP during World War II.

A 70-reel microfilm edition, *The World War II Letters of United States Women,* to be published by Scholarly Resources, Inc., is in preparation.

1.8 Naval War College
Department of the Navy
686 Cushing Road
Newport, RI 02841-1207

The Naval Historical Collection of the Naval War College contains an archive with manuscripts and oral histories. Recently the archivist began an oral history project on the WAVES in World War II. Thus far, interviews with 18 women have been conducted, and memorabilia have been assembled whenever possible. The following oral histories are on record in transcript form.

Mary Caswell, hospital corps
Arlene Chilson, gunnery instructor

Dorothy Council, officer
Mary E. Hawthorne, officer
    Includes papers, 1944-86. 2 boxes.

The boxes contain biographical data; naval orders, 1964; a subject file
on the WAVES, including pamphlets, programs, newletters, 1944-45;
miscellaneous memorabilia, including citations, imprints, programs, newspapers, 1960-68; and photographs, including a photograph album and
scrapbook, 1944-70.

Winifred Love, officer
Mary McCoy, officer
Tina McNiel, storekeeper
Dorothy R. Midgeley, recreation specialist
Doris Nemitz, yeoman
Eileen O'Connor, yeoman
Doris O'Toole, pharmacist's mate
Gabrielle Pouliot, master-at-arms
    Includes papers, 1944-68. 0.5 box.

The box contains imprints, including "A Short History of the U.S.
Naval Training School (WR), Bronx, NY" and "Our Days at the U.S. Naval
Training School, Bronx, NY"; the WAVES songbook and prayer; a press
release, 1945; transcript of a radio interview, 1944; and a certificate. The
box also holds photographs of Waves marching and the June 1944 class
at the U.S. Naval Training School, The Bronx, NY; WAVES ninth birthday
celebration, 1951; Adm. Forrest Sherman's funeral procession, 1951; and
President Harry S. Truman and Winston Churchill, 1952.

Edith Smith, yeoman
Virginia Smith, hospital corps
Elizabeth Sullivan, yeoman
Esther Villeneuve, storekeeper
Nelli Waite, storekeeper
    Includes papers, 1943-46. 0.5 box.

The box contains copies of discharge and separation papers, 1946;
certificates and pass, 1945; newspapers, NAVAIRSTA, Atlanta, 1944; invita-
tions and menus, 1943-45; photographs of WAVES regiment, Hunter
College; and a Navy prayer book.

Jean Yarnell, Link trainer instructor

2. Middle Atlantic[2]

2.1 Franklin D. Roosevelt Library
511 Albany Post Road
Hyde Park, NY 12538

The library is part of the National Archives and Records Administration and is listed here for reference; a description of its holdings relating to military women appears in the next section of the volume.

2.2 Columbia University
Oral History Research Office
Butler Library
New York, NY 10027

This leading oral history archive contains more than 15,000 hours of tape-recorded reminiscences, generated from its own projects or donated by others. Most of these interviews have been transcribed, but some collections await funding for that purpose. Despite the size of the holdings in this center, the only oral histories at Columbia relating to military women of the World War II period are that of Col. Ruth Cheney Streeter, Director of the Marine Corps Women's Reserve, and several of Jacqueline Cochran, Director of the Women Airforce Service Pilots (WASP).

Cochran, Jacqueline.
Interview conducted in 1960, 63 pp.

This interview, conducted for the Columbia University Oral History Research Office aviation project, covers Cochran's experiences in obtaining a pilot's license, the Australian race, instrument flying, aviation medicine, women ferry pilots in World War II, the WASP, jet flying, world records, the FA-1, and Northeast Airlines. It also includes her recollections of Gen. Henry H. Arnold and Howard Hughes. Interviewer: Kenneth Leish.

Cochran, Jacqueline.
Interview conducted in 1973, 257 pp.

This interview covers Cochran's relations with the U.S. Army Air Forces, military aeronautics, American women air pilots, Cochran's meetings with General Eisenhower, her efforts to persuade Eisenhower to run for President, fundraising for his Presidential campaign, and post-Presidential con-

tacts. Interviewer: John Wickman. (The original transcript is at the Dwight
D. Eisenhower Library.)

Cochran, Jacqueline.
Interview conducted in 1976, 134 pp.

This interview covers women flyers for the British military, 1940-41;
the origin of the WASP, including lobbying efforts for that organization;
Cochran's recollections of Gen. Henry H. Arnold; and postwar lobbying
for benefits for women flyers for the military in World War II. Interviewers:
Maj. John Shiner and Capt. Robert Bartanowicz. (The original transcript
is at the U.S. Air Force Academy in Colorado Springs, CO.)

Streeter, Ruth Cheney, 1895-1990
Interview conducted in 1979, 366 pp.

This interview, conducted for the Columbia University Oral History Program, deals with Colonel Streeter's life before, during, and after her tour
as Director of the Marine Corps Women's Reserve (MCWR) in World War
II. She tells of the formation of the MCWR; her selection and duties as
Director; MCWR personalities, events, and training; and assignments of
the women reservists. Interviewer: Dr. John T. Mason, Jr. (A copy of the
transcript is held by the U.S. Marine Corps Historical Center.)

2.3 Hunter College
Wexler Library
695 Park Avenue
New York, NY 10021

The archives at Hunter College in New York City contain two small
boxes of unprocessed material related to the WAVES. These boxes
hold photographs, news clippings, correspondence, and miscellaneous documents. The former Bronx campus of Hunter, home of
the WAVES boot camp, is now Lehman College.

2.4 Lehman College Library
250 Bedford Park Boulevard West
Bronx, NY 10468-1589

The enlisted Waves were trained at the U.S. Naval Training School
(WR) at Hunter College, The Bronx, NY (now Lehman College),
as were some members of the Marine Corps Women's Reserve and
the SPAR. In the collections at the Lehman College Library are the
following relevant documents.

Personal Papers

Freid, Bernice Sains
Papers.

Freid's reminiscences (four pages) detail her arrival at boot camp, innocul-
ations, training, meals, clothing, watch duty, inspection, Jewish Waves,
and her final days as a Wave. The collection also includes two booklets,
a WAVES songbook, an orientation handbook, and postcards. Another of
Freid's reminiscences details her shore leave and gives a profile of a typical
Wave (three pages); it includes a brochure of the Service Women's Center
at the Biltmore Hotel, a photograph of Regiment 42, and postcards. A
letter to Freid's parents, dated September 25, 1944, describes the schedule
at boot camp.

Johnson, Helen A. Tice
Postcards.

Kuehner, Mary Breninger
Postcards.

Mounts, Malvina McDowell Mace
Papers.

Mounts's papers include a postcard from WAVES training, photographs,
WAVES brochures, and 33 WAVES/Navy song lyrics.

Spohr, Winifred Fien
Papers.

A letter that Spohr wrote to her parents, August 19, 1944, details the life of
a Wave on the Hunter campus; the collection also includes news clippings.

Stahley, Roberta Silvester
Papers.

Stahley's papers include letters to her family from the Hunter campus,
June–July 1943; orders to active duty and a memorandum regarding uniforms; a news clipping about her assignment to Hunter; two drawings;
postcards; the June 1943 issue of *Conning Tower* (vol. 1, no. 7); instruction
materials; a brochure from Radio City, "For Service Women in NYC"; and
a map.

Thompson, Ellen Mooney
Papers.

Ellen Mooney Thompson's papers are composed of photocopies of WAVES programs, a booklet, Thompson's identification card, news items, a map showing station boundaries, and a letter detailing the life of a Wave.

Oral History Interviews

The Lehman College Library holds five oral history interviews conducted with former Waves (not identified by name).

Publications

Bennett-Telcott, Richard. *U.S. Naval Training School (WR), The Bronx, New York, New York.* Somerville, MA: Letter-Booklets, 1943. 24 pp. (photocopy).

Munch, Janet Butler. "Making WAVES in the Bronx: The Story of the U.S. Naval Training School (WR) at Hunter College." *The Bronx Historical Society Journal* 30 (Spring 1993): 1-15.

U.S. Assistant Chief of Naval Personnel for Women. *The WAVES: Records of the Assistant Chief of Naval Personnel for Women, 1942-1972.* Wilmington, DE: Scholarly Resources, Inc., 1991. 20 rolls of 35mm microfilm with guide.

U.S. Department of the Navy, Bureau of Naval Personnel, Women's Reserve #88a. *U.S. Naval Administration in World War II.* Washington, DC: Historical Section, Bureau of Naval Personnel, 1946. 9 microfiche.

U.S. Naval Training School (WR), The Bronx, New York. #88b. Washington, DC: Director of Naval History, Bureau of Naval Personnel, 1946. 7 microfiche.

U.S. Naval Training School (WR), Public Relations Office. *Navy Service, A Short History of the United States Naval Training School (WR), The Bronx.* New York: The School, 1945. 190 pp.

Photographs

There are a number of photographs scattered in the collections and grouped separately.

2.5 U.S. Army Military History Institute
Carlisle Barracks, Building 22
Carlisle, PA 17013-5008

The U.S. Army Military History Institute collects, preserves, and provides to researchers source materials on American military history. It holds more than 7 million items, including nearly 1 million photographs. No other agency has as extensive a collection relating exclusively to the role of the military in the development of the United States.

The institute receives materials from Army libraries as well as from individual donors. Its coverage ranges over fields allied to the military, such as law, science, medicine, economics, geography, and sociology, and others. Original sources are an important part of the holdings. They are represented by the papers of hundreds of prominent generals, junior officers, and enlisted men and women from colonial times to the present.

Approximately 10 percent of the institute's total collection is accessible by computer, much of it relating to the Civil War and World War II. The most effective way to retrieve specific material is to seek the help of a reference archivist. The following holdings reflect the lives of World War II military women.

Personal Papers

Craighill, Margaret D.
Papers, 1942–46. 31 boxes.

Colonel Craighill was the first woman doctor to serve as an officer in the Army Medical Corps assigned to the Army Surgeon General in World War II. She was consultant for WAC health and welfare and inspected health conditions in every major theater. This file is very valuable for the quantity of material it contains on WAC preventive medicine, medical statistics, physical standards, diseases, nutrition, physical fitness, abstracts of meetings, and history of the Women's Medical Unit.

Olson, Betty M.
Papers, 1942–45. 1 box.

Olson was a member of the first WAC unit to enter France after D-day. She became secretary to Maj. Gen. Frank S. Ross, Chief of Transportation, European Theater of Operations, September 1944–October 1945. Her letters and memoirs cover basic training at Fort Des Moines, IA; work at post headquarters, Hampton Roads, VA; and assignments in Paris and Frankfurt, Germany.

Smith, Jean
Papers, 1913–20 and 1944–49. 1 box.

This WAC officer's letters and papers include letters written from British civilians and military personnel, 1913–20; a manuscript about WAC activities in Australia, New Guinea (Papua, Hollandia), the Philippines, and Japan during World War II; and clippings about education and women's activities in postwar Japan.

Temple, Jane
Papers, 1944–45. 1 box.

This collection includes radio scripts written by Temple, a WAC officer, and broadcast to patients in Battey General Hospital, issues of newspapers and a newsletter, orders, and documents.

Wayman, Martha A.
Papers, 1942–46. 2 boxes.

Starting with WAAC training at Fort Des Moines, IA, Wayman's personal letters to her family describe her everyday life while she was stationed in various U.S. training centers, and then in Australia, New Guinea, the Philippines, and Japan.

McCann Collection

The McCann Collection of Women in Uniform, 1938–44. 2 volumes.

This collection contains brochures and news clippings compiled by the McCann family on Wacs, Waves, Wafs, Spars, Army nurses, and women Marines, including some articles on military women in Canada, Europe, Britain, and the U.S.S.R. during the war.

Army Service Experiences Questionnaire

The institute's ongoing survey of World War II veterans by means of an 18-page questionnaire has, thus far, netted 5,000–6,000 responses. Each response is kept in a separate folder along with any memorabilia that may have been included. The institute has received more than 70 responses from former Wacs and Army nurses. Their responses have been filed by name in cases where the primary military unit of assignment could be identified.

Oral History Interviews

In 1971 the institute implemented a debriefing program covering senior retired officers. Completed transcripts are maintained in the Manuscript Archives Branch. The following cover women officers of the World War II period.

Army Nurse POWs

These oral histories of 11 Army nurses and 2 dietitians who were prisoners of war in the Philippines in World War II are also available at the U.S. Army Center of Military History in Washington, DC.

Hallaren, Col. Mary A., 46 pp.

This WAC leader included among her assignments command of the first group of enlisted women sent to the European theater in July 1943. She became WAC Staff Director of the Army Air Forces in Europe and was appointed third WAC Director in 1947, serving until 1953. She led the postwar effort toward integration of women into the regular Army.

Streeter, Col. Ruth Cheney, 66 pp.

Colonel Streeter was Director of the Marine Corps Women's Reserve in World War II. Her recollections as given in this interview are separate from her oral history sponsored by the Columbia University Oral History Program (see holdings of the Marine Corps Historical Center).

2.6 St. Vincent College
Center for Northern Appalachian Studies
Latrobe, PA 15650-2690

Dr. Richard Wissolik conducted oral history interviews with women working in factories during World War II and with six or seven Army and Navy nurses. From these he produced a book of edited interviews, *Out of the Kitchen,* published in 1994 by the Center for Northern Appalachian Studies. The tapes of the interviews have been placed in the center archives, along with computer disks containing the unedited transcripts.

3. District of Columbia[3]

3.1 Bethune Museum and Archives, Inc.
1318 Vermont Avenue, NW
Washington, DC 20005

The Bethune Museum and Archives (BMA) is a nonprofit institution dedicated to the collection, preservation, and interpretation of African-American women's history. Access to the manuscript collection in the archives is by appointment only. Researchers must submit a written request, stating topic of research and days available. For specific reference questions, the archivist may be contacted by telephone and will provide information as time allows.

Items in the collection that bear on the experiences of black U.S. military women in World War II are as follows.

Personal Papers

Burrell, Prudence Burns
Papers. 1 large box.

This box contains a careful historical record compiled by former Lieutenant Burrell, Army Nurse Corps, on the training and assignments of the black Army nurses in World War II in the United States and overseas, with photographs. The history is displayed on boards, showing Army nurses grouped by station and rosters, sometimes accompanied by news accounts. Designed as an educational display, the boards provide accurate and quite extensive information.

Roundtree, Dovey Johnson
Papers, 1938-48. 1 cubic foot.

Roundtree was one of the first 39 black WAAC officer candidates at Fort Des Moines in 1942. She later became an ordained AME minister and then an attorney. Her papers include articles that she wrote on her World War II experiences as well as news clips, photographs, a scrapbook, and a WAC newsletter.

Smith, Ethel Heywood
Papers. 3 linear inches.

The papers of this member of the Women's Army Corps include official correspondence, photographs, and a large scrapbook.

Records

National Council of Negro Women
Records. 278 linear feet.

This collection documents a wide variety of subjects, including civil rights, education, employment, feminism, health, housing, and women's issues. Materials include correspondence between founder Mary McLeod Bethune and many other black women, including WAC and Army Nurse Corps members in World War II, specifically Frances Futtrell, Dovey Johnson, Lucile Miller, and Thelma Brown, the WAC officer in charge of the black women's Army band.

Also in this collection are files labeled "WAVES," "WACS," and "War Department." These contain documents on the admission of black women into the WAVES and SPAR; correspondence relating to black women and the WAC; documents concerning the treatment and experience of black women in the WAC; references to the Cadet Nurse Corps; copies of the *Aframerican Women's Journal* with articles on and by Wacs and Army nurses; and a "Who's Who" of black women officers.

Oral History Interviews

Jackson, Margaret Young
Interview conducted on June 22, 1987.

This enlisted member of the Women's Army Corps served in the United States and was later a member of the 6888th Central Postal Directory Battalion, which served in England and France. She tells of life in a black women's company during the war and also of her experiences in Birmingham, Rouen, and Paris. Interviewer: Eleanor Stoddard.

Lewis, Lorraine
Interview conducted on February 22, 1989.

This enlisted member of the Women's Army Corps served in the United States during the war and stayed on as a noncommissioned officer, serving in Frankfurt and then Paris under Eisenhower in SACEUR, and then was transferred to Japan. Disabled by a stroke, she returned for medical treatment to the States and was discharged from the Army in 1958. She recounts her service life and her love of the Army. Interviewer: Eleanor Stoddard.

3.2 Center for Air Force History
170 Luke Avenue, Suite 400
Bolling Air Force Base
Washington, DC 20332-5113

One of the chief missions of the Center for Air Force History is to write the history of the U.S. Air Force and its predecessor agencies. These agencies include the Army Air Corps and the Army Air Forces that existed in World War II. The center holds a collection of papers, documents, and oral history transcripts, many of these on microfilm, as well as a library. The microfilm collection reproduces much of the collection of original documents at Maxwell Air Force Base, Montgomery, AL. Not all of those documents have been purchased on microfilm by the center because of cost.

Researchers using the center should call first for an appointment, stating the area of interest. Those with a special interest in Air-Wacs (approximately two-fifths of the Women's Army Corps) or Women Airforce Service Pilots (WASP) will find microfilmed copies of relevant papers and documents in the following areas.

Women's Army Corps (WAC), Air-Wacs

WAC Air Reserve Plan of Air Defense Command
WAC Detachment at Eagle Pass, Army Air Field, Eagle Pass, TX
WAC History
WAC Inspection Manual
WAC: I Troop Carrier Command: Transcript of Interview with Maj. R. H. Kerr, WAC Staff Director, by Lt. Rose Leibbrand, A-2, July 1943, 4 pp.
WAC Officers: Graduates of Special Service Schools on Duty Within Continental United States, August 1943
WAC Program in the Army Air Forces prepared by WAC Branch, Military Personnel Division (highlights in development of Wacs in key jobs, prepared by Lt. Col. Betty Bandel), November 1945
WAC Recruiting Plan

Army Air Forces (AAF)

USAF Historical Division, *The Army Air Forces in World War II,* vol. 7, *Services Around the World,* section 5, "Women in the AAF," pp. 503-541

Women Airforce Service Pilots (WASP)

Women Airforce Service Pilots, AAF Tactical Center WASP Training Course, April–September 1944

Women Airforce Service Pilots, AAFs Training Command: History and Supporting Documents of the WASP Program under the Direction of Jacqueline Cochran in World War II, 1942-45

Women Airforce Service Pilots, AFMDC Wasps at Alamogordo, September-December 1944

Women Airforce Service Pilots, Eastern Flying Training Command: History of Wasps in the Eastern Flying Training Command, 1943-44

Women Airforce Service Pilots, First Air Force

Women Airforce Service Pilots, Fourth Air Force

Women Airforce Service Pilots, Second Air Force: History of Wasps in the Second Air Force, 1944

Women's Auxiliary Ferrying Squadron, AAF Training Command: Miscellaneous correspondence, 1942-43

Women's Flying Training, AAF Training Command, Training Command Memorandums, 1943-44, Statistical Report on Classes, October 4, 1943-August 4, 1945

Women Pilots Division AC/AS OCAR Diaries

Women Pilots in the Air Transport Command

Women Pilots in the Ferrying Division, Air Transport Command, July 1941-December 1944

Women Pilots of the AAF: AAF Historical Study #55, "Women Pilots of the AAF, 1941-1944"

The center holds the following papers and publications that contain information on Col. Jacqueline Cochran, Director of the WASP during World War II.

Papers—Col. Jacqueline Cochran

Arnold, Gen. Henry H., Commander of Army Air Forces
Papers at Library of Congress (partially on microfilm).

General Arnold's papers include correspondence, interview material, articles, excerpts from *Congressional Record,* biographical data, and photographs, with references to Jacqueline Cochran.

Publications—Col. Jacqueline Cochran

Johnson, Lt. Col. Ann R., with introduction by Jacqueline Cochran. "The WASPs of World War II." *Aerospace Historian* 17 (Summer/ Fall 1970): 76-82.

Cannon, Edmund. *Women Air Force Service Pilots in World War II.* Washington, DC: Congressional Research Service, November 6, 1975.

Oral History Interview

In this interview, which is on microfilm, Ann Hamilton Tunner, wife of Lt. Gen. William H. Tunner and former Wasp, recalls her life, including her entry into pilot training in Tulsa, OK; interview by Colonel Cochran; further training in Houston, TX, on P-47 and P-40; numerous ferrying missions throughout the United States; travel with General Tunner; work in military government in Japan; and testimony before Congress to attempt to obtain VA benefits for Wasps.

Publication

Simpson, Albert F. *USAF History of Women in the Armed Forces: A Selected Bibliography.* Washington, DC: U.S. Air Force, Office of Air Force History, June 1976.

3.3 Library of Congress
Manuscript Division
First Street and Independence Avenue, SE
Washington, DC 20003

The Manuscript Division contains two directories that proved useful in providing leads to collections of papers relating to military women in World War II. These were as follows.

Hinding, Andrea, and Sheldon Bower, eds. *Women's History Sources: A Guide to Archives and Manuscript Collections in the United States.* 2 vols. New York: R. R. Bowker Company, 1979.

National Union Catalog of Manuscript Collections. Washington, DC: Library of Congress, 1959-92. The indexes, 1959-84, were prepared by Chadwick-Healy Inc., Alexandria, VA, in 1994. Indexes for 1985-92 were prepared by the Library of Congress.

The Manuscript Division also contains the following collection.

Hobby, Oveta Culp, 1905-95
Papers, 1941-52. Approx. 2,200 items.

This material pertains to Hobby's work with the War Department during World War II when she was Chief of the Women's Interest Section of the War Department Bureau of Public Relations (1941–42) and Director of the Women's Army Corps (1942–45). The collection includes general correspondence files, scrapbooks, photographs, articles, press releases, news clippings, and miscellaneous printed matter. This personal collection is the only one in the Manuscript Division pertaining to military women in World War II.

3.4 National Archives and Records Administration
Seventh Street and Pennsylvania Avenue, NW
Washington, DC 20408

National Archives and Records Administration
8601 Adelphi Road
College Park, MD 20704-6001

The addresses of the Washington, DC, area National Archives facilities are included here for reference, but a discussion of their holdings relating to military women appears in the next section of the volume.

3.5 Office of the Coast Guard Historian
2100 Second Street, SW
Washington, DC 20593

The Office of the Coast Guard Historian contains a large collection of papers, documents, publications, and finding aids on the history of the U.S. Coast Guard, as well as a library. Researchers must make an appointment to use its resources. The collection of material on the World War II SPAR is found in 10 boxes and a number of separate file folders, books, scrapbooks, and photograph collections. The boxes are neither numbered nor labeled very descriptively, but they are placed together in the following order.

First box: SPAR Women. This miscellaneous collection includes SPAR "Hunter Boots," a reunion book; an early report to Congress on SPAR formation; talks to trainees; rosters of officers; home addresses of women officers; age groups and states of origin; recruiting plans; an insignia chart; a report on Alaska for duty; a SPAR songbook; reports in manuscript form of status, 1943 and 1944; Report on Post-War Opportunities for Service Personnel (H. Doc.

344, 78th Cong.); a four-chapter draft entitled "The Establishment of the Women's Reserve of the U.S. Coast Guard" (unpublished); and many excellent photographs and negatives.

Second box: Women. This box contains a large photographic collection of individual Spars arranged by name and also of ceremonial occasions. It is a large photographic collection.

Third box: Women: SPAR Officer Training. This box holds a collection of lectures, courses (on organization, personnel, and ships), transfers, dispatches, and correspondence.

Fourth box: World War I. This material pertains to the World War I period.

Fifth box: Women: Spars—World War II. This box contains personnel papers, regulations, memorandums, executive orders, and correspondence of Lt. Comdr. Ineva Meyer, Enlistment Assignment Division.

Sixth box: Women: SPAR Officer Training. This box holds insignia, aids to navigation, and materials relating to social hygiene (syphilis).

Seventh box: Women: SPAR Officer Training. This box contains information on training schools; copies of training manuals; copies of manuals on the organization of the Army, Navy, Marine Corps, and Merchant Marine; and copies of manuals on ships, aircraft, and ordnance.

Eighth box: Women. In this box are materials relating to training at Bainbridge, MD, a written chronology of women in the Coast Guard, photographs, and other miscellaneous material.

Ninth box: Women (Spars). This box holds mostly photographs. It includes some correspondence from 1943.

Tenth box: Women. This box contains a photocopy of *Three Years Behind the Mast: The Story of the United States Coast Guard SPARS* by Lt. Mary C. Lyne and Lt. Kay Arthur, USCGR (W), n.p., n.d. It also includes memorandums, orders, and many photographs.

Separate items (unboxed). Eight file folders are organized as follows: "40th SPAR Reunion"; "SPAR Officer Training" (procedures for regimental staff); "SPAR Officers Training Course" (academic lectures and reports); three file folders of newspaper clippings; one large file folder of photographs; and "Facts About the SPARs" (photocopy of *The Coast Guard at War,* vol. 22, *Women's Reserve,* prepared in the Historical Section, Public Information Division, U.S. Coast Guard Headquarters, April 15, 1946).

Miscellaneous separate items. U.S. Coast Guard magazine, and anthology of World War II articles pertaining to Spars; file on the 40th SPAR reunion; three books, *50th Anniversary, 1942-1992* (paperback, n.p., n.d.), *General Training Course for SPARs* (Groton, CT, n.d.), and *Handbook for Yeomen and Storekeepers* (Groton, CT, 1943); three personal photograph albums; one scrapbook of news clippings; three personal scrapbooks; and one large scrapbook of manuscripts on carbon paper, including "History of Women's Reserve, 13th Naval District" (1946), 152 pp., and "History of District Coast Guard Personnel Office and Military Morale and Captain's Office, 13th Naval District" (1945), 84 pp., written and prepared by the U.S. Coast Guard Personnel Office.

Publications

The following publications are available from the Coast Guard Historian's Office:

Lyne, Mary C. and Arthur, Kay. *Three Years Behind the Mast: The Story of the United States Coast Guard SPARS.* N.p., n.d. 126 pp.

Thomson, Robin J. "The Coast Guard & the Women's Reserve in World War II." Commandant's Bulletin, October 1992. (insert)

U.S. Coast Guard. *The Coast Guard at War,* vol. 22, *Women's Reserve.* Washington, DC: U.S. Coast Guard, Public Information Division, April 15, 1946. 259 pp.

U.S. Coast Guard. *Facts About SPARs.* Washington DC: U.S. Coast Guard, 1943. 22 pp.

Videotaped Interviews

Videotaped interviews with retired Coast Guard women officers can be viewed at the Coast Guard Historian's Office. These include the following women from the World War II period: Dorothy Stratton, Helen Schleman, Eleanor L'Ecuyer, and Carol Cottrell.

3.6 Smithsonian Institution
National Museum of American History
Constitution Avenue between 12th and 14th Streets, NW
Washington, DC 20560

In addition to artifacts, the military history collection of the National Museum of American History contains the following items related to World War II military women.

Personal Papers

Hugo, Alice

This collection contains "WAC Island," an unpublished manuscript by Alice Hugo, a member of the WAC. (It is also available in the Iowa State University Archives.)

Pollard, Clarice

This collection consists of the memoirs of a member of the WAAC/WAC. (See also East Texas Research Center, Stephen F. Austin State University.)

Sullivan, Celeste Noland

Sullivan was a model and public relations representative for the WAAC/WAC. The collection consists of clippings.

Oral History Interview

May, Col. Geraldine; Riley, Col. Emma Jane

A teacher from the Air Force Academy conducted this joint oral history interview with Col. Geraldine May and Col. Emma Jane Riley. Both women had been in the armed services in World War II and later joined the new Department of the Air Force. Colonel May became Women in the Air Force (WAF) Director in 1948, and Colonel Riley became WAF Director in 1957. This interview was conducted in 1990.

3.7 Smithsonian Institution
National Air and Space Museum (NASM)
Seventh Street and Independence Avenue, SW
Washington, DC 20560

The archives of the National Air and Space Museum contain several collections on military women under the following headings.

NASM Biographical Files

These files contain biographical information (both documents and photographs) on aviation personalities, including women involved in military aviation. They are arranged alphabetically by name. A researcher would need to know names of women for access to the file.

NASM WASP Technical File

This file contains miscellaneous material relating to the WASP.

The U.S. Air Force Pre-1954 Still Photograph Collection

This collection contains photographs of military women, including Wasps, Wacs, and Army Air Corps nurses.

Wasps Binder: Pictures of Life and Training of the Wasps, Acc. 1989-0123

This scrapbook of Bernice Falk Haydu (class 44-W-7) contains photographs, class rosters, graduation data, a WASP songbook, an original Miss Fifinella color sketch by Walt Disney, and other items.

3.8 U.S. Army Center of Military History
1099 14th Street, NW
Washington, DC 20005-3402

A major mission of the Center of Military History (CMH) is to write the official history of the U.S. Army. A closely related effort is under way to foster the study of military history on the part of the academic community and the general public.

Researchers should make an appointment with the appropriate office before visiting the center. There is a wealth of material, and anyone with a general research interest is urged to request retrieval help. The staff can provide useful guidance, although the discovery of a specific piece of information is usually left to the researcher.

Field Program and Historical Services Division (FP)

The Field Program and Historical Services Division, known as FP, maintains collections of published and unpublished material dealing with the history of the U.S. Army. A 40,000-volume library contains selected publications, including books and monographs published by the center, as well as government and commercial publications, Army regulations, technical and training manuals, foreign publications, and others.

The FP collection contains approximately 2,000 unpublished manuscript histories of U.S. Army operations worldwide for the 1940–45 period. The collection also contains biographical sketches of general officers, historical resumes of current and abandoned U.S. Army installations (incomplete), select Army training exercises, special reports, interviews, and other documents. For anyone researching the history of WAAC/WAC units or individuals, this collection could provide useful background as long as locations and other specific associations were known.

Oral History Interviews

Oral histories were first used in World War II to supplement official written records. These "after action" interviews of participants in battles were used with other sources (maps, reports, photographs) in historical monographs and broader publications. Such oral histories have been continued in later wars. In 1970 the Senior Officer Oral History Program was established to convey to younger officers the qualities and experiences that had made the careers of retiring officers successful.

The center contains no oral history transcripts of women who served in the Women's Army Corp in World War II. Some interviews of that period conducted by Army historians can be found at the U.S. Army Military History Institute, Carlisle Barracks, PA (see the listing for the institute).

The center does have in its holdings, however, approximately 300 interviews with members of the Army Nurse Corps. The transcripts of these interviews tell the stories of Army nurses serving under a host of war conditions. Many narrators from World War II have been recorded, including women serving in every theater:

European, Mediterranean, Pacific, Middle East, and China-Burma-India. They include the histories of 27 Army nurses stationed at Pearl Harbor on December 7, 1941, and a significant number who were prisoners of war in the Philippines.

Three of the interviews were conducted with Army Nurse Corps historians. Anyone interested in using the transcripts should first contact the center.

Publications

The chief publications of the Center of Military History that concern military women are the following.

Bellafaire, Judith A. *The Army Nurse Corps.* U.S. Army Center of Military History (CMH) Pub. 72-14. Washington, DC: U.S. Army, n.d. 32 pp.

Bellafaire, Judith A. *The Women's Army Corps.* CMH Pub. 72-15. Washington, DC: U.S. Army, n.d. 28 pp.

Piemonte, Robert V., and Cindy A. Gurney, eds. *Highlights in the History of the Army Nurse Corps.* Rev. ed. Washington, DC: U.S. Army Center of Military History, 1987. 94 pp. This chronology covers the years 1775–1984.

Morden, Bettie J. *The Women's Army Corps, 1945-1978.* CMH Pub. 30-14. Washington, DC: U.S. Army, 1990. 543 pp.

Treadwell, Mattie E. *The Women's Army Corps.* The United States Army in World War II, Special Studies. CMH Pub. 11-8. Washington, DC: U.S. Army, 1954. 841 pp.

The last two publications are comprehensive and detailed official accounts of the growth of the Women's Army Corps from its inception in 1942 to its dissolution in 1978. The books cover the evolving organization of the WAC; its relationship with the men's Army; changes in policy and regulations relating to women; struggles and contributions of leading WAC officers; and step-by-step progress in achieving closer equality of responsibilities, roles, and ranking with male counterparts.

3.9 U.S. Naval Historical Center
Washington Navy Yard
Ninth and M Streets, SE
Building 57, Third Floor
Washington, DC 20374-0571

The Naval Archives can be used by researchers to put their work in context. The archivists will assist with research but will not do the research themselves. They can help researchers find their way through a well-defined group of collection categories, as follows.

Waves' Papers, ACNP(W) (Assistant Chief of Naval Personnel for Women)

The collection includes immediate office files for the WAVES Directors, 1942–72 (Mildred McAfee to Robin Quigley).

CHINFO (Chief of Information) Speech Files

This collection contains copies of speeches given by Mildred McAfee.

Officer Biography Collection

The collection contains biographical information on the lives and naval careers of women Navy officers plus a few notable nonofficers (all WAVES Directors plus later female admirals).

Personal Papers

This collection includes the personal papers of many Waves at all ranks.

World War II Command File

The files of the Under Secretary of the Navy include press releases relating to Navy women, chronologically arranged. This collection also includes authors' articles, advance copies, and manuscripts on Navy women, filed under name of author.

Aviation History Collection

Organized by naval aviation commands, this collection contains a history of naval shore establishments where Waves were stationed. Approximately one-third of the Waves in World War II were in aviation (BuAir). The researcher needs to know the station to which a Wave was assigned in order to use this excellent but underused source.

Uniform Board Records

Series VIII: Women's Reserve and Nurse Corps records, 1942-82, and regulations on uniforms are included in this collection.

Records Relating to Hospital Ships

Fourteen hospital ships were in use during World War II. Most of this file consists of textual records and photographs related to the U.S.S. *Comfort,* which took part in the Okinawa campaign and was hit by a kamikaze in April 1945, suffering significant losses to medical and other ship personnel.

Navy Nurse Corps Records

Office of the Director, Navy Nurse Corps
Records, 1881-1981 (chiefly 1908-77).

These records contain the immediate office files of the Director of the Navy Nurse Corps for 1908-77.

U.S. Naval Institute Oral History Interviews

This collection consists of three volumes of transcripts of oral history interviews with the following WAVES officers:

Crandall, Elizabeth B., 1970
Hancock, Joy Bright, 1969 and 1970
Horton, Mildred McAfee, 1969
Kitchen, Etta Belle, 1969
Lenihan, Rita, 1970
Palmer, Jean, 1969
Rich, Frances, 1969
Rigby, Eleanor Grant, 1970
Shelly, Mary Josephine, 1970
Wilde, Louise K., 1969
Wiley, Tova Petersen, 1969

Also included are transcripts of interviews with Senator Margaret Chase Smith, 1971; Dorothy Constance Stratton, Director of the SPAR, 1970; and Robin Quigley, ACNP(W).

Naval Historical Center Oral History Collection

Approximately 25 oral history interviews with World War II Waves and Navy nurses are on file, about one-half of them in transcript form. Tapes can be heard only with permission. Some of the interviews were conducted by personnel of the Naval Historical Center and some by local high school students as part of a project. Ten transcripts were donated to the center by Eleanor Stoddard; these cover seven WAVES officers and three enlisted Waves.

Ready Reference File

This file contains published sources used for general reference. Selected headings are "Women in Military," "Women in Navy," "Blacks in Navy," "Navy Nurses," and "Nurse POWs."

Note: The Navy Library, in the same building, contains administrative histories and other unpublished material providing background for decisions. Examples are "Women in the Navy"; "Negroes in the Navy"; and "History of the Naval Reserve Midshipmen's School (WR), Northampton, MA," prepared for inclusion in the History of Representative Field Activities of the Bureau of Naval Personnel, World War II. The library also contains the administrative history of the Bureau of Medicine and Surgery and numerous related books and journals relating to the World War II period.

3.10 U.S. Navy
Bureau of Medicine and Surgery
23d and E Streets, NW
Washington, DC 20372-5300

Oral history interviews of members of the Navy Nurse Corps have been conducted by Dr. Jan Herman, BUMED historian, as part of an ongoing project. The following are currently available for use in transcript form.

Oral History Interviews

Bernatitus, Ann
Oral history interview conducted January 25, 1994.

Bernatitus's account covers her prewar Navy nursing and assignment to duty in Manila. At the outbreak of World War II, when the Cañacao Naval

Hospital was destroyed, Bernatitus went to Sternberg Hospital (Army) and then to Santa Scholastica Musical College, where her Navy group established a hospital. She was the only Navy nurse ordered to Bataan, where she worked as an operating room nurse along with 25 Army nurses. Transferred to the Malinta Tunnel on Corregidor, she was evacuated on May 3, 1942, along with 11 Army nurses, on the submarine *Spearfish*. Returning to the States, she went on speaking tours for war bonds and was awarded the Legion of Merit. She saw duty in the Okinawa campaign in April 1945. Her later duty in the Philippines and in Dairen, Manchuria, involved retrieval of POWs. She stayed in the Navy Nurse Corps after World War II. This is a full and valuable account of Bernatitus's life as a Navy nurse.

Billings, Jeanne Brand
Oral history interview conducted August 23, 1992.

Billings was a member of the WAVES assigned as a medical historian to the Navy Bureau of Medicine and Surgery in Washington, DC, in World War II. During 1944, working for the bureau, she wrote histories of the Allied offensive in the Pacific, using immediate, fresh data from the field. In this interview, she describes the process and techniques of putting the accounts together and mentions fellow historians.

Brown, Josie Mabel
Oral history interview conducted by Brown's niece, Rachel Wed-eking.

This narrative was obtained from this World War I member of the Navy Nurse Corps just before her death. Her first assignment was to the Naval Hospital, Great Lakes, IL, in the midst of the flu epidemic. Out of 173,000 men on the station, 6,000 were stricken and died rapidly. This brief but graphic account provides vivid descriptions of the infected patients, the morgue stacked with bodies, and 16-hour workdays.

Danner, Dorothy Still
Oral history interview conducted December 3 and 4, 1991.

Danner describes her pre-World War II career in the Navy Nurse Corps and her assignment to Cañacao Naval Hospital in the Philippines. She describes the crisis when war came, her move to Santa Scholastica, and her imprisonment at Santo Tomas and Los Baños. The interview provides a good account of Danner's coping methods and hardships in Los Baños and the dramatic rescue by U.S. forces of the prisoners there in February 1945. (See also "Reminiscences of a Nurse POW," based on this oral history, in *Navy Medicine,* May-June 1992.)

Erikson, Ruth
Oral history interviews conducted in 1994 and 1995.

This former Director of the Navy Nurse Corps tells of her experiences in the 1930s at the Naval Hospital, San Diego, CA, and on the hospital ship *Relief* in the late 1930s; describes the 1941 attack on Pearl Harbor, where she was stationed at the naval hospital; and describes her experiences treating American POWs liberated in Japan, 1945, and treating Japanese survivors of the Nagasaki bombing in late August 1945.

Gibson, Madge Crouch
Oral history completed December 1, 1995.

Crouch entered the Navy Nurse Corps in 1944 and was first assigned to duty at the Naval Hospital, Norfolk, VA, and then at the National Naval Medical Center, Bethesda, MD. Later, aboard the U.S.S. *Benevolence* in Tokyo Bay, she treated American POWs liberated from the Tokyo area.

Pribram, Kathryn Van Wagner
Oral history interview conducted January 6, 1995.

This member of the Navy Nurse Corps was 1 of the 12 graduates in the first training class of Navy flight nurses in January–February 1945. She was among the first air-evacuation nurses to bring the wounded by plane back from the Iwo Jima battlefield.

Ramsey, Helen Pavlovsky
Oral history interview conducted by telephone, April 15, 1994.

Ramsey was a member of the Navy Nurse Corps in World War II. In the interview she describes her duty at Naval Base Hospital No. 12, Netley, Hants, England, from February 1944 to September 1944. Formerly the Royal Victoria Hospital, the U.S. Navy took it over from the U.S. Army to be a receiving hospital for casualties from the Normandy landings. The narrator describes preparations for D-day, buzz bombs, receipt of the first casualties, use of sulfa and penicillin. (See also "Navy Nurses Remember the Invasion" in *Navy Medicine,* May–June 1994.)

St. Pierre, Bertha Evans
Oral history interview conducted May 20, 1992.

This member of the Navy Nurse Corps in World War II was serving in Manila when war broke out. She was captured by the Japanese and imprisoned in Santo Tomas, then transferred to Los Baños in the Philippines. The interview provides sharp detail on living and working conditions in the prison camps and St. Pierre's eventual rescue.

Personal Papers

The bureau also holds the following collection.

Cobb, Laura
Papers (in process).

Cobb was a member of the Navy Nurse Corps, World War II. She was chief nurse over other Navy nurses at Santo Tomas prison in Manila, Philippines, and then at Los Baños. Her papers cover her career in the Navy Nurse Corps and include memorabilia from the war experience, including the rescue at Los Baños.

3.11 U.S. Marine Corps Historical Center
Washington Navy Yard
Ninth and M Streets, SE
Building 58
Washington, DC 20374-0580

The Marine Corps Historical Center contains 2,400 processed collections of personal papers of individual marines as well as a library and art collections. The resources of the center are available to researchers by appointment. Those who are seeking data on members of the Marine Corps Women's Reserve in World War II will find the following collections.

Personal Papers

Penning, Anne Cooper
Papers, 1943-44. 1 box.

The papers include newspapers; copies of the newsletter *The Pendleton Scout,* 1943-44; a handbook; Penning's service record book; and other memorabilia.

Stanley, Mariana Trice
Papers, 1943-45. 1 box.

This collection includes rules and regulations of women's barracks, Norfolk, VA; Stanley's dog tags; emblem; photographs; recruiting booklet; and *USMCWR Yearbook,* Camp Lejeune, New River, NC, 1943-44.

Streeter, Ruth Cheney
Papers, 1942-47. 2 boxes.

Colonel Streeter's papers include correspondence and clippings from her time as Director, Marine Corps Women's Reserve, plus an unpublished manuscript, authored by Colonel Streeter and Katherine A. Towle, "History of the Marine Corps Women's Reserve: A Critical Analysis of Its Development and Operation, 1943-1945."

Stremlow, Mary V.
Notes for MCWR histories, 1917-77. 24 boxes.

Stremlow's notes consist mostly of extensive background data pertaining to World War II and later but also contain material on the earlier history of Marine Corps women. The papers are very systematically arranged in numerous clearly marked folders. See Col. Mary V. Stremlow, U.S. Marine Corps Reserve, *A History of the Women Marines, 1946-1977* (Washington, DC, 1986). See also Capt. Linda L. Hewitt, USMCR, *Women Marines in World War I* (Washington, DC, 1974).

Wilson, Edna S.
Journal, June-July, 1944.

Excerpts from Wilson's personal journal detail her life as a new recruit in the MCWR, basic training, and feelings associated with being a female marine.

Records

Marine Corps Women's Reserve
Orders, 1942-46. 15 boxes.

This collection contains background for history and drafts of the publication by Maj. Pat Meid, USMCR, *Marine Corps Women's Reserve in World War II* (Washington, DC, February 13, 1964), now out of print. The collection consists of orders, promotions, uniform regulations, instructions on courtesy and barracks discipline, officer and enlisted personnel training, course outlines, correspondence, rosters of personnel, and much more. It also includes a large collection of excellent photographs.

Oral History Interviews

Transcripts of the following oral history interviews are available, subject to restrictions on use. It may be of special interest to know that files also contain transcripts of 32 interviews conducted with women who served in the Marine Corps in World War I.

Gridley, Lily Hutcheon, 1908-93
Interview conducted in 1988, 44 pp.

Gridley was a lieutenant colonel in the Marine Corps Women's Reserve, 1942-46, and in the Marine Corps Reserve, 1949-65. This interview covers Gridley's early legal career, her service as the first woman Marine Corps legal officer in World War II, her return to civilian life, her subsequent recall to active duty, and her promotion to major and assignment as legal assistance officer in Marine Corps Headquarters. Permission required to quote. Interviewer: Eleanor Stoddard.

Hale, Mary Janice, 1915-
Interview conducted in 1989, 50 pp.

Hale was a lieutenant colonel in the Marine Corps Women's Reserve, 1943-48, and in the Marine Corps, 1948-64. In this interview, she discusses her decision to join the Marine Corps Women's Reserve in World War II; recruit training; leadership training at officer candidate school; duties as an officer at Camp Lejeune, NC; assignment to Hawaii as an education officer; good working relations with male marines; ongoing service with the regular Marine Corps after the 1948 integration act; service as a training officer at Parris Island, SC, 1949; assignment to Quantico, VA, officer training; assignment to Marine Corps headquarters for officer recruitment; and assignment as an executive officer to DACOWITS. Permission required to quote. Interviewer: Eleanor Stoddard.

Hamblet, Julia Estelle, 1916-
Interviews conducted in 1991, 54 pp. and 51 pp.

Hamblet was a colonel in the Marine Corps Women's Reserve, 1943-46 and 1946-48, and in the Marine Corps, 1948-65. Hamblet's first interview covers her decision to join the MCWR; training in the first class of marine officer candidates at Mount Holyoke, MA, in February 1943; assignment to Hunter College, NY, as training adjutant; assignment to Camp Pendleton, CA, as executive officer of her company; assignment to Quantico, VA, on the general staff; assignment to Cherry Point, NC, as CO of a reserve group; discharge from service in April 1946 and move to London; and acceptance of the offer to head the postwar Marine Corps Women's Reserve. Permission required to quote. Interviewer: Eleanor Stoddard.

The second interview with Hamblet covers her role in organizing the postwar Marine Corps Women's Reserve; pursuit of a master's degree at The Ohio State University; her phaseout as Director of the MCWR in 1948 and assignment to Pearl Harbor, HI, in G-1 statistics; assignment as chief officer for women officer training at Quantico, VA; appointment as the second Director of Women Marines, 1953; assignment as military secretary to Commander in Chief, Allied Forces, Southern Europe, Naples, Italy,

1959; assignment to Parris Island, SC, as CO of training for women recruits, 1962; retirement in 1965; and career in U.S. Office of Education, 1965-78. Permission required to quote. Interviewer: Eleanor Stoddard.

Smith, Edna Loftus
Interview conducted in 1981, 63 pp.

Smith was a lieutenant colonel, USMC service, 1943-63. In this interview, she discusses her World War I service as a Navy yeoman, naval aviation in the 1920s and 1930s, her duty in the Bureau of Aeronautics during World War II, Marine Corps aviation personalities, MCWR training in World War II, and Robert Sherrod and the history of Marine Corps aviation in World War II. Open. Interviewer: Benis M. Frank.

Streeter, Ruth Cheney, 1895-1990
Interview conducted in 1979, 366 pp.

Cheney was a colonel, USMCR, USMC service, 1943-53. This indepth interview with Colonel Streeter, conducted for the Columbia University Oral History Program, deals with her life before, during, and after her tour as Director of the Marine Corps Women's Reserve (pp. 206-285). Colonel Streeter talks of the formation of the MCWR; her selection and duties as Director; MCWR personalities, events, and training; and assignments of the women reservists. Open. Interviewer: Dr. John T. Mason, Jr.

Towle, Katherine A., 1898-1986
Interview conducted in 1970, 309 pp.

Towle was a colonel, USMC service, 1943-46 and 1948-53. This interview, conducted with Colonel Towle for the Regional Oral History Office, University of California, Berkeley, covers mainly her association with that university until her retirement in 1965 as dean of students and vice chancellor for student affairs. This memoir also covers Colonel Towle's reminiscences of her two tours of Marine Corps duty. In 1943 she was commissioned directly from civilian life and assigned to key posts with the MCWR until 1946, when she returned to Berkeley. In 1948 she was recalled to active duty as the first Director of Women Marines, serving until 1953, when she returned to Berkeley with increased responsibilities. Permission required to cite or quote. Interviewer: Harriet S. Nathan.

4. Southeast

4.1 Women In Military Service For America Memorial Foundation, Inc. (WIMSA)
5510 Columbia Pike, Suite 302
Arlington, VA 22204

In addition to collecting, preserving, and displaying artifacts related to the experience of U.S. military women, WIMSA's mission is to become a source for academic research. Questionnaires have been sent to as many women veterans as possible, and already l00,000 women have responded and been registered. Using the master computer register, a researcher will be able to identify names of individuals, military units, and hometowns as well as to obtain considerable information on service records. The WIMSA collection also contains 40 oral history interviews of military women, with transcriptions, that were conducted by the Colonial Dames and donated to WIMSA.

4.2 George C. Marshall Foundation
Drawer 1600, VMI Parade
Lexington, VA 24450-1600

The foundation contains the papers of several women who served in the Women's Army Corps in World War II as well as considerable material in the Marshall Papers on the role played by General Marshall in the formation and subsequent history of the WAAC and the WAC. As a special program, the foundation offers scholarships to college seniors to do research and write papers based on material in its archives. Two of these papers relate to military women.

Personal Papers

The papers of and relating to World War II military women are as follows.

Bagbey, Lelia Cocke
Papers, 1942–45. 6 file folders.

Bagbey was a member of the WAAC and the WAC. She was trained at Fort Des Moines, IA, and subsequently became the recruiting officer at Fort Jackson, SC. She was later assigned to Camp Seibert, AL, and saw overseas duty in Brisbane, Australia, and in Manila, where she managed translators and interpreters assigned to question Japanese prisoners.

Brockenbrough, Rebecca L.
Papers and correspondence, 1942–45. 264 items and 1 box.

Brockenbrough was a member of the first WAAC officer candidate class at Fort Des Moines, IA. She subsequently served at Camp J. T. Robinson,

AR; Camp Conway, AR; and Fort Oglethorpe, GA. She was assigned to overseas duty in Salisbury, England, and in Paris and Fontainebleau, France.

Brockenbrough's papers include transcripts of two oral history interviews conducted by Eleanor Stoddard on February 26, 1987, and March 22, 1988, covering Brockenbrough's World War II experience.

See also Martha Averett, "The Women's Army Corps in Europe During World War II: The Service of Rebecca L. Brockenbrough," George C. Marshall Scholarship Program, April 1988.

McGee, Martha Rector
Papers, 1942–43. 2 file folders.

This member of the first officer candidate class at Fort Des Moines, IA, was later assigned to Little Rock, AR, on the WAAC recruiting staff. Her papers consist of letters, including one from Oveta Culp Hobby with signature; magazines; and news clippings.

Marshall, George C., 1880–1959
Papers, 1932–60. 115 feet.

In this large collection of papers and correspondence are many items covering General Marshall's role in the establishment and administration of the WAC and the formation of requisite policy.

Turner, Susanna P.
Papers, 1942–46. 1 box.

A member of the first officer candidate class at Fort Des Moines, IA, Turner was selected for command and general staff school and retired as a lieutenant colonel in the WAC in 1946. She taught enlisted women, served at the Pentagon in ordnance and the Signal Corps, and was then stationed overseas in London, Versailles, and Berlin; from there she returned to Pentagon duty. Later she was head of St. Catherine's School in Richmond, VA, and administered an Episcopal college in Liberia, West Africa. Most folders contain correspondence from Turner to her mother.

See also Cecilia Hook, "Creation and Perception of the Image of the WAC, 1942–44," George C. Marshall Scholarship Program, 1993.

Oral History Interview

Hobby, Oveta Culp
Transcript of interview conducted by Forrest C. Pogue, August 28, 1963.

This interview covers Hobby's experiences in testifying before Congress on the WAAC bill, being appointed Director of the WAAC, and working with General Marshall in setting policies for the WAAC and the WAC. Hobby also discusses the question of sending women to North Africa in 1943, uniforms, and her relationship with Eleanor Roosevelt.

4.3 National Association of Women Veterans, Inc.
P.O. Box 10114
Atlanta, GA 30319-0114

Evelyn M. Monahan and her associate Rosemary Greenlee have set up a foundation to house their collection of more than 1,000 oral history interviews of World War II military women, many conducted by telephone; 95,000 questionnaires; and 80,000 letters. Most of the interviews are 1½ hours long (some are longer; some are shorter). Only 15 have been transcribed. Monahan and Greenlee have also received uniforms, unit histories, and other forms of memorabilia. Monahan plans to write a book using this material and is seeking a suitable archive to preserve it once her book is finished.

4.4 The Women's Army Corps Museum
Fort McClellan
Anniston, AL 36205

The Women's Army Corps Museum presents the history of women in the Army from the inception of the WAAC/WAC in 1942 to the present. It contains extensive exhibits arranged in historical sequence, displaying uniforms, copies of key legislation, photographs and biographies of the 9 directors of the WAC as well as 6,000 artifacts, and a library of approximately 400 books relating to the WAC. There is also a research collection for use by serious scholars upon prior arrangement, as follows.

Historical Reference Files

Through the use of a card catalog, researchers can find copies of unit orders, policy papers, training programs, lesson plans, official documents, regulations, planning documents, statistics, and much more.

Personal Scrapbooks

More than 300 scrapbooks show life as it was in World War II. They contain photographs, personal notes, promotion orders, news clippings, views of the WAC by the hometown press, and activities at stations in the United States and overseas.

Other Printed Material

This is a miscellaneous collection of recruiting posters and papers, files of newspapers, pamphlets, magazines, military post papers, and works of art by and about Wacs.

Videotaped Interviews

Most of the nine WAC directors, including Oveta Culp Hobby, are included in these videotaped interviews. Many other WAC leaders are captured on tape. There are, however, no transcribed oral history interviews. Visitors to the museum may watch the video-taped interviews, which vary in length. The interview with Hobby runs for approximately 30 minutes.

4.5 Air Force Historical Research Agency
HQ AFHRA/SR
600 Chennault Circle
Maxwell Air Force Base, AL 36112-6424

As the repository for Air Force historical documents, the agency contains more than 60 million pages on the history of the service and accessions approximately 2 million pages of historical material each year. The collection is also recorded on 16mm microfilm. Most of the collection is open to the public. Aside from extensive use by the Air Force, the collection has been used by scholars; students; and writers of books and monographs, master's theses, doctoral dissertations, magazine articles, and television and movie scripts.

The collection at Maxwell Air Force Base is divided into two broad categories: (1) unit histories of Air Force organizations and (2) special collections consisting of monographs, oral history transcripts, end-of-tour reports, personal papers of Air Force personnel, reference materials on the early period of military aviation, command working documents, collections of various organizations (U.S. Army, British Air Ministry, German Air Force), and material relating to U.S. Air Force activities in wars in Southeast Asia and the Persian Gulf.

5. Middle West

5.1 Detroit Public Library
Burton Historical Collection
5201 Woodward Avenue
Detroit, MI 48202

The library's historical collection is open to the public. Patrons are encouraged to take extensive notes since there is no public photocopying facility available for manuscripts.

The Burton Historical Collection holds the following set of papers relating to World War II military women.

Moore, Anna Sherman
Papers. 6 boxes.

This Air-Wac entered service in December 1943 and served for 27 months. With a degree in library science, she had worked in the Detroit Public Library before the war and returned there after the war. Following basic training at Daytona Beach, FL, she served at Kessler Field, MS, for the duration of her service. The portion of her papers relating to World War II consists of a series of letters to her mother, Mrs. Sherman Moore, from December 1943 through March 1946 (boxes 1 and 2). The other boxes contain articles on Detroit history, research notes on Great Lakes steamships, and high school and college themes.

5.2 Bowling Green State University
Center for Archival Collections
Jerome Library, Fifth Floor
1001 East Wooster Street
Bowling Green, OH 43403

The Special Collections within the Bowling Green State University Archives contain well-organized material on three World War II military women. There are no restrictions on the use of these collections, which are as follows.

Klein, Mary Frances Goldmann
Papers, 1942–46. 3 linear feet (on microfilm).

Included in this collection are scrapbooks and files containing correspondence, official Army documents, brochures, news clippings, and photographs relating to Klein's service in the WAAC and the WAC. Starting as an enlistee, she soon became an officer and began recruiting. In August

1944 she was sent overseas, serving in England and occupied Germany. The material is described as "most valuable . . . as it pictures the war through the very observant and compassionate eyes of a woman in the service. . . . [It is] useful for its sensitive portrayal of the United States, England, France, and Germany during World War II." A 2-hour taped interview (not transcribed) with Klein is included in the collection.

Kronfield, Josephine Suter
Scrapbook, 1942–45.

This WAVES enlistee was trained as an aviation metal smith at the Naval Air Technical Training Center, Norman, OK. Her scrapbook contains news clippings and some excellent photographs.

Panning, Annie Turnbull, 1902–82
Papers. 6 boxes.

This collection contains a wealth of material on the WAC, 1943–49. Panning was called to active duty in February 1943, trained at Daytona Beach, FL, and became a cook. Stationed first at Kessler Field, MS, she was ordered overseas in May 1945 to France and later to Bremerhaven, Germany. In 1947 she returned to Fort Monmouth, NJ, and was discharged in March 1949. The first two boxes contain personal and military correspondence, scrapbooks, WAC newsletters, news clippings, and books. The last four boxes contain extensive photographs, mostly of events in wartime Europe.

5.3 The State Historical Society of Wisconsin
816 State Street
Madison, WI 53706-1488

The library of The State Historical Society of Wisconsin is the largest in the United States devoted to North American history. The library's holdings cover all aspects of the history of the United States and Canada; these include many doctoral dissertations and the second largest newspaper collection in the nation. The archives contain more than 39,000 cubic feet of manuscripts, among them some valuable holdings on U.S. military women, as follows.

Papers

Chapelle, Georgette Meyer, 1918–65
Dickey Chapelle Papers, 1933–67. 18 boxes. 5 tape recordings.

The papers of Georgette Meyer Chapelle, a photographer and writer, who was one of the first women foreign correspondents to cover World War II, the Korean and Vietnam wars, and other worldwide military struggles, are included in the Dickey Chapelle Papers. Georgette Chapelle's work was published in leading U.S. magazines. Her papers include biographical material, news clippings, photographs, personal correspondence, taped interviews, and drafts of two autobiographies. Chapelle's articles reported on 20 or more countries and areas, including her own 1955-57 imprisonment in Hungary.

Cooper, Signe Skott
Papers, 1943-46. 1.5 cubic feet.

The papers of this Army nurse concerning her World War II service and that of family members include her correspondence from Fort Belvoir, VA, and from India, 1944-45. Included are notes on other Wisconsin nurses, among them Ellen Gertrude Ainsworth, the only Wisconsin nurse killed in action. There is also correspondence of her brother, who served in Europe and the Philippines, and her father, a civilian employed by the Army to interview Germans.

Gates, Marcia L., 1915-70
Papers, 1942-45. 0.5 cubic feet.

Marcia Gates was an Army nurse who served on Bataan and Corregidor in World War II and was held by the Japanese in the Santo Tomas prison camp in Manila until 1945. Included are scrapbooks containing correspondence, photographs, clippings; a collection of internment camp newspapers (Internews); a travel diary; other memorabilia; and an obituary.

Sanders, Luida E., 1917-
Luida and Lewis Sanders Papers, 1941-52. 2 boxes.

These papers of a Wisconsin brother and sister, mostly relating to their Army service during World War II and the Korean war, include correspondence with family and friends and materials from Luida Sanders's service in the WAC—gossip sheets, diary, materials on duty, personal notes, and orders.

Records

Wisconsin Nurses Association, Districts 4 and 5
Records, 1906-85. 13 boxes.

The records of the Milwaukee area district nurses associations, until their merger with the Wisconsin Nurses Association in 1928 and later, include

documents on the mobilization of nurses for civilian and military duty in
World War II.

Oral History Interviews

The State Historical Society of Wisconsin undertook an oral history
project to capture the experiences of Wisconsin women on the
homefront and in the military in World War II. Interviewees were
from a broad cross section of racial and ethnic backgrounds and
rural and urban life. They worked both inside and outside the
home. All the interviews have been transcribed. Full abstracts with
biographical data are provided. Interviews conducted with 30 military women are as follows.

Marine Corps Women's Reserve (MCWR)

Allord, Lorraine (NCO)
Duff, Betty (enlisted)
Howards, Annette (enlisted)
McKinstry, Virginia L. (Kastner) (enlisted)
Murphy, Ernestine (NCO)

Army Nurse Corps (ANC)

Baehr, Elizabeth
Cooper, Signe Skott
Johnson, Elizabeth
Nix, Hazel
Rabideaux, Lucille
Romaine, Katherine

Navy Nurse Corps (NNC)

Lange, Mary K. (Air-Evac)

Women's Army Corps (WAC)

Collins, Martha (NCO)
Davenport, Judy (enlisted) (She and her mother were the first
    mother-daughter team to join the WAAC.)
Day, Gladys (enlisted)
Hargraves, Priscilla (enlisted)
Hendersin, Dolores (enlisted)
Pascale, Marge (enlisted)

Sanders, Luida (enlisted)
Sarenac, Milka (enlisted)
Schlosser, Geraldine (enlisted)
Schurch, Frieda (enlisted)
Siekert, Vera (enlisted) (Air-WAC)
Wilke, Juanita (officer)

Women Accepted for Volunteer Emergency Service (WAVES)

Boxill, Marjorie (enlisted) (transferred from SPAR to WAVES)
Keating, Dorothy (enlisted)
Kobishop, Mae (enlisted)
Washinawatok, Gwendolyn (enlisted)

Women Airforce Service Pilots (WASP)

Loufek, Julia
Mosher, Dorothy

5.4 University of Illinois at Urbana–Champaign
University Archives
19 Library
1408 West Gregory Drive
Urbana, IL 61801

During World War II there was a WAAC training program at the University of Illinois at Urbana for 1 year. The archives contain the following material relating to that program.

Pease, Theodore Calvin, 1887–1948
Papers, 1915–44. 3 linear feet.

Among the papers of this history professor are reports and correspondence relating to history courses for Waacs.

5.5 Grout Museum of History
503 South Street
Waterloo, IA 50701

In 1994 this museum conducted 22 oral history interviews on videotape with Iowa men and women, focusing on their World War II experiences, both in the military and on the homefront.

Two of these women were with the WAVES. The tapes have not been transcribed but are available for viewing at the museum.

5.6 The University of Iowa Libraries
Iowa Women's Archives
Iowa City, IA 52242

At present, the Iowa Women's Archives of The University of Iowa Libraries has just one collection on military women of the World War II period. The staff are interested in collecting more such papers and encourage donors to get in touch with them. The current very complete and well-organized holding is this one:

Lichty, Marion Cox, 1915–
Papers, 1942–89. 2 boxes.

Lichty was a member of the first WAAC officer class at Fort Des Moines, IA. By 1951 she had been promoted to lieutenant colonel. Her career with the WAC lasted until 1946, during which period she served in personnel, training, and recruitment assignments, part of the time in the Air Service Command at Paterson Field, OH. In 1948 she applied for and received an appointment in the U.S. Air Force Reserve. In 1950 she was assigned to Washington headquarters, then transferred to the Strategic Air Command (SAC) in Omaha, NE, in 1955. She retired from active duty in 1965 and became a member of the Retired Reserve. Her papers include a considerable number of military documents, useful for background.

5.7 University of Missouri-Columbia
Western Historical Manuscript Collection
23 Ellis Library
Columbia, MO 65201

This collection comprises the manuscript holdings of both the University of Missouri and the State Historical Society of Missouri. The holdings are wide ranging and eclectic and include more than 13,000 linear feet of paper records, more than 7,000 rolls of microfilm, and approximately 4,800 audiocassettes and videocassettes, tapes, films, and recordings. The only collection of significant material relating to women in the military is the following.

World War II Letters, 1940–46
3,467 folders.
Collection number 68.

The collection is made up of correspondence from U.S. military men and women to friends and relatives all over the country, mostly to people in Missouri. Approximately 75 of the letters were written by Wacs, Waves, Spars, and Army and Navy nurses. Most of the letters were sent from overseas—from Europe, the Philippines, New Guinea, or other Pacific areas. Most of the letters stand alone with no other correspondence from the same individual.

5.8 Harry S. Truman Library
U.S. Highway 24 and Delaware Street
Independence, MO 64050-1798

The library is part of the National Archives and Records Administration and is listed here for reference; a description of its holdings relating to military women is in the next section of the volume.

5.9 State Historical Society of North Dakota
North Dakota Heritage Center
612 East Boulevard Avenue
Bismarck, ND 58505

Block, Irma A.
Papers, 1937–68. 7 folders.

This member of the Army Nurse Corps was on duty at Schofield Barracks Army Hospital the morning of the Japanese attack on Pearl Harbor. Her collection consists almost entirely of 150 photographs relating to her Army and postwar careers.

U.S. Navy Enlisted Waves of North Dakota
Scrapbook.

This scrapbook of newspaper clippings details the enlistment and activities of more than 65 North Dakota and Minnesota women who joined the WAVES in World War II.

5.10 Dwight D. Eisenhower Library
200 Southeast Fourth Street
Abilene, KS 67410

The library is part of the National Archives and Records Administration and is listed here for reference; a description of its holdings relating to military women is in the next section of the volume.

5.11 The Ninety-Nines, Inc.
Library and Archives
Amelia Earhart Lane and East Terminal Drive
P.O. Box 59965
Will Rogers World Airport
Oklahoma City, OK 73159

The Ninety-Nines is an organization of international women pilots, established by Amelia Earhart in 1929. Their records and other materials are gathered in the Women in Aviation Resource Center at the Will Rogers World Airport. The center includes historical material from early in the 20th century on women in aviation. In its collection are considerable data on individual members of the WASP, including separate interviews on videotape (not transcribed).

6. Southwest

6.1 Texas Woman's University
Blagg-Huey Library
P.O. Box 23715
Denton, TX 76204-1715

The Blagg-Huey Library at Texas Woman's University began collecting the biographies of great women in 1932. Since then, this collection has grown to 42,000 books, 2,500 cubic feet of manuscript collections, 19,000 photographs, and a woman's periodical collection. Much of the material is on microform.

The library holds a remarkable WASP Collection, 1942–45, as well as a few manuscript collections of women in other World War II services. The WASP Collection documents 67 women who served as Women Airforce Service Pilots (WASP) and 3 who served with the Women's Auxiliary Ferrying Squadron (WAFS). Many collections have been donated very recently, and some of them are fragmentary. The following list comprises the more extensive holdings.

Records of Wasps

Christian, Jeanne Richey (WASP class 43-W-4)
WASP records. 3 cubic feet.

This collection contains WASP veterans association material.

Kelley, Lillian Ruth "Dixie," d. 1975 (WASP class 44-W-9)
Records. 1 cubic foot.

Nicol, Marjorie (WASP class 44-W-9)
Letters and records, 1944-. 5 folders.

Nicol's letters describe her training experiences. Her records include *A Handbook for Women Student Pilot Trainees* (1944) and a journal with details of a WASP trip to Russia in 1990 to visit Russian women pilots.

Richards, Faith Buchner (WASP class 43-W-4)
Records. 1 cubic foot.

WASP Reports
Looseleaf notebooks and photocopies.

This collection includes base histories, medical considerations, training memorandums, a WASP handbook, a history of the Air Transport Command, and other reports.

Watson, Margaret Harper (WASP class 44-W-1)
Records. 5 folders.

Women Airforce Service Pilots
Records, 1943-45. 25 cubic feet.

These records include correspondence, president's papers, photographs, news clippings, and subject and biographical files pertaining to the veterans' organization and the experiences of women who served as Wasps.

Personal Papers of Wasps

Bennett, Madeleine Allaire (WASP class 43-W-7)
Collection. 0.5 cubic feet.

Bennett's collection comprises biographical material, correspondence, papers, photographs and artifacts. Bennett received the DAR Medal of Honor in 1994.

Bosca, Caro Bayley (WASP class 43-W-7)
Correspondence, 1943-44. 8 folders.

Dalrymple, Mildred (WASP class 44-W-4)
Memoirs and memorabilia. 0.5 cubic feet.

Deaton, Leoti (WASP chief establishment officer)
Papers, 1976–86. 1 cubic foot.

Ebersbach, Dorothy Ellen, 1914– (WASP, class 43-W-5)
Papers and photographs. 7 folders.

Edwards, Mary Catherine Quist (WASP class 44-W-7)
Letters, 1943–44. 3 folders.

Granger, Byrd Howell (WASP)
Papers. 9.5 linear feet.

A writer, educator, and aviator, Granger was also an archivist for the WASP. She collected many vital records and photographs and left research notes for her book, *On Final Approach: The Women Airforce Service Pilots of W.W.II.* (Scottsdale, AZ: Falconer Publishing Co., 1991).

Gray, Marjorie (WASP class 43-W-1)
Papers, 1936–90. 3.5 cubic feet.

Hixson, Jean F. (WASP class 44-W-6)
Papers and photograph album. 1.5 cubic feet.

Hodgson, Marion Stegeman (WASP class 43-W-5)
Papers, 1943–. 3 cubic feet.

Hunter, Ziggy, 1912-1990
Papers and research materials. 21 cubic feet.

Hunter was a journalist, pilot, and WASP flight instructor. The collection includes research files and material pertaining to the efforts of Hunter and Jewel Estes to locate former Wasps. It also holds Hunter's research files compiled for her unpublished historical novel about Wasps (no manuscript on file) and interviews on tape relating to her novel.

Knight, Florence, 1919–93 (WASP class 43-W-3)
Papers, 1943–50. 4 folders.

Knight's papers include official correspondence, her pilot's log book, news clippings, and a copy of Jacqueline Cochran's "Final Report on Women's Pilot Program."

Loop, Paula, 1916–44 (WASP class 43-W-2)
Papers.

Loop died in a military plane crash, July 7, 1944. Her papers include postcards, letters, photograph album, and Air Force records.

Luts, Helen Jane Trigg (WASP class 43-W-8)
Papers, 1943–86. 1 cubic foot.

McCormick, Jill, 1916– (WASP class 43-W-5)
Papers. 1 cubic foot.

Nielson, Laurine Y. (WASP class 43-W-3)
Papers, 1943–86. 1 cubic foot.

Severson, Helen Jo Anderson, 1918-1943 (WASP class 43-W-5)
Photographs and papers. 6 folders.

Severson died in a plane crash just before graduation. This collection includes biographical information, letters, documents, photographs, and news clippings.

Simpson, Janet Hutchinson (WASP class 44-W-6)
Papers. 18 folders.

Steele, Katherine Landry (WASP class 44-W-7)
Papers, 1930s–90s. 2 cubic feet.

Strother, Dora Dougherty (WASP class 43-W-3)
Papers. 4.5 cubic feet.

Weatherby, Marvine (WASP class 44-W-4)
Letters, 1943–44. 1 folder (photocopies)

Wise, Lucille Doll (WASP class 43-W-7)
Papers. 0.5 cubic feet.

Wyall, Mary Ann Martin (WASP class 44-W-10)
Papers and scrapbook. 1.5 cubic feet.

Smaller collections of Wasps' memorabilia

Alexander, Marion Cleveland (class 44-W-5)
Boxberger, Lena Seetin Cusack (class 43-W-6)
Burri, Dorothy Johnson
Carmichael, Mickie (class 44-W-4)
Champlin, Jane Dolores (1917–43) (class W-4) (died in training)
D'Hooghe, Solange (class 43-W-5)
Estes, Jewel (class 44-W-10)
Fenton, Isabel Stinson
Folk, Eleanor Bryant (class 43-W-7)
Gery, Ellen H. (class 43-W-2)
Gorman, Gretchen J. (class 43-W-3)
Hailey, Lois Brooks (class 43-W-3)
Haydu, Bernice (class 44-W-7)
Hayes, Hazel
Head, Alberta
Jenks, Joan Trebtoske (class 43-W-4)
Jones, Winnie Lee (1919–46) (class 44-W-7)
Marsh, Clara Jo Stember (class 44-W-3)
Minton, Madge Rutherford (class 43-W-4)
Nelson, Esther L.
Rountree, Martha Harmon (class 44-W-5)
Schwager, Gloria DeVore (class 44-W-3)
Tanner, Doris B. (class 44-W-4)
Thompson, Marjorie Sanford (class 43-W-5)
Wardle, Sarabel D. Booth, "Sue" (class 44-W-6)
Werber, Margaret M. (class 44-W-10)
Wise, Lucille Doll (class 43-W-7)
Wood, Betty Taylor (class 43-W-4)
Yonally, Lillian Lorraine (class 43-W-7)
Zerlaut, Jacqueline Riley (class 44-W-10)
Ziler, Lois Hollingsworth

Papers and Records of Wafs

The Blagg-Huey Library holds the collections of three members of
the Women's Auxiliary Ferrying Squadron (WAFS), as follows.

Love, Nancy
Collection. 0.5 cubic feet
Collection. 1 folder.

These two collections contain a limited amount of material on Love, who organized and directed the WAFS and later was director of women pilots in the Air Transport Command in World War II. The first collection is primarily photographs, and the second includes papers and photographs.

Nelson, Esther L.
Scrapbook and pilot record.

Sharp, Evelyn
Photograph and biographical profile (copy).

One of the original Wafs, Sharp was killed in 1944 in a P-38 plane crash.

Papers and Records of Other Military Women

Andrews, Ela Beth
Photographs and records. 0.5 cubic feet.

This collection consists of memorabilia. Andrews was 1 of 51 dietitians selected to serve in the Army in World War II. She died in 1990.

Carter, Edith M. Loughlin
Papers, 1942-46. 1 foot, 9 inches.

Personal effects and personal papers document Carter's career as a Wac in World War II.

Dobbs, Vivian Lynn
Papers, 1943-45. 9 folders.

Material from the World War II experience of Vivian Dobbs, a Marine Corps Women's Reserve enlistee, includes her letters home, news clippings, songs, and photographs.

Pilkey, Rita
Papers, 1943-45. 1 foot.

These photographs, letters home, and news clippings relate to Pilkey's 2-year stint in World War II as club director for American Red Cross service clubs on American bases in China.

Russell, Phyllis Tyre
Records, 1949-50. 1 folder.

Russell's records consist of her memorabilia as a member of the Marine Corps Women's Reserve in World War II.

Publications

Among the publications in the library (also available at Maxwell Air Force Base in Alabama) are the following.

Cochran, Jacqueline, with Floyd Odlum as Wingman. *The Stars at Noon.* Boston: Little, Brown, 1954.

Cochran, Jacqueline. *Jackie Cochran: An Autobiography.* Toronto and New York: Bantam Books, 1987.

Oral History Interviews

Women's Collection staff members have conducted oral history interviews with a number of Wasps and other World War II military women. Interviews last from 1 to 6 hours. Those conducted to date, not all of them transcribed, are as follows.

Wasps

Chaffey, Kay Gott
D'Hooghe, Solange
Deaton, Leoti
Fender, Grace Clark
Garrett, Penelope Peirce
Hailey, Lois Brooks
Haydu, Bernice
Johnson, Nancy
Lewis, Dorothy Swain
Richards, Faith Buchner
Ringenberg, Margaret
Seymour, Dawn
Steele, Kaddy Landry
Strother, Dora Dougherty
Thompson, Marjorie Sanford
Wyall, Marty
Young, Millicent Peterson
Ziler, Lois Hollingsworth

Note: The library also holds the transcript of an interview with Jacqueline Cochran conducted by Kenneth Leish in 1960: "The Reminiscences of Jacqueline Cochran" (New York: Oral History Research Office, Columbia University, 1975) (microfiche).

Wafs

Watson, Florence Miller

Wacs

Carter, Edith Loughlin

6.2 Stephen F. Austin State University
East Texas Research Center
Steen Library
P.O. Box 13055, SFA Station
Nacogdoches, TX 75962-3055

The East Texas Research Center contains several relevant collections, including material on the Army Administration School located on the Stephen F. Austin campus during World War II. The following collections are available.

Army Administration School, Nacogdoches, TX
Women's Army Corps, Branch No. 1
2 scrapbooks, 1943–44.

These two large scrapbooks contain newspaper clippings, photographs, graduation programs, news of school events, and human interest stories about the Wacs. The school, the first of its kind in the United States, was established in February 1943 to train Wacs for administrative jobs in the Army. The college provided quarters, classrooms, and offices. Army officers and WAC officers served as instructors and directors. Twelve classes, more than 2,000 women, graduated from the school. At graduation, each class presented a program for the public; titles included "Two Knights in a Day Room," "Why I Joined the WAAC," "WAC's a' Poppin'," and "WAC Tracks." The local WAC branch also published a newspaper called *Tag Echo*.

Bezanson, Marguerite Crouse, 1909–
Papers, 1943–45. 1 box.

This WAAC officer was ordered to active duty in January 1943 as an instructor at the Army Adminstration School at the university. She later became a personnel officer, public relations officer, special services officer, and assistant adjutant. In January 1944 she was made commander of the headquarters company and ended her service as a captain. Her collection consists chiefly of special orders relating to her service career. It also contains an untranscribed oral history interview.

Swank Family
Papers, 1942–45. 1 box.

This collection contains materials relating to the Marine Corps careers of Harry Swank and Mary Foster Swank during World War II. In March 1943 Mary Foster joined the Marine Corps Women's Reserve. She went through basic training at Hunter College in New York City and was stationed in Washington, DC, North Carolina, and California. She was one of four women reservists who were receptionists to the American delegation at the U.N. conference in San Francisco in 1945. Her collection includes general items, such as news bulletins and a Bible issued to service personnel.

Oral History Interview

Pollard, Clarice Fortgang, 1918–
Transcript of oral history interview, 34 pp.

Pollard discusses basic training as a Waac, training at the Army Administration School in Nacogdoches, her impressions of life in a small town, a WAAC variety show, and her feelings upon returning 40 years later.

Photographs

The archives hold 48 photographs directly relating to Wacs at Stephen F. Austin State University.

7.   West Coast[4]

7.1 University of Washington Libraries
Manuscripts and University Archives Division FM-25
Seattle, WA 98195

The University of Washington Archives has received the memorabilia of a few military women of the World War II era. The collections are the following.

Market, Hazel
Papers and photographs.

A member of the WAVES in charge of network radio for the WAVES during the war.

Miller, Mary A.
Letters, 1942–45.

These letters were from a member of the Army Nurse Corps in Great Britain.

Moran, Mary Adelaide
Papers, 1942–51. 2.5 inches.

Mary Moran was a member of the first officer candidate class at Fort Des Moines, IA, in July 1942. She became an officer over enlisted women in various posts. Her papers contain letters, military orders, photographs, clippings, and memorabilia.

7.2 Judah Magnes Museum
2911 Russell Street
Berkeley, CA 94705

The museum has conducted and transcribed oral history interviews with three Jewish women veterans of World War II. Further details on these interviews and other memorabilia in the museum's collections were not provided.

7.3 Hoover Institution on War, Revolution, and Peace
ATA Archive
Stanford University
Stanford, CA 94305

Jane Plant Spencer was one of the Air Transport Auxiliary (ATA) pilots who flew all types of military aircraft for the British in World War II, and she is involved in the ATA History Project. A study in Britain of the ATA by Paula Roberts discusses the women who made up roughly 10 percent of the ATA pilots. The Roberts study, along with various books, articles, and other memorabilia, is in the Hoover Institution's ATA collection. Spencer has been seeking funds for oral history interviews with the remaining women to add to the collection.

7.4 California State University, Long Beach
Library Archives
1250 Bellflower Boulevard
Long Beach, CA 90840

The university's Oral History Program has developed a number of collections, including significant ones on women in the military and on the homefront in World War II. The oral history collections are part of the university archives and can be used by researchers who make personal visits. Tapes and transcripts of oral history interviews of the following military women are available.

Women's Army Corps (WAC)

Bickelhaupt, Barbara (enlisted)
Brockenbrough, Rebecca (officer)
Campbell, Joan Malkenson (enlisted)
Corbin, Mildred (enlisted)
Jackson, Margaret Young (enlisted)
Jagger, Georgiana Norsk (enlisted and officer)
Jeffrey, Helen Smolich (NCO)
Lewis, Lorraine (NCO)
McCutcheon, Evelyn Krouse (NCO)
Sachs, Martha Schuchart (officer)
St. Peter, Virginia (enlisted and officer)
Steinberg, Florence Fink (enlisted)
White, Sylvia Marsili (officer)

Women Accepted for Volunteer Emergency Service (WAVES)

Dietz, Loretta Marilley (enlisted)
Dougherty, Margaret (officer)
Echols, Gladys Marsheck (enlisted)
Hayford, Margaret Randall (enlisted and officer)
Nessler, Elsa Stamm (enlisted and officer)
Pearson, Vera Maxine (enlisted)
Peets, Elizabeth (enlisted) (later WAC officer)
Taft, Frances Prindle (officer)
Updegraff, Margery (officer)
Wolensky, Irene (officer)

Marine Corps Women's Reserve (MCWR)

Gridley, Lily Hutcheon (officer)

Hale, Mary Janice (officer)
Hamblet, Julia Estelle (officer)
Leon, Florence Pratt (NCO)
Winton, Jean Carpenter (enlisted and officer) (in process)

Army Nurse Corps (ANC)

Aron, Katherine
Forrest, Nola
Moore, Flora
Myers, Eleanor June
Rosenbaum, Ruth Rabkin

Navy Nurse Corps (NNC)

Brauninger, Amy Mulford
Mattie, Zena

American Red Cross (ARC)

Vetter, Elisabeth
Wyper, Margaret Verhoeff

The interviews with the 37 women listed above were conducted by Eleanor Stoddard as part of an independent study project during the 1985–94 period.

The Homefront

The Calfornia State University, Long Beach, oral history archives also contain 42 bound transcripts of interviews with women who worked in the California shipyards and aircraft factories during World War II. The original tapes plus a few additional untranscribed interviews are with this group. See the book based on these interviews: Sherna Berger Gluck, *Rosie the Riveter Revisited: Women, the War, and Social Change* (Boston: Twayne Publishers, 1987).

NOTES

© 1996 by Eleanor Stoddard

1. South Kingston High School Library
   South Kingston, RI 02879
   Contact: Linda P. Wood

   In the 1980s, students in the Honors English Program at the South Kingston High School conducted oral history interviews with Rhode Island women who had experienced World War II in the military and on the homefront. The students produced a book from tapes and transcripts, presenting the testimony of 29 narrators from a number of perspectives, entitled *What Did You Do in the War, Grandma?* (1989). The library is open only during the school year and on school days.

2. Martha Schultz
   582 Third Avenue
   Troy, NY 12182

   Martha Schultz, a high school teacher, started conducting oral history interviews of military women in connection with her teaching program. By 1995, she had conducted interviews with 43 women—8 from World War I and 35 from World War II. Her collection includes tapes of interviews with Wacs, Waves, one or two marines, two Spars, a few Wasps, some Army and Navy nurses, and one employee of the United Nations Relief and Rehabilitation Administration (UNRRA). Schultz's tapes have not been transcribed. After she has written a few articles, Schultz will donate her tapes to the University of Southern California archives.

3. Dr. Janet Sims-Wood
   Moorland-Spingarn Research Center
   Howard University
   Washington, DC 20059

   Dr. Sims-Wood conducted oral history interviews with four African-American women who had been members of the Women's Army Corps in World War II. These interviews were part of a study of the whole life experience of each of these women, including her life as it unfolded after the war. This research was undertaken for Dr. Sims-Wood's doctoral dissertation, entitled "We Served America Too!" She plans to put her tapes in an archive, as yet unselected.

4. Osborne Publisher, Inc.
   2464 El Camino Real, Suite 99
   Santa Clara, CA 95051
   Contact: Carol L. Osborne

   Carol Osborne and her associate Bobbi Troutt, pioneer female pilot, have been collecting information on aviation history for years. Most of their work consists of videotaping men and women pilots; 250 such interviews have been accomplished to date. Osborne has also published two books on aviation history, one of which was a biography of Amelia Earhart coauthored by Osborne and the famous flier's sister, Muriel Earhart Morrissey. Osborne has conducted interviews with former Wasps, but World War II was not the focus. She is producing a CD-ROM on women in aviation for educational and other purposes.

MUSEUMS, FILM AND GRAPHIC ARCHIVES, AND EDUCATIONAL RESOURCES

Clare M. Cronin

Although archives and libraries are the most obvious places to find documents related to women in the military, there are other sources—such as museums, film and graphic archives, and educational resources—that should not be missed. Together they hold the wide variety of documents produced during World War II, including letters, diaries, scrapbooks, objects, photographs, films, sound recordings, maps, and official government records.

In this paper I wish to address two groups of people: those who would like to contribute objects, papers and photographs, or time to museums or archives; and those who are planning to use these special resources to do research on American military women in World War II.

CONTRIBUTING TO MUSEUMS AND ARCHIVES: DONATIONS, LOANS, AND VOLUNTEERING

Donations

Why donate? Maybe you are moving to a smaller apartment and do not have room to keep all your old wartime souvenirs, photographs, or papers. Maybe you have no family to pass things along to. Or maybe you want to make sure that the story of the work that you and your friends did is remembered. Many people decide to give their possessions to a museum or offer their documents to an archive. If this sounds as though it is something you would like to do, wonderful!

Before you make a donation, first find out if the institution wants the items you have. Do not just pack a box and send it off. Nearly all archives have a "collections policy," a long-term plan and procedure for what the staff will collect and care for. Museums also have collections policies as well as "collections plans." These are even more specific as to what types of objects will be collected and are based on considerations of space as well as on what types of items already exist in the collection. A museum's collections *policy* may state, for example, that military vehicles will be collected; the collections *plan* would specify that only pre-Korean war vehicles will be added to the collection. If your offer is not part of their plan, they may not be able to accept the object, and that particular repository may not be the best place for your donation. If you offer your dress uniform to a museum and find that it turns the offer down, do not be offended. The museum may already have 12 other uniforms exactly like yours. Ask the staff if they can recommend other institutions that might be interested in or looking for a dress uniform. And do not think just in terms of uniforms. The museum may be thrilled to have your souvenirs or insignia. Personal items, diaries, letters, scrapbooks, fatigues, bathing suits, and even makeup, stockings, and underwear might be welcomed by a museum or archive trying to build its collection on women in the military. Shop around!

Investigate the institution to which you might make a donation. Try to visit it. Find out what types of exhibitions and holdings it has, how long it has been open to the public, and what kind of financial support it has. Ask about storage facilities and staff. Who is on the board of directors? After determining what the museum, archive, or historical society collects, decide if some of your things might best be given to one place and other items to another. Find out who gets to see or use the collections and how many researchers come during an average year. Inquire when your donation will be available for research and what collection it will become part of. Visit the research room if possible, and ask for a guide to the holdings to see what else is in the collection.

Donors who do not do their homework run the risk of being taken advantage of by people who solicit items for a "museum" but then sell the objects to dealers for the money. Or they may select a museum without a solid financial footing that eventually folds and loses its holdings though auction to private collectors.

If you are giving a large collection, you may need to make provisions for a bequest or financial gift to accompany the collection simply to accommodate the museum whose budget is so tight that it can not afford to process incoming gifts or arrange for increased

This woman Marine is one of many military women working as parachute riggers, Cherry Point, NC, November 1943.

National Archives, Records of the U.S. Marine Corps (127-GN-6126)

storage space. Ask about this in advance. Perhaps you can arrange with your friends or your veterans' organization to start a fund-raising drive. Do not let such financing scare you off; the problem does not apply to all museums and certainly not to most donations.

One of the things to ask yourself is whether you have clear title to the potential donation. If you want to give your uniform to a museum, but you have already given the jacket to your daughter, your daughter may be able to legally prevent the donation of the jacket on the grounds that it was given to her. And if you have been involved in a divorce and want to give your husband's old field jacket away, you may not legally be able to do so without his consent. These issues do not usually create a problem, but every now and then questions of ownership do arise.

When making a donation to a museum or archive, you will need to be familiar with a few terms that will come up. I want to explain these very briefly.

Deed of Gift

A deed of gift is a legal agreement drawn up between you and the institution that lays out the terms for the gift of your object or papers. If there are restrictions (such as requirements for care, display, or disposal), tax valuations, or questions of credit, they should all be spelled out in the deed of gift. In short, if you feel very strongly about something, GET IT IN WRITING! And keep a copy of it.

Valuation for Tax Deductions

Donations to nonprofit organizations, such as museums or archives, are usually tax deductible. You will want to put a valuation on the objects you are giving. Valuations are 1) the cost of the object, 2) the cost plus a percentage of the appreciation in value, or, most often, 3) the current fair market value. You can consult sales and auction catalogs for similar objects or documents to determine an appropriate value. You should also do this for determining insurance value if you are making a loan. You could try asking dealers for valuations, as well, because military memorabilia are very collectible nowadays; many dealers will give you a value, however, expecting to purchase the objects from you. The American Society of Appraisers, a national association, can put you in contact with certified appraisers.

Standards of Care

Make sure that the institution to which you are giving has facilities for storage and can regulate light, temperature, and humidity. Ask about its preservation program. Does it have a conservator on the staff, or does it contract out this type of work? Who monitors the storage conditions and the objects for signs of deterioration, and what type of training has that person had? For loans, these questions are especially important, particularly for fragile objects such as textiles (uniforms) and documents (letters, diaries, scrapbooks, film, and photographs).

Permanent Exhibition

Do not expect that objects you give to a museum or historical society will be on permanent display. Good museums will not guarantee this. Fragile objects on display, such as photographs or textiles, should be rotated at least once a year to ensure that objects are not damaged from exposure to light, humidity, or stress of mounting. Just because an object is not on exhibition, however, does not mean that no one will ever see it or appreciate it. Researchers often examine these collections, and objects are loaned to other museums for their displays.

Keeping Collections Together

Many museums will no longer guarantee that your collection of objects will be kept together, although they usually try to be as obliging as possible. One object may deteriorate to the point that it can no longer be kept. Certainly do not expect that everything will always be exhibited together; sometimes this is not feasible. If you have a uniform and personal effects you used as a nurse in the Pacific and the museum decides to do an exhibit on women's military footwear, obviously it would only wish to display your shoes. Again, try to be flexible.

Disposal

In recent years, some museums have found it necessary to dispose of their collections for various reasons. Art museums, for example, sometimes auction off their artworks. The museum community usually requires that funds from these sales be used to purchase other artworks, but as revealed by a few well-publicized legal cases, several art museums are using the funds to add to their endowments; this angers the heirs of the original donors who believe that the art should remain in a public venue rather than be auctioned into private hands. Such sales have not happened so much with history museums, archives, or historical societies, but there is potential for concern. It is more common for history museums to try to arrange trades with other museums or, very rarely, with dealers to obtain other objects of like value. Funds from objects that are sold are used to purchase other objects or to ensure the care of the rest of the collection. If you have strong feelings about how your donation should be disposed of in the event that that question arises (and it does not arise very often or very lightly), make sure your concerns are covered in the deed of gift. But again, be flexible. Disposal is a very serious question that is undertaken only after long, thoughtful discussions among the curatorial staff and oftentimes among the director and the board of trustees, as well.

Copyright and Right of Reproduction

If you are giving letters, papers, photographs, films, or personal objects, make sure to let the museum know whether you are also transferring the rights to copy, reproduce, or photograph the items. With respect to objects, film, photographs, letters, diaries, or manuscripts, there are two property rights involved in a donation: 1) transferring ownership of the physical item itself, and 2) transferring ownership of the intellectual content of the material you made, wrote, or produced yourself. This second property right involves copyright, the right to authorize others to reproduce or use your creation. Particularly with archival material, which researchers may later wish to reproduce in publications, make sure that the transfer or retention of these rights is in writing to avoid any confusion. Most museums and archives prefer unrestricted gifts and the transfer of copyrights to allow the fullest unhampered use of their holdings. If you wish to place a restriction or retain copyright, be flexible and give your reasons: you think that the film or diary is so important that someone will be willing to pay for the right to reproduce or use the material in a television documentary or for a film script, and you want your grandchildren to get the money. If your donation does not realistically fall into this category, transfer copyright as well as physical ownership to allow the freest use of the material by others.

Finally, if you are giving your possessions, be prepared to give a little of yourself. Even if you are not asked, write or record details of your service. You may want to give facsimiles of your military records if you have them. Tell about your training. What did it entail? Where did you receive it? Whom did you train with, and who trained you? Record the type of work you did. You may think that all you did was work at a typewriter. Well, what kinds of things did you type? Whom did you work for? How long did you work each day? And where were you? What were your responsibilities? Who were your friends? What did you do while off duty? What type of religious or social activities did you pursue? What did your family think of your military service? What did you do after your service? A museum may have 12 dress uniforms, but a uniform connected to a real person and having a documented history behind it means a lot more and allows the staff to display the object more effectively, with fuller, more personal captions and labels. If you have trouble writing things down, see if a friend or family member can help you. You may even want to speak into a tape recorder if you find it difficult to write. Your history will not only be of interest as a record to go with the uniform, but it may also be a source of interest in and of itself to researchers and archivists.

Loans

If you do not want to give your possessions away, you may want to let museums know that you would be willing to loan them for short-term exhibitions or to allow an archive to borrow them so the staff can make copies of them. Today with excellent color copies possible, you might consider keeping the copy and donating the original material or vice versa. In the museum field, "short-term" can mean anything from 6 months to 10 years! Here are a few things to know about loans.

Permanent Loans

In the past, some museums accepted what they called "permanent loans," loans of objects for display for an indefinite length of time with the unwritten understanding that the object would be given to the museum upon the lender's death. Good museums do not do this anymore for a variety of reasons. There have been cases in which a parent died, and the children took the object from the museum and sold it to a dealer. If you want your heirs to have something, let them have it. If you intend that a museum should have something of yours after your death, PUT IT IN WRITING! Or give it to the museum now. It is really not fair to expect museums to spend time and money caring for your objects and then, in the end, not to bequeath these objects to the museums. Set a closing date on any loan, a date by which the object is to be returned to you. This will save lots of headaches and possible misunderstandings.

Chief Petty Officer Cy Rhodell Angell, USNR, one of the first four women to qualify for this rank, proudly wears her new insignia as she goes about her duties in the office of the Commander in Chief, U.S. Fleet. Photograph released June 2, 1944.

National Archives, General Records of the Department of the Navy, 1798-1947 (80-G-45657)

Custody Receipt

If you send an object to a museum for any reason, make sure you get a custody receipt. This is simply a document stating your name and address, the fact that the museum currently has your object, the intended uses for the object, when the museum received it, and, usually, when the object will be returned.

Loan Agreement

If you are asked to loan an object to a museum, you should be given a loan agreement. This is a legal contract between the museum and the lender. It discusses who is in charge of insuring the object, how the object will be transported and who will pay for transport, if photography of the object is permitted, if photographs may be published, what credit the lender will have on exhibition labels and in brochures and catalogs, and most important, when the object will be returned! If an object is very fragile, you may want to impose restrictions on how it will be displayed (i.e., under glass, with low lighting, or for only a certain period of time).

Special Considerations

Insuring the Object

Most museums will take on the responsibility for insuring the object according to the lender's valuation. You may say, "oh, it's only an old mess kit; it isn't worth much." Well, if nothing else, it has sentimental value. And military memorabilia, such as insignia, equipment, and uniforms, are valued by collectors. Put some sort of a price value on it, even if it is only a few dollars. Find out if your personal property insurance covers the objects when lent to a museum. Think in terms of theft or damage caused by mishandling, fire, or flood. You can waive insurance by putting it in writing.

Transporting the Object

Transportation is usually arranged and paid for by the museum that is borrowing your objects. There are moving and shipping companies that work specifically with museum objects; most museums use one of these. If you have only letters, documents, or small items, the museum or archive may ask you to send them by registered or express mail.

Photography Permission

If a museum wants a record of an exhibition in which your objects appear or wants to produce a catalog to go along with the exhibition, it will need to ask your permission to take photographs of your objects. Use your judgment. If an object is very faded and fragile, you may permit it to be photographed for the catalog but not while exhibited. You may not want it to be photographed at all. Whatever you decide, make sure it is in writing!

Credit Lines

These lines of identification are simply the information used on labels or in catalogs to show that the object belongs to you. Most museums require that they be credited when they loan an object.

There is no reason why you, too, should not be acknowledged. The style is up to you. You can use nicknames, if you prefer, or a title. Some people like to include their state and town, although most prefer just their name. Ask the museum if there is any particular formula or style it uses. Also, you may want to require that a copy of the exhibition brochure or catalog be sent to you so that you will have a record of where your possessions have been displayed.

Contact Information

Make sure that the museum has an address and telephone number where its staff can contact you! If you have a summer home in Florida, but your permanent residence is in Oregon, make sure that the museum has both addresses. If you move, make sure you send a change of address, and call to make sure the museum has received it. I know this seems obvious, but too often people forget to notify the museum, and when museum representatives try to return objects to a lender or call with a question, they have no idea where to look. If you are going on vacation for an extended period of time and a daughter or neighbor is looking after your property while you are gone, tell the museum IN WRITING the name and address of the person looking after things for you and what authority that person has to make decisions affecting your objects. That way, if questions or problems come up, the caretaker can either resolve them or inform you to contact the museum.

Volunteering

As a final note, if there is a museum, archive, or historical society near you, find out if it needs volunteers. Nearly every such institution in the country operates on a very tight budget and welcomes any help it can get! Be specific about what type of work you would like to do, but do not expect it to be guaranteed. Ask if there are any projects under way. For example, the National Park Service was restoring a destroyer in Boston, and they were glad to have a group of World War II naval veterans to help them scrape rust and put things in order. If you are going to volunteer, be fair, and guarantee a set amount of time each week. Do not give 2 hours on Tuesday this week and a half hour next Friday. A half day 2 days a week or 1 whole day each week is best to make sure that you have time to complete a project. And do not decide to skip your scheduled time because you do not feel like going in. Such absences really are not fair. Think of volunteering as a real commitment, almost like a job. No one expects you to turn up if you are on your annual vacation or if you get sick, but take the commitment seriously.

Many of the curators and archivists I have spoken with have mentioned that groups of women veterans have been of great help to them, whether by raising funds, helping as guides, giving uniforms or other objects, or collecting and preparing the stories of their individual experiences to add texture to the collection. If you are in touch with any members of your old unit, see if there is something you can all do together.

Sources for Researchers: Film and Graphic Archives, Museums, and Educational Resources

I am going to list a few places that might be useful to people researching the subject of military women in World War II, focusing specifically on film and graphic archives, museums, and educational resources. Please note that this list is just a jumping-off point, the tip of the iceberg. It is not complete, but it should get you started and will hopefully lead to other sources as well. Always call or write an institution to find out when it is open for research and to collect other information that may ease your work, such as reproduction fees or the name of the staff person who may assist your research.

Film and Graphic Archives

There are a number of places that hold film and photograph collections; I have tried to include the major collections below. Other sources for photographs are the archives of colleges and universities and most commercial archives, such as Bettmann and Time-Life. Particularly good sources are women's colleges and the historically black colleges. Check nursing and medical schools that may have sent alumnae to the services or the Red Cross or may have had members in the Cadet Nursing Corps. Try public libraries, too, particularly those in large cities, such as Boston, Chicago, and New York. They usually have archival and photograph collections and can put you in touch with other local sources. There are also several directories to commercial photographic sources, including David Bradshaw and Catherine Hahn, *World Photography Sources*

(New York, 1982) and Fred W. McDarrah, ed., *Stock Photo and Assignment Source Book* (New York, 1984).

National Archives and Records Administration
Motion Picture, Sound, and Video Branch
8601 Adelphi Road
College Park, MD 20740-6001

Still Picture Branch
8601 Adelphi Road
College Park, MD 20740-6001

The National Archives probably has the best, most extensive holding of films, photographs, maps, and posters (as well as textual records) dealing with World War II; so if you are doing research, start here. Discuss with staff the procedures for acquiring reproductions or copies. For more detailed information, see the following section of the volume, which outlines relevant National Archives holdings, and request the General Information Leaflet (GIL) No. 33 *Motion Pictures & Sound and Video Recordings in the National Archives* and GIL No. 38 *Information for Prospective Researchers About the Still Picture Branch of the National Archives.* You may obtain these free leaflets from National Archives, Publications Distribution (NECD), Room G-9, Seventh and Pennsylvania Avenue, NW, Washington, DC 20408.

Library of Congress
Motion Picture Reference Branch
First Street and Independence Avenue, SE
Washington, DC 20540-4840

The reference room staff have various manual and online catalogs and free explanatory leaflets for prospective researchers. One of these databases (MUMS) is on the Internet as part of the Library of Congress electronic information system, but this database is not comprehensive for the motion picture holdings. The types of material include fiction, documentaries, and scattered newsreel collections. Access to the holdings is primarily by title of the motion picture, and viewing is restricted to researchers engaged in a project that will lead to a publicly available work or to university students with a letter from a professor endorsing their research project. Only some items may be copied, and a leaflet discussing the restrictions is available.

Prints and Photographs Division
First Street and Independence Avenue, SE
Washington, DC 20540-4840

The prints and photographs staff have catalogs and finding aids. The material on World War II and women would include homefront photographs, posters, and cartoons. Staff prefer that you make an appointment in advance, particularly if you have never worked with their holdings. Some reproductions may be purchased.

Brown University Library
Anne S. K. Browne Military Collection
Box A
Providence, RI 02912

The library holds a collection of illustrations relating to the military history of all countries and eras, not specifically of women. Prints include 10,000 black-and-white photographs and some color images. Staff will answer mail and telephone requests, and you can visit by appointment. There is a fee for reproductions.

Celeste Bartos International Film Center
Department of Film
Museum of Modern Art
11 West 53d Street
New York, NY 10019-5498

There are limited hours for research by appointment and for serious scholars only. Film screening fees range from $2.50 to $15 per hour, depending on the type of film being viewed. The center's holdings are primarily commercial films and do not focus on women in World War II. If, however, a researcher wishes to examine contemporary depictions of military women during the war, this is a potential resource. The center can also provide a guide to film distributors for those searching for programming.

Mount Holyoke College Archives
Dwight Hall
South Hadley, MA 01075

The relevant collection is called "the War Collection" and includes a variety of materials related to Mount Holyoke and wars from the Civil War to the Persian Gulf. Objects include scrapbooks and photographs and relate to civilian relief efforts as well as to the WAVES, Marine Corps Women's Reserve, and WAAC. More information can be accessed online through a national database, OCLC. Reproductions can be arranged.

National Air and Space Museum
Photo Archives Division
MRC-322
Washington, DC 20560

The Air and Space Museum has collections of photographs of Air Force operations from pre-1944 to the present, including WASP activities. It welcomes donations. To do research, call for an appointment and a research application. Photographs may be reproduced for publication by permission and for a fee.

Smith College
Archives/Sophia Smith Collection
Northampton, MA 01060

The archives contains many photographs, both official and off duty, of Waves in training at Smith during World War II. Also non-WAVE war activities of civilian women students. Other non-World War II photographs include images of the Smith women's unit in France during World War I. The Sophia Smith Collection covers general women's history. Prints and slides can be reproduced for a fee. Photographs may be used for publication for a fee; call for more information. The archives does contain a few artifacts, but these are an exception, and because of limited storage space, it would rather not acquire more.

Texas Woman's University (TWU)
Blagg-Huey Library
Special Collections
P.O. Box 23715
Denton, TX 76204-1715

Inquiries may be made by telephone or mail; appointments are not required but recommended. Black-and-white photograph reproductions are available for a fee. You will need to consult the collections staff for publication permission. TWU has an extensive collection dealing with the WASP, including documents, photographs (both official and personal), and scrapbooks as well as uniforms and equipment, such as parachutes and watches. Some objects and photographs relating to the WAFS are also available. The special collections also include records and uniforms relating to the other women's services of World War II, including the WAC, ANC, women Marines and Marine Reserve, SPAR, and Red Cross. TWU also holds belongings and papers of military women who served in other actions, including Vietnam and the Persian Gulf.

U.S. Army Military History Institute
Carlisle Barracks, PA 17013-5008

Open to the public. Appointments are not required. The collection holds a wide variety of photographs, including many of the WAC and ANC and also some of civilian women employed by the Army during wartime. Reproductions can be ordered for a fee. Researchers can also arrange to make reproductions using their own equipment. Many photographs are in the public domain and can be published. Consult the archivist.

U.S. Coast Guard
Historian's Office
2100 Second Street, SW
Washington, DC 20593-0001

The Coast Guard has an extensive photograph archives, which includes photographs of SPAR activities. They usually pull and photocopy photographs on requested topics to send to researchers, who can then purchase reproductions. Researchers may make appointments to go through the archives themselves. You will need to request publication permission information.

U.S. Marine Corps Historical Center
Personal Papers Collection
901 M Street, SE
Navy Yard, Building 58
Washington, DC 20374-5040

Some photographs are found within collections of personal papers, which are usually filed by the name of the individual and sometimes under the unit heading. Donations receive an acknowledgment but not a deed of gift, and papers will be filed by the name of the marine who served rather than by that of the donor (if they are different individuals). Files are cross-indexed. The official Marine Corps photograph collection primarily contains combat footage and very little on women. There are a few films that are currently being inventoried and transferred to the U.S. Marine Corps University Audio/Visual Department at Quantico, VA. They are in very poor condition and are currently inaccessible.

Museums: Objects and Exhibitions

There are a number of museums with collections on women in the military and World War II. Museums do not collect just uniforms anymore. They also have personal equipment, vehicles, airplanes, and communications equipment that women veterans may have used during their service. Many museums also have some archival-type materials, such as newspapers, magazines, diaries, letters, photograph albums, scrapbooks, and dinner menus—anything that a veteran may have picked up, seen, or used. Most museums are also understaffed and have small budgets, so call in advance if you wish to look at objects in the collection. It may be a good idea to see a museum as a visitor before making an appointment to see a curator.

I have tried to list those museums with the most extensive collections of women's material, but there are many others. There are two publications that would be worth examining for listings of other museums and collections not given here. The best is the directory put out by the **American Association of Museums (AAM)**, 1225 I Street, NW, Washington, DC 20005. Another publication is Kenneth Hudson and Ann Nicholls, *The Directory of Museums and Living Displays* (New York, 1985).

An often-overlooked source is local and regional historical societies, which can be traced through the **American Association for State and Local History**, 530 Church Street, Suite 600, Nashville, TN 37219. They publish a list of member societies in their *Directory of Historical Agencies in the United States and Canada.* These societies often hold small collections of objects. You never know what you might find on your own doorstep.

If your search leads you farther afield, you can ask the AAM to assist you in contacting collections worldwide. You can also write to the **International Council on Museums (ICOM)**, maison de l'UNESCO, 1 rue Miollis, 75732 Paris, CEDEX, France. If you are trying to reach a museum in a particular country, try contacting the country's embassy in the United States. Usually there is a department of cultural affairs that can help.

American Red Cross
Historical Collection
National Headquarters
Washington, DC 20006

The Red Cross is not a branch of the military, but it has a collection of uniforms and some information on Red Cross workers in World War II. The collection is stronger for World War I, but it has very small holdings and no actual museum. It is very important to call in advance for an appointment.

Company of Military Historians
North Main Street
Westbrook, CT 06498

They have some women's uniforms and a room with an exhibition on women in the military. Most holdings on women are small and postwar. They do accept donations and assign value for tax deductions. Contact them for more information, and call for an appointment if you want to do research.

Massachusetts Military Research Center
739 Washington Street
Quincy, MA 02169

This museum will be opening in 1996 and will include facilities for research, conferences, and reunion groups. The collections on women in World War II are extremely small, limited mostly to photographs and articles. The museum is interested in acquiring artifacts of American military women and accepts donations, which are tax deductible. Researchers, prospective donors, or visitors may call or write for further information or assistance.

Military Museum of Southern New England
125 Park Avenue
Danbury, CT 06810

This museum has a small collection of uniforms and personal effects and a more extensive collection of vehicles and equipment.

The museum has very little on women but is interested in acquiring artifacts. Call in advance to confirm hours and changing exhibits and to find out how to make a donation.

National Air and Space Museum
Aeronautics Department
Room 3312, MRC-312
Washington, DC 20560

The Air and Space Museum has uniforms and objects related to WASP duties as well as other World War II artifacts. Researchers should call or write to discuss requirements. Donations are welcome.

National Museum of American History
Division of History of Technology
Military History Collection
NMAH MRC-620
Smithsonian Institution
Washington, DC 20560

This collection consists of military uniforms, equipment, flags, ordnance, art, and personal objects from the Civil War to the present, with a good collection of WAC and ANC uniforms and insignia. Work is under way to make the collection accessible on the World Wide Web, America Online, and other electronic media such as CD-ROM. The staff welcome information on proposed donations, but please first send a description of the item in writing and a photocopy or photograph if feasible.

National Museum of American History
Naval History Division, MRC-620
Washington, DC 20560

The division has uniforms and a few personal objects relating to the WAVES, SPAR, and women Marines of World War II. It also has a few photographs and archival materials, but very little. The collection includes objects relating to women in the military from World War I to the present. The division welcomes donations, especially of records, letters, diaries, and objects if the donor is willing to include a few details about her service and personal history. Please call for an appointment in advance.

National Museum of American Jewish Military History
1811 R Street, NW
Washington, DC 20009

The museum has some photographs and memorabilia for a 1997 exhibition but very little else. It is not accessible for research. Donations are welcome. The museum has a very small staff and welcomes anyone who cares to become a volunteer, particularly veterans.

Pima Air and Space Museum
6000 East Valencia Road
Tucson, AZ 85543

Researchers wishing to do work in the collection or archives should call in advance for an appointment. Exhibitions include a WASP and nurse's uniforms from World War II as well as a larger display on women in aviation and space exploration. There are over 200 aircraft, including those of the type flown by the WASP and WAFS. Donations are welcome, and the curator is working with a local WASP group to improve holdings. Photographs may be taken of the objects in the collection if arranged in advance. Photographs in the archival collection may be reproduced on a case-by-case basis.

U.S. Air Force Museum
1100 Spaatz Street
Wright-Patterson Air Force Base, OH 45433-7102

This is the central museum for the United States Air Force; it consists of a research center with archival and graphics materials and a museum collection. It has women's uniforms, insignia, and a display in the World War II area on WASP service. The museum also has many examples of Army Air Forces equipment, including the various types of planes flown by the WASP. The research center has archival information and a few photographs. Contact the research center for more information; staff will refer you to a curator and the collections for further research. An appointment is required.

U.S. Army Center for Military History
1099 14th Street, NW
Washington, DC 20005-3402

The Center for Military History is the central body for the U.S. Army Museum system. There are many Army museums around the country, relating to various branches of the service. Anyone planning to do work related to the U.S. Army in World War II should start here. There are two separate divisions of the center, a historical division and a museum division. There is a separate WAC museum (described below).

U.S. Coast Guard Museum
U.S. Coast Guard Academy
15 Mohegan Road
New London, CT 06320-4195

The Coast Guard collection is about 30 years old. It covers Coast Guard history from the Revenue Service to the present day and has very few objects related to the SPAR. The museum is very interested in acquiring objects from veterans. Give a description of the objects to be donated to the curator, who will then submit it to the collections review committee.

U.S. Marine Corps Historical Center
901 M Street, SE
Navy Yard, Building 58
Washington, DC 20374-5040

The museum is located in the Navy Yard near the U.S. Navy Museum, although the historical holdings are stored in Quantico, VA. There is a small collection of objects related to the women Marines in World War II, which consists mostly of uniforms, including utility types, and some personal objects and accessories. Researchers may make appointments to examine the collection and should explain in advance what they are looking for. Donations are welcome, particularly of utility garments and personal objects and accessories.

U.S. Navy Museum
Washington Navy Yard
Ninth and M Streets, SE
Building 76
Washington, DC 20374-0571

Exhibits are open to the public. The women's uniform holdings in the collection are small and incomplete. Donations are welcome, particularly of accessories (handbags and shoes) and utility clothing. The museum has women's items from World War I to the present. Call in advance for an appointment and to discuss research needs.

War Memorial Museum of Virginia
9285 Warwick Boulevard
Newport News, VA 23607

The museum has an extensive collection of uniforms, including those for women, and exhibitions. It also holds many posters related to military women as well as to other women in war work (for example, members of the Red Cross and Labor Service). It has a collection of films (primary and secondary). There is also a photograph archive. Call for an appointment to do research and for information on making donations.

West Point Museum
United States Military Academy (USMA)
West Point, NY 10996

Researchers should call Monday through Friday for appointments to view the collections. The exhibitions are open to the public and cover U.S. military history as well as the history of the Military Academy. There are uniforms and equipment mostly of nurses but also of Wacs in the section on World War II. Women are represented in other segments as well. Curators are able to direct researchers to additional sources. Arrangements can be made to photograph the collection. Photographs, manuscripts, and other documents are part of the special collections division of the library at the Academy.

Women In Military Service For America Memorial Foundation, Inc. (WIMSA)
5510 Columbia Pike, Suite 302
Arlington, VA 22204

This is a memorial center currently under construction at the gateway to Arlington National Cemetery. The memorial will include an education center, a register of women in the military, and exhibits on the history of women in America's armed forces from the Revolution to the present. The register will include the name, photograph (when available), and individual story of each woman's

military service, active duty, National Guard, and Reserve service—
past, present, and future. The anticipated opening of the memorial
is October 1997. The collection of artifacts is growing, and the
staff are actively soliciting donations from women veterans. Call
for further information on the opening, donations, content of the
holdings, and research possibilities. WIMSA has a catalog of posters,
books, videotapes, and other items related to women in the military
and available for purchase.

The Women's Army Corps Museum
Building 1077
Fort McClellan, AL 36205-5000

The museum's exhibits cover women's involvement with the
U.S. Army from the Revolution to the present. The collection
includes objects, uniforms, and original memorabilia from World
War II to the present day, including underwear, accessories, ban-
ners, decorations, and field equipment. The collection covers not
only the WAC, but also women's involvement in other services,
such as the Navy, the Navy Yeomanettes of World War I, the women
Marines, and the American Red Cross. It also contains British, Viet-
namese, and other foreign uniforms. The museum's archival holdings include documents from the Revolutionary War era as well as
albums, films (primarily training films), a few photographs, and oral
histories. Researchers should call for an appointment. Prospective
donors should contact the museum before sending items to see
what is currently being sought.

Finally, collecting military memorabilia is a popular hobby in
the United States today. You may want to see if there are any dealers
of militaria who have hard-to-find uniform or equipment pieces,
old field manuals, or rare editions of books on military history. If
they do not have anything in stock, they may be able to recommend
another source, or they can keep an eye out for the object you are
looking for. Women's uniforms and equipment can sometimes be
found in the stock of these dealers, but very few people are collecting this type of item.

Educational Resources

In addition to the places mentioned above, there are a variety
of other research opportunities available to you. You may want to

contact the **public affairs** departments of the respective armed services through the Pentagon in Washington, DC. They will be able to put you in touch with their historian's offices and archives, which publish their own histories and booklets. The public relations departments can also usually assist you in reaching veterans' organizations that might be able to send you newsletters or unit histories or suggest members who would be willing to talk to you about their experiences. The **U.S. Army**, for example, publishes a guide called *U.S. Army Veterans' Associations*, which lists contact addresses for many veterans organizations, including those for the Women's Army Corps and Army Air Forces. Other places you might contact include the Veterans of Foreign Wars, the American Legion, the American Gold Star Mothers, the United Service Organizations (USO), and the Normandy Foundation.

The **Women's Army Corps Museum** offers a booklet, *A Date With Destiny*, describing the holdings of the museum and the history of the WAC. They may have a catalog of other available publications, as well.

The **Dover Publishing Company** offers a book of paper dolls, *Great Fashion Designs of the 1940s* designed by Tom Tierney, which includes not only drawings of fashions by Chanel, Dior, and other haute couturiers, but also depictions of uniforms worn by the WAC, WAVES, and other women's units, with a few paragraphs describing the role of women in the war. It can sometimes be found in gift shops and bookstores.

The **MINERVA Center**, headed by Linda Grant DePauw, publishes a quarterly journal, *MINERVA: Quarterly Report on Women and the Military,* and a quarterly Bulletin Board with articles about current events and issues relating to women in the military. *MINERVA* covers women of all nations and eras and their relationship with the military as service members, dependents, supporters, and victims. The center recently received a book for review, *Women and War* by Fiona Reynoldson (New York, 1993), aimed at children, ages 10 to 14, which discusses women of all nations during World War II.

The **National Women's History Project** (7738 Bell Road, Windsor, CA 95492-8518) has a list of recommendations for readings, films and videotapes, and other materials about women and the military. The staff also publish a catalog of other women's history materials, including a collection of oral histories, *"What Did You Do in the War, Grandma?"* and a videotape series on women in American life, which includes a segment on World War II and the beginning of the cold war era.

They recommend contacting the **Women In Military Service For America Memorial Foundation, Inc.** (WIMSA) (address given in "museums" section), which has a catalog of posters, books, videotapes, and other items related to women in the military that are available for purchase.

Finally, the **National Archives Office of Public Programs** has a World War II catalog listing many different teaching units, videotapes, and publications, which may be of value to educators and students as well as the general public: *World War II Resources from the National Archives and Its National Audiovisual Center.* These materials cover a range of topics in U.S. wartime history and have segments on women. The most relevant items include topical teaching units, such as *The United States at War: 1944* and *World War II—The Home Front,* and booklets, such as *Broadsides and Posters from the National Archives, Holocaust: The Documentary Evidence,* and *Powers of Persuasion: Poster Art from World War II.* The many poster reproductions include commemorative posters of the Army Nurse Corps and the WAC. Various audiovisual records are also available for purchase. They are described in Select Audiovisual Records leaflets: *Pictures of World War II, Voices of World War II, Pictures of African Americans During World War II,* and *Captured German Sound Recordings.* The free World War II resources catalog and the Select Audiovisual Records leaflets are available from the National Archives Trust Fund, Publications Distribution (NECD), Room G-9, Seventh and Pennsylvania Avenue, NW, Washington, DC 20408.

Now that you are armed with this brief introductory information, you are encouraged—veterans and researchers alike—to pass the word along to your friends and, by all means, to get in touch with these institutions and give them whatever support or help that you can. The wartime role of women has often been undervalued. Women deserve to be represented and remembered. While museums and other archival organizations are willing to try to preserve the evidence that it was "a woman's war, too!," they can only accomplish this with your help.

DOCUMENTING WOMEN'S SERVICE
National Archives and Records Administration

The formal discussion of published and unpublished sources documenting U.S. women's military service in World War II continued in this session with presenters elaborating on the wartime holdings of the National Archives and Records Administration. These records were created, collected, or captured by agencies or authorities of the federal government and are more voluminous than either those of previous wars or the war-related holdings of nonfederal archives and historical societies. They detail the development of the women's units, the biases and impediments faced by servicewomen, and the progress made by women within the established military bureaucracy.

In the first paper, DeAnne Blanton provided an overview of the National Archives and its holdings and stressed the institution's commitment to public accessibility of materials. Her descriptions of finding aids and the archival research process were also instructive. She surveyed the major groups of textual documents (including military service records and Presidential papers), electronic files, still pictures, and films and newsreels relating to servicewomen in World War II and invited prospective researchers to use these rich materials. Marcia R. Haley and Eleanor Stoddard contributed sections to the paper.

Barbara Lewis Burger outlined the general holdings of the National Archives Still Picture Branch and highlighted the pictorial records generated by military and civilian agencies as part of the government's effort to document the global conflict, shape public opinion, and keep the country apprised of the course of the war. Her illustrations of women in uniform were drawn from these collections. She provided useful information about the archival organization of photographs and posters as well as aids and strategies to help facilitate research.

Jennifer A. Nelson focused on the complex wartime image of America's servicewomen portrayed in the edited and unedited government films housed in the Motion Picture, Sound, and Video Branch of the National Archives. She emphasized the value to viewers of learning to read the cultural meanings of films established through the interplay of overtexts and subtexts while cautioning against interpreting past images from current perspectives. She recommended researching production files and scripts for additional interpretive insights. Annotated lists of National Archives finding aids are appended to her paper.

The session was chaired by DeAnne Blanton, an archivist specializing in military records at the National Archives and Records Administration and author of a prize-winning article on women soldiers in the Civil War.

INVITATION TO SCHOLARSHIP
An Introduction to Records in the National Archives

DeAnne Blanton

In the field of military history, until relatively recently, the extensive and varied contributions of women to the armed forces and war efforts of the United States were largely overlooked or ignored. While scholarly interest in women's military history has increased markedly over the past 10 years or so, large gaps remain in the current historiography. Additional research needs to be done, particularly in regard to women's groundbreaking efforts during World War II. Indeed, the door is wide open to further indepth, primary research. The National Archives and Records Administration, with its myriad and, in many cases, untapped resources, invites such research.

The National Archives is the guardian of the permanently valuable records of the United States government. Founded in 1934, the institution physically protects and makes available to the American people the basic records of the three branches of the federal government. The records mostly date from the 1770s to the 1960s, with some earlier and later documents, and mostly originate from federal agencies, the federal courts, the military, and Congress. Through these records, the National Archives documents the history of the nation since the First Continental Congress. Overall, the institution holds approximately 4 billion pieces of paper and millions of photographs, maps, electronic files, microfilm reels, motion pictures, and other items.

More records are in the National Archives documenting World War II than for any of the previous wars fought by the United States. The records reflect the scale and scope of both U.S. involvement in the war and the war itself. Most of the records pertaining to World War II in general were either created, collected, or captured by agencies and authorities of the federal government. Most of the

World War II records specifically concerning women in the military were created by the various branches of the U.S. Armed Forces. The majority of these records are textual (paper), but the National Archives has significant holdings of motion pictures and still pictures relating to servicewomen. There are also some electronic files.

A primary mission of the National Archives is to make these and other records available to government agencies, the scholarly community, and the general public. Access to records, whether textual or special media, is typically unproblematic. World War II records are not subject to privacy restrictions, for the most part. Unless the records are still security classified, researchers may have access to them. Most World War II-era records are now declassified, but researchers should keep in mind that some still pictures and motion pictures may be copyright protected.

There are generally two paths to follow in researching records in the custody of the National Archives, regardless of the type or format of the records. Researchers seeking specific items or specific documents may call, write, fax, or e-mail the appropriate reference unit. Individuals who wish to perform extensive research should visit the National Archives in person; although reference units are staffed to assist you with your research, they cannot undertake substantive research for you. The reference branches holding World War II records are located at the National Archives at College Park, 8601 Adelphi Road, College Park, MD 20740-6001.

Before beginning research, it is helpful to have the scope of your project clearly defined. Know in advance what is sought. Develop an idea of what branch of the military might have created records of interest. All records in the custody of the National Archives, regardless of type or format, are arranged according to the record group concept. A record group is a collection of records created or collected by a single entity. For example, Record Group (RG) 24 is the Records of the Bureau of Naval Personnel. Within record groups, discrete sets of interrelated documents are called series. (Specific series are identified in the following pages with bold type.) In RG 24, **general correspondence, 1925–45,** and **microfim copies of muster rolls** are examples of series.

The National Archives has many published inventories, each providing a description of a specific record group and its series and outlining the administrative history of the organization or agency that created or accumulated the records. These inventories are sometimes found in large reference libraries as well as at the

National Archives. The *Guide to Federal Records in the National Archives of the United States* (Washington, DC, 1995), provides a general overview of the holdings of the National Archives at large. This publication is widely available in public libraries and is also on the Internet at the National Archives' World Wide Web site (http://www.nara.gov). The National Archives has also published a very concise and widely available finding aid that is useful in researching military women: *American Women and the U.S. Armed Forces: A Guide to the Records of Military Agencies in the National Archives Relating to American Women*, compiled by Charlotte Palmer Seeley, Virginia C. Purdy, and Robert Gruber (Washington, DC, 1992). This guide is available for purchase from the National Archives Trust Fund, P.O. Box 100793, Atlanta, GA 30384. It may also be found in large reference libraries.

The following paragraphs present some, but not nearly all, of the unclassified and declassified records in the National Archives relating to the contributions of American servicewomen to victory in World War II.[1] You will find a list of record groups cited, arranged by number and title, in appendix A to this paper.

Textual Records

Paper records relating to servicewomen in World War II were almost exclusively created by the two arms of the U.S. Armed Forces: the Department of the Navy and the Department of the Army. (Within the Department of the Navy were the U.S. Marine Corps and, for the duration of the war, the U.S. Coast Guard. Within the Department of the Army was the Army Air Corps.) The textual records that hold information about World War II servicewomen are so extensive that only highlights can be presented here.

Researchers should note that many of the textual records were originally created for administrative or operational reasons, not for the purpose of historical documentation. Thus, many of the files are bureaucratic in nature. Unfortunately, very few of the textual records relating to women in the military during World War II are filed together nicely under a big label that reads "servicewomen." Many of the most pertinent records about military women are buried within voluminous high-level correspondence series. Research using World War II textual records can be quite time consuming.

However, if the researcher perseveres, the hunt through the records can be rewarding. As a whole, the textual records relating to

World War II servicewomen trace the conception, implementation, and development of the various women's units such as the WASP (Women Airforce Service Pilots) and the WAC (Women's Army Corps). Textual records provide information about the biases and impediments faced by military women. The records also track the progress women made and the praise they ultimately earned from high-level Army and Navy brass. Additionally, the textual records provide a sense of the underlying administrative and bureaucratic culture of the World War II American military.

Department of the Navy. Servicewomen in the Navy were assigned to the WAVES (Women Accepted for Volunteer Emergency Service). Records about the WAVES pertain to enlistment, placement, training, housing, assignments, courts-martial, medals and awards, discipline, marriage, pregnancy, nonpreferential treatment, and discriminatory practices against African-American women. The records include correspondence, statistics, regulations, evaluations, reports, and legislative and administrative histories.

Correspondence series in RG 19, Records of the Bureau of Ships; RG 74, Records of the Bureau of Ordnance; and RG 24, Records of the Bureau of Naval Personnel, are pertinent in researching the roles of the WAVES. An additional useful records series in RG 24 is the **regulations governing women accepted for Volunteer Emergency Service, July 1942–November 1945.** The most valuable information about the WAVES is located in the high-level office files, general correspondence, and final reports of RG 80, General Records of the Department of the Navy, 1798–1947. Likewise, high-level correspondence files in RG 38, Records of the Office of the Chief of Naval Operations, include documentation about the WAVES. In RG 24, **muster rolls of ships and shore establishments . . . , 1898–1956,** provide names and ranks of Waves.

Servicewomen in the Marine Corps were assigned to the MCWR (Marine Corps Women's Reserve). In RG 127, Records of the U.S. Marine Corps, the **muster rolls, 1798–1945,** reveal names of, and remarks concerning, women who served in the MCWR. Other personnel records in RG 127 relate to the qualifications, duties, and training of the MCWR. The **general correspondence, 1943–1945,** series of RG 72, Records of the Bureau of Aeronautics, includes similar information.

Women in the Coast Guard were part of the SPAR, a popular acronym for the Coast Guard Women's Reserve, based on the Coast Guard motto: *Semper Paratus*—Always Ready. In RG 24, the **gen-**

eral correspondence, 1925–1945, holds documents outlining personnel policies toward and the training of Spars.

Many World War II–era Department of the Navy records, particularly those of the U.S. Marine Corps and the U.S. Coast Guard, are not yet part of the National Archives. Researchers interested in the WAVES, MCWR, and SPAR should also contact the Naval Historical Center, the Marine Corps Historical Center, and the U.S. Coast Guard Historian's Office.

Department of the Army. Researchers will find an abundance of information on Army women since the vast majority of the World War II–era Department of the Army records reside at the National Archives.

Servicewomen in the Army were assigned to the WAAC (Women's Army Auxiliary Corps) and to its successor, the WAC (Women's Army Corps). Records about the WAAC and WAC cover subjects such as race relations and discriminatory practices against African Americans, health, training, qualifications, allotments, pay, benefits, rights and privileges, recruitment, assignments, morale, living conditions, courts-martial, marriage, and pregnancy. Some records provide numerical strengths of units, and others trace the development of the WAAC and WAC through historical reports.

Correspondence series in the following record groups relate to the WAAC: RG 407, Records of the Adjutant General's Office, 1917–; RG 218, Records of the U.S. Joint Chiefs of Staff; RG 165, Records of the War Department General and Special Staffs; RG 160, Records of Headquarters Army Service Forces; and RG 107, Records of the Office of the Secretary of War. RG 107 also holds the useful **"Report on the Suitability of Military Occupations for WAAC Auxiliaries, n.d."**

Records relating to the WAC are found in correspondence files of RG 218. Useful records in RG 407 include the **operations report file, 1940–1948.** WAC reports are found in RG 332, Records of U.S. Theaters of War, World War II, and in RG 338, Records of U.S. Army Commands. Additionally, records of the Control Division in RG 160 contain documentation of several negative propaganda campaigns against the WAC, orchestrated by Army servicemen.

In RG 18, Records of the Army Air Forces, the **general correspondence, 1939–1942,** of the commanding general, headquarters, is useful in tracing the origins of women's service in the Army Air Corps. This series also contains information about the Air WAC, specifically concerning assignments, duty stations, and male attitudes toward the service of women.

Women pilots during World War II were organized into the WAFS (Women's Auxiliary Ferrying Squadron), the WFTD (Women's Flying Training Detachment), and WASP (Women Airforce Service Pilots). Records of the Chief of Staff in RG 165 include useful information about the WAFS and the WASP. In RG 407, the **unclassified general correspondence, 1940–1954,** holds references to the WASP. Correspondence series in RG 18 pertain to orders and regulations, target towing, utilization and training, status, strengths, assignments, discipline, and recruiting of World War II women pilots. There are few significant records series relating to the WFTD.

For information about women who worked in military intelligence capacities, such as linguistic specialist or spy, use RG 226, Records of the Office of Strategic Services (OSS). Additionally, in RG 319, Records of the Army Staff, the **formerly security classified general correspondence, 1946–1950,** of the Office of the Director of the WAC contains references to 88 women in the WAC who worked for the OSS.

Medical Personnel, Navy and Army. Records relating to nearly every facet of women's medical involvement during World War II can be located at the National Archives. Records relating to the Navy Nurse Corps (NNC) and the Army Nurse Corps (ANC) are the most prevalent.

References to women dentists, physicians, and surgeons in the Navy and Marine Corps are found in the **general correspondence, 1925–1945,** of RG 24. This series is also useful for information about the assignments of Navy nurses. RG 52, Records of the Bureau of Medicine and Surgery, includes **records relating to the history of the Navy Nurse Corps, 1908–1975,** which is useful in researching the work of women in the NNC. Some references to Navy flight nurses are in the multiple correspondence files of the Office of the Secretary of the Navy in RG 80. Detailed records about women Navy nurses who became prisoners of war are in RG 389, Records of the Office of the Provost Marshal General, specifically in the series **correspondence, camp reports, diaries, rosters, and other records relating to Americans interned by Germany and Japan during World War II, 1942–1946.**

Histories and statistical information pertaining to the ANC, covering topics such as morale, training, and work conditions, are included in RG 112, Records of the Office of the Surgeon General (Army). Further ANC documentation is located in the following series and record groups: **annual reports of the divisions of the Surgeon General's Office, 1942–1949,** in RG 112; annual reports of the ANC in RG 332; **historical manuscript collection** in RG 319; and **unclassified general correspondence, 1940–1954,** in RG 407. Records of the Surgeon General's Inspection Branch and multiple series of personnel records in RG 112 provide war reminiscences of, and reports by, ANC women in both the Pacific and European theaters. Detailed information about Army nurses detained as POWs are found in records of the War Crimes Branch in RG 153, Records of the Office of the Judge Advocate General (Army), and in the **statistical tabulations relating to casualties, prisoners of war . . . , 1940–1953,** in RG 407.

Records of Army medical units, 1942–1954, in RG 338, consist of historical and annual reports, unit histories, and general orders pertaining to Army women nurses, doctors, and other medical personnel. Administrative records, including reports and histories concerning the work of women physicians and flight nurses, are located in correspondence files in RG 18.

To access and obtain more information about World War II textual records in the custody of the National Archives, contact the Archives II Reference Branch, Textual Reference Division. For further information on textual records and personal papers in other repositories, see Eleanor Stoddard, "A Traveler's Guide to Chronicles of Military Women: World War II" in the preceding section.

Electronic Records

There are two electronic records series relating to servicewomen in World War II. The first of these is a computerized version of the **Army serial number file, 1938–1946,** in RG 407. These records hold vital statistics and military service data about enlisted servicemen and servicewomen in the Department of the Army. The records provide demographic and other descriptive information about Army personnel, including members of the WAC.

Also, there are three electronic records files with responses from two attitude surveys of U.S. Army nurses and Wacs, taken in January and February 1945, in the **American Soldier Studies** series. The surveys deal with multiple issues, including treatment, condition, and use of Army women, and are part of RG 330, Records of the Office of the Secretary of Defense. The **American Soldier Studies** represent one of the first attempts to collect and analyze data on public opinion and to conduct statistical analyses on the attitudes of soldiers, recruits, and combat veterans.

For further information about these computerized records, contact the Center for Electronic Records, NSX, Room 5320, National Archives at College Park, 8601 Adelphi Road, College Park, MD 20740-6001.

Still Pictures

Photographic documentation of women in World War II is extensive. Of the approximately 1 million World War II photographs held by the National Archives, thousands of the images are of women in the military. Researchers should keep in mind that photographs, like textual records, are not necessarily arranged by subject.

Several hundred photographs documenting the recruitment, training, and employment of Waves and NNC women are found in RG 80, series **G**. Additional photographs of Navy nurses on the job are located in RG 52, series **G**. Several hundred photographs of women Marines, performing a variety of jobs, are within RG 127, series **GS**. Approximately 400 photographs of Spars are filed in RG 26, Records of the U.S. Coast Guard, series **G**.

RG 111, Records of the Office of the Chief Signal Officer, series **SC** and **SCA,** include several hundred photographs relating to recruitment, training, and duty assignments of Wacs and the ANC, at home and abroad. More Army nurse images are part of RG 112, series **SGA**. Photographs of virtually all types of servicewomen, including Wafs and Wasps, are among the files in RG 208, Records of the Office of War Information, series **LO, LU, MO,** and **N**. Series **WWT** in RG 86, Records of the Women's Bureau, includes approximately 2,500 photographs of women working in various occupations, including the military.

WAC, ANC, and NNC recruitment posters are part of series **PA** in RG 44, Records of the Office of Government Reports. WAVES recruitment posters are located in series **DP** and **PO** in RG 24.

To research photographs and posters, contact the Still Picture Branch. A more detailed discussion of still pictures in the National Archives is included in this section in Barbara Burger, "Women at War: Still Pictures Relating to U.S. Women in the Military during World War II." For a discussion of still pictures in other institutions, see Clare Cronin, "Museums, Film and Graphic Archives, and Educational Resources," in the preceding section.

Motion Pictures

There are over 60 edited films and many more reels of unedited motion picture footage relating to World War II servicewomen. Although most films are black-and-white, a few appear in color. These films are primarily located in Record Groups 18, 111, 208, and 428, General Records of the Department of the Navy, 1947–. The films represent female participation in all branches of the armed forces and cover topics such as training, work-related activities, official ceremonies, and recreation. Recruitment films also exist. A few films specifically address the roles and contributions of African-American servicewomen.

In addition to the government-created films cited above, the National Archives possesses a large collection of commercially produced newsreels. The newsreels contain some publicity of, and human interest information about, servicewomen. Uniforms are one of many popular topics. Many of these newsreels may be copyrighted or contain copyright proprietary material.

To access motion pictures and newsreels in the National Archives, contact the Motion Picture, Sound, and Video Branch. A more detailed discussion of this topic is included in this section in Jennifer A. Nelson, "Reading Cultural Text in Government Films: Women, Image, and the World War II Experience." For information on motion pictures in other repositories, see Clare Cronin's paper in the preceding section.

The National Personnel Records Center[2]

There is one category of textual records that deserves special mention—military service records, or personnel jackets, for World War II servicemen and servicewomen. They are housed in St. Louis, MO, in the Military Personnel Records facility of the National Personnel Records Center, which is administered by the National Archives. These records, though in the physical custody of the National Archives, remain in the legal custody of the branch of service that created them.

Records Holdings. The National Personnel Records Center maintains the military personnel records of veterans who are discharged, retired, or deceased. The major exception is the records of living, retired Army veterans, which are retained by the Department of the Army until the veteran's death. The records of both women and men veterans are filed together according to the branch of service, name, service number or social security number, and approximate dates of service. The military records on file at the center begin with the specific dates of each service as follows:

AIR FORCE   Officers and enlisted, September 25, 1947
                     (the date the Air Force was established)

ARMY   Officers separated July 1, 1917
                     Enlisted separated November 1, 1912

COAST GUARD   Officers separated January 1, 1929
                     Enlisted separated January 1, 1915

MARINE CORPS   Officers and enlisted separated January 1,
                     1905

NAVY   Officers separated January 1, 1903
                     Enlisted separated January 1, 1886

Military personnel records for individuals separated before these dates are found in the holdings of the Archives I Reference Branch, Textual Reference Division, National Archives and Records Administration, Washington, DC 20408.

Requesting Records. Requests for copies of military personnel records must contain enough information to identify the record from among the more than 70 million on file at the center. The information needed to locate a record includes the veteran's full name, service number, branch of service, and approximate dates of service. Requesters seeking women's records should remember to provide the name(s) under which she served as well as her current name. Unit(s) of assignment and the veteran's date and place of birth can also be helpful, especially if the service number is not known.

The 1973 Fire. On July 12, 1973, a fire at the National Personnel Records Center destroyed about 80 percent of the records for Army personnel discharged between November 1, 1912, and January 1, 1960, and about 75 percent of the records for Air Force personnel with the surnames of Hubbard through "Z" discharged between September 25, 1947, and January 1, 1964. Among the records involved in the fire were those of women who served in the Army during World War II. If a woman remained in the Army until after

1960, however, or if she later enlisted in the Air Force and her last name fell in the first half of the alphabet, her record would probably have been stored in another area. Duplicate copies of the destroyed records were not maintained, but alternate record sources are available at the center for use in reconstructing a record of military service when a particular personnel record cannot be located. These auxiliary records include final pay vouchers, special orders, enlistment ledgers, morning reports, rosters, and sick reports.

Access to Records. Access to military personnel records on file at the National Personnel Records Center is restricted under the provisions of the Privacy Act, but veterans of World War II may obtain a copy of their individual service records or their reconstructed file. If a veteran is deceased, the next of kin may obtain a copy. Limited information from the military personnel records at the center is releasable to the general public without the consent of the veteran or a deceased veteran's next of kin. Such information is intended to strike a balance between the public's right to obtain information from federal records, as outlined in the Freedom of Information Act, and the veteran's right to privacy as defined by the Privacy Act. Researchers may obtain the following information by citing the Freedom of Information Act:

name
age (date of birth)
dates of service
source of commission
rank/grade and date attained
marital status
city/town and state of the last known address and the date of
   the address
serial/service number (does not include the social security
   number)
photograph
place of induction and separation
duty assignments
dependents (including name, sex, and age)
records of court-martial trials (unless classified)
military education/schooling
information about decorations and awards earned

For deceased veterans, the place of birth, place of death, and place of burial are also releasable.

Veterans and researchers should note that the military personnel record was created as an administrative record and does not contain detailed information about the veteran's participation in such things as military battles or daily unit activities. That type of information is included in organizational records such as after action reports, deck logs, and unit histories, many of which are in the holdings of the Archives II Reference Branch. Researchers who want access to organizational records (e.g., the morning reports stored at the National Personnel Records Center) must obtain permission from the appropriate military service department.

All requests pertaining to military personnel records or organizational records located at the center should be sent to the National Personnel Records Center (Military Personnel Records), 9700 Page Avenue, St. Louis, MO 63132-5100.

Presidential Libraries

The Presidential Library System is administered by the National Archives and Records Adminstration, and the records retained in the libraries are in the legal custody of the National Archives. A Presidential library holds both personal and professional papers of the President, papers of the President's associates in the White House, and papers of the First Lady. Essentially, a Presidential library holds documentation of the life, times, and administration of a 20th-century President. Three Presidential libraries house a small quantity of records relating to servicewomen in World War II.

The Franklin D. Roosevelt Library, the nation's first Presidential library, has some textual records and a few photographs of World War II servicewomen. In the President's Official File, there is correspondence of the Roosevelt administration concerning every branch of women's service in World War II. In the Eleanor Roosevelt Papers, there are references to Oveta Culp Hobby, the WAAC, the Air WAC, and other women in defense of the nation. The library also has 30 photographs of women in the armed forces. The library is in Hyde Park, NY.

The Harry S. Truman Library holds two major sources for researching military women in World War II. One of these is the personal papers collection of Westray Battle Boyce Long, a World War II WAC officer. Her papers include biographical material and records relating to the history of the WAC. The other source consists of the papers kept by Harry S. Truman when he was a U.S. Senator.

In these senatorial papers, there is constituent correspondence relating to the WAVES and the WASP. The library is in Independence, MO.

The Dwight D. Eisenhower Library includes extensive holdings relating to World War II military women. General Eisenhower's papers hold scattered items relating to the WAC. In the library's collection of 20th-century military records, there are files relating to the WASP. Papers of the following individuals hold a variety of useful information: Jacqueline Cochran, head of the WASP; Ruth Briggs, the WAC secretary to Gen. Walter Bedell Smith; and Margaret Chase, a Red Cross volunteer.

Additionally, the Eisenhower Library holds 250 collections under the heading "World War II Participants and Contemporaries Papers." A number of these collections pertain to the WAC, including the papers of Edith M. Davis, who served as a WAC commander at SHAEF (Supreme Headquarters, Allied Expeditionary Forces). The library is in Abilene, KS.

For further information about these and other records in the Presidential libraries, see appendix B. For access to records in the Presidential libraries, researchers should contact the individual libraries directly. Each library can provide a guide to its holdings upon request.[3]

NOTES

1. I wish to thank Barry Zerby, Kenneth Schlessinger, and Terri Hanna for leading the breakout sessions on individual service branch records during the conference and for providing additional information regarding the textual records section of this paper. Appreciation also goes to Margaret Adams and Ted Hull for conferring with me on computerized records; Barbara L. Burger, on still pictures; and Jennifer A. Nelson, on motion pictures.
2. Marcia R. Haley, branch chief at the National Personnel Records Center, St. Louis, MO, contributed this section of the paper.
3. The research of Eleanor Stoddard was useful in writing this section of the paper (see her paper in the previous section for a select inventory of historical collections elsewhere in the country). Her annotated description of records in the Presidential libraries appears in appendix B. You will note that these records have been described in greater detail than the other textual records described in this paper because collections in the Presidential libraries are not as voluminous as those held by the Office of the National Archives and can, therefore, be afforded more comprehensive treatment. This level of detail suggests the richness of information found in all National Archives records.

APPENDIX A: List of Record Groups Cited

18	Records of the Army Air Forces
19	Records of the Bureau of Ships
24	Records of the Bureau of Naval Personnel
26	Records of the U.S. Coast Guard
38	Records of the Office of the Chief of Naval Operations
44	Records of the Office of Government Reports
52	Records of the Bureau of Medicine and Surgery
72	Records of the Bureau of Aeronautics
74	Records of the Bureau of Ordnance
80	General Records of the Department of the Navy, 1798–1947
86	Records of the Women's Bureau
107	Records of the Office of the Secretary of War
111	Records of the Office of the Chief Signal Officer
112	Records of the Office of the Surgeon General (Army)
127	Records of the U.S. Marine Corps
153	Records of the Office of the Judge Advocate General (Army)
160	Records of Headquarters Army Service Forces
165	Records of the War Department General and Special Staffs
208	Records of the Office of War Information
218	Records of the U.S. Joint Chiefs of Staff
226	Records of the Office of Strategic Services
319	Records of the Army Staff
330	Records of the Office of the Secretary of Defense
332	Records of U.S. Theaters of War, World War II
338	Records of U.S. Army Commands
389	Records of the Office of the Provost Marshal General
407	Records of the Adjutant General's Office, 1917–
428	General Records of the Department of the Navy, 1947–

APPENDIX B: Records in the Presidential Libraries

Franklin D. Roosevelt Library
511 Albany Post Road
Hyde Park, NY 12538

The Franklin D. Roosevelt Library, the nation's first Presidential library, contains over 200 separate collections, including the President's personal and family papers, papers covering his public career, papers of Eleanor Roosevelt, and those of many Roosevelt associates in public and private life. Materials in the library are grouped by type of material—manuscripts, microfilm, and oral history transcripts. Researchers wishing to use the library's materials are requested to make advance application. The staff, however, will provide answers by mail or fax if the requested information is brief.

Items relating to military women in World War II can be found under the following headings:

Personal Papers

The President's Official File (OF), 294 pp.

OF 18E: Women's Reserve of the U.S. Marine Corps
OF 21M: Women's Reserve of the U.S. Coast Guard
OF 25JJ: Women's Army Auxiliary Corps
OF 357E: Women's Army Corps Service Medals
OF 379B: Women's Auxiliary Naval Reserve

Eleanor Roosevelt Papers

There are alphabetical card index entries for the papers, and under the general headings of Correspondence with Government Departments and Personal Correspondence, arranged by year, are the following names bearing on the World War II military service of women:

Oveta Culp Hobby
Women in Defense
Women's Air Corps
Women's Army Auxiliary Corp
Women's Defense Cadets of America
Women's Volunteer Reserve Corps
World War II, Armed Forces, Women: 30 photographs

Harry S. Truman Library
U.S. Highway 24 and Delaware Street
Independence, MO 64050-1798

The archives in the Harry S. Truman Library contain the extensive papers of President Truman as well as material on a number of individuals whose lives touched his career. There are materials in two collections of personal papers and in two oral histories that relate to servicewomen in World War II:

Personal Papers

Harry S. Truman, Papers as Senator and Vice President, Box 216.

This box includes constituent correspondence on Waves and Wasps, including references to Jacqueline Cochran.

Westray Battle Boyce Long Papers, 1933–62. 5 boxes.

Westray Battle Boyce was a leading WAC officer in World War II and became director of the WAC at war's end (July 12, 1945 to March 4, 1947). She had previously held an important position with the Rural Electrification Administration. Her papers include biographical material, items relating to her wartime service in the WAC, correspondence both personal and general, many news clippings and articles, and correspondence on the history of the WAC and its 20th anniversary in 1962.

Oral Histories

These two transcripts of interviews may contain references to the status of military women.

India Edwards
    Head of the Women's Division of the Democratic National Committee.

Katie Locheim
    Head of the Women's Division of the Democratic National Committee.

Dwight D. Eisenhower Library
Abilene, KS 67410

The Dwight D. Eisenhower Library, established to preserve the papers, books, and other historical materials relating to President Eisenhower, includes a research room, archival stacks, and offices.

Within its extensive holdings are items and collections relating to World War II military women. The following are especially worth noting:

Personal Papers and Textual Records

Dwight D. Eisenhower Papers, 1916-52.

Scattered throughout General Eisenhower's pre-Presidential papers are items relating to women's service during World War II, such as a memorandum from Oveta Culp Hobby on the distribution of WAC personnel, correspondence between General Eisenhower and Everett Hughes on Wacs, and a 110-page diary maintained by Kay Summersby, June 1, 1944, to April 30, 1945.

Dwight D. Eisenhower Library: Collection of 20th-century military records, 1918-50.

Briggs, Ruth
Papers, 1942-54.
>   This member of the WAC was secretary to Gen. Walter Bedell Smith. Most of this collection consists of 326 well-identified photographs. Additionally, it contains identification cards, passes, booklets, and other items. Briggs retired from the service as a lieutenant colonel.

Chase, Margaret
Papers, 1942-60. Approximately 1,100 pp.
>   This American Red Cross volunteer served in North Africa and Europe during World War II. Included in her papers are four diaries covering the 1942-45 period plus personal correspondence. She comments on the social life at Allied Forces Headquarters and on the type of women who served with the Red Cross and the treatment they received.

Cochran, Jacqueline
Papers, 1932-75. 379,000 pp.
>   Cochran was a noted aviatrix, the only woman to fly a bomber across the Atlantic during World War II. She urged the U.S. Air Force to use women as pilots and became head of the Women Airforce Service Pilots (WASP), training over 1,000 women for active duty flying.

Air Transport Auxiliary (ATA) series. 5 boxes.
>   This material documents Mrs. Cochran's work with the Air Transport Auxiliary (ATA), a branch of the British Royal Air Force.

Women Airforce Service Pilots (WASP) series. 28 boxes.
>   This material, covering the period 1941-72, includes correspondence, directives, reports, and printed data relating to the WASP

program. Other series, such as the General File and the Ninety-Nines, should also be checked.

McKeogh, Michael J. and Pearlie
Papers, 1941–48. 400 pp.

Pearlie Hargrave McKeogh was a member of the WAC and served as a driver in General Eisenhower's headquarters in North Africa and at SHAEF in London and Paris during World War II. She married Michael McKeogh, an enlisted aide to General Eisenhower, during the war. A major portion of this collection consists of 374 photographs. Also found is a small quantity of correspondence and photocopies of articles.

Series I, Historical Studies, Air University, Box 15. WASP History, 75 pages.

Series II, Library Reference Publications, Box 23. Office of the Surgeon, Headquarters 5th Army, "The Medical Story of Anzio," September 25, 1944, with descriptive paragraph.

Report describes 5th Army medical service during combat operations at Anzio, Italy, lists casualties among nurses, and mentions actions resulting in the first awards of the Silver Star to women in the U.S. Army. Cites several examples of women serving and dying in military service.

World War II Participants and Contemporaries Papers. Over 250 collections.

These collections have been received from individual donors, including civilians on the homefront. A number pertain to Wacs. One of the largest WAC collections is that of Edith M. Davis documenting her service as commander of a WAC detachment at SHAEF and USFET (U.S. Forces, European theater after July 1, 1945). Aside from her own correspondence and memorabilia, her file contains reminiscences of other Wacs and letters by Mary Medcalfe Rexford, a Red Cross Clubmobile worker. A list of individual donors is available at the library.

Aurand, Henry S.
Papers, 1873–1967. 58,200 pp.

Memorandums of General Aurand's staff conferences held while he was commander of 6th Service Command, Chicago, IL, contain numerous references to issues concerning the WAAC personnel under his command plus WAAC news clippings. His report *History of Normandy Base Section: D-Day to V-E Day* contains a two-page description of the WAC Detachment, Headquarters, Normandy Base Section, of which he was commanding general.

Women's Army Corps

These records at the Eisenhower Library duplicate those held at the National Archives.

Supreme Headquarters, Allied Expeditionary Force, Office of the Secretary General Staff, Records, 1943–45 (microfilm). See file "324.5 Employment of WAC and ATS Personnel."

U.S. Army, U.S. Forces, European Theater, Historical Division, Records, 1941–46 (microfilm). Pertinent file folders relate to WAC concerns, including "534. WACs in the ETO-History, 3 monographs, 1942–1944."

U.S. Army, U.S. Forces, European Theater, General Board: Reports, 1942–46. The General Board was established in June 1945 to prepare an analysis of the strategy, tactics, and administration employed by the U.S. forces in the European theater during World War II. Box 2 contains Study Number 11, "Study of the Women's Army Corps in the European Theater of Operations," Vols. I, II, and III, approximately 500 pp.

Oral Histories

Cochran, Jacqueline, 257 pp.

Contains almost no commentary on the World War II period.

Jehl, Sue Serafian, 48 pp.

WAC member of General Eisenhower's headquarters at SHAEF. Comments on her assignment and other activities, personnel, and Eisenhower's relationship with Kay Summersby.

Scott, Inez G., 34 pp.

Wac assigned to 21st car company in North Africa in 1943 and later to Office of the Commander in Chief. Background on WAAC company's assignment to North Africa and descriptions of incidents involving her and General Eisenhower.

WOMEN AT WAR
Still Pictures Relating to
U.S. Women in the Military
During World War II

Barbara Lewis Burger

They were mothers, daughters, sisters, and wives from many walks of life and from various ethnic and religious backgrounds who, when the need was greatest, became soldiers, sailors, aviators, marines, and coast guardsmen in the United States military. Perhaps they joined the armed services to help defend their country and for the cause of freedom worldwide. Maybe they sought to help hasten the return of loved ones, release a man for combat duty, have an occupation, or to enrich themselves and develop as individuals. Or perhaps they wanted to travel and fulfill a desire for adventure. Whatever their reasons, their service during World War II contributed to the war effort and opened up opportunities for women in the military. Today, the history of these servicewomen is preserved among the millions of documents in the National Archives, including in its pictorial records.

Home to millions of photographs accumulated by federal agencies, the National Archives maintains and preserves these pictures because they are official records of the activities of our government and because of the value of the information they contain. Although photographs are found in various units in the National Archives, the vast majority are in the custody of the Still Picture Branch. The branch traces its genesis to the early days of the National Archives, when a decision was made to establish a separate division to administer still photographic archives, reproduction, and research.

The primary emphasis of the unit was initially on copying paper records in the Archives, microfilming projects, and documenting the new facilities. Efforts moved quickly into accessioning the permanently valuable records of the government. The earliest accessions were from the War, Navy, and Interior Departments. Included in these early transfers were pictures from World War I, photographs of American Indians, and aerial photographs (aerial photographs are now in the custody of the Cartographic and Architectural Branch). The end of the Depression and the closing of many New Deal agencies resulted in the addition of large numbers of records to the holdings of the branch, and with World War II's conclusion, the branch experienced a similar surge of photographs as many civilian war agencies completed their work. The Still Picture Branch continues to accession records. Most recently the branch received Army, Navy, Air Force, and Marine Corps photographs covering the war in Vietnam, photographs from the Department of Housing and Urban Development, and images from the photograph library of the United States Information Agency.

Over 1 million of the approximately 8 million photographs maintained by the Still Picture Branch were taken during World War II. An estimated 10,000 of the roughly 15,000 graphic arts (posters) in the branch were created during the war. Most were produced under government photography and art programs. Included in the branch's holdings are thousands of images relating to servicewomen.

From the outset, the government made a concerted effort to document the war for strategic and historical purposes. At the same time, it established mechanisms to help shape and influence public opinion. Both the government and the press were interested in keeping the public abreast of the course of the war, and photography was one medium used to help accomplish these varied needs.

Almost the entire government turned its energies toward documenting the war. Many long-established civilian agencies directed their staffs toward recording their expanded functions, and newly organized agencies quickly formed units to document their wartime responsibilities. The military, which has a long tradition of photographically documenting its wide-ranging activities, immediately geared up for war duties. Hundreds of military photographers were assigned to take official and technical pictures. Press photographers, under military supervision, also covered combat operations. Technological advancements facilitated photographers' ability to cover the war. Improved cameras, lenses, and films could better capture the chaos of combat, and cameras became more portable. These changes allowed combat photographers in particular to get into the thick of the action. Military and government officials and the press found access to images was accelerated due to radio facsimile transmission of photographs and other improved delivery systems. World War II became the most photographed of all the wars. Photographers captured the war from all points of view: from battlefield events and homefront activities to government programs and projects.

Most of the wartime photography in the Still Picture Branch was generated by six major programs conducted by the five military services (Army, Navy, Coast Guard, Marine Corps, and Army Air Forces) and by one civilian agency, the Office of War Information. In general, photographic coverage of women in service varies little from agency file to agency file. For the most part, each program recorded recruitment efforts, training programs, accommodations, types of uniforms, job assignments both overseas and domestic, and recreational activities. All of the records feature individuals, many of whom are identified. But by no means are any of the files comprehensive in their coverage of either the war or women's service, nor are there photographs of every individual who served in the military.

This paper describes the holdings of the armed services and the Office of War Information as they pertain to the service of women. In addition, the Women's Bureau, another civilian agency, is discussed because of the relevance of its photographic coverage of women in the work force during the war. The records of the Office of Government Reports are also included because they are a major source of World War II posters. Researching all these records is fairly straightforward. Most are arranged by subject and can be accessed by organizational entity and other topics or by surname (i.e., WAC, SPAR, Nurses, Women, Negro, Recruitment, etc.). In a couple of instances a subject index must be used to locate necessary access points. And as with any research, knowing as much as possible about the subject in question may lead to additional research approaches. Information about the locations where individuals or units were deployed, types of occupations, unit histories, and any significant events may help facilitate research.

The Army

The 4-by-5 photograph shows a Wac dressed in trousers, combat jacket, and helmet with a pack strapped to her back stepping gingerly off the landing craft onto the French shore. It is July 1944, and according to the caption, 1st Sgt. Nancy E. Carter is

First Sgt. Nancy E. Carter was the first member of the first regular WAC unit to land in Normandy. (111-SC-191451-s)

the first member of the first regular WAC (Women's Army Corps) unit to land in Normandy. In the beginning, Carter and her fellow Wacs camped out in an apple orchard, slept on cots, ate field rations, and washed in cold water carried in helmets. Upon landing, they immediately went to work as clerks, typists, and telephone operators.

In another photograph, three Wacs are shown. Surely, their smiling faces belie the discomfort they must be feeling. After all, the Air Wacs are wringing out their clothing after their tent collapsed during a rainstorm. Even the hazy look of the photograph gives a sense of moisture still in the air. But like their male counterparts, Pfcs Ines Kirkman and Billy Vinyard and Cpl. Glenna Cooper evidently learned to make do with conditions on Leyte Island in the Philippines. It was the rainy season, and living conditions were unexpectedly horrendous. The photograph is dated December 27, 1944, a date that suggests that these Air Wacs were among the first Wacs to arrive on Leyte, an area still being strafed by enemy fire, some 36 days after the first wave of U.S combat troops.

Three Air Wacs wring out their clothing on Leyte Island. (111-SC-265222)

These two photographs are fairly typical of the many photographs documenting the activities of women in Army units—WAC, Army Nurse Corps, and Army Air Forces WAC—that are among the **Records of the Office of the Chief Signal Officer (RG 111, Series SC and SCA).** The Signal Corps directed the Army's photographic program—the most extensive of all the services—and consequently is the source of the greatest documentation of Army activities. Its photography program was so comprehensive that by war's end, the Army Pictorial Service library held more than 500,000 images. In addition, Signal Corps photographs accounted for about one-half of all the pictures published in the press.

It is therefore not surprising that a collection of such size contains considerable documentation of the roles of women. There are at least 2,000 photographs relating to women in service. Subjects pictured include recruitment, training, and duty assignments both at home and abroad. Pictures of African-American women serving in the WAC and Army Nurse Corps are also included in the records. Captioning information for the photographs in these two series is generally adequate, but because of security concerns, units and locations are often not given. There is a subject index to Series SC; Series SCA is arranged by subject. WAC and Nurses are only two of many possible subject headings that can be researched.

The photograph on the next page shows seven women lounging against a jeep. A cross, probably red (this is a black-and-white photograph), stands out clearly on the armband of the woman on the far right. According to the caption, the women are field hospital nurses who arrived in France via England and Egypt. The picture is in the records of the Army's Surgeon General.

Although the Signal Corps had principal responsibility for documenting the Army during the war, other Army organizational units maintained their own files and often acquired Signal Corps pictures. Such is the case with the Army's Surgeon General. Hence, the **Records of the Surgeon General—Army (RG 112, Series SGA)** is another source for photographs of Army nurses. Among the approximately 1,100 photographs documenting Army Medical Corps activities in Europe and of Army medical personnel are a few images showing Army nurses.

Field hospital nurses who arrived in France via England and Egypt. (112-SGA-44-10842 [War & Conflict #921])

The Navy

"LT (jg) Harriet Ida Pickens and ENS Frances Wills, first Negro WAVES to be commissioned." The caption for the photograph of two uniformed African-American women proudly smiling reveals little of the significance of the occasion. For African Americans, the commissioning ceremony on December 21, 1944, was a momentous occurrence. Finally, after years of pressuring, the Navy, which had been steadfast in its refusal to recruit black women, acquiesced. Pickens and Wills graduated from WAVES training at the Naval Reserve Midshipmen's School (WR) at Smith College, and the enlistment of black women began a week later.

At first glance, there was nothing unusual about the slightly under-exposed next photograph. Like many others among the Navy's photographic files, it shows an obviously exhausted nurse. A perusal of the caption reveals that it is a picture of Ens. Jan Kendleigh on duty in the Marianas. A quick check of surrounding images further reveals a mini photo-essay within the larger file. Altogether there are 12 photographs showing Kendleigh administering to casualties, waiting to evacuate injured marines, being briefed by the pilot ferrying her and her charges to the fleet

"LT (jg) Harriet Ida Pickens and ENS Frances Wills, first Negro WAVES to be commissioned." (80-G-297441 [African Americans in WWII #159])

hospital, recording information on patients charts, and checking on the injured. Ensign Kendleigh, as it turns out, was the first Navy nurse to fly into Iwo Jima to aid in the evacuation of casualties. When Kendleigh landed at the airfield on Iwo Jima, it was under mortar attack. Kendleigh had to first take shelter in foxholes until the enemy positions could be wiped out.

Navy nurse Ens. Jan Kendleigh on duty in the Marianas. (80-G-48979)

Although its photography program was not as extensive as the Army's, the Navy Department photograph files are nearly as voluminous. The **General Records of the Department of the Navy, 1789–1947 (RG 80, Series G)** consists of more than 700,000 photographs. A significant percentage of these images are from World War II. The two photographs described above are among several hundred documenting the recruitment, training, and employment of women in the WAVES and the Navy Nurse Corps.

The General Photographic File is the principal file in this record group, and it is there that one may find the two photographs described above. The file is particularly rich in documentation of the variety of occupations available to women in the WAVES. Coverage is strongest in those areas where women made their greatest impact: communications, aviation, weather forecasting, and photography. Most of the photographs bear full captions, but the information is not as detailed or as robust as some of the other agency captions. There is a subject index to the file.

Noteworthy also are the **Records of the Bureau of Medicine and Surgery (RG 52, Series G and NNU).** The records of this Navy unit contain over 300 photographs showing facilities and treatment at U.S. Navy hospitals in France and England. Included are a small number of photographs of Navy nurses on duty and Navy Nurse Corps uniforms of the period. The **Records of the Bureau of Naval Personnel (RG 24, Series DP and PO)** is an excellent source for examples of the kinds of posters used to encourage and recruit women into the WAVES.

The Coast Guard

"If I can't shoot the enemy myself, at least I can release a man who can." So spoke GM3c Marie Deppen when asked in 1943 about her service in the SPAR. We know a lot about Deppen because along with six photographs in the folder bearing her name are a lengthy caption and a newsclipping. Deppen, 21 years old and a sharpshooter, joined the WAVES in 1942 and transferred to the SPAR in 1943. She was highlighted, undoubtedly, because she was in charge of the Coast Guard armory repair shop in Philadelphia and was one of the few women in service to hold a gunners mate rating. Although she was not permitted to use weapons, Deppen was able to put her familiarity with guns to good use and in doing so replaced a man who became a gunner at sea.

The six photographs showing a uniformed Deppen are just a few of the approximately 400 photographs of Coast Guard women in the **Records of the U.S. Coast Guard (RG 26, Series G).** The interesting feature of Coast Guard photography is that Coast Guard photographers were encouraged to portray the individual. As a result, the records contain many portraits often with very detailed captions about the person pictured. Also, the files are fairly compre-

GM3c Marie Deppen, of the SPAR, was one of the few women in the service to hold a gunners mate rating. (26-G-20,481)

hensive in terms of showing the variety of occupations in which women were employed. The records also include photographs of Spars engaged in recruitment and publicity campaigns. Many of the photographs were obviously staged, and by today's standards the publicity photographs border on cheesecake. The objective of the publicity campaigns was not only to attract recruits (10,000 women volunteered) but also to publicize the important work of the Coast Guard. The Coast Guard records are arranged by subject, with a heading for women.

The Marine Corps

T. Sgt. Selma "Rusty" Olson is the daughter of a retired Marine Corps quartermaster sergeant who approved of Olson's enlistment on her 20th birthday in April 1943. When her photograph was taken in 1945, Olson was a crew chief of an aviation repair group. The photograph shows Olson with her eight-member crew servicing a North American Mitchell B-25 bomber at Cherry Point, NC. These marines were just a few of the nearly 40 percent of the Women's Reserve who held jobs in aviation.

Marine T. Sgt. Selma "Rusty" Olson and her crew service a B-25. (127-N-8927)

Several hundred photographs documenting women Marines working in many of the 200 jobs to which they were assigned, as well as engaged in recruitment activities and training programs, are in the **Records of the U.S. Marine Corps (RG 127, Series GS).** The series is arranged by subject, and there is a category for women Marines. There are no images of African-American women Marines in this series; the first African-American enlistee joined well after the war's end, in 1949.

The Army Air Forces and the Women Airforce Service Pilots

The Army Signal Corps records (described above) contain a few photographs of Air Wacs and members of the Women's Auxiliary Ferrying Squadron (WAFS), a predecessor of the Women Airforce Service Pilots (WASP). The bulk of Army Air Forces photography for World War II, however, has not been transferred to the National Archives and is presently on loan to the Archives Division, Air and Space Museum of the Smithsonian Institution. As a result, pictorial documentation on the role of women in the air units is very sketchy. Fortunately, the records of two civilian agencies, the Office of War Information and the Women's Bureau, fill in some gaps in coverage.

Office of War Information

If the subject matter were not so grim, you might pause to admire the chiaroscuro effect. The photograph shows a nurse giving a transfusion to a soldier. Two glowing candles provide the only light as she goes about her work. Neither the nurse nor the patient is identified; the information provided merely indicates that they were somewhere in France at a frontline hospital.

The sign on the desk in the next photograph reads: "Captain D. H. Raney, A.N.C," but it is the earnest expression on the face of the nurse that catches the eye. Further examination of the attached caption reveals that in May 1945, Captain Raney was one of only five African-American captains in the Army Nurse Corps and was head of a nursing staff at Camp Beale, CA.

The third photograph shows veteran aviator and director of the Women's Auxiliary Ferrying Squadron (WAFS), Nancy Harkness Love. "Once the women begin delivering planes to Army bases," Love explained on another occasion about the job of ferrying military aircraft, "they seldom have more than six or eight hours

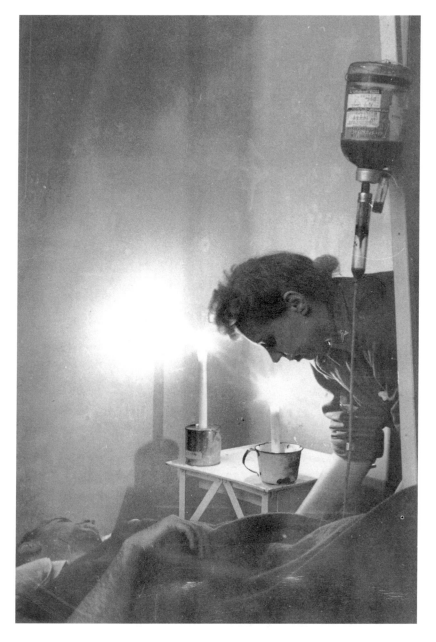

Somewhere in France at a frontline hospital, a nurse gives a transfusion to a soldier. (208-N-37380-77)

Capt. D. H. Raney, Army Nurse Corps. (208-PU-161K-1 [African Americans in WWII #147])

of rest between flights. They're forever hopping off to some remote part of the country, dropping off their planes and coming back by whatever means they can find, to hurry off with other planes."

The three photographs and the poster described here are from the **Records of the Office of War Information (RG 208, Series LO, LU, MO, NP, PMO, and PU).** The Office of War Information (OWI) was established in 1942 to coordinate government information on the war. To achieve its objectives, OWI used press, radio, motion pictures, and still photography resources. OWI's Domestic Operations Branch disseminated information within the United States, while the Overseas Operations Branch's domain was all countries outside the continental United States, with the exception of Latin America.

"Be a Marine . . . Free a Marine to fight." This recruiting poster features a portrait of a woman Marine painted by artist

Nancy Harkness Love, Director of the Women's Auxiliary Ferrying Squadron (WAFS). (208-N-4222 [208-PU-120Y-1])

Recruiting poster for the Marine Corps Women's Reserve. (208-PMO-296)

Douglas Crockwell. The original painting hung in the office of the Director of Women Marines until 1977.

The 200,000 images in the records of the Office of War Information constitute a pictorial history of the war, both on the U.S. homefront and on the battlefields. Included in the records also are posters and cartoons promoting conservation, war bonds, increased production, security issues, and recruitment. OWI's Negro Press Section photographs provides considerable documentation of the contributions of African Americans to the war effort. Of particular note for this paper are the many images of black women serving in the military. Many of the pictures in the series were taken by black photographers, some of the first hired by the government.

Although several series within this huge record group provide limited documentation of the activities of women in the Army, Navy, Marine Corps, WAFS, and WASP, the six series listed above offer the most direct access to several hundred images. The records in most of the series referred to are arranged by subject; for the others a subject index is available.

The Women's Bureau

"That feminine touch. Looking a bit bewildered by the bevy of charmers who've 'invaded' the mechanical field, this enlisted man prepares to turn over his duties in the maintenance of aircraft." The group of women in this photograph replaced men who were then freed for duty at sea or abroad. Aviation was one area in which women in all the services found ready occupations. Reaction to women in the services was mixed, and undoubtedly a few men were mystified. But many more probably reacted just as one Coast Guard coxswain: "We welcome them. They give us our one and only chance for the job we want,—the sea."

This photograph is one of about 2,500 photographs in the **Records of the Women's Bureau (RG 86, Series WWT)** showing women working in various occupations during World War II, including defense industries and all the branches of the armed forces. The photographs are arranged by subject.

Posters

"WANTED. More Navy Nurses."

In addition to the record groups described above, the **Records of the Office of Government Reports (RG 44, Series PA)** is a

*A group of women prepare to take over maintenance responsibilities for aircraft.
(86-WWT-60-7)*

Recruiting poster for the Navy Nurse Corps. (44-PA-2296)

source for World War II posters. Within the office, the Division of Public Information assembled and distributed propaganda materials relating to campaigns and programs promoting the war effort. Among the division's records are several thousand posters used in recruitment, including many directed toward women such as *"WANTED. More Navy Nurses."* In order to preserve and safeguard original posters, researchers must view color slide reproductions. The color slides of posters in RG 44, Series PA, are arranged by subject.

In conclusion, this paper highlights only the primary resources for still picture documentation of women in service in World War II. Other wartime agency files and series, although not included, are often good supplemental sources that should not be overlooked especially by researchers interested in indepth and exhaustive research. Persons interested in researching the records described in this paper and other records maintained by the Still Picture Branch are invited to contact the branch for assistance or additional information (NNSP, Room 5360, National Archives at College Park, 8601 Adelphi Road, College Park, MD 20740-6001).

BIBLIOGRAPHY

MacGregor, Morris J. *Integration of the Armed Forces, 1940-1965.* Defense Studies Series. Washington, DC: Government Printing Office, 1981.

Stremlow, Mary V. *Free A Marine to Fight, Women Marines in World War II.* Marines in World War II Commemorative Series. Washington, DC: History and Museums Division, Marine Corps Historical Center, U.S. Marine Corps, 1994.

Thomson, Robin J. *The Coast Guard and the Women's Reserve in World War II.* Washington, DC: Coast Guard Historians Office, U.S. Coast Guard, 1992.

Treadwell, Mattie E., *The Women's Army Corps.* The United States Army in World War II, Special Studies. U.S. Army Center of Military History Pub. 11-8. Washington, DC: Government Printing Office, 1954.

Women in World War II. Fact Sheet. Washington, DC: 50th Anniversary of World War II Commemoration Committee, Department of the Army, n.d.

APPENDIX
National Archives Publications
Describing Still Picture Branch Holdings

Burger, Barbara Lewis. "American Images: Photographs and Posters in the Still Picture Branch," *Prologue: Quarterly of the National Archives,* 22 (Winter 1990): 353-368.

————— , comp. *Guide to the Holdings of the Still Picture Branch of the National Archives and Records Administration.* Washington, DC: National Archives and Records Administration, 1990.

————— , comp. Select Audiovisual Records, *Pictures of African Americans During World War II.* Slide set and leaflet. Washington, DC: National Archives and Records Administration, 1993.

Burger, Barbara Lewis, William Cunliffe, Jonathan Heller, William T. Murphy, and Les Waffen, comps. *Audiovisual Records in the National Archives of the United States Relating to World War II,* Reference Information Paper 70. Washington, DC: National Archives and Records Administration, revised 1992.

General Information Leaflet 38, *Information for Prospective Researchers About the Still Picture Branch of the National Archives.* Washington, DC: National Archives and Records Administration, revised 1994.

Heller, Jonathan, ed. *War & Conflict: Selected Images from the National Archives, 1765-1970.* Washington, DC: National Archives and Records Administration, 1990.

READING CULTURAL TEXT IN GOVERNMENT FILMS
Women, Image, and the World War II Experience

Jennifer A. Nelson

*In no country has such constant care been taken as in America
to trace two clearly distinct lines of action for the two sexes
and to make them keep pace one with the other, but in two
pathways that are always different.... Hence it is that the
women of America, who often exhibit a masculine strength
of understanding and a manly energy, generally preserve
great delicacy of personal appearance and always retain the
manners of women although they sometimes show that they
have the hearts and minds of men.*

— *Alexis de Tocqueville,*
Democracy in America,
Volume II, 1840

Tocqueville's reputation as a shrewd observer and interpreter of
American culture and its society rests partially in the fact that
his writings have stood the test of time. Though sometimes sweep-
ing, his generalizations remain relevant and contain provocative
insights that may guide our understanding today. Tocqueville recog-
nizes the dichotomy between human nature and false appearances,
between the true and the cosmetic, and the part that this relationship plays in fashioning the constructs of gender roles in America.
He says that because of the rigid distinction between that which
is female (an undefined condition here) and that which is masculine
(here intellectual and energetic in heart and mind), women must
appear to conform to the accepted order of the gender code so
that they may leave intact, though camouflaged, and express, when
prudent, the true nature of their equally aggressive minds and

hearts. To appreciate Tocqueville's insight and to reach such understanding, one must learn to peel apart image from substance, to identify and "read" the layers of meaning inherent in cultural texts of all types.

One of the most intriguing sources of cultural texts is motion picture film. Archivists, museum curators, and documentary producers as well as the Academy of Motion Pictures, Arts, and Sciences have long been well acquainted with this fact. Thematic study of film yields much information about the meanings and influences of gender upon cultural dynamics. This perspective has fostered many perceptions about "starlets" and their film characters, influenced how film industry moguls package female images, and explained audience attraction to films that feature popular feminine icons. Much less attention has been directed toward those comparatively few commercial films that have shown women engaged in traditionally masculine activities.

Where can the scholar look to find film representations of women's dual existence as identified and described by Tocqueville? Where can we locate a rich collection of films that provide images and texts relevant to Tocqueville's cultural analysis of gender? Where, during what time, and under what circumstances did women, en masse, show their gritty ambition and breach the gender gap? Did this happen without public controversy? Who were these women, and how were the full expressions of their hearts and minds documented on film?

Answers to these questions lie within collections that hold and preserve historical films. Whereas any film can be described as "historical"—in that all films are created within time and usually contain some sort of overt or veiled interpretation about known conditions in the cultural world, past or present, which general audiences can identify as realistic or nearly realistic—only certain films are truly historical in the academic sense. These films either are expressly created to candidly record real events as they happen or are scripted productions that possess obvious intrinsic value as reflective of, or as commentary upon, a historic event or era such as the Second World War. One can easily argue that the greatest number of historical films ever created concern World War II.

Among the richest of World War II film depositories is the National Archives and Records Administration. It is within the motion picture holdings of the National Archives that the diligent scholar researching World War II film will find evidence that, as volunteers to the various branches of the United States Armed Forces, women assumed work and career roles traditionally reserved for men. Historical World War II film betrays a complicated social and psychological fact about America's servicewomen. It shows that in subtle but significant ways these women functioned both as "feminine" and "masculine" because of the ways the military at large incorporated gender-associated social expectations inherent in the cultural hegemony of the period. Here is Tocqueville's delicate but aggressive American woman. Her gender is distinguished from that of the male soldier by segregated organizational affiliations, uniform styles, and formal service status. Yet she is "present and accounted for," remains active, and works intently toward accomplishing the mission of her unit.

Cultural messages about American servicewomen are buried in historical film. Learning to "read" these messages, to identify layers of meaning, and then to examine images and to sift those explicit and implicit artistic impressions through our present-day perspectives in the hope that fresh ideas about yesterday will emerge, is a thoroughly difficult and daunting but highly rewarding task. "Reading" motion picture images for meaning is an intellectually and emotionally interactive experience, a dynamic activity, between audience members and film. "Reading" is more than viewing; it is the act of ingesting meaning contained within images and then digesting meaning—developing an understanding of the meaning of images, now shaped by audience interpretation—through analysis.

We, as members of the audience as well as critics and scholars, should consider a few words of caution concerning our "reading" of cultural images, specifically the excavation of gender meaning from layers of cultural text and production and script elements inherent in film. Oftentimes when interpreting images, especially those that depict the past, we unconsciously foist current social and political contexts upon them. We must take care to know our personal and cultural biases—we can never be entirely free from such opinions—and understand how those perspectives inform our analyses, especially if we bring relevant personal experience to bear upon our interpretation. If we are careful, even ploddingly so, and are aware of our personal as well as academic reasons for pursuing explication of gender images in film, we can see with reasonably clear vision the breadth and depth offered in these cultural texts.

Further, we will understand that culture reflects the often contradictory beliefs and expression of peoples whose perceptions of their historical experience may naturally change over time. Culture is not static, nor is it usually composed of simple or rational philosophic formulas. Oftentimes analysis of cultural meaning cannot be measured but must be sensed and explicated while acknowledging that, when discussing "rules" of cultural analysis, "the exception to the rule" may easily be found while remaining the exception. Thus, one or more "readings" of cultural images may contain several components that may seem to directly contradict one another. This condition is natural to cultural analysis, given the nature of culture. In this spirit, we will find and become well acquainted with Tocqueville's American women in military service. First, however, we must physically locate the motion pictures that will facilitate this meeting and then, within the context of gender studies, apply specific analytical techniques to reading these texts.

Before analyzing motion picture film for cultural meaning, the scholar must locate and view a suitable film. Two search methods prove helpful to researchers who utilize the National Archives' film and video holdings. First, if the researcher prefers to conduct a subject-related search, regardless of whether film exists as edited or unedited, the researcher should examine the National Archives' many motion picture card catalogs. Each catalog indexes, usually by subject but in some instances only by item number, those films within a specific numeric record group (RG) containing records from a specific federal agency, commission, or donation to the National Archives gift collection.

Moving images pertaining to American women in the military during World War II include, but are not limited to, gender and race segregation at meals and other activities; recreational activities such as dodgeball, softball, basketball, and horseshoes; attendance at religious services; daily life routines; classroom and on-the-job training at installations such as Fort Oglethorpe and Fort Knox; ceremonial functions and reviews; stations overseas in England, France, Italy, Japan, Germany, and North Africa; work as technicians, medical assistants and nurses, mechanics, and office and radio personnel; the experiences of African-American women in the military; and the work of women in the American Red Cross. Of some interest may be a portion of an edited film showing the Navy Yeomanettes in World War I. A researcher will also find film footage showing many aspects of military life experienced by the

Marine Corps Women's Reserve, the Women's Army Auxiliary Corps (WAAC) and the subsequent Women's Army Corps (WAC), the Women Accepted for Volunteer Emergency Service (WAVES), the Women Airforce Service Pilots (WASP), the Women's Auxiliary Ferrying Squadron (WAFS), and the Coast Guard's SPAR.

The other most common search method is to research only those catalogs that describe edited films or those that describe unedited film. The researcher should focus upon specific card catalogs that contain references to each type of film. Only the main card catalog contains references to both types; the majority of films contained therein, however, are edited films and may be copyrighted. After selecting the card catalog(s) of interest, the researcher should proceed with a subject search as described above.

If the researcher requires uncopyrighted original sources or silent stock footage, unedited film showing American women in the military during World War II can be found in the following catalogs of the Army Air Forces, Army Signal Corps, and Navy: RG 18, Records of the Army Air Forces (the CS 18 index); RG 111, Records of the Office of the Chief Signal Officer (the ADC and LC Signal Corps collections); and RG 428, General Records of the Department of the Navy, 1947-. Whereas a few color film items exist in the holdings, the vast majority of films are in black-and-white format.

On the other hand, the researcher wishing to view and duplicate edited films is encouraged to determine the current copyright holder and arrange permission for use directly with the copyright holder. (The National Archives cannot guarantee the copyright status of any film.) Edited films relating to U.S. women in the military during World War II are located in the following catalogs: RG 208, Records of the Office of War Information; RG 200 PN, Paramount Newsreels in NARA's Donated Materials; and RG 111 M, Records of the Office of Chief Signal Officer. Virtually every item includes sound; most films range from 1 to 10 minutes in length. All exist in black-and-white format. Reference finding aids relating to American servicewomen are available through the National Archives Motion Picture, Sound, and Video Branch (see appendixes to this paper).[1]

After obtaining the film, how can the researcher analyze its meaning or method of conveying its message? The researcher must learn to "read" the film: to identify, extract, and interpret overtextual and subtextual messages inherent in it. This technique is fundamental to interpretation of cinematic, literary, and every other form of artistic work. Whatever the genre, messages come to us as overtexts and subtexts.

The overtext is the declared intent of the piece. For example, in the case of many WAC recruitment films, the overtext addresses society's purported need for more women to join military service, explains why women who join the WAC are not wasting their time, and describes the benefits that await those who respond. The overtext is the obvious message contained in, or the purpose in creating, the film. The subtext, on the other hand, is less obvious. Whether it lies deeper within, or soars above, the film's formulaic patterns, it is hidden. The subtext usually seeks either to underscore or to undercut the overtext through use of image and word choice and even the omission of ideas.

Whether the subtext seems to support or to contradict the overtext depends entirely upon the purpose of the film, the cultural elements inherent within the film, and any bias-laden "reading" of the film by the audience experiencing the film. Whereas the overtext controls the direction of the film (e.g., the plot or the narrative), the subtext speaks to the hearts and minds of the audience. Subtextual messages are powerful elements; no matter what the content of the overtext, the subtext almost always delivers the greater intellectual and emotional impact. Because of this, gender-infused subtextual meaning in film deserves analysis, especially in historical film (edited or unedited) relating to women in the military.

How overtexts and to what degree subtexts appear in film depends largely upon whether the film is edited or unedited. The most significant factor distinguishing edited from unedited film is the determination of where, by what means, and how deeply the subtexts are hidden. In some instances, subtext may not exist at all.

Edited films about American servicewomen during World War II found in National Archives holdings reflect every conceivable recruiting angle used by the Department of War and provide perspectives on the media's attempt to temporarily popularize, as well as contain, women's roles in the war. Edited film is "packaged." The overtexts and subtexts are substantial parts of that packaging. Audiences may enjoy these productions more than screenings of unedited film because the package engages them.

Whereas creation of the overtext as part of the packaging is always deliberate, creation of subtext is not always deliberate. Generally, when the subtext distinctly supports the overtext, it seems that creation of the subtext is intentional because the packaging clearly links the texts. However, when the subtext seems to contradict the overtext, it is always harder to determine whether the subtext does so by design.

Deliberate undercutting of the overtext may be evident. If, for example, a film that is presumably intended to encourage public support for a specific political program is to be shown to an audience that will not likely accept the premise or purpose of the film (its overtext), the film may contain subtexts that somehow encourage the audience to feel less threatened or offended by the overtextual messages. Sometimes this type of relationship between over- and subtext will be achieved by subtle comic portrayal within the subtext so the audience will accept the overtext with humor rather than reject it with disgust.

Undeliberate undercutting of the overtext, however, may be evident in a film that reflects social or political, even religious, biases imbedded in the culture that fostered the film and its overtext. For example, a film that instructs a community of individuals to "love their neighbor" may contain words that define the audience's relationship to the "neighbors" such that an "us versus them" perspective is established and the intent of the film as presented by the overtext cannot be achieved. In this sense, the subtext undercuts the overtext while the purpose of the overtext, as created by the filmmaker, remains genuine. How subtexts are defined—as either supportive or undercutting of the overtext, whether deliberate or unintentional—will depend upon the cultural biases that audience members bring to their "reading" of a film's subtext(s).

Unedited film, often called "raw footage," provides interesting candid footage that tells a story and, free of packaging and sensationalism, shows the audience scenes and conditions in an extemporaneous fashion. The meaning of the overtext often is captured by the audience's general acceptance of the idea—either introduced while they observe the film or presumed before viewing—that the events shown on unedited film occurred in real time. The only manipulations or contrivances placed upon the subject by the cameraman are those regarding choice of subject and duration of time spent in filming the subject. Interpretation of the subtexts, where they exist in raw, unedited film, is born from individual and group reactions of audience members to the film. In this sense, the audience may impose its own subtextual meanings upon the film and, in so doing, actually create the subtext spontaneously. The import of those meanings is not created by camera manipulation, scripting, or post-production magic but through the audience's general acceptance, or the filmmaker's acceptance, of unedited film as "raw" evidentiary information. Its documentary nature suggests that, despite variations in interpretations of the meaning of events shown in unedited film, the facts have been recorded and are indisputable. In short, "what one sees" is "what one gets," because with unedited film there is a less contrived relationship between the overtext and subtexts and a more honest representation of the reality being filmed. This sense of realism coupled with the audience's subjective reading of images makes unedited film a powerful medium.

Thus, with unedited film the relationship between overtexts and subtexts showing the World War II experiences of U.S. women in the military is one that we may believe shows the past as it occurred. The stark visual contrasts provided by the black-and-white format of unedited footage taken from this era, especially if it is silent, focuses the audience's attention on the actions of women as they are shown training, marching on parade, transcribing and processing documents, attending church services and recreational gatherings, and testing armaments. The overtexts and subtexts may be, or seem to be, unified. The natural, uncontrived images reflect natural, uncontrived experiences—full of accidental occurrences and subtle surprises. Stock footage oftentimes shows the familiar; the familiar does not shock. Messages and lessons that buttress common assumptions and interpretations about the experiences of women in uniform are the ones that most often compose the subtext of unedited film featuring such women.

The difficulty posed by subtextual gender-related messages in or imposed upon unedited film can also be discussed in terms of apparently natural human tendencies to find meaning where none, or little, actually exists and to impose order and patterns upon that which, for whatever reason, withstands analytical treatment. For example, depending upon the thoughts we bring to gender-associated dress codes and related social stigmas, stock footage scenes that show Navy Waves engaged in drilling and marching while dressed in stiff-looking skirts and shoes will likely elicit today either amusement or disgust. What if it appears that the women are enjoying themselves? What if they do not seem to mind their own discomfort and perspiration? What if they seem disgruntled? The film probably does not represent a cultural or political agenda concerning the meaning of women's military experiences during World War II; does the audience expect an agenda? With unedited film it is difficult, sometimes exceedingly so, to distinguish elements that are intentionally misleading from those that are coincidental, unimaginably simplistic, somehow incomplete, or naturally unflattering. However, the ever-insistent human impulse to interpret and apply meaning to every perceived condition is ever present. Wherever subtext does not exist within film (edited or unedited), the audience will create subtextual meaning as they develop their own interpretations while viewing a film.

With edited film, the relationship between overtexts and subtexts showing World War II experiences of U.S. women in the military is tightly knit for several reasons. Subtextual messages contained in edited film may be difficult to de-layer, but the audience can sense or infer their existence because these messages are part of a packaged presentation. Edited film, in some respects, is less daunting to the observer than is unedited film because the former usually possesses a discernable artistic form, even if "impressionistic." The audience knows that there is a beginning, a middle, and an end to a relatively formulaic, uncomplicated plot. Characters, setting, and language are seldom complex.

However masked by artistic direction, the overtexts of most edited films intend to entertain and to "sell" commercial products as well as political and social ideas. Whether we, as audience members, are comfortable with the meanings inherent in certain images linked to over- and subtexts, we recognize and understand the meanings of subtextual messages even if we do so only on a subconscious level. The import of the subtextual rests squarely on the shoulders of those often stubborn cultural assumptions that are familiar to the audience, and it is this familiarity that markets or "sells" the film to the audience. This dynamic relationship also generally prevents the audience from identifying the cultural subtextual fuel that empowers the overtextual plot. In short, we are drawn to understand how the plot—the overtext—progresses and why it does so; we are not prompted to question subtextual reasons underlying why the plot makes sense to us.

When performing cultural analysis upon edited film, the researcher may find it taxing to try to distinguish when, where, and to what extent a subtext supports the overtext. This exercise provides the proverbial map and shovel, however, for excavating hidden subtexts and their related messages. For example, in an Office of War Information recruitment film called *Glamour Girls of 1943*, several male actors present an overtext. They purport to "play the devil's advocate" by presenting statements declaring the dire consequences that await the social order because of female volunteer enlistment during World War II. The assertions offered by these men provide the narrator with an opportunity to explain and dismiss the men's fears as misguided and then to talk about the reasons why women should enlist. As characters within the movie, these men ask, "If my wife works, people will think I can't support her"; "Oh, I don't mind my wife working, but who's gonna run my home?"; and "It's okay now, but what about after the war? The women'll have all the jobs."

Upon careful analysis, it seems that these statements may serve a purpose beyond that of providing a prompt for the narrator's discussion. There is subtext, to be sure, in both the double-edged quality of the statements and their relation to the overtext. While the overtext suggests that the men's comments were scripted only to raise issues so they could be addressed and resolved in the minds of audience members, the simple mention of these not-so-subtle socioeconomic and political issues carries a strong reminder to the audience of gender divisions, biases, and accepted social norms— in general, common beliefs about "the way things should be" and what women should and should not do. Subtextual messages, especially of this kind, are powerful. They encourage cultural hegemony by speaking directly to deeply ingrained beliefs about the United States' social order, which has been taught to every member of the audience born in the United States. The messages are not over-intellectualized; in fact, they often dodge intellectual processes. This is precisely why subtextual messages can be communicated so effectively.

In some instances, examination of a film for its over- and subtextual messages will show that the film contains several conflicting subtexts: Some agree with the overtext, and others either do not agree with the overtext or do not agree with one another. In a general sense, upon stripping away the overtext—which addresses the need for escalated enlistment of women into military service— the jumbled subtexts seem to reflect the coexistence of aspirations that sometimes differ between males and females as well as mimic the confusion and uncertainty felt by Americans about future economic and social gender divisions.

Superb examples of these discordant cultural and critical elements are found in the 1944 WAC recruitment film entitled *It's Your War, Too*. The overtextual as well as several subtextual messages encourage women to join the military and to consider that their enlistment could lead to postwar careers. As Wacs, women could experience wonderful things immediately, irrespective of economic class affiliation. They could travel (one scene shows a Wac riding a camel in what appears to be a North African desert), represent the U.S. Armed Forces in ceremonies at home and abroad, learn marketable skills, become physically fit, and, in the company of others, pursue their country's serious mission. One set of subtexts suggests to young American women that their ambitions are natural and admirable and that they should develop and utilize their personal strengths, not be ashamed of their bodies, and look for opportunities, such as volunteering for the military, to improve self-confidence.

Another set of subtexts supports this broad, positive view of women's volunteer military service and seeks to gain the attention of women who may harbor resentment at exclusion from male-dominated sectors of the work force or from the armed forces in general. Toward the conclusion of the film, a Wac glances at the camera and then glances a second time, holding her gaze steady, and, maintaining an appearance and tone denoting criticism, erroneously states, "In World War I, we were on the sidelines." Admittedly, the script misrepresents history. In fact, women volunteered for many organizations, such as the Red Cross and the Navy (Yeomanettes), during World War I. Indeed, the notion of volunteerism by American women originated well before the post-Civil War proliferation of philanthropic organizations and existed even during the American Revolution. Of course, the most likely purpose of the statement was not to mislead but to encourage women to see themselves as the strong pioneers that they had always been and, accordingly, to join the WAC in what was to become part of a watershed movement in broadening roles for women. It is interesting to note that the title of the film itself suggests that American women should be reminded that they may or should assist the war effort.

A different set of subtexts in *It's Your War, Too* offers less noble messages for American women. In one instance the narrator instructs prospective recruits to forget rumors they may have heard suggesting that Wacs could not wear makeup, good stockings, or attractive hairstyles or engage in recreational activities. While the narrative voice, which provides the overtext, seems to tell women that they can retain their individuality while in the service, the subtext simultaneously reminds women of their seemingly large concern for cosmetics and clothing and viewers of the notion that women could not function as dedicated workers because of the perceived softness and luxury of domestic life. A scene showing a Wac in full makeup "touching up" her lipstick application, while glancing happily and approvingly into a compact mirror, supports the subtextual message.

In another instance of gender-laden subtext, the narrator identifies possible candidates for women's volunteer service. He names "Mary Jones," "Jane Doe," "the Idle Housewife," and "the Girl Next Door." The titles are generic at best. At worst, they presume women's unappreciative enjoyment of middle-class leisure. The sequence of images that accompany this role call provides additional subtextual messages that underscore ideas about women's unconcerned, even lazy, lifestyles. Shown first, "Mary Jones" appears startled by the narrator's voice as he interrupts her bridge game. "Jane Doe," a young woman sporting a carefully coiffed hairstyle, earrings, and heavily applied makeup, quickly glances up from her reading. Then "the Idle Housewife," surprised as she purchases a matinee movie ticket, turns to face the camera. Finally, the youthful "Girl Next Door," adorned in a hat and surrounded by a fashionably large soft collar, gazes vacantly into the camera as she slowly sips a malted drink through a straw. The lighting and costuming (and perhaps even frosted camera lens filters) used in filming the "Mary Jones" and "the Girl Next Door" segments created a "soft" image— the essence of a life obviously untouched by the rough masculine world of work and warfare. The audience may even have wondered if "the Girl Next Door" could have graduated from WAC training if she had enlisted.

Whereas these four images may simply have represented negative stereotypes against which potential volunteers could have compared themselves favorably before deciding to "join up," the stereotypes themselves are heavily laden with gender-specific meanings that were, no doubt, meant to cast the popular middle-class domestic feminine ideal in a less than flattering light. Whereas such use may be described as creation of unintentional subtext, it should be noted that these stereotypes and the connotations they bear are found in the popular literature and early advertising of 19th-century America and would not have been unfamiliar to the mid-20th century American psyche.

These old stereotypes equate domestic womanhood with luxury and idleness and, as used in this particular film, denote that this carefree and unpatriotic lifestyle does not respect necessary wartime sacrifices. The "Girl Next Door" may make amends for her excesses, though; she may serve her country by courageously agreeing to leave her domain and accept relatively unthreatening and appropriate, feminine work in the WAC. Yet, while this effort certainly was then, and is shown in the film to be, daring, the movie does not portray women's work in the WAC as requiring skills that deviated far from those that women generally had performed at home or on the farm. It is fair, therefore, to wonder about the meaning that these images held for audiences that viewed this and other recruitment films as well as about their effect within a larger social context. What did these subtextual messages, so closely linked to cultural ideas about gender, tell young men and women about women's roles and the meaning of femininity as they watched this and other recruitment films that were shown in theaters nationwide during the spring of 1944?

Overtexts and subtexts may be located within other elements of edited film besides the combination of image and scripted dialogue. Dialogue alone can provide over- and subtexts. For example, it is interesting to note that throughout *It's Your War, Too* the narrative tone vacillates between the masculine and the feminine and their respective gender-associated characteristics. Whenever narration describes the mission of the WAC, how women's volunteer service aids the general purpose of the Allied effort, and general recruitment needs, a male voice is used. Because this voice sounds official and utilizes direct language, it seems to express the collective will of military authority. Significantly, the male narrator states that WAC service could lead to civilian careers for women in postwar America. Whereas in many respects this claim was actualized, it is important to note that in an official recruiting film, women were not encouraged to believe that the military would utilize their services following the armistice, let alone allow women to enlist in a peacetime army.

During other segments of this film, a female voice assumes a narrative role that differs substantially from that of the male narrator. Using a less formal tone, one reminiscent of "girl talk," this voice speaks directly and at some length to women about the quality of WAC life as "novel and interesting." The idea that the WAC lifestyle is "all work and no fun," she says, "is strictly Axis propaganda."

As if a colleague, friend, or hostess, she invites women to imagine, then join, the fun and dedicated WAC organization. Elsewhere in the film, women's voices declare their allegiance to the WAC, pledging to "live up to the legends of our fighting men" and the national cause. Yet they imply nothing about their own achievements or a desire to champion their own honor. In *It's Your War, Too* the female voice, whether linked to the narrative or to the scripted dialogue, does not inspire awe for the sacrifices or leadership abilities exhibited by women during World War II. Rather, the film shows the audience that the dedicated Wacs "always retain the manners of women" and the "great delicacy of personal appearance." If an immortal Tocqueville had read from the text of this film, he probably would have recognized the Wac.

One remaining source of insight into over- and subtexts can be found only outside of film. It will be left only to diligent researchers to attempt to read the cultural meanings inherent in these specific texts. Production files and scripts are rich in information regarding production, distribution, and political and social issues relative to a film. Use of production files may either help or hinder the creative process of modern historians developing philosophical interpretations of overtexts and subtexts. These documents (which record specific decisions and changes regarding scripting, general film production, and distribution) may thoroughly dispute or support a theory about cultural meaning in a film because they may contain information that reveals the intentions and biases of the film's script writer(s), director(s), and producer(s). These files reveal facts that the viewing audience could not blindly intuit from the film, yet the essence of these facts finds its way onto the screens and into the minds of the audience.

Production files and related documents sometimes become part of film collections. When researching government films and donated motion picture items at the National Archives, production files can be located and examined as part of the historical record. The file pertaining to *It's Your War, Too* provided helpful information and broadened the film's subtextual perspective.

When *It's Your War, Too,* which Warner Brothers originally filmed under contract to the War Department in 1942, was recreated into a shorter public release film in March and April of 1944, the War Department insisted that two changes be made to the script before military officials would approve distribution of the film. One change altered a statement made by General Eisenhower, who is shown near the beginning of the film. The original line uttered by Eisenhower was "One Wac can do *certain* jobs as well as one man" (italics added). The changed line, read by a narrator for the general, states, "One Wac can do many jobs as well as one man." It is interesting to note that the claim expressed in Eisenhower's revamped statement is underscored by General Marshall's speech, which concludes the film and was written specifically for this production. Marshall says, "There are hundreds of important Army jobs which women can perform as effectively as men. In fact, we find that they can do some of these jobs much better than the men." Together, Generals Marshall and Eisenhower (with some rescripting for the latter) seemed to describe women as nearly equal to men in their usefulness and ingenuity.

Concerning a second change to the script, for reasons that cannot be determined, a powerful narrative statement was stricken and not replaced, contrary to the case of every other revised or removed line. The line read, "The Army needs thousands more, thousands of women, *proud* to take their share in shaping the history of their country." A careful reading of these subtexts suggests that *It's Your War, Too* strikes a careful sociopolitical balance between moderately controversial and traditional treatments of gender. One must conclude, though, that the script leans further toward the traditional—the pedestal—perspective of women and feminine characteristics. The film praises the fortitude, but not the power, of women.

A reading of government films as cultural text within the context of gender-studies analysis reveals an important characteristic about these films. Taken together, the overtexts and the subtexts clearly present "a mixed bag" of social messages. In short, recruitment films—especially as seen in *It's Your War, Too*—simultaneously praise and discount women's capabilities. These edited films, as well as many segments taken from popular newsreels of the time, discuss women's abilities in terms of the presence or absence of masculinity. The productions loosely identified women's volunteer service as "masculine" in deed but not "masculine" in spirit. Viewers sense almost a nervous quality in the recruitment films, in their stiff and awkward messages that describe not only how a woman could perform so many tasks traditionally reserved for men but also how a woman could not be evaluated by the same standards believed to measure a man's masculinity, especially as a soldier.

In some instances these issues are dismissed by a few jocular remarks, either scripted dialogue or narrative, that suggest that women's volunteer military service is less than serious, a fad that will be forgotten once the men return from war and all social life returns to "normal." Such assumptions and comical remarks, too, are subtextual messages that dictated to woman that, despite the fact that they had accomplished much during the war, their feminine social roles could not accommodate the masculine work ethic—a construct that ranked a male individual within the macrocosmic economic and political order. Women, naturally unfit for this environment, were to exercise their influence within the microcosmic domestic sphere and refer to the macrocosmic world vicariously through the position of their men.

The WAC's pledge, as presented by *It's Your War, Too,* to "live up to the legends of our fighting men" reflects the traditional belief that, during wartime, American women assist and relieve men while men assist and direct the nation. Ideas about how gender roles structure and inform participation in specific types of military and national service, depending upon how service is associated with gender, are deeply rooted in American experience. The mission of war and focus upon the contribution to war effort, as explained thoroughly in Michael C. C. Adams's book *The Great Adventure: Male Desire and the Coming of World War I* (Bloomington, IN: 1990), amplifies the notion that women's duties as wives and mothers are set apart from men's duties as breadwinners and protectors. In this sense, women cannot appear in government-produced film as anything but a helpmate sprung from the homestead. At most, the subtexts of edited government films do not convey much more than a commitment to introducing U.S. women, within rigidly defined boundaries, into the realm of the masculine war machine.

Reading historical film is "a way of reading the past—not just reading the scenes recorded and the faces immobilized into permanent images, but the past as culture, as ways of thinking and feeling, as experience."[2] We find in archived government film, in historical film, important texts that furnish meaning and substance for interpretations of our cultural beliefs and identities. Although film texts yield messages that reinforce the cultural hegemony concerning divisions of work and gender-assigned roles, in many ironic respects the overtexts and several subtexts that exist within unedited government film show that the experiences of U.S. women in the military during World War II successfully challenged traditional wartime presumptions about gender roles in America. Women acted in defense of their fighting men, of the United States, and of the Allied effort at large. Women acted decisively to exercise their personal needs for involvement in critical issues that touched them and others they knew, for broadening their understanding of the world and their capabilities as human beings, and for experiencing the satisfaction of knowing that they had accomplished important work.

If researchers step back from the analysis of subtexts and minute details, they can see in government films how, where, and why women found their motivations to volunteer for military service. Women quietly disregarded the idea that their work was masculine in deed but not masculine in spirit and, instead, developed a twist on this notion. Women publicly embraced the subtle philosophy that work that was "masculine" in deed was "feminine" in spirit. Historical film captures many complex elements of women's experiences in World War II. The texts that film provides may be used to discover new interpretations of the lives of American women or to reinforce ideas about that which is known or accepted. In the texts of historical film showing U.S. women in the military during World War II, we find evidence of a character common among American women and apparently persistent through time. Women in volunteer military service, while preserving great delicacy of personal appearance and retaining the manners of women, did not betray what Tocqueville observed long ago: American women possess ambitious and powerful hearts and minds.

NOTES

1. Only in a few instances will researchers find meaning in the catalog title codes "CS," "LC," "ADC," "M," "PN," and "NPC," which mean, respectively: "combat subject," "library copy," "Army depository copy," "miscellaneous," "Paramount Newsreel," and "Navy Photographic Center." These codes are helpful only in referring to a specific card catalog when not identifying its particular record group.
2. Alan Trachtenberg, *Reading American Photographs, Images as History: Mathew Brady to Walker Evans* (New York: 1989), p. 288.

APPENDIX A

Motion Picture, Sound, and Video Branch Card Catalogs

The Motion Picture, Sound, and Video Branch of the National Archives maintains a variety of card catalogs describing its holdings. Many of these card catalogs were produced by the agencies that created the records; others were compiled by National Archives staff. The branch possesses about 7.5 million catalog cards, some of which are made available on microfilm or microfiche.

Moving Images

Main Card Catalog. The main card catalog describes both government and commercially produced newsreels, public information films relating to federal agencies' missions and work, and documentary films covering a wide range of subjects. The earliest film dates from 1894, with the bulk dating from 1915 through the early 1970s. About 10,000 separate titles are included in this catalog and are arranged by record group (RG), title, and credits and alphabetically by subject headings. Subject headings are loosely based on the Library of Congress cataloging system.

Ford Film Collection Catalog (RG 200 FC). This card catalog, in conjunction with summary sheets, describes edited and unedited material donated to the National Archives by the Ford Motor Company in 1963. The collection covers a broad range of "Americana," with particular emphasis on the development and impact of the automobile. Dates range from 1915 to 1956. There are approximately 5,000 titles in the collection. The *Guide to the Ford Film Collection in the National Archives* is available, but it does not provide detailed item-level descriptions of the material. The guide may be purchased through the National Archives, Publications Distribution (NECD), Room G-9, Seventh and Pennsylvania Avenue, NW, Washington, DC 20408.

Universal Newsreel Catalog (RG 200 UN). This catalog, available on index cards and on microfilm, describes edited stories and outtakes of Universal's worldwide coverage for the period 1929–67. Approximately 150,000 titles are described on more than 600,000 cross-reference cards arranged in 13 broad subject categories, each of which is subdivided more specifically. There are approximately 125 rolls of Universal Newsreel microfilm. Summary sheets, arranged chronologically, are also available. Reference copies of the entire collection—as well as some outtakes—are available for viewing on videotape.

United States Air Force Catalog (RG 342). This catalog includes a broad range of aviation and Air Force footage dating from 1900 through the 1970s. About 10,000 titles are described on numerically arranged cards.

Army Air Forces Special Film Project (18 SFP) Catalog. This catalog describes outtakes from the Army Air Forces production *Thunderbolts* and covers activities of the 12th Army Air Force in Europe in 1944 and 1945. It includes 800 titles arranged alphabetically by title and by subject heading; 16mm color prints are available for most subjects.

Army Air Forces Combat SUBJECTS/Signal Corps Army Depository Film (RG 18 CS/111 ADC/111 LC). This card catalog describes unedited and camera record footage covering all theaters of military activity during World War II, the occupation of Germany and Japan, the war crimes trials, and the Korean war. Approximately 15,000 titles are described alphabetically by title and by subject heading in an arrangement based loosely on the Library of Congress cataloging system; 35mm black-and-white prints are available for all 18 CS subjects and for the 111 ADC series.

Navy Catalog (RG 428 NPC). This catalog describes unedited and camera record footage covering Navy activities from World War II through 1965. It includes about 10,000 titles and is available both in card and automated form.

Atomic Energy Commission Catalog (RG 362). This catalog describes unedited film covering testing and research procedures at various Commission field installations from 1950 to 1953. About 220 titles are arranged by film number and alphabetically by subject heading.

Marine Corps Catalog (RG 127). This microfiche catalog describes unedited and camera record footage shot mostly by Marine Corps units from World War I to about 1960. It includes approximately 60,000 subjects and is filmed on microfilm aperture cards.

Sound Recordings

Main Sound Catalog. This catalog briefly describes both government and privately produced sound recordings from a variety of sources and consists of radio broadcasts, speeches, interviews, actuality sound, documentaries, and oral history and public information programs. The earliest recording is from 1896, but most recordings date from 1935 to the present. Titles are described numerically and by personal name reference.

National Public Radio (NPR) Catalog (RG 200 NPR). This microfiche catalog indexes NPR news and public affairs broadcasts from 1971 to 1978. Indexes are by program title, name of speaker, subject keyword, subject classification, and geographic location. Reference copies are available on audiocassette.

Milo Ryan Phonoarchive Collection Catalog (RG 200 MR). This catalog describes 5,000 recordings primarily of CBS-KIRO radio broadcasts from 1931 to 1977, which were originally maintained at the University of Washington. The collection consists of news and public affairs programs, actualities, speeches, interviews, wartime dramas, and daily World War II news programs. Two published finding aids are available: *History in Sound: A Descriptive Listing of KIRO-CBS Collection of Broadcasts of the WWII Years* (1963) and *History in Sound: Part II* (1972). Catalog cards contain brief content summaries and are more detailed than the published guides. Most entries are available on reel-to-reel reference tapes.

ABC Radio Collection Catalog (RG 200 ABC). This catalog describes 27,000 radio broadcasts of news and public affairs programs from 1943 to 1971. The catalog is arranged chronologically by date of broadcast and thereunder by program series, title, keyword, or personal name reference.

NASA Audio Collection Catalog (RG 255). This catalog describes 1,400 NASA sound recordings dating from 1952 to 1975 and consisting of air-to-ground communications, astronauts' voices, public affairs programs, press conferences, speeches, and mission highlights. Some transcripts are available.

Supreme Court Oral Argument Collection (RG 267). This catalog describes 5,000 sound recordings of oral arguments presented before the U.S. Supreme Court from October 1955 to April 1978. Cases argued are indexed in published volumes of *U.S. Reports*, which are available in the research room. Case citations by title, volume, and *U.S. Reports* page number are required to locate recordings through the Court-prepared finding aid, which is arranged alphabetically by case name and thereunder chronologically. Reference copies are available.

APPENDIX B

Finding Aids Created by the National Archives Regarding Women in the Military

The finding aid folder "Women in the Military" is available in the Motion Picture Research Room. The finding aid generally describes the broad scope of films and images relating to women in the military contained in the holdings of the Motion Picture, Sound, and Video Branch. Included is a list of select films arranged by record group number. This finding aid is available to researchers during established research room hours. To find out how to obtain copies of motion picture, sound, or video items or for information about the contents of the finding aid folder, please call the staff of the Motion Picture, Sound, and Video Branch (301-713-7060), or visit the research room located on the fourth floor of the National Archives at College Park, MD.

Select pages from the recently published National Archives subject catalog *World War II on Film, A Catalog of Select Motion Pictures in the National Archives* (1994) might also be of interest to researchers. This catalog may be purchased through the National Archives, Publications Distribution (NECD), Room G-9, Seventh and Pennsylvania Avenue, NW, Washington, DC 20408.

LEADING THE WAY

The hundreds of thousands of women who served in the armed forces during World War II blazed a remarkable trail. Their little-known but pioneer experiences as servicewomen, veterans, and private citizens are documented in personal stories and public records that deserve recognition.

In the first paper of the session, Cynthia Neverdon-Morton used archival sources and interviews with veterans to highlight the efforts of African-American and Japanese-American servicewomen to secure the "Double V" (victory against fascism and nazism abroad and racism at home). Despite all-too-familiar encounters with racial prejudice and discrimination, these women strove to compile exemplary service records as proof of their able and loyal support of their country and entitlement to all the rights of citizenship.

Mary V. Stremlow's paper provided a historical account of the social, political, economic, and military factors preventing large numbers of World War II servicewomen from viewing themselves as legitimate veterans and taking advantage of the health-care and cash benefits due them. The Department of Veterans Affairs' poor preparation for the equitable handling of women's claims was also discussed. Stremlow stressed the urgency of locating veterans, informing them of their rights, and improving the quality of their lives by granting them full access to all earned benefits.

In the final paper, Mary E. Haas observed that military women were proactive during the war in seizing opportunities to serve their country, expand their knowledge and sense of self-worth, and increase society's awareness of their roles and accomplishments. She expressed alarm that students—especially girls—have seldom been taught the inspirational story of these women because school texts and curricula are distressingly silent. She called upon women veterans of World War II to volunteer once again to help strengthen democracy by demonstrating through their own stories the contributions that can be made when individuals are not limited by stereotype or apathy.

The session was chaired by Mary E. Haas, professor and educator of prospective social studies teachers at West Virginia University and author of numerous works on women and war.

Securing the "Double V"
African-American and Japanese-American Women in the Military During World War II

Cynthia Neverdon-Morton

Introduction

World War II ushered in a new era of social, economic, and political complexities for minorities in the United States. Emotionally charged media campaigns called upon minorities to participate as the nation shifted to a wartime economy and strengthened its military capability for a worldwide conflict. Yet discrimination and segregation shadowed the involvement of African Americans, the largest minority group in the United States, and Japanese Americans, who were still viewed by many Americans as an extension of Japan on American shores. Because race and class divisions were magnified and somewhat transformed, historians identify the era as a watershed in race relations.

During the war years, continuing discrimination against African Americans and the internment of Japanese Americans brought into sharp focus the negative racial policies and practices of the United States. While ignoring their own racially motivated acts of oppression and destruction, the Germans and the Japanese were quick to point out that Jim Crow laws, Oriental exclusion laws, and race riots were clear indicators that racism abounded in the United States. As a direct result of the war, the national and international attention given to the evolving racial consciousness further energized the victimized groups. African Americans, in particular, protested for radical and pervasive changes. Nevertheless, even as the war drew to a close, racism at home and the varied responses to it remained an explosive issue.

Rosalind Rosenberg argues successfully that another key issue of the 1940s was the relationship between gender and race in

American society.[1] Because of their efforts to gain acceptance in the military and inclusion in wartime industries, black and Japanese-American women were often in the national spotlight.

As we reconstruct the history of the era, we hear the voices of its participants. We read their writings—letters to governmental officials, petitions, organizational resolutions, and conference reports. We talk with them. We listen to their anecdotes. We relive with them their feelings of accomplishment and disappointment.

Before and during the World War II era, African Americans faced more opposition than any other minority group because of their ethnic and racial background. Just as African Americans were exploited under slavery, they were still being exploited under Jim Crow segregation as a source of cheap labor and psycho-social advantage for white Americans. Hence, they were denied civil rights and the opportunity to elevate themselves individually and collectively. During the same period, a racially and culturally diverse America was struggling to accept the reality that its diversity was not a threat to its ideals and principles but a strength to be nurtured.

As the United States' role in the world conflict expanded, African Americans and others willingly responded to the nation's call for workers on the homefront and recruits in the military. But it was not unconditional service; the thousands of African Americans who worked for victory expected that America would reward their patriotism and service by including them in all economic and social gains. African Americans did not want to hear empty visionary promises. They desired immediate visible progress toward true democracy at home.

To ensure that progress, they mobilized for the "Double V," victory against fascism and nazism abroad and victory against racism at home. Black women, who historically labored under the oppressive double burden of race and gender, accepted the "Double V" commitment and personalized it by proclaiming "Double V begins with me." These women clearly understood that until racial equality was achieved, gender issues were secondary.

Aiding the "Double V" cause was the black press, which kept its largely black readership informed of racial progress and problems. There were 230 black newspapers publishing on a regular basis in 1940. Nearly every major city, including Baltimore, Washington, DC, Chicago, New York, Philadelphia, and Atlanta, could boast of a black-owned press, which refused to compromise its commitment to its readers.

Increased participation in the industrial work force and the military initiated change at a faster pace. Coupled with that change, an increasing black exodus from the rural South transformed many communities in both the North and urban South into powder kegs primed for the flame of racism. Some exploded during the war years in places such as Livingstone, LA, and Detroit, MI. Other communities remained outwardly calm until the fifties and later.

The history of Japanese Americans in the United States was also marked by discrimination. In spite of early intelligence findings indicating that the majority of Japanese Americans were not security threats and posed no real danger to the United States, the press and patriotic organizations fueled anti-Japanese feelings and called for their removal from the Pacific coast. Economic desire to control Japanese property, racial bias against any person of color, and jockeying for political power motivated many in California and on the west coast to demand the internment of Japanese Americans. Bowing to political pressures, Roosevelt signed Executive Order 9066, the first step toward stripping civil liberties from Japanese Americans; citizenship was no longer of any consequence.

During the early months of 1942, Japanese Americans were removed from the western coastal area and forcibly interned in 10 camps in 7 states, stretching from inland California to Arkansas. In February 1943, to quell Japan's assertions that World War II was a racial war, all internees were required to respond to loyalty questionnaires. The intent was to determine eligibility for work furloughs and to register nisei, Japanese Americans who had been born in the United States, for the draft. According to definitions provided by the War Department, issei were a generation removed, born in Japan; nisei, two generations removed and American citizens; and kibei, those who returned to Japan, after having been born in the United States, for the purpose of an education, which immersed them in Japanese culture and language.

Responses to two questions ended up dividing the Japanese-American community. Question 27 of the "War Relocation Authority Application for Leave Clearance" asked women, "If the opportunity presents itself and you are found qualified, would you be willing to volunteer for the Army Nurse Corps or the WAAC?" Elderly issei and nisei women with young children wondered if a "yes" answer to the question meant they would be drafted. Of 300 tallied forms from Japanese-American women interned at Tule Lake, CA, 125 answered "yes" to question 27, and 175 answered "no." Of the

125 women who answered "yes" to question 27, only 50 were rated qualified. The other 75 were disqualified because of their age or because they had children. Some of those who answered "no" gave the following reasons: applying for repatriation to Japan, would like to know English better, parents object, husband objects, and health not good.[2]

Question 28, "Will you swear unqualified allegiance to the United States and forswear any form of allegiance or obedience to the Japanese emperor, or any other foreign government, power or organization?," was particularly disturbing for the issei, persons born in Japan and not yet naturalized as U.S. citizens. They were being asked to renounce the only government that recognized them; during the 1940s, issei were not ruled eligible for U.S. citizenship. Because of the likelihood that question 28 would contribute to increased tension and confusion in the camps, it was revised in 1943 to read "Will you swear to abide by the laws of the United States and take no action which would in any way interfere with the war effort of the United States?"[3]

Unfortunately, by the time the question was revised, the damage had been done. "Yes/yes," "no/no," or any combination of the two responses divided Japanese Americans into antagonistic factions. Beginning in September 1943, based on answers to the two questionnaires, most who were deemed disloyal were relocated yet again to Tule Lake, where a section of the camp was reserved for them. In keeping with expected behavior within the family, many women went to Tule Lake because their husbands, fathers, or sons were declared disloyal.

A limited comparison of African-American and Japanese-American experiences during the 1940s reveals that the interests and civil rights of both groups, against a backdrop of service in the armed forces, intersected at a crucial time in U.S. history. The two oppressed groups had an opportunity to reach across racial lines and unite in protest against national thought and action that relegated both groups to second-class citizenship.

A 1942 Office of War Information survey of African Americans in Memphis, Atlanta, Chicago, and New York supported the belief that many African Americans felt an affinity with Japanese Americans because they were also a dark-skinned race. Only 25 percent of the black respondents felt they would be any worse off under Japanese rule than they were as American citizens. Of the respondents who were willing to express their true sentiments, 9 percent felt that they would be better off under Japanese rule.[4] Easily, the percentages could have been higher. Given the racial tensions of the time, it is likely that some of the respondents were fearful of repercussions if they expressed their true feelings.

Survey conclusions drawn by War Department officials state

> Japan is a colored race assertedly trying to oust the white man from exploiting the colored races of the Far East. The sympathy of the Negro for this point of view should not be underestimated. He knows what it is to be kicked around because of color. Better to show that Japan is no democracy. That masses of Japanese are worse off than anyone in America—even share-croppers. That Japan is doing her part in China just what Hitler is doing in conquered Europe. That giant Japanese banking and commercial houses are in partnership with the military to exploit everyone—their own as well as conquered peoples.[5]

Japanese Americans—in their desire to stabilize their position in a country where, though American born, they were considered the enemy—disassociated themselves from the black civil rights struggle. Yet, in spite of (and ironically, in many cases, due to) segregation and discrimination, African Americans and Japanese Americans at the end of the war years each possessed a greater sense of group cohesiveness and empowerment than they had previously and were dedicated to effecting positive change in the social, political, and economic systems of the United States.

When compared to the number of white women who served in the military during World War II (over 360,000), the number of black and Japanese-American women was extremely small, 4,600 and approximately 350 respectively. The exact number of Japanese Americans is difficult to ascertain because they served in integrated units where their racial identity was not routinely noted. The total enlistment of black women was limited to 10 percent of the white women, while the WAC quota for Japanese Americans was set at 500. Reactions to the negative implications of quotas and racism were often viewed as primary factors influencing the low enlistment rates of the two groups.

Beyond inclusion, the greater significance of their involvement was the modification of national racial policies. The women, through their valor and competence in the military sphere, were able to raise the social consciousness of the nation as it pertained to race and gender issues. When the war ended, these women willingly exploited their newly gained knowledge and skills to build and strengthen their families and communities.

Army Nurse Corps (ANC)

In any war a primary concern is treatment and care of the wounded. In 1901, to meet that concern, the Army Nurse Corps was established as an auxiliary under the Army Reorganization Act, which formalized women's roles as nurses. With the outbreak of the Second World War, the War Department relied upon the Red Cross to recruit and certify nurses for the corps. Parfenia Jones Butler, a member of the first contingency of black nurses sent overseas in 1943, indicated that as a student at Tuskegee Institute in Alabama she had supported Red Cross activities. Therefore, it was natural for her to say "yes" when a national Red Cross nurse approached her in 1941 to become part of a year-long training program for the ANC. As the nurse supervisor for the x-ray technicians and acting nursing director at John Andrew Hospital in the town of Tuskegee, she felt qualified, skilled, and responsible; she viewed military service as an opportunity to represent her race and acquire additional skills.[6]

Butler joined in September 1941, but she was not the first black nurse to enter military service during the war years; Della Raney Jackson was accepted in April 1941. A quota of 56 black nurses was established by the Army in January 1941. Quotas were established to limit black involvement and were a result of the racism of the time. By March, under the leadership of Mabel K. Staupers, executive secretary of the National Association of Colored Graduate Nurses, a campaign to remove the quota was fully operational. The quota was not lifted until July 1944, when the military faced a health care emergency due to a nursing shortage. By the end of World War II, 512 African Americans and approximately 12 Japanese Americans had served as Army nurses. The Navy did not begin to accept black nurses until the war was almost over. Phyllis Daley, in March 1945, was the first of only four black nurses commissioned by the Navy.

Parfenia Jones Butler states that in spite of the Army's segregation policies, sparse accommodations, and limited recreational activities, she had a number of rewarding military experiences. The most memorable was her service overseas. In Monrovia, Liberia, she was "challenged to use her creative ability" to provide quality nursing care with limited medical supplies. The knowledge she gained in treating tropical diseases and controlling malaria proved valuable during her subsequent graduate studies.[7]

Butler also served in England, nursing German prisoners of war. In October 1944, after allegations that only African Americans were required to nurse the Germans, Eleanor Roosevelt requested verification from the War Department. Throughout the Presidential terms of her husband, Eleanor remained an advocate of social justice, challenging national social thought and practices. War Department officials, answering her query, cited the location of the 168th Station Hospital, with 211 black nurses, as the determining factor for the assignment. They affirmed that "[t]he selection of the 168th Station Hospital for this task was not made because it had negro nurses."[8]

The assignment was to last only as long as the prisoner-of-war problem was acute. The War Department indicated that several hundred white nurses were also caring for POWs. According to Butler, black nurses understood that under the Geneva Convention prisoners of war were to receive care. Often, discriminatory practices by white Americans, not the German patients, created a hostile workplace for the black nurses.

A 1945 survey of 577 nurses revealed that black and white nurses with overseas experiences shared many of the same concerns—poor housing conditions, unfair promotions, and too many restrictions on social life. There were also similarly held perceptions of treatment based on gender. In responding to the question, "Do you feel that women are discriminated against in the Army because of their sex?," 17 percent said "yes, quite a bit"; 50 percent "yes, a little"; 30 percent "no, not at all"; and 3 percent gave no answer.[9] But the burden of race—whether overseas or in the United States—rather than gender presented the most hardships for black women.

The treatment of black nurses at the POW camp in Florence, AZ, prompted protest on their behalf by the National Association for the Advancement of Colored People (NAACP). Forced to eat in segregated settings, the nurses were reported to have been humiliated before the German prisoners. They refused to eat in the separate dining hall until told by their commanding officers that they must obey the direct orders of their superior officers.[10] Despite the efforts of the NAACP, the National Council of Negro Women (NCNW) (under the leadership of Mary McLeod Bethune), and other national groups, segregation in the armed forces remained an unresolved complaint.

African-American protest strategies varied according to the organization's goals and programs. Some groups such as the NCNW were labeled accommodationist because they chose to effect change by working within accepted political and social guidelines. More often than not, they were represented on governmental committees and supported interracial cooperation. Other groups adopted a more militant and proactive stance, demanding immediate changes in discriminatory military policies. Letter-writing campaigns, petitions to governmental officials, mass meetings, fiery editorials in the black press, and the appointment of legislative lobbyists were some of the specific strategies utilized by the various groups.

The nursing shortage, both in the military and on the homefront, prompted Congress to enact legislation to finance the training of nurses. The Bolton Act of 1943, introduced by Frances Payne Bolton (D-OH) as a new amendment to the Nurse Training Bill, established the U.S. Cadet Nurse Corps, which would be administered by the Public Health Service. The overwhelming response to the act by black women confirmed that many were willing to take advantage of meaningful training opportunities that would prepare them for service to their nation and personal advancement. A Women's Bureau report estimated almost 2,000 black women joined the Cadet Nurse Corps through April 1945. The enrollment at Freedmen's Hospital School of Nursing in Washington, DC, rose dramatically after the passage of the Bolton Act: 77 in 1939; 78 in 1942; 116 in 1943; and 166 in 1944.[11]

Nisei women also aspired to become nurses because of the field's prestige and available job opportunities. Because nursing was viewed as a care-giving field, it was considered acceptable for Japanese-American women. Though many of the nisei preferred employment in the civilian sector rather than enlisting in the military, more than 200 Japanese Americans enrolled in the Cadet Corps.

Yet the shortage of trained nurses remained such a concern that congressional efforts to enact an Army Nurse Draft Bill began. Black national spokespersons and organizations were divided as to whether they should support the bill. All agreed that if such a bill were to pass, it must contain antidiscrimination and antisegregation clauses.[12] V-E Day occurred before the bill gained enough momentum for passage. The Army-Navy Nurse Act of 1947 established the Nurse Corps as a permanent military entity with potential for promotion to lieutenant colonel/commander. In 1949, using a nucleus of World War II ex-Army Nurse Corps members, the Air Force established its Air Force Nurse Corps.

Women's Army Auxiliary Corps (WAAC)

With congressional approval of Public Law 5554 on May 14, 1942, the Women's Army Auxiliary Corps (WAAC) was formed. After President Roosevelt signed the bill, Oveta Culp Hobby was sworn in as Director of the corps. Initially, 30,000 women applied for admission to the WAAC. However, based on their qualifications and established guidelines, only 770 were selected to report for training to Fort Des Moines, IA, in July. Of the 440 chosen as officer candidates, 40 were black women. There were always more black and Japanese-American women in the WAAC/WAC than in any other service. Of the 440 officer candidates, 99 percent had been successfully employed in civilian life. Most were 25 to 40 years of age, with 16 percent younger and 10 percent older. One in five was married, usually to a serviceman, and some were mothers with grown children. The majority of the women (90 percent) were college trained, with some holding multiple degrees.[13]

The educational training of the black women spanned from 2 years of high school to doctorates in philosophy. They were teachers, photographers, chiropodists, lawyers, students, professional entertainers, journalists, housewives, cooks, librarians, beauticians, seamstresses, and social workers.[14] Black America was consciously sending its best to represent the race. As Jeanne Holm, author of *Women in the Military: An Unfinished Revolution*, has so accurately observed, it was inconsistent and illogical that the corps desired a small, elite group of women with technical skills and formal training to perform unskilled work.[15] Even more inconsistent and illogical was the requirement that black women have the same qualifications as white women; once enlisted they were subjected to discriminatory practices and often placed in jobs where their skills were not fully utilized.

In keeping with the Army's racial policies, the early classes of black officer candidates at Fort Des Moines were segregated during training. In spite of their small number and elite status, these women were segregated through distinctive seating arrangements in the mess hall and classrooms, separate hours for the use of select recreational facilities, such as the swimming pool, and separate quarters. Largely due to protest from the black leadership, most of the segregation policies affecting officers were reversed in November 1942. Still, the most glaring form of discrimination was apparent in the type of postgraduation duties assigned to the officers. White officers were given regular posts while many of the black officers held assignments usually reserved for noncommissioned officers. Black enlisted women were always segregated during basic training and assigned to segregated field units commanded by black commissioned or noncommissioned officers. Beginning in 1943 exceptions to the segregation policies were made for enlisted women attending specialist and technical schools. The women, regardless of race, trained and lived together at the schools.

Ironically, the segregated units did have some positive outcomes. They were commanded by black female officers, permitting some to gain military leadership skills while serving as role models for younger, more inexperienced recruits. Gladys Carter, a member of the 6888th Postal Directory Battalion, recounted the pride she felt as she watched Charity Adams [Earley] lead the battalion. She stressed that only racism kept Adams at the rank of major when most battalion leaders were colonels.[16] Adams agreed that race kept her from achieving faster promotions and higher rank.[17] Overwhelmingly, black servicewomen's lives were negatively impacted more by their color than by their gender.

According to figures released by Oveta Hobby's office in February of 1943, anticipated discrimination still did not deter some from volunteering. On active duty were 791 African Americans: 292 at Fort Huachuca, AZ, and 499 in training at Fort Des Moines, IA. There were 47 black officers: 6 at Fort Huachuca, 23 on recruiting duty at Service Command Headquarters, 2 at WAAC Headquarters in Washington, DC, and 16 at Fort Des Moines. Listed on inactive duty were 1,194. The three specialist schools at Fort Des Moines provided training for administrative specialists, motor transport personnel, bakers, and cooks.[18]

Dovey Johnson Roundtree, recruiter for the WAAC, stated that "Quite a few of the Army specialists schools which service-women could attend admitted Negroes. Those who qualified made good records. The cryptographic and allied Signal Corps courses, and the Army Physiotherapy schools were never open to our WACS."[19]

Recruiting Japanese Americans

"The Japanese Question" of inclusion in the military resurfaced in January 1943. Before 1943 the policy forbade the acceptance of any Japanese, regardless of citizenship status, for service in the armed forces. After it was determined that nisei men were eligible to serve, Hobby and John J. McCloy, Assistant Secretary of War, issued a joint memorandum stating that Japanese-American women would also be accepted.[20] The War Relocation Authority (WRA) reported to Colonel Hobby that the potential pool of applicants was the approximately 11,040 married and 10,374 unmarried women between 18 and 45 living in the 10 relocation centers. A count of the number of persons with occupations of interest to Director Hobby was conducted: editors and reporters, 13; pharmacists, 12; physicians and surgeons, 6; teachers, 228; trained nurses and students, 124; managers, 129; clerical workers, 2,541; stenographers and typists, 254; chemists, 1; college teachers, 4; dentists, 1; lawyers, 1; social workers, 13; librarians, 4; draftsmen, 1; optometrists, 3; laboratory technicians, 8; and religious workers, 30.[21]

According to Mei Nakano in *Japanese American Women: Three Generations, 1890–1990,* nisei women, influenced by cultural norms, as a rule, did not further their education beyond high school. Males in the family were given first preference for higher education, particularly if available funds were a factor. Professional careers were extremely limited for women; a few were available in health care and science. Most who were employed, like black women, were in domestic service and farm labor. Others were clerical workers or seamstresses or were employed in ethnic enterprises. More often than not, Japanese-American women were expected to marry and bear children.[22]

By March 1943, 151 Japanese-American women had registered at the Gila River Relocation Center in Rivers, AZ; 56 had indicated interest either in the WAAC or Army Nurse Corps. Reports from other relocation centers also indicated the number of women interested in military service. Serious planning had to begin in order to ensure a smooth intake program for those finally selected. Those who were interested insisted that they were willing to enlist only if they were fully integrated into the WAAC. To them, separate Japanese-American units were not acceptable. The reasons for their decision were stated as

1. Japanese are all we see here [in the internment camps].
2. Because we are mostly concerned with adjusting ourselves to others.
3. Racial distinction.

4. This is a democracy, we are American citizens. There is no sense to segregation.
5. Rather take basic training with any group and then serve with combat team.
6. At home we were spread out through the Caucasian race. It smacks too much of race segregation.[23]

A meeting with a representative group revealed more about the women's perceptions of race and their place in the racial hierarchy of the United States. They asked if Chinese girls and "colored girls" were kept in separate units. When told the "colored were," their response was "Well, we don't want to be classed with negroes."[24]

Because it was deemed economically impractical to segregate a potentially small number of Japanese-American recruits, policy decisions were necessary. If these women were integrated into existing white companies, what type of precedent would that set for other minorities? Would a favorable decision for the Japanese-American women lead to charges of discrimination from African Americans? Based on past occurrences, it was expected that black women would protest, involving the black press if they were unjustly treated. The issue was "kicked upstairs" to WAAC headquarters for further discussion and resolution.[25] It was finally ruled that segregating Japanese-American women was unnecessary because it would "increase racial friction and complicate administration."[26]

Once the decision to enlist Japanese-American women was finalized, recruiting centers were encouraged to assist in identifying promising candidates. An initial enrollment quota of 500 was set, and a formula was devised for assigning the recruits to service commands. Physical standards for the women were to be the same as for other applicants, except for a minimum height of 57 inches and minimum weight of 95 pounds. All of the applicants had to demonstrate proficiency in both written and spoken English. Because of the amount of required planning time, the enlistment of women of Japanese ancestry was to begin when general enlistment for the Women's Army Corps (WAC) was authorized following its conversion from an auxiliary corps (WAAC) to full military status in the summer of 1943.[27]

Before the official intake of recruits began, women wrote directly to the War Department seeking admission. Mary Uyesaka, in her letter to Colonel Hobby, expressed the belief that all Americans, regardless of race, color, or creed, should fight together in the military and work together on the homefront. As an American citizen, she expressed her desire to join the WAAC.[28] Lt. Ruth Fowler, in a short memorandum to Hobby, indicated that the letter was typical and the sentiments representative of the approximately two letters a week they received from Japanese-American women.

When the induction process finally began for Japanese-American women, additional policy had to be formulated. Photographs were taken at the December 13, 1943, induction of Iris Watanabe (the first evacuee Wac), Sue Ogata, and Bette Mishimura. Given the negative images of Japanese fostered by the media and the fact that most Japanese Americans were still in relocation centers, a question arose as to whether publicity about the induction would negatively impact future recruiting efforts among white women. Again, the War Department became involved. John J. McCloy ruled that there was nothing objectionable about WAC induction photographs of women of Japanese ancestry.[29]

During the period from July 28, 1943, to January 31, 1944, 13 Japanese-American women enlisted, the first on November 9, 1943. Basic training reports from Fort Des Moines, where the first recruits were sent, indicated that there were no significant problems and "no evidence of discrimination." However, primarily due to cultural constraints, administrative delays, and the increasing availability of employment opportunities, the enlistment figures for nisei women remained low. One of the main deterrents was the influence exercised by parents over Japanese-American women. In some cases there were delays in processing the Provost Marshal General reports required of Japanese-American women enlisting in the corps.[30] Nevertheless, by mid-1943 qualified women, aided by a WRA media blitz touting their skills, left relocation centers for employment in cities throughout the United States. Many of the women were employed in private industry while others held government jobs.

In *Strangers From a Different Shore*, Ronald Takaki asserts that World War II intensified a feeling of "twoness" for many Japanese Americans—an awareness of having an American public persona, displaying the cultural habits of Americans, and of having a private persona, preserving the culture and language of Japan. Borrowing the "twoness" concept from W.E.B. Du Bois, the noted black social scientist and philosopher, Takaki explores the ambivalence felt by the nisei as they strove to become respected American citizens while remaining loyal to their families' customs and traditions.[31]

To overcome the women's reluctance to volunteer, educational programs relating to women and the WAC were presented at the relocation centers.

When WAC headquarters' staff began recruiting/factfinding trips to relocation centers in spring 1943, they were met with fear, hatred, and suspicion. At the Tule Lake Relocation Center, more so than at any other center, strikes and violence were commonplace. The segregation camp housed 18,000 Japanese Americans—issei, nisei, and kibei. Before World War II, the nisei, who were in many cases more Americanized, considered the kibei "too Japanesey" and questioned their loyalty to America. The conflict between the kibei and nisei heightened during the internment period.

Resistance movements sprang up in the various camps. Steven A. Chin in *When Justice Failed: The Fred Korematsu Story* identifies four forms of protest: (1) the filing of lawsuits to question the legality of the internment, (2) noncompliance with camp regulations, (3) campaigns demanding the restoration of constitutional rights before induction into the military, and (4) renunciation of American citizenship.[32]

At Tule Lake, a hotbed of resistance, it was reported that a nisei woman was beaten because she expressed a desire to become a Waac. In order to allay fears and curb violence between the issei, nisei, and kibei, all meetings regarding the WAAC were open, with parents and kibei attending if they wished. No person was allowed to actually sign any enlistment document. The meetings were held only to assess interest in the WAAC, disseminate information, and hopefully dispel any myths and rumors about the WAAC.

Given the humiliation and sense of betrayal felt by many Japanese Americans, why did some Japanese-American women seek to join the military? Sue Ogata stated, "I joined the WACs to prove my Americanism."[33] Before the war she did not realize that she was "different." For others "It was the right thing to do" or "I would do anything to get out of the camp." "To avoid bringing *Haji* (shame) to the family" was another reason given.[34] Clifford Uyeda concludes, "that there seemed no absolute right or wrong reason; the only right was the right to choose. Each individual made his/her choice, and lived the consequence. Ultimately, the decisions were all based on individual reactions to their own country treating them as enemy aliens rather than as loyal subjects."[35]

Regardless of the reasons for volunteering, the women were determined to prove their loyalty and patriotism. More than 300 nisei women served in the WAC, performing a number of duties in integrated units. The War Department, in an effort to elicit positive reactions to the enlistment of Japanese Americans, high-lighted the activities of a special unit of the WAC. In November 1944, 47 nisei Wacs were trained as translators at the Military Intelligence Service Language School (MISLS) in Fort Snelling, MN. Also assigned to the company were three white women and one Chinese American. The 1946 order decreeing "no more enlisted WACs overseas" did not reach Fort Snelling in time to halt the dispatch of 13 of the linguists to the Allied Translator and Interpreter Section in Tokyo. These women were given a choice: They could either return to the States and remain in the service or be discharged and remain in Japan under a 1-year contract. All 13 accepted the civil service offer. The MISLS WAC Detachment was deactivated in 1946.

The NAACP, other national organizations, and interested black women continually objected to racial segregation for African Americans in the armed forces. The official rationale for segregation in the WAC was that the Army was not a sociological laboratory; it would leave the administration of various training camps to the officers in charge. More often than not, racial policies reflected the prejudices of camp commanders and the social climate of the camp's location. Below the Mason-Dixon line and further south, segregation policies became more rigid in the camps and surround-ing towns.

Even though African Americans were establishing distinguished military records, the War Department and laypersons still debated the question of whether they should serve in integrated units. Also questioned was the extent to which black soldiers should interact with Europeans during overseas tours. Arthur Sulzberger of the *New York Times* recommended that colored troops be moved out of the rural areas of Europe and into urban ports. Persons living in rural areas, Sulzberger felt, did not possess the same biased views of African Americans as did those in the more populated urban areas. He believed that the rural residents, particularly the girls, were "very much attracted to the colored people" and stated that the natives found the African Americans to be quieter and gentler than the whites. James P. Warburg disagreed with Sulzberger. In a letter to Elmer Davis, Director of the Office of War Information,

Warburg wrote, "Actually, I think it is a mistake to send colored troops here and transplant into this country a problem which we have been unable to solve at home." He anticipated problems if something were not done to keep the black troops out of England, namely, that African Americans would justifiably become angry once they compared their treatment in Europe with the oppression they experienced in the United States.[36]

Recruitment Problems

Racial attitudes of white Americans did impact the recruitment of people of color; at no time were the enlistment quotas for African Americans or Japanese Americans met. Letter after letter in various files of War Department officials from minority members of the armed forces and the general public recounted stories of rejection and ill-treatment because of race.

In the early years, some like Florence H. Santos of Providence, RI, clamored for admission to the WAAC. Santos was not chosen for the first group but remained determined to become a Waac. In a letter to the War Department she wrote,

> Dear Sir:
>
> *Push* has come to *shove* all over the world, and fast!
> I took the mental exam for the W.A.A.C. candidacy and haven't heard another word. Can't they erect one extra cot and throw in an extra handful of beans and raise the number of candidates to 441? God and I will do the rest.
>
> Seriously
> Florence H. Santos
> 109 Faith Street
> Providence, R.I.
>
> P.S. Why doesn't the Army give commissions to college graduates? The Navy does.[37]

The first letter written by Wac Thelma Lee O'Kelley to Mary McLeod Bethune also conveyed her enthusiasm and readiness to serve. Subsequent letters, however, document the negative psychological impact of discrimination. In her first letter, Thelma related her disappointment at seeing so few black women in the WAC. When she decided to join the service, she wrote, she met a great deal of opposition from family and friends. She related that 98 percent of the opposition came from men, consistent with a national survey. She believed that an aggressive recruiting plan for the WAC, led by the black press, would increase the number of black Wacs and help the other three branches—Coast Guard, Navy, and Marines—to recruit African Americans.[38]

In Private O'Kelley's second letter to Mrs. Bethune, her discontent was apparent. She now witnessed the impact of Jim Crow policies, noting the closure of the Huachuca School of Physiotherapy and the return of all of the black students to Fort Des Moines with a promise of another school becoming available at a later date. According to O'Kelley, over 1,000 white women had been commissioned and transferred to the Medical Corps while only 11 black women were enrolled in the physiotherapy program. She pointed out that nine government schools operated for whites, while Huachuca was the only one opened for African Americans, and it was discontinued in the middle of its second class. She recognized that if the class had continued, the training received by the students would have provided them with a highly marketable skill for postwar America. No longer did she fill her correspondence with recommendations for increasing the number of black women in the WAC. Instead, (now Private First Class with one stripe) O'Kelley wanted information about the National Council of Negro Women to share with others.[39] She now better understood why so many "of our girls" were not willing to join the WAC.

In spite of discriminatory patterns, some who joined felt the advantages outweighed the disadvantages. Dovey Roundtree supported the "pro" position when she wrote,

> The adjustment in the matter of living together and working as a team was one of the greatest benefits our women—All Service-Women—gained from their military service. The Hup-two-three-four of infantry drill, the classroom lectures and tests, the thrill of being one of hundreds of women marching in step at a retreat parade, the sharing of company miseries caused by swollen feet and tetanus shots all crystallized to make a common denominator in experience for many who but a few years ago had nothing in common but their sex. A bond of sisterhood and understanding developed among all members of the Women's Army Corps, in spite of the general Army policy of separating Negroes and Puerto Ricans (colored) from Americans other than colored. Indians, Chinese, Japanese, and light-colored Puerto Ricans were classified as white.[40]

Black women continued to pressure for full desegregation of the armed forces for women and men. In 1946, on the occasion of the third anniversary of the WAC, the Alpha Kappa Alpha Sorority (AKA), an all-black organization with undergraduate chapters based on college campuses, graduate chapters, and a national administrative arm, wrote to President Truman requesting that he issue a directive to abolish segregation in all WAC units. They wrote, "Negro women have served valiantly in this war and deserve to be accorded first-class citizenship without being segregated from all other American women citizens in the Women's Army Corps." They stated that separate was not equal, but a form of discrimination. The letter appealed to Truman's sense of morality and concern for the image of the United States, but he did not issue Executive Order 9981, desegregating the armed forces, until 1948. *Full* official desegregation was not realized until September 1953, when the last segregated schools operated by the armed forces (for dependents of military personnel) were integrated.

Women's Reserve of the U.S. Navy (WAVES)

Because of their small numbers, black volunteers who joined the WAVES (Women Accepted for Volunteer Emergency Service) were not segregated in units. As early as July 1943, AKA worked to have black women enlisted in the Navy. Thomasina Walker Johnson, legislative representative for the sorority, called for black women to support the action. The sorority was just one of many organizations that agitated for a change in policy.[41] Historian Benjamin Quarles, however, credits AKA's legislative council's continuous pressure as the deciding factor. Forced to yield to concerted pressure from the War Department, Members of Congress, and citizens, the Navy began to accept black women on October 19, 1944. The total number permitted to enlist was to correlate with the needs of the service. Frances Willis, Harriet Ida Pickens, and Jean A. Freemen were the first three black WAVES officer graduates. After completing their training at the Naval Reserve Midshipmen's School in Northampton, MA, the women were commissioned. Based on available records, it would appear that no Japanese-American women served in the WAVES. Again, it must be noted that Japanese-American women were fully integrated into units and thus were not classified by race.

Coast Guard Women's Reserve (SPAR)

The Women's Reserve of the Coast Guard was signed into law on November 23, 1942. The branch was titled the SPAR, using the first letters of the Coast Guard's motto, "*Semper Paratus*—Always Ready." Olivia Hooker, the first African American admitted to the SPAR, originally planned to enlist in the Navy. As a member of Delta Sigma Theta Sorority, Inc., she assisted in the campaign to lift the color ban in the Navy. Once black women were able to join, she noted no one took advantage of the opportunity. Determined to take advantage of the opportunity herself, she attempted three times to enlist at the local Navy recruiting station but met obstacles each time. Finally, she decided to try the Coast Guard. Again, efforts were made to discourage her. However, the Coast Guard recruiters were no match for her determination at that point. Olivia Hooker was sworn in as the first black Spar, serving from March 9, 1945, to June 26, 1946, and she was one of the last to be discharged.

Before the SPAR disbanded, four other black women volunteered. Together, the five black women developed a support system that enabled them to get the most from the military experience. While serving in fully integrated units, Hooker remembers isolated acts of racism, but on the whole, she states that the experiences of the five were generally positive.

The number of volunteers for the Navy and Coast Guard remained low due to the timing of the decisions to accept African Americans. Also of importance was the fact that the three services—Army, Navy, and Coast Guard—attempted to recruit from the same pool of black applicants. When the color line began to fade in the services, the women had options that were not available in earlier years. If treatment and advancement were perceived to be better in one service than in the others, the women chose the one with better advantages. In addition, some excellent military candidates were lost when they opted for the training provided by the U.S. Cadet Nurse Corps. The nursing skills would enable them to compete for better jobs after World War II.

Because industry demands opened long-closed employment doors, black women, in increasing numbers, selected homefront jobs. For African Americans, well-paying blue collar jobs in manufacturing offered the greatest job security and potential for upward mobility. For many of the women, the chance to move from a service position, often at the lowest rung, was more economically enticing and presented greater hope for a family than enlistment in the military.

Marine Corp's Women's Reserve (MCWR)

The Marine Corps did not accept black or Japanese-American women during the war years. The Women's Armed Services Integration Act of June 12, 1948, incorporated women as part of the regular Marine Corps and ensured the permanency of women's support roles in all the services. A goal of 1,000 officers and 18,000 enlisted women was set by the Marines. When A. Philip Randolph, member of the Committee Against Jim Crow, questioned if black women were to be included, the reply was "If qualified for enlistment, negro women will be accepted on the same basis as other applicants."[42] It was not until September 8, 1949, that Annie E. Graham of Detroit, MI, earned the distinction of becoming the first black woman Marine. A day later Ann E. Lamb enlisted in New York. Both women were sent to the boot camp at Parris Island, SC. Annie L. Grimes was the third to join in 1950. All three were integrated into existing units.[43]

Postwar Years

Approximately 370,000 women served in the armed forces during World War II, 2 to 3 percent of all military personnel. The 4,600 black volunteers represented approximately 1 percent of the total number of women; the percentage of Japanese-American women, of which there were about 350, was even lower—.009 percent. A survey of women veterans in 1946 revealed that they experienced readjustment difficulties similar to those of enlisted men. The study does not provide racial data, even though the survey sample included African Americans. It was noted that special problems arose because women were part of a veteran population for the first time. If the white female veteran and her concerns were obscured because of the attention given to the white male veteran, Japanese-American and black female veterans' concerns were, for the most part, invisible.

In a 1945 memorandum to John J. McCloy, Truman K. Gibson, Jr., Civilian Aide to the Secretary of War, detailed factors differentiating postwar problems for white and black soldiers.

1. African Americans would find it more difficult to secure GI Bill loans and educational subsidies from private commercial agencies.
2. During the war years, many of the industries traditionally closed to African Americans remained closed to them, while those that hired African Americans were subject to massive cutbacks once the war ended.
3. As a result of military service, illiteracy was greatly reduced among African Americans. As a direct result, more counseling was needed to ensure that new skills acquired by the black soldiers would benefit them in civilian life.
4. Migration from the South would likely increase if information about increased opportunities in the South was not readily available.[44]

Civilian organizations also became involved in postwar planning for returning veterans. Beginning in August of 1945, the National Association of Colored Graduate Nurses, Inc., served as a liaison agency for the American Nurses Association's Guidance and Placement Service and the U.S. Employment Service in the placement of returning veteran nurses. At the end of World War II, 512 black nurses were members of the ANC and were assigned to 5 general hospitals, 11 station hospitals, 3 regional hospitals, and 13 overseas units. The majority, 388, held the rank of second lieutenant; 115 were first lieutenants; and 9 held the rank of captain.[45]

As the war drew to a close, the key question for some servicewomen was whether or not they should remain in the military. Lt. Susie A. Pinkley, ANC, elicited the assistance of James C. Evans, Assistant Civilian Aide to the Secretary of War, in her quest to remain on active duty. In January 1946 she expressed the desire for an overseas assignment, a transfer to Camp Beale, CA, or relocation to some place where black nurses were stationed. As support for her request, she cited the fact that her husband, a disabled veteran, had died in December 1945. By March of 1946, while stationed at Fort Devens, MA, she felt she was treated "nicely" at her current base but was not afforded an opportunity to serve on ship duty. In her words "a new project is brewing and several colored nurses signed for it, and if we are not chosen or discharged before that time some one will explain to me why."[46] In June of 1946 she was stationed at the Tuskegee Airfield Hospital and shared her growing dissatisfaction with the military. In another letter to

Evans, she wrote, "I am expecting to get discharged soon. I am tired of the Army and its discrimination."[47]

Not all of the black members of the ANC vacillated as to their intent. Lts. Earlyne A. Harrison, Constance Carithers, Helen C. Johnson, Olga Ford, and Marion Walters, in a March 1946 telegram to the War Department, stated they wished to "stay in service indefinitely."[48]

A 1947 report by Public Affairs, Inc., entitled *Our Negro Veterans* detailed the many readjustment problems faced by black male veterans; no indication was given as to black female veterans. Problem areas for returning veterans were jobs, housing, and education. Discrimination and the urgency on the part of white America to revert to "normal" prewar conditions contributed to the severity of the concerns for black veterans. Many African Americans returned to communities undergoing rapid change, where the focus was on securing victory on the homefront.

Many of the servicewomen, African Americans and Japanese Americans, ended their military careers with greater appreciation for their capabilities and willingness to assist in effecting change for their race. While many stepped back into traditional life styles, marrying and rearing children, some sought ways to manage both homes and careers, rejecting what the dominant culture defined and celebrated as the traditional gender patterns of behavior. For black women, who were often required to assume many roles in order to protect the family, choosing one or both options was not as difficult a decision as it was for Japanese-American women. Instead of deliberating about the choice, black women thought more about how best to prepare for fulfilling career and personal goals.

The GI Bill

Approved by the 78th Congress on June 22, 1944, the Servicemen's Readjustment Act of 1944, popularly known as the GI bill of rights, provided financial subsidies for returning veterans, covering housing, educational, and private enterprise goals. Lowell and Prudence Burns Burrell's utilization of the GI bill was typical. Prudence joined the Army Nurse Corps in 1942. In 1945, while stationed in the Philippines, she married 1st Lt. Lowell Burrell. Together they established the goals they hoped to achieve once the war was over. With the assistance of family members, they selected a house in

Detroit and purchased it with a guaranteed mortgage. Upon discharge from the corps, Prudence used the GI bill to complete credits for her B.S. degree with a certificate in public health from the University of Minnesota School of Public Health. Her employment history chronicles an impressive career in health services and education.

The Burrells and many other black veterans credit the GI bill with affording them the opportunity to acquire additional education and thus giving them a competitive advantage in the job market. They saw the completion of undergraduate degrees, the acquisition of advanced degrees, and the attainment of certificates from specialized training programs as a sure road to upward mobility. Education, as it had been in the past, was viewed as highly significant in the struggle for personal and racial advancement.

Dovey Roundtree's and Olivia Hooker's surveys on the use of the GI bill by other female black veterans highlight the value of additional skills and degrees. Use of the GI bill figured prominently in the personal success stories of many of the women. Some returned to college or enrolled in training programs; some, like Lucia M. Pitts, secured loans to start their own businesses; and some, even as late as 1988, applied for GI-bill-guaranteed home mortgages. Because of the GI bill's potential to radically effect change in the status of black America, community-based black organizations and the press implemented various strategies to encourage black veterans to take full advantage of the bill.

Fearing the impact of those changes, some southern whites campaigned against the bill. The great migration by African Americans from the South had already significantly depleted its menial labor force. Congressman John E. Rankin (D-MS), known as "Negrophobic," saw in the passage of the GI bill the further decline of the South's black population and, therefore, its economic base. He attempted to block the passage of the bill, fearing that African Americans, particularly males, would use it to further their education or to refuse low-paying jobs and collect unemployment compensation until they could acquire a better-paying job. More than 1 million black men served in the armed forces during World War II and thus were entitled to veterans benefits if not ruled ineligible because of a discharge rating of undesirable or dishonorable.[49] Clearly, he believed the bill would eliminate some of the control southern whites retained over African Americans and thus over the retention of a multitiered social, economic, and political system in the South, popularly summarized as "Jim Crow" segregation.

Rankin was not the only person concerned about possible changes in the racial hierarchy used to order life in the United States. The Intelligence Office of Army Services Forces, beginning in mid-1945, collected extensive data on race relations and what it termed "Communist" efforts on behalf of African Americans. The office was particularly concerned about acts of individual and group physical violence and unrest in urban areas and communities near military installations.

That same fear also motivated white Americans to encourage the dispersal of Japanese Americans leaving the relocation centers. Once the exclusion order was rescinded in 1944, most of the Japanese Americans began the long trek back to the west coast. Tule Lake, the last of the internment camps, closed in March 1946. Approximately 43,000 of the former internees relocated to other areas of the country, including the Midwest, the east coast, and the Deep South. Upon their discharge, the nisei female veterans joined the homeward movement. Contrary to their prewar fear that if they joined the military, they would jeopardize their opportunity to later marry, most married; some went to college; and some chose to remain in the military.

Postwar Military Service

In planning for the postwar years, the executive and legislative branches of the government formulated national defense goals in keeping with the nation's new role of world leader. As of September 1949, the number of minority women in the armed forces remained comparatively small. There were 335 black women in the Army, the most in any of the services. Of that number, 241 were enlisted women and 94 were officers, 6.5 percent and 1.7 percent of the total. As during the war, the Army Nurse Corps still had the largest number of officers at 84. Advances made by African Americans in the Army were directly attributed to implementation of clauses in the Gillem Board Report. The board was appointed by President Truman to study the role of African Americans in the military during World War II. Based on the need for efficiency in the postwar military, integration in the armed forces was accepted, and the 10-percent quota was abandoned.[50]

Conclusion

In spite of the United States' rejection of their citizenship rights, black and Japanese-American women participated in the defense of the nation both at home and abroad. In postwar America, united with others in their respective communities, black women, more so than Japanese-American women, had no qualms about presenting their war records as proof of their loyalty to and support of the United States. Those war records, they felt, entitled them to all America had to offer. Yet, as they left separation centers, some were met with overt hostilities. Parfenia Jones Butler waited 3 days in a train depot at Fort Bragg for a train that would accept black soldiers. The bitterness she felt is still heard in her voice when she recounts the experience. As they returned home, Japanese Americans also encountered hostility, such as signs proclaiming, "No Japs Allowed, No Japs Welcome."[51] Even though both groups of women confronted discriminatory practices and stereotypes during the war years, they were at no time able to put aside racial and group objectives to coalesce around common goals. They did consistently and diligently pursue their own group approaches, however, which they hoped would guarantee desired results.

For both groups civil rights was the focus for the fifties and sixties. African Americans organized to resist continuing discrimination and segregation while the Japanese Americans sought interethnic unity with other Asian Americans, citizenship for issei, reparation for the internees, and an end to exclusionary immigration laws. Now was the time to fight the war for social justice, a war yet to be fully won.

NOTES

© 1996 by Cynthia Neverdon-Morton

1. Rosalind Rosenberg, *Divided Lives: American Women in the Twentieth Century* (New York, 1992), p. 122.
2. Robert A. Wilson and Bill Hosokawa, *East to America: A History of the Japanese in the United States* (New York, 1980), p. 227; War Relocation Authority, Application for Leave Clearance, Folder: Enrollment of Japanese American Women in WAAC, box 49, Office of the Director of Personnel and Administration, Records of the War Department General and Special Staffs, RG 165, National Archives, Washington, DC (hereinafter, records in the National Archives will be cited as RG___ , NA).
3. Wilson and Hosokawa, *East to America,* p. 228.
4. "Survey of Intelligence Materials Supplement to Survey No. 25, Bureau of Intelligence, Office of War Information," p. 5, Folder: Office of War Informa-

tion, box 226: Oakland Port of Embarkation to Officer Candidate School, Office, Assistant Secretary of War, Civilian Aide to the Secretary, Subject File 1940-47, Records of the Office of the Secretary of War, RG 107, NA.

5. Memorandum for the Office of Facts and Figures, Apr. 3, 1942, p. 3, Folder: Office of Facts and Figures, box 226: Oakland Port of Embarkation to Officer Candidate School, Office, Assistant Secretary of War, Civilian Aide to the Secretary, Subject File 1940-47, RG 107, NA.

6. Parfenia Jones Butler, Feb. 8, 1995, telephone interview.

7. Ibid.

8. Memorandum to Assistant Secretary, General Staff, Oct. 26, 1944, Folder 211: Classified General Correspondence, 1942-47, Office of the Chief of Staff, RG 165, NA.

9. "What Returnee Nurses Say About Their Overseas Experience," American Soldier in World War II Survey, p. 20, Survey 192 A and B, Records of the Armed Forces Information and Education Section, Records of the Office of the Secretary of Defense, RG 330, NA.

10. Report of the Acting Secretary, National Association for the Advancement of Colored People (NAACP), Feb. 9, 1945, Folder 329: Military Training, 1943-45, box 21, series 5, Records of the National Council of Negro Women (NCNW), Bethune Museum and Archives, Washington, DC; Roy Wilkins to John J. McCloy, Assistant Secretary of War, Jan. 9, 1945, Folder: NAACP-1, box 221, Office, Assistant Secretary of War, Civilian Aide to the Secretary, Subject File 1940-47, RG 107, NA.

11. *Negro Women War Workers,* Bulletin No. 205, Women's Bureau, U.S. Department of Labor, 1945, p. 13, Folder: U.S. Department of Labor-Women's Bureau 1946, box 35, series J, Bethune Museum.

12. NAACP Press Release, Jan. 11, 1945, Folder 329: Military Training, box 21, series 5, Records of the NCNW, Bethune Museum.

13. Jeanne Holm, *Women in the Military* (Novato, CA, 1983), p. 28.

14. "Brief History of Negro Women in the Army—Talk to be made at the New York Public Library Commemorating National Negro History Week on 13 February 1947," p. 2, Folder 536: Women's Army Corps, 1945-47, box 38, series 5, Records of the NCNW, Bethune Museum.

15. Holm, *Women in the Military,* p. 22.

16. Gladys Carter, Jan. 25, 1995, telephone interview.

17. Charity Adams Earley, Feb. 17, 1995, interview at the Doubletree Hotel, Crystal City, Arlington, VA.

18. Memorandum from Col. Oveta Culp Hobby, WAAC Director, to Truman K. Gibson, Jr., Feb. 12, 1943, Folder: Women's WAC, box 258 Women's Army Auxiliary Corps to WPA, Office, Assistant Secretary of War, Civilian Aide to the Secretary, Subject File 1940-47, RG 107, NA. The memorandum states that there were 45 black officers, but the figures elsewhere in the memorandum and other sources indicate 47 black officers.

19. Dovey Johnson Roundtree, unpublished manuscript, p. 3.

20. Memorandum from Hobby and McCloy, Jan. 13, 1943, Folder: SPWA 291.2, Office of Director of Personnel and Administration, RG 165, NA.

21. Letter from E. M. Royall, Acting Director of the War Relocation Authority, to Hobby, Jan. 26, 1943, Folder: SPWA 291.2, Office of the Chief of Staff, RG 165, NA.

22. Mei Nakano, *Japanese American Women: Three Generations, 1890-1990* (Berkeley, CA, 1990), pp. 117-118.

23. Memorandum from William L. Tracy, 1943, Folder: SPWA 291.2, Office of the Director of Personnel and Administration, RG 165, NA.

24. Report of WAAC Officer Margaret E. Deane's Visit to Japanese Relocation Center at Hunt, Idaho, Exhibit A, Mar. 8, 1943, Folder: SPWA 291.2, Office of the Director of Personnel and Administration, RG 165, NA.

25. Memorandum from T. B. Catron to the Assistant Secretary of War, Mar. 12, 1943, Folder: SPWA 291.2, Office of the Director of Personnel and Administration, RG 165, NA.

26. Memorandum from John M. Hall to Assistant Chief of Staff, Apr. 10, 1943, Folder: SPWA 291, Office of the Director of Personnel and Administration, RG 165, NA.

27. Memorandum from the Adjutant General's Office to Commanding General, Each Service Command, July 28, 1943, Folder: AG 291.1, Office of the Chief of Staff, RG 165, NA; Holm, *Women in the Military*, p. 54.

28. Mary Uyesaka to Hobby, Mar. 17, 1943, Folder: SPWA 291.2, box 49, RG 165, NA.

29. McCloy to Dillon S. Myer, Dec. 28, 1943, Folder: SPWA 291.2, Office of the Director of Personnel and Administration, RG 165, NA.

30. Memorandum from Hobby to the Secretary of War, "Report on Enlistment of Japanese-American Women in the Women's Army Corps," Feb. 17, 1944, Folder: SPWA 291.2, Office of the Director of Personnel and Administration, RG 165, NA.

31. Ronald Takaki, *Strangers From a Different Shore: A History of Asian Americans* (New York, 1989), pp. 214-215.

32. "Kibei Nisei," *Nikkei Heritage* 3 (Fall 1991): 5.

33. Nakano, *Japanese American Women*, p. 170.

34. Clifford Uyeda, "Reflections, Fifty Years Later," *Nikkei Heritage* 5 (Spring 1993): 5.

35. Ibid., p. 7.

36. James P. Warburg to Elmer Davis, Sept. 1, 1942, Folder: WDCSA 291.21, box 189, Records of the War Department, Chief of Staff, Security classified, 1944-45, RG 165, NA.

37. Florence H. Santos to the War Department, July 18, 1942, Folder: SPWA 291.21, RG 165, NA.

38. Pvt. Thelma Lee O'Kelley to Mary McLeod Bethune, Friday noon, n.d. (ca. 1943, early 1944), Folder 391: Correspondence O 1946-49, box 26, series 5, Records of the NCNW, Bethune Museum.

39. Pfc. Thelma Lee O'Kelley to Bethune, n.d., Folder 391: Correspondence O 1946-49, box 26, series 5, Records of the NCNW, Bethune Museum.

40. Roundtree, unpublished manuscript, p. 2.

41. Judy Barrett Litoff and David C. Smith, *We're in This War, Too: World War II Letters from American Women in Uniform* (New York, 1994), pp. 78-79; Zatella R. Turner, "Alpha Kappa Alpha Sorority's Wartime Program," *The Aframerican Woman's Journal* 3 (Summer 1943): 23, Folder 11 AWJ, box 2, series 13, Records of the NCNW, Bethune Museum.

42. Henry I. Shaw, Jr., and Ralph W. Donnelly, *Blacks in the Marine Corps,* History and Museums Division, Headquarters U.S. Marine Corps (Washington, DC, reprinted 1988), p. 56.

43. Ibid., pp. 56-57.

44. Memorandum from Gibson to McCloy, May 21, 1945, Folder: Post War Employment Film, Filipinos to Post War Planning, Office, Assistant Secretary of War, Civilian Aide to the Secretary, Subject File 1940-47, RG 107, NA.

45. Memorandum from Lt. Col. Edna B. Groppe, ANC, Assistant in the Office of the Surgeon General, Army Services Forces, to Gibson, July 26, 1945, Folder: Army Nurse Corps A.N.C., Negro Soldier Injunction to Nurses, Office, Assistant Secretary of War, Civilian Aide to the Secretary, Subject File 1940-47, RG 107, NA.

46. S. A. Pinkley to Mr. Evans, Mar. 7, 1946, Folder: Army Nurse Corps A.N.C., Negro Soldier Injunction to Nurses, Office, Assistant Secretary of War, Civilian Aide to the Secretary, Subject File 1940-47, RG 107, NA.

47. S. A. Pinkley to Mr. Evans, June 11, 1946, Folder: Army Nurse Corps A.N.C., Negro Soldier Injunction to Nurses, Office, Assistant Secretary of War, Civilian Aide to the Secretary, Subject File 1940-47, RG 107, NA.

48. Telegram from Lt. Olga Ford to Office of Civilian Aide War Department, Mar. 4, 1946, Folder: Army Nurse Corps A.N.C., Negro Soldier Injunction to Nurses, Office, Assistant Secretary of War, Civilian Aide to the Secretary, Subject File 1940-47, RG 107, NA.

49. John Egerton, *Speak Now Against the Day: The Generation Before the Civil Rights Movement in the South* (New York, 1994), p. 221; Reemployment and Selective Service Special Monograph No. 13, Vols. 1-2 (Washington, DC, 1949), p. 108.

50. "The Negro in the Army: A Special Report Prepared by the Office of the Civilian Aide to the Secretary of the Army," 15 pp, April 1949, Folder 330: Military Training 1947-49, box 22, series 5, Records of the NCNW, Bethune Museum.

51. Takaki, *Strangers From a Different Shore,* p. 405.

WOMEN AS VETERANS
Historical Perspective and Expectations

Mary V. Stremlow

The facts would be interesting but not really disturbing if the health and standard of living of so many women were not at stake. For nearly half a century, large numbers of women who served honorably in the American armed forces in World War II did not consider themselves veterans. Most failed to apply for the benefits and health care they had rightfully earned. Those impertinent enough to seek help often found that the Veterans Administration dispensed benefits to women according to a different set of rules than used for men. The question is: Why did the women accept less?

We are told that World War II women veterans did not expect to be rewarded for doing their patriotic duty. Men claimed their benefits. Were they not patriotic? We are told that women did not recognize themselves as veterans because they were not actively involved in combat. Yet not all men were combatants. We are told that the women thought of their World War II service as temporary—merely their contribution to the war effort. They returned home eager to get on with their lives. The men, too, were anxious to return home and get on with their lives, but they knew their rights and claimed them.

Using 1994 figures published by the Department of Veterans Affairs (VA), we find that there are 1.2 million female veterans, making up 4.4 percent of the total U.S. veteran population.[1] Despite the rapidly growing number of women in the military, World War II women still constitute the greatest proportion of women veterans. As a guide, consider that there are 329,000 women veterans aged 65 or over and 327,000 under 35.[2]

Historically, women have not been identified as veterans or received VA benefits at the same rate as men. In fact, before the census of 1980, no figures were available. When it was found that there were nearly twice as many women veterans as originally thought, Congress commissioned Louis Harris to conduct a survey of women veterans. The results were troubling; it was discovered that 57 percent of the women did not know they were eligible for VA benefits or health care.[3]

The need to study World War II female veterans goes beyond the realm of academic exercise. The situation is this: A substantial number of them could dramatically improve the quality of their lives if they took advantage of the available federal benefits. The problem lies in finding them and convincing them that, as a nation, we value their service. The VA, veterans organizations, advocates for women veterans, and advocates for the aging female population are determined to locate the women, inform them of their rights, and improve their accessibility to VA-provided health care, mental health care, and cash benefits. These women also need to know that many inequities have been eliminated.

The VA Advisory Committee on Women Veterans repeatedly recommends greater outreach to women veterans. Before manufacturers or retailers market their products, they first assess the targeted consumers' needs and motivations. I suggest that the social, political, religious, and economic factors that defined the generation of women who joined the military in World War II, combined with the sometimes fuzzy perception of their military status, produced a corps of reluctant veterans. To be effective, outreach efforts must consider all these factors. Since people do not act in a historical vacuum, it is shortsighted to explain away the attitudes of older women veterans within the time frame of 1941 to 1995.

In the musical *My Fair Lady*, Dr. Higgins laments, "Why can't a woman be more like a man?" Among the myriad answers that come to mind, one bears directly on this discussion. Women have been socialized to play the supportive role. Women who enlisted in the armed forces in the Second World War, regardless of their social, economic, geographic, ethnic, or religious background, had a common gender view. Men were doers; women were helpmates. Men's work mattered. But other than motherhood, women's work was trivial, irrelevant, sometimes even silly.

Women were expected to share the reflected praise and rewards showered on their fathers, husbands, and children. For a recent example of this sentiment, consider the obituary of Rose Fitzgerald Kennedy, "daughter of a congressman, wife of an ambassador and mother of a president."[4] For pre-World War II women, it was unseemly to expect personal recognition or benefit for a job well done. It was unladylike to demand compensation for service. And should a woman dare ask and be refused, it was shrewish to persist. Shakespeare had it right. Othello won Desdemona by boasting; Kate won Petruchio by shutting up.

Even women raised in the relatively modern first half of the 20th century were accustomed to a political system that did not regard them as full-fledged citizens. Their rights were not God-given but were bestowed, usually grudgingly, by men through a series of constitutional amendments, laws, and judicial decisions. When the Founding Fathers were designing the republic, women were excluded from deliberations "to prevent deprivation of morals and ambiguity of issues."[5]

The British common law tradition adopted by the United States held that a woman could not have a legal existence apart from her husband's. Women could not vote, serve on juries, or hold public office. A married woman could not own property, sue or be sued, or work without her husband's permission. In *Bradwell* v. *Illinois* (1873) a judge wrote that women and men have separate spheres and different personalities and that women's naturally disqualify them from many jobs. Granting women fewer rights than men was accepted judicial logic until long after V-J Day.

Audacious women, citing the passage of the 14th amendment, tried to vote in the 1872 election. The Supreme Court in *Minor* v. *Happersett* (1874), however, ruled that it was possible for people to be citizens without being able to vote because the states could decide who would be permitted to vote. The decision went on to say that if *the people* wanted women to vote, they would press their elected representatives to pass the enabling legislation. The implication was that the phrase *the people* did not include women.

Women's citizenship was elusive. It was dependent upon their husbands' status. During World War I, American-born women, but not men, married to Germans were stripped of their citizenship and labeled enemy aliens. Even after the passage of the 19th amendment, which finally granted women's suffrage in 1920, women married to aliens still could not vote. Furthermore, until 1934 the law provided that a man married to an alien could pass on his citizenship to his children but a woman could not.[6] In the United States during World War II, we saw natural-born female citizens interned in relocation camps with their Japanese husbands. So it appears that it was an easy transition for female Americans who had accepted a limited version of citizenship to later accept the similar notion that they were not real veterans.

Organized religion, as well, carefully prescribed women's place. During the heyday of the women's rights movement in the late 19th century, clergymen quoted Bible passages to reinforce the tenet that the subjection of women is God's will. St. Paul wrote, "Let the women learn in silence with all subjection." When writing about women, the mid-19th-century Catholic spokesman Orestes Brownson stated, "Without masculine direction or control, she is out of her element, and a social anomaly, sometimes a hideous monster."[7]

For centuries churchmen preached that women should be unobtrusive, mild, dependent, and conscious of their God-given weakness. Submission and silence were admirable feminine virtues even in the mid-20th century. Thus, hand in hand, the church and the law conditioned women to accept a subordinate position, and the workplace affirmed their inferior standing.

In the 19th century, women, treated as temporary workers, were offered less money and responsibility than men. Minority women almost exclusively held jobs as domestics or farm workers with low wages and no benefits. The tradition that men were the providers carried over into the 1930s; even predominately female unions signed contracts permitting unequal pay for the sexes. During the Depression, women were routinely exhorted not to steal jobs from men.

Women were expressly barred from some occupations. Twenty-six states had laws prohibiting the employment of married women. Both before and after World War II, prominent corporations such as IBM and Detroit Edison were among those who enforced policies banning the hiring of married women. In the 1920s Columbia and Harvard Law Schools excluded women as did the New York City Bar Association until 1937. From 1925 to 1945 medical schools in the United States had a 5-percent quota on female applicants. In 1939, 21 states had no minimum wage laws for women.[8] The Equal Pay Act, mandating equal pay for women and men doing the same job, was not passed until 1964; Title VII of the Civil Rights Act, which barred sex discrimination in hiring, firing, promotions, and working conditions, did not become law until the same year.[9]

Against this background of disparity—social, political, religious, and economic—we can begin to understand why American women who broke through stereotypical barriers to serve in the armed forces expressed little dissatisfaction about the lack of recognition they received for their contribution. Lucille Spooner Votta, a psychiatric nurse who in World War II treated GIs in the Philippines, summed it up: "I never really felt I deserved all that I got. I feel that I was lucky to be involved at that time, and I was glad to participate. I just thank God."[10]

The military experience itself made it clear from the beginning that women were not precisely members of the armed forces in the same way as men. The organizations were different: The most basic regulations governing their everyday lives were different. As a matter of law, significant benefits were withheld from females. Because the history of women in the military has been well documented, the aim here is solely to point out certain anomalies that caused a majority of women to accept the premise that since they were not really soldiers, they were not really entitled to all veterans benefits.

The creation of the Army and Navy Nurse Corps at the turn of the century marked the entrance of women into the armed forces. Their status, while official, was ambivalent and has been described as quasi-military (they were neither enlisted nor commissioned). During World War I many nurses were sent abroad, where they served under combat conditions. Some were wounded, and others died from diseases. Since they were not accorded rank, they were simply called "nurse." If you were to visit a national cemetery today, on the headstone of a World War I nurse you would find the inscription "nurse" where you would expect to find the veteran's rank.

In 1917 the Navy and the Marine Corps recruited women Yeomen (F), and Marines (F) who joined the war effort as clerks, drivers, switchboard operators, translators, fingerprint experts, camouflage designers, draftsmen, and bacteriologists. When the war ended, they were released but not without reminders that they were not quite legitimate veterans. "*Ex-military* members" was an often-used label.

Only the Marine Corps granted servicemen's benefits to its women. The Marines (F) were entitled to insurance, a $60 bonus, medical treatment, and burial in Arlington National Cemetery.[11] The Navy, on the other hand, intended to give the Yeomen (F) "good" or "ordinary" discharges until Rear Adm. Charles McVay interceded on their behalf, giving them entitlement to honorable discharges.[12]

Holding honorable discharges, however, did not make eligibility for certain veterans' benefits any easier to prove. Even for nurses disabled in the line of duty, health care was difficult to obtain. Other benefits were just as slippery. In 1924 a bill introduced by Representative John McKenzie to provide adjusted compensation for war veterans specifically excluded women until former Yeomen (F) enjoined the American Legion to lobby with them. But perhaps the most telling rebuff was the government's initial refusal to pay World War I female veterans for the time they had spent incarcerated as prisoners of the Germans.[13]

The quasi-military standing of Army and Navy nurses prevailed for another 20 years. Shortly after the end of World War I, nurses were granted "relative rank," a cosmetic change that allowed them to wear the insignia of officers from second lieutenant to major but denied them the pay and privileges of rank. These inequities were finally corrected in 1944. But the law has yet to be written that could compensate for the special indignity of a more personal nature reserved for pregnant, unwed Army nurses who until World War II were separated with dishonorable discharges. Women were treated like convicted criminals for behavior not only tolerated but deemed of little account in men.[14]

And yet, despite a history of inequitable treatment, women enlisted in the military in unprecedented numbers to do their part in World War II. The truth was that they received more training, more responsibility, and more freedom in the armed forces than they would ever have received at home or in private industry. They were grateful for the privilege to serve, and that privilege was its own reward.

The decision to recruit women was made with a certain reluctance, but the emergency left little time for reflection. The times were reminiscent of the antislavery era, when "male reformers were not always happy about having female colleagues, believing the ladies were best off at home. . . . But the need for timely workers became so great that women were admitted by some groups with the hope that they would confine themselves to suitably feminine roles."[15] The authors of Public Law 554, which established the Women's Army Auxiliary Corps (WAAC) in May 1942, had something similar in mind when they argued that the women would serve in an auxiliary *with* the Army and not *in* the Army.

The notion of the WAAC was ill conceived and caused ongoing confusion about the veteran status of its members. These early female military members were finally recognized as veterans in 1977, but in the interim they missed 24 years of eligibility. The potential to use some benefits, such as the GI bill, was lost entirely.

The Women Airforce Service Pilots (WASP), courageous pilots who made aviation history in the 1940s by flying everything from Piper Cubs to Mustang fighters and B-17 Flying Fortresses, were forced to fight the bureaucracy and United States Congress before winning military status in 1977. After prolonged acrimonious debate, fueled and stoked by organized opposition led by the VA and American Legion, the WASP amendment to the GI Bill Improvement Act was passed when Congressman Olin E. Teague, longtime chairman of the House Veterans Affairs Committee, had a last-minute change of heart. He compared the discharge notice of Wasp Helen Porter to his own and found they both read, "honorably served in active Federal Service in the Army of the United States."[16] The elation of victory, however, was tempered by the humbling experience of begging for recognition and by the memory of the 38 Wasps who were killed in crashes or while towing targets but were never accorded death or burial benefits.

To its credit, the Navy learned from the mistakes made by the Army and dismissed the idea of an auxiliary. Legislation signed by the President on July 30, 1942, established the Women's Reserve, granting military status but meager benefits to the future Waves. According to Jean Ebbert and Marie-Beth Hall, authors of *Crossed Currents: Navy Women from WWI to Tailhook*,

> women killed or injured on active duty were not entitled to the same benefits granted to male reservists; rather, they would receive those prescribed by law for U.S. civil employees. Thus the women were excluded from a lump-sum death gratuity to beneficiaries, retirement pay, and compensation or hospital care from the Veterans Administration. In these distinctions Congress and the Navy implicitly treated women as female civil servants while placing them under full military control.[17]

In November 1943 the restrictions were lifted, and women were granted the same benefits as men in the Navy. But a study of the history of women's use of their veterans benefits reveals the damage done by the ambiguity of their status throughout the war and the ensuing 30 years.

Enlistment standards were more stringent for women than men. They had to be older, better educated, and of certified good character. Arguably the most divisive issue, however, was the biased treatment of dependents. For the most part, women's family members were nonpeople. In an early recruiting booklet enumerating the "Advantages of being a Marine," one benefit, "Family Allowances—Same as to men," was lined out in pen. On the next page, the pay, rent, and subsistence allowance for officers with dependents was crossed out.[18] It would be nearly 30 years—May 14, 1973—before the Supreme Court, in the *Frontiero* v. *Richardson* decision, would rule that servicewomen were eligible for all benefits, privileges, and rights granted servicemen under the same circumstances. Furthermore, former or retired servicewomen could file claims for retroactive payment of with-dependents quarters allowances for periods of active duty during which they were married but did not receive the increased allowances.

Adding to the illusion of quasi-military organizations for women was the appointment of female directors who, though they had very little real authority, were often perceived to be the ultimate

Women Marines aboard this World War II transport plane get a bird's-eye view of the Hawaiian Islands, May 13, 1945.

National Archives, Records of the U.S. Marine Corps (127-N- 124152)

leader of female members. It was not unusual for male marines to wrongly suggest that the women had their own Commandant. Women worked side by side with men but had their own company commander. They even had their own acronyms. Women were not soldiers, sailors, or Coast Guardsmen. They were Wacs, Waves, and Spars. The Marines insisted that their women were marines and should be identified as such, but in fact it is hard to find a reference to them as other than "women Marines."

Considering the social, political, and economic customs that were so readily accepted, combined with the narrowly defined conditions of military service imposed during World War II, it is a wonder that women veterans applied for any benefits at all. As a rule, before leaving the service, they were not invited to outposting lectures where their benefits would have been explained. Few remember receiving a separation physical examination, an omission that made service-connected disability difficult to prove.

Upon arriving home, women exchanged their uniforms for aprons and maternity clothes. They seemed little interested in changing the status quo, and there was not much talk of political action. Full equality was not a priority for the majority of women. Surprisingly, the female press and leading women's advocates were nearly mute on the subject. A magazine article written in early 1945 told the story:

> The Wac in this war, like her sisters not in uniform, "will always be a civilian at heart." Service in the Wac will increase her femininity, and her hopes to settle down to the peace and security of a home and family. . . . In fact, the most important post-war plans of the majority of women in the Wac include just what all women want—their own homes and families.[19]

Surveys quizzing returning servicemen about their "dream girl" produced predictable results. Tops on every list was a homemaker with a fondness for children. GIs felt it was the girl's duty to make a home for fighting men coming back from foreign soil. One survey revealed that only 8 percent wanted a "brainy girl," and only 7 percent wanted a "business girl who could take care of herself." While the nation poured out its gratitude to male veterans, the women took their traditional place, basking in reflected glory.[20]

They were given little reason to join the men on center stage. They were turned away from veterans organizations and VA hospitals, being told they were not veterans. In an oral history, one woman confided, "After we were married, my husband wrote for my Victory Medal, as he was always proud of my service. They wrote back that I wasn't entitled to it, and that was the first time I knew that I wasn't in the army."[21]

The VA was no better prepared to deal with women than was the War Department. A male-only mindset permeated all facets of benefits delivery. The hospitals did not have the appropriate staff, equipment, medications, or desire to treat women. Furthermore, the basic design of most of the facilities caused problems related to privacy and dignity. Male veterans were welcome regardless of the cause of their medical concerns. Women, especially those needing gender-related treatment, were routinely told to go to their own doctor. Many never returned to the VA.

There is evidence suggesting that postwar VA regional offices acted as distinct entities when settling claims, which produced uneven results for women veterans. Since service-connected disability compensation is related to employability, some adjudicators denied claims in the belief that women did not need the money to which they were entitled because they had working husbands.[22]

Married women veterans were treated differently from men when applying for GI home loans. The loan was granted based upon a husband's income regardless of his veteran status. The woman veteran was viewed as a working wife whose income was merely supplemental and not stable. Apparently few took advantage of this popular benefit. In June 1946 the *New York Times Magazine* reported, "No women veterans' applications for GI house loans have been received in this region. . . . None . . . has applied for a GI business loan."[23]

Women did use the education benefits but were denied the dependents' allowance, even if their husbands were permanently incapable of self-support due to physical or mental disability. The exclusion continued until 1972 when Public Law 202 provided that for all VA benefits, the term "wife" or "widow" would include the husband or widower of a female veteran.

And they died as they lived—in anonymity. For years, women veterans were buried in national cemeteries along with their husbands—just as civilian wives. And their names are engraved on the reverse side of the headstone—just as the civilian wives'—without mention of military service.

All of this was allowed to happen despite a strong veterans lobby that could have made a difference. But women were not part of it. With only a few exceptions, they were not welcome at post meetings and were encouraged, instead, to participate in the ladies auxiliary. The arrangement, while it may have been preferable socially, slowed down the quest for equity.

After World War I, thousands of Yeomen (F) joined the American Legion, often forming their own posts.[24] The more experienced male veterans opened legislative doors for the women and taught them the ways of lobbying. But after World War II, it was not unusual to hear women recount disappointing stories of being prohibited from marching in uniform in parades with veterans organizations. Acceptance took a very long time. In *American Women and World War II*, Doris Weatherford wrote, "The Carter Administration, in response to growing feminism in the late 1970s, tried to pressure the VFW into admitting women veterans on an equal basis, but administration officials were shouted down at the VFW convention."[25]

World War II women veterans are the product of their heritage, their military standing, and their postwar experience. It is not surprising that the majority, even as late as 1982, had no idea they were entitled to benefits. Despite aggressive outreach since then by the VA and the elimination of many barriers to service, today only 2 percent of World War II female veterans receive compensation compared to 10 percent of female Vietnam veterans. Nor is it surprising that an unfortunate generational rift developed when women veterans of the Vietnam war launched a drive to erect a monument when no such honor had yet been paid to the women who served in earlier wars.

Recognition and reward—the concepts were foreign. The outcome was predictable.

NOTES

© 1996 by Mary V. Stremlow

Special thanks to Joan Furey, R.N., M.A., Director, Women Veterans Program Office, Department of Veterans Affairs, for the statistics she provided, especially on female usage of veterans benefits; to Linda Spoonster-Schwartz, R.N., M.S.M., Chair, Vietnam Veterans of America Veterans Affairs Committee, for sharing her research and writings on problems faced by women veterans; and to Thomas Zamary, Director of the Department of Veterans Affairs Regional Office in Buffalo, NY, for a chronological summary of legislative changes that affected the benefits for women veterans and their dependents.

The author's previously published works, *A History of the Women Marines, 1946-1977* (Washington, DC: History and Museums Division, Headquarters, U.S.

Marine Corps, 1986), *Coping With Sexism in the Military* (New York: The Rosen Publishing Group, 1990), and *Free A Marine To Fight: Women Marines in World War II* (Washington, DC: History and Museums Division, Headquarters, U.S. Marine Corps, 1994) were also used.

1. Department of Veterans Affairs, *Statistical Brief; Projections of the U.S. Veteran Population: 1990-2010* (May 1994), p. 2.
2. Ibid., p. 5.
3. Louis Harris and Associates, *Survey of Female Veterans: A Study of Needs, Attitudes and Experiences of Women Veterans.* IM&S M 70-85-7, Study no. 843002, 1985.
4. Barbara T. Roessner, "Was Rose Ever Allowed To Bloom?," *Buffalo News,* Jan. 28, 1995, p. C7.
5. Virginia Sapiro, *Women in American Society: An Introduction to Women's Studies,* 2d ed. (Mountain View, CA, 1990), p. 106.
6. Ibid., p. 108.
7. Miriam Gurko, *The Ladies of Seneca Falls; The Birth of the Woman's Rights Movement* (New York, 1974), p. 9.
8. Carol Hymowitz and Michaele Weissman, *A History of Women In America* (New York, 1978), pp. 303-314.
9. Sapiro, *Women in American Society,* p. 108.
10. Linda P. Wood and Judi Scott, *What Did You Do in the War Grandma?: An Oral History of Rhode Island Women during World War II* (South Kingston, RI, 1989), p. 39.
11. June E. Willenz, *Women Veterans; America's Forgotten Heroines* (New York, 1983), pp. 16-17.
12. Jean Ebbert and Marie-Beth Hall, *Crossed Currents: Navy Women from WWI to Tailhook* (Washington, DC, 1993), p. 16.
13. Willenz, *Women Veterans,* p. 15.
14. Jeanne Holm, *Women in the Military: An Unfinished Revolution,* rev. ed. (Novato, CA, 1982), p. 71.
15. Gurko, *Ladies of Seneca Falls,* p. 33.
16. Sally Van Wagenen Keil, *Those Wonderful Women in Their Flying Machines* (New York, 1979), pp. 347-348.
17. Ebbert and Hall, *Crossed Currents,* p. 37.
18. U.S. Marine Corps, *Be A Marine ... Free a Marine to Fight: U.S. Marine Corps Women's Reserve,* recruiting brochure (n.d., pre-July 1945).
19. Melissa S. Herbert, "Amazons or Butterflies: The Recruitment of Women into the Military during World War II," *MINERVA: Quarterly Report on Women in the Military,* 9 (Summer 1991): 61.
20. Doris Weatherford, *American Women and World War II* (New York, 1990), pp. 309-310.
21. Michelle A. Christides, "Women Veterans of the Great War," *MINERVA,* 3 (Summer 1985): 121.
22. "Dealing With a Legacy of Neglect," *DAV Magazine* (October 1986): 7.
23. Weatherford, *American Women and World War II,* p. 104.
24. Telephone interview with Erle Cocke, Jr., past national commander of the American Legion, Jan. 11, 1995.
25. Weatherford, *American Women and World War II,* p. 103.

WORLD WAR II AND PROACTIVE WOMEN

Mary E. Haas

A s the last speaker of the conference, I have come to realize that I bring a very different perspective to our topic from that of previous presenters. In my work as an educator, I play the role of an intermediary. Virtually all of my time is spent instructing prospective elementary teachers about issues and strategies related to the teaching of social studies. In this career, I have had the opportunity to come to know what the current generation has learned from their public school and university courses about women in general and about women in the military in particular.

I must unfortunately report that most of the young women and men in my classes over the past 9 years have shown little understanding of women's history and often no knowledge of women who have served in the military—one young woman in the reserves and another who was a drill sergeant in the U.S. Marines were exceptions. Most have even failed to recognize the connection between civilian women entering the labor force on the homefront during World War II and America's war efforts. If my sample of college seniors from five different states (New Jersey, Pennsylvania, Maryland, Virginia, and West Virginia) is in any way representative of students in other states, we might well be wondering about its cause. I have also been struck by the fact that, when giving presentations to educators at national meetings, participants are aware of the roles that men played in World War II but surprisingly lacking in information about the numbers of women who served and the extent of their struggles and accomplishments. Has there not been an increased emphasis on the teaching of social history and the inclusion of ordinary people, including women, in that history over the past 20 years?

I have discovered in my studies that the roles that women have played in the military tend to fall into three categories: victim, reactive participant, and proactive participant.[1] War has always had a broad impact on women's lives, but the massive world wars of this century provided special opportunities for women to assume proactive roles. In this paper I will focus on the development of that role during World War II.

Proactive women typically see a problem, consider the consequences of actions they might take, and select a course of action. They assume control and responsibility for their lives rather than wait for something outside their sphere of influence to happen. Some are, as is to be expected, more aggressively proactive than others.

Beginning in World War I, proactive women legally entered military service through both active recruitment and support organizations, such as the Red Cross. But immediately after the war, all but a few nurses were forced out of the military. Between the wars, laws were changed to prohibit women's service even though famous generals like John J. Pershing and George C. Marshall advocated a formal military role for women.[2] Fear, ignorance, and sexist prejudice won out, and women had to find other avenues for their talents and energies.[3]

World War II acted as a catalyst for increasing the numbers of proactive women. It gave women an opportunity to aid their nation while acquiring new skills, enhanced self-concepts, and the satisfaction of helping to achieve the national goal of winning the war. The sudden demand for both civilian and military workers during World War II provided women with opportunities to work in jobs not normally open to them. The government encouraged women not only to fill jobs on the homefront, while financing child care centers to enable mothers to work, but also to volunteer for military service. And they did.

Proactive women joined the Women's Army Auxiliary Corps (WAAC), Women's Army Corps (WAC), Women Accepted for Volunteer Emergency Service (WAVES), Women's Reserve of the Coast Guard (SPAR, from the motto *"Semper Paratus*—Always Ready"), Women Airforce Service Pilots (WASP), Marine Corps Women's Reserve, Army Nurse Corps (ANC), and Navy Nurse Corps (NNC). Those who were more highly proactive worked for British intelligence and as ferry pilots for Britain prior to America's formal entry into the war.

The pioneers of World War II knew that they had to succeed if other women were to have the same opportunity to serve. The original group of Wasps were among the most successful pilots of their day and experienced a dramatic change in their lives when they became pilots for the military. The first 440 WAAC officers were women of accomplishment: 99 percent had been employed; 90 percent had attended college. They all set a high standard that the more than 350,000 women who served in the military during the war strived to maintain.

When the largest percentage of these women returned to civilian life, they did not cease to be proactive. Their varied encounters with people and experiences in the military had given them confidence in their abilities. Even the women who married and no longer worked outside the home were proactive as they reared their families and helped in community organizations. Because of servicewomen's contributions, women's accomplishments received greater public attention. When women used the GI bill to pursue professional and educational advancement, the nation also benefitted. Through their patriotic service, these women displayed the true quality and full meaning of citizenship.

It is troubling that Americans born after the end of World War II have so little, if any, knowledge of the honorable service that these women gave. Even worse is the seeming oversight on the part of the press, which covered servicewomen's efforts during the war, to honor these veterans during many of the anniversary celebrations.

When I speak to teachers and prospective teachers about women and the military, I am usually pleased with their interest and am delighted to hear the undergraduates express a desire not to continue supporting curricula that omit women and their accomplishments. But I often wonder where they will get the knowledge they will need to teach their young charges. It is very difficult for teachers to find information on this topic, particularly at the local level. No matter how interesting and meaningful the information in this conference has been for each of us, we deceive ourselves if we think that teachers can teach what they have not learned or what states, communities, professional educational organizations, or publishers have not been aware of or made available to them.

How, then, can the history of the WAC, WAVES, SPAR, Marines, and WASP possibly survive? An examination of the textbooks used at the K–12 levels as well as my own personal observations confirm that knowledge and even awareness of these women's units are slipping away quickly. Additionally, the first edition of the National

Standards for United States History, published in 1994 as a guide to what teachers should include in the study of history for grades 7-12, contained only one reference to women and World War II; it recommended discussing the effects of World War II on gender roles and the American family. The single activity suggested to attain this goal was to analyze images of such working women as "Rosie the Riveter" and decide why they were portrayed in this way and if the images were complimentary ones. It is not my purpose to find fault with these efforts but to alert people, educators and female veterans of World War II alike, to go out and be proactive so that this conference will be more than just a pleasant, fleeting memory. Only when the adage "Women's work is never done!" is taken to heart and acted upon can the fading images of these servicewomen and their contributions be burned once again into the minds and pride of Americans.

But why does this story about proactive women in World War II need to be learned? What is the rationale for teaching it? I propose that the following ideas form the basis of our discussion: it is better for an individual to be a proactive participant than either a victim or a reactor; and democracy succeeds only when large numbers of its citizens are proactive.

Democracy is not a particular form of government that can be created and set into motion once and for all time. Instead, it is a dynamic process, created anew and sustained through the acts of each person every single day in response to changing historical conditions. There is a direct parallel for me between fighting to preserve democracy from foreign dictators and fighting to protect democracy from domestic undemocratic ideas and actions, particularly those stemming from prejudice and discrimination, which promote inequality and lack of opportunity for people. In order for individuals to act proactively in defense of democratic principles and values, they must be exposed to these ideals and come to believe that they will benefit both themselves and the common good. Only then will individuals work to ensure that others are accorded the same rights and privileges.

The world has changed greatly since the days of World War II, but it is still necessary that every individual grow up and develop into an active citizen with a democratic perspective. This is especially significant for our nation today as the social and geographic mobility of our people threatens to separate and divide us.

With this realization, we must determine what the important subjects are and how they should be taught both within and outside the classroom, within and outside the curriculum. We might ask, for instance, how many people have put their lives on the line for reading, mathematics, or science. Very, very few, of course, compared to those who have done so in the name of democracy. In the past, our efforts to promote democracy have sometimes failed; we must ask if we are in danger of failing new generations of children and immigrants.

It is our hope that through learning, which is predominately an individual activity, society will come to adopt the important common principles that ensure life, liberty, and happiness for all of its members. Unfortunately, there are many young people who lack the opportunity or appropriate stimuli to learn about the power that democracy affords them and how to use it legitimately and responsibly.

Democracy will not be preserved if youth fail to be educated, learn only part of their history, or are deprived of the wisdom that experience can offer. In our particular case, we do not advocate teaching about women and the military in order to turn our daughters into warriors. We do it so that our children, by gaining a larger perspective of the capabilities of American women, may come to better understand themselves. Our children need to see how people face challenging situations and how they act to solve difficult problems.

Studies show that many more girls in their teens accept negative stereotypes and develop negative views of their future than boys do. They continue to see themselves as victims, often reacting violently to physical and emotional violence against them; they do not learn how to become proactive. A female social studies educator recently encouraged me to include some of my work on teaching about women and war in a book of readings. Her comment to me was simply, "The girls need it." It is also important for today's young men to learn to confront their sexist views and stereotypes, just as male soldiers had to do in World War II. They need to know that women fought in wars and endured conditions similar to men and that cooperation, not supremacy, leads to success.

During World War II, servicewomen's weapons were patience, care, cooperation, leadership, determination, and endurance. In spite of postwar technological advances, the veterans' best weapons remain the same. Their mission today, however, is to inspire and inform the uninformed and to help researchers and educators to tell their story.

I have always been inspired by the veterans I have met. Recently, I became acquainted with Ada Henderson, who left a very small community in rural Georgia to join the WAAC and later the WAC; she served in England, typing orders for the D-day invasion, and completed her service in France. She told me of going to the veterans' section in the cemetery where she has a plot, seeing statues of male veterans representing all branches of the service, and proceeding to the cemetery office to complain about its unfairness in not recognizing female veterans. The officials told her, "This is not a liberated cemetery." "Well it will be," she replied. About 6 months later she returned and observed that a statue of a nurse had been added. Delighted, she went back to the office where the staff explained that, because they could not erect statues for all of the service ladies, they had picked a nurse to represent them. Ada's

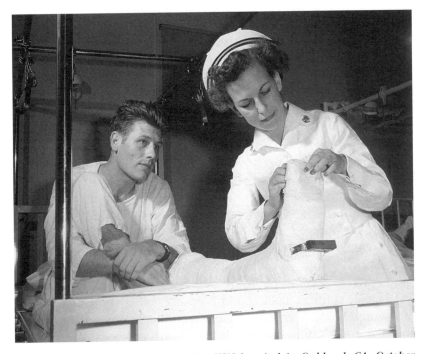

A Navy nurse attends patient at the USN hospital in Oakland, CA, October 17, 1944.

National Archives, General Records of the Department of the Navy, 1798-1947 (80-G-288570)

reply was "That's the greatest thing you could have done. They are the women who suffered the most during the Second World War, and I am pleased that you chose a nurse. All I wanted was a woman."

There are a number of actions that women veterans can take to help preserve the memory of and bring public recognition to the outstanding service that women provided to win World War II. As a researcher and educator, I suggest the following activities, in ascending order of difficulty.

1. Register your service with the Women In Military Service For America Memorial Foundation. Write to WIMSA, 5510 Columbia Pike, Ste. 302, Arlington, VA 22204.

2. Organize your own records in a scrapbook, photograph album, or picture frame. Label and date pictures and letters. Include a short statement that says what your military service has meant to your life.

3. Share your finished product with friends and family. Do not wait for a special request; offer to loan your materials to local museums or libraries for display. Many school children visit such displays, and sadly, many displays lack the important contributions of women. Designate on the display and in your will someone or some organization at the local, state, or national level to receive your records when you die.

4. Celebrate Grandparents Day by duplicating photographs and records, and present a family history book to your grandchildren. Be certain that it includes your military service. Make note of any famous people that you met during your service, and give your impressions of them. This information will complement what is read in texts or history books.

5. Provide a copy of your discharge papers to your heirs, and instruct them to have your grave marked with a military marker even if you plan to be interred in a family plot. Cemeteries are important sources of historical and genealogical information and provide wonderful opportunities to educate younger generations.

6. Speak up, and ask the local and regional news media how they plan to continue telling the story of women during World War II. If they try to tell you the celebration is over, remind them of their future obligation to faithfully present the entire story. Suggest that they do a followup segment if they already have done a feature; journalists often do that.

7. Contact teachers and instructors in schools, colleges, and universities, and ask them what they are teaching about women and World War II. Suggest to teachers of lower grades that they look at Mary E. Haas and Janet K. Tipton, "Studying World War II in the Elementary School," pp. 18–19, and "Pull-Out Feature I: The Study of World War II," pp. 1–4, both in *Social Studies & the Young Learner* (November/December 1994). Volunteer to be interviewed or to speak to classes. In 1994 I connected a fourth-grade teacher with a lady who had been a young teen in a small neighboring community during the war. She talked about what her life was like then; the children's interests and responses thrilled both the presenter and the teacher. She has since written about her experiences for her own children and grandchildren.

8. Consider writing your own story. Even if you do not have a book-length manuscript, you may try to publish in one of the many state cultural or historical society magazines that contain short articles or columns devoted to memories. If you need assistance, contact a good local reporter or a university department of history, English, or journalism. Honors and graduate students often need ideas and inspirations for their projects. More than a few university professors are pursuing the study of women in World War II because someone asked them for their skilled assistance in a project that proved more fascinating than first imagined.

9. Contact publishers of school textbooks and biographies for young readers, and suggest that they publish the stories of the women who served America during World War II. Today many children's books about the Holocaust are available. Just as the Holocaust is an important topic, so too are the stories of those proactive women who helped end Nazi racism and genocide through the Allied victory. I would like to be wrong in stating that, among all the books for young girls about nursing, there is not one that tells the story of a military nurse in the 20th century. Certainly no books tell of a pilot who became a Wasp. I am certain, however, that we would all agree that biographies of such women as the WAC's Lt. Col. Charity Adams Earley, the Navy's Capt. Joy Bright Hancock, and the Air Force's Maj. Gen. Jeanne Holm would truly inspire today's young girls.[4]

Soon after the attack on Pearl Harbor, a song with a simple melody and a strong march beat became very popular. It included a phrase indicating that the song was Uncle Sam's reply on behalf of all Americans to the attack on Pearl Harbor. The song's title, repeated often within the piece, still serves as our rallying call.

> We did it before and we can do it again.
> And we will do it again.
> We've got a heck of a job to do,
> but you can bet that we'll see it through. . . .
> We did it before and we can do it again.
> And we will do it again.

The National Archives and participants in this conference deserve thanks for their efforts in gathering, preserving, and making known the important history of women in World War II. I would like to conclude by thanking our veterans and asking them to volunteer again and again and again so that subsequent generations, and girls in particular, will learn that they can—and must—become proactive, too. Only then will they have the opportunity to prevail in their war against stereotypes and personal apathy so both they and democracy can survive and develop in this changing world.

NOTES

© 1996 by Mary C. Haas

1. In Nelly P. Stromquist's (ed.) *Encyclopedia of Third World Women* (New York, 1996), see Mary E. Haas, "Women and War."
2. See Jeanne Holm, *Women in the Military: An Unfinished Revolution* (Novato, CA, 1992).
3. Margaret Mead was quick to remind her audience, when questioned at an appearance at Indiana University, that the fear of women taking jobs from men and its resultant discrimination were exacerbated during the Great Depression.
4. Charity Adams Earley, an African-American school teacher with graduate training, became the first African-American woman commissioned as an officer in the Women's Army Corps (WAC). Major (later Lieutenant Colonel) Adams was the commanding officer of the decorated 6888th Central Postal Directory Battalion, which served in Europe during the war. She tells her own experiences and those of many African Americans who served in the WAC in *One Woman's Army: A Black Officer Remembers the WAC* (College Station, TX, 1989).

   Capt. Joy Bright Hancock was one of two women to serve the Navy in both World War I and World War II. During World War II she made it possible for women to serve in many different roles. She remained in the WAVES until 1953 and became the third Assistant Chief of Naval Personnel for Women. Captain Hancock, more than any other individual, was responsible for the establishment of the WAVES as a component of the Navy. She related much of her background and naval experience in *Lady in the Navy: A Personal Reminiscence* (Annapolis, MD, 1972).

Maj. Gen. Jeanne Holm's distinguished and long career with the Air Force became historic when she was the first female to earn the rank of major general. A strong advocate of women's service, Major General Holm is considered the most knowledgeable individual on the role of women in the United States military and is the author of *Women in the Military: An Unfinished Revolution* (Novato, CA, 1992).

LIST OF ACRONYMS

AA/AAA/AAC	Antiaircraft artillery units
AAF	Army Air Forces
AFB	Air Force Base
ANC	Army Nurse Corps
ARC	American Red Cross
ASF	Army Service Forces
ATA	Air Transport Auxiliary
ATC	Air Transport Command
ATS	Auxiliary Territorial Service
BPR	Bureau of Public Relations
CAA	Civil Aeronautics Administration
CAP	Civil Air Patrol
CBI	China-Burma-India theater
DOD	Department of Defense
ETO	European Theater of Operations
MCWR	Marine Corps Women's Reserve
MISLS	Military Intelligence Service Language School
MOS	Military Occupational Specialty
NAACP	National Association for the Advancement of Colored People
NCNW	National Council of Negro Women
NNC	Navy Nurse Corps
OCS	Officer Candidate School
OWI	Office of War Information
POW	Prisoner of war
ROTC	Reserve Officers Training Corps
SHAEF	Supreme Headquarters, Allied Expeditionary Forces
SPAR	"*Semper Paratus*—Always Ready" Coast Guard motto
SWPA	Southwest Pacific Area
USFET	U.S. Forces, European Theater
USO	United Service Organizations
VA	Department of Veterans Affairs

WAAC	Women's Army Auxiliary Corps
WAC	Women's Army Corps
WAF	Women in the Air Force
WAFS	Women's Auxiliary Ferrying Squadron
WAFT	Women's Auxiliary Ferry Troop
WASP	Women Airforce Service Pilots
WAVES	Women Accepted for Volunteer Emergency Service
WD	War Department
WFTD	Women's Flying Training Detachment
WRA	War Relocation Authority

SOURCES FROM THE
NATIONAL ARCHIVES FOR
FURTHER RESEARCH

Most of the publications listed below are described in a free catalog, *WWII Resources From the National Archives*. The catalog describes books, posters, teaching aids, videotapes, and gift items relating to World War II.

To request the free catalog or purchasing information, write to or call the National Archives, Publications Distribution (NECD), Room G9, Seventh and Pennsylvania Avenue, NW, Washington, DC 20408 (telephone 202-501-7190/1-800-234-8861; fax 202-501-7170).

Information about National Archives publications, still pictures, motion pictures, and sound recordings is also available on the World Wide Web. The URL for the National Archives and Records Administration home page is http://www.nara.gov.

The two slide sets may be purchased from the National Technical Information Service (NTIS), 5825 Port Royal Road, Springfield, VA 22161; their World Wide Web URL is http://www.fedworld.gov/ntis/nac/nac.htm.

Burger, Barbara Lewis. "American Images: Photographs and Posters in the Still Picture Branch," *Prologue: Quarterly of the National Archives* 22 (Winter 1990): 353–368.

———, comp. *Guide to the Holdings of the Still Picture Branch of the National Archives.* Washington, DC: National Archives and Records Administration, 1990.

———, comp. Select Audiovisual Records, *Pictures of African Americans During World War II.* Slide set and leaflet. Washington, DC: National Archives and Records Administration, 1993.

Burger, Barbara Lewis, William Cunliffe, Jonathan Heller, William T. Murphy, and Les Waffen, comps. *Audiovisual Records in the National Archives of the United States Relating to World War II*, Reference Information Paper 70. Washington, DC: National Archives and Records Administration, revised 1992.

Chalou, George, ed. *The Secrets War: The Office of Strategic Services in World War II*. Washington, DC: National Archives and Records Administration, 1992.

Gellert, Charles Lawrence, comp. *The Holocaust, Israel, and the Jews: Motion Pictures in the National Archives*. Washington, DC: National Archives and Records Administration, 1989.

Hartmann, Susan M. "Women in the Military Service." In *Clio Was a Woman: Studies in the History of American Women*, edited by Mabel E. Deutrich and Virginia C. Purdy. Washington, DC: National Archives and Records Administration, 1980 (out of print; available in many libraries).

Heller, Jonathan, ed. *War & Conflict: Selected Images from the National Archives, 1765-1970*. Washington, DC: National Archives and Records Administration, 1990.

————, comp. Select Audiovisual Records, *Pictures of World War II*. Slide set and leaflet. Washington, DC: National Archives and Records Administration, 1990.

O'Neill, James E., and Robert W. Krauskopf, eds. *World War II: An Account of Its Documents*. Washington, DC: National Archives and Records Administration, 1976.

Seeley, Charlotte Palmer, comp. *American Women and the U.S. Armed Forces: A Guide to the Records of Military Agencies in the National Archives Relating to American Women*. Revised by Virginia C. Purdy and Robert Gruber. Washington, DC: National Archives and Records Administration, 1992.

Serene, Frank H. *World War II on Film: A Catalog of Select Motion Pictures in the National Archives*. Washington, DC: National Archives and Records Administration, 1994.

CONTRIBUTORS

Regina T. Akers

Regina Akers is an archivist with the Naval Historical Center's Operational Archives. She previously served as an archives technician in both the Still Picture Branch and Motion Picture, Sound, and Video Branch of the National Archives. Ms. Akers holds a B.A. degree from The Catholic University of America and an M.A. degree from Howard University, where she is currently pursuing a doctorate in history. Her numerous presentations and published articles address the role and experiences of women in the military during World War II. Her master's thesis is entitled "The Integration of Afro-Americans into the WAVES, 1942–1945." Ms. Akers is active in the Mid-Atlantic Regional Archives Conference, Oral History Mid-Atlantic Region, and the Association of Black Women Historians.

DeAnne Blanton

DeAnne Blanton is an archivist with the Archives I Reference Branch at the National Archives Building in Washington, DC. She previously worked in the Military Reference Branch. Ms. Blanton holds a B.A. degree from Sweet Briar College and an M.A. degree from Wake Forest University. She has published articles pertaining to military women and other subjects in *Prologue: Quarterly of the National Archives* and in *MINERVA: Quarterly Report on Women and the Military*. She received the 1993 Sara Jackson Award for her *Prologue* article entitled "Women Soldiers of the Civil War." Ms. Blanton is a member of the Mid-Atlantic Regional Archives Conference.

Barbara Lewis Burger

Barbara Burger is a senior-level archivist with the Still Picture Branch at the National Archives at College Park. She has written four National Archives publications, including the *Guide to the Holdings of the Still Picture Branch of the National Archives*. For this publication, Ms. Burger received the 1992 Mid-Atlantic Regional Archives

Conference (MARAC) Finding Aids Award. She previously served as assistant chief for reference of the Still Picture Branch and assistant to the director of the Special Archives Division. She holds a B.A. degree from Howard University and an M.S.L.S. from The Catholic University of America. Ms. Burger is a member of numerous professional organizations, including MARAC, Phi Alpha Theta, the D.C. Picture Group, and the Association of Black Women Historians.

D'Ann Campbell

D'Ann Campbell is dean of the College of Arts and Sciences and professor of history at Austin Peay State University in Tennessee. She previously held administrative and professorial positions in history and women's studies at Indiana University and served as visiting professor of military history at the U.S. Military Academy. Dr. Campbell has written a book entitled *Women at War with America: Private Lives in a Patriotic Era* and three dozen articles on social and military history. A Phi Beta Kappa graduate from Colorado College, she earned her doctorate in history at the University of North Carolina. Dr. Campbell has presented over 120 papers on social and military history to a wide variety of audiences, served on editorial boards and on national professional committees, and reviewed both NEH grant proposals and manuscripts for publication in books and journals.

Clare M. Cronin

Clare Cronin earned her bachelor's degree from Smith College and master's degree in museum studies from The George Washington University. She has worked at the United States Marine Corps Museum and assisted with two exhibitions at the National Museum of American History. She is presently serving as consultant for an upcoming exhibition at the United States Holocaust Memorial Museum. Her current research interests include military social history and women's history from the 19th century to the present.

Linda Grant De Pauw

Linda Grant De Pauw is an established scholar in women's, military, and early American history. She holds a bachelor's degree from Swarthmore College and a doctorate from The Johns Hopkins University. Dr. De Pauw has been teaching since 1962 and currently serves as professor of history at The George Washington University.

Her books have been nominated for and received awards from such organizations as the American Historical Association and the American Library Association. She has written articles for popular and scholarly journals, historical anthologies, and the *Young Reader's Companion to American History*. In 1983 Dr. De Pauw created *MINERVA: Quarterly Report on Women and the Military* and later founded The MINERVA Center, Inc., a nonprofit foundation dedicated to promoting women's military studies. From 1965 to 1984 she was director of the First Federal Congress Project, which is producing the multivolume *Documentary History of the Federal Congress, 1789-1791*; she now chairs the project's board of advisers. Dr. De Pauw frequently addresses both popular and scholarly audiences and serves as historical consultant to a wide variety of enterprises undertaken in both the public and private sector. Her most recent project is *Battle Cries and Lullabies: A Brief History of Women in War*.

Dorothy Jeanne Gleason

Capt. Dorothy Jeanne Gleason, USCGR (ret.), was sworn into the U.S. Coast Guard in early 1943 and entered boot camp at Hunter College (the designated WAVES Training Station) in The Bronx, NY. After being assigned to the 9th Coast Guard District in Cleveland, OH, she was recommended for Officer's Candidate School, Pay and Supply, in Palm Beach, FL, and commissioned on June 14, 1944. Captain Gleason was assigned to Manhattan Beach Training Station, Brooklyn, as deputy disbursing officer until the station was closed in 1946. She finished out her active duty at Coast Guard Headquarters in Washington, DC. In 1949 she rejoined the Coast Guard and served as spokesperson for the SPAR before the Senate and House Committees seeking to enact remedial legislation for the forced broken service that occurred between 1947 (when the Spars were automatically discharged) and 1949 (when new legislation allowed their reentry). Captain Gleason remained in the ready reserve program until 1978, serving in various administrative units as well as for 2 years at Coast Guard Headquarters as the Commandant's adviser on the women's program. Simultaneously with her Coast Guard Reserve service, Captain Gleason enjoyed a successful civil service career that included 24 years as head of employee-management relations at the Naval Ordnance Laboratory in White Oak, MD. She has held office at all levels in the Reserve Officers

Association and served as a member of the board of directors of the Retired Officers Association. She remains active in programs pertaining to the Coast Guard Reserve.

RitaVictoria Gomez

RitaVictoria Gomez is assistant professor of history at Anne Arundel Community College in Maryland. She is currently completing her doctorate at The George Washington University with a dissertation entitled "Clipped Wings: Women and the Army Air Forces, 1939-1952." Her B.A. and M.A. degrees were awarded by Pace University and California State University, Sacramento, respectively. Ms. Gomez has served in a variety of teaching and research capacities in academia and the military. Her interest in the history of women and minorities is long-standing. She has presented numerous papers at professional conferences, reviewed books and other publications for military and other journals, written related articles for newspapers, appeared widely on radio and television talk shows, and taken part in women's studies panels. As a historian in the Center for Air Force History, Bolling Air Force Base, Ms. Gomez is currently writing the official history of women in the Air Force.

Mary E. Haas

Mary Haas is associate professor of curriculum and instruction in the College of Human Resources and Education and adjunct associate professor of geography at West Virginia University. Her Ed.D. degree is from Indiana University. Dr. Haas has broad classroom experience as both a social studies teacher for grades 7-9 in Michigan City, IN, and a university professor of undergraduate and graduate courses in social studies methods, instructional strategies for use in a wide range of disciplines (including economics and geography), curriculum construction, and teacher training. Her extensive teaching, administrative, and professional responsibilities include directing graduate research, serving as newsletter editor for the West Virginia Council for the Social Studies, acting as National History Day judge, and participating in numerous conference program and planning committees. Dr. Haas has been a prolific contributor to the burgeoning literature in her field. She has coauthored a book and instructor's manual on *Social Studies and the Elementary/Middle School Student* and published chapters, articles, book reviews, and educational simulations in newsletters, ERIC publications, journals, textbooks, and educational guides and materials. Much of Dr. Haas's work has focused on women and war, and she has approached her topic from the dual perspective of what and how we teach young people about war and whether women have a unique perspective toward war.

Marcia R. Haley

Marcia Haley is chief of the Air Force Reference Branch at the National Personnel Records Center in St. Louis. She has been employed by the National Archives since 1974 and worked in its Records Reconstruction Branch, the Navy Reference Branch, and the Reference Service Support Branch. Ms. Haley holds a B.S. degree in social studies education from Southeast Missouri State University.

Terri Hanna

Terri Hanna is an archivist with the Archives II Textual Reference Branch at the National Archives at College Park. She previously worked in the National Archives Suitland Reference Branch. She holds a B.A. degree from George Mason University. Ms. Hanna is a member of the Mid-Atlantic Regional Archives Conference and serves as membership coordinator for the National Archives Assembly.

Mary B. Johnston

Mary Blakemore Johnston interrupted her studies at Emory and Henry College in Emory, Virginia, to join the WAAC on December 8, 1942. Her 3 years in the Army were spent at posts in the southern states and overseas in New Guinea and the Philippines. After the war, she completed work for her bachelor's degree and did postgraduate work at the Presbyterian School of Christian Education. In 1947 she married Dr. William C. Johnston, a physicist who had worked on the Manhattan Project. In 1977, after raising four children, she completed work for a master's degree in counseling education at George Mason University in Fairfax, VA, and worked as a licensed professional counselor until her retirement in 1990.

Judy Barrett Litoff

Judy Barrett Litoff is professor of history at Bryant College in Smithfield, RI. She and Dr. David C. Smith have devoted the last decade to locating and collecting the letters written by U.S. women, both military and civilian, during World War II. Their accumulated manuscript holdings consist of 30,000 wartime letters and constitute the largest collection of its kind in the world. A microfilm edition of these letters, to be published by Scholarly Resources, Inc., is in preparation. Dr. Litoff and Dr. Smith are the co-authors of four books on Women and World War II: *We're In This War, Too: World War II Letters from American Women in Uniform* (Oxford, 1994); *Since You Went Away: World War II Letters from American Women on the Home Front* (Oxford, 1991; paperback ed., University Press of Kansas, 1995); *Dear Boys: World War II Letters from a Woman Back Home* (University Press of Mississippi, 1991); and *Miss You: The World War II Letters of Barbara Wooddall Taylor and Charles E. Taylor* (University of Georgia Press, 1990). They are co-editors of *American Women in a World at War: Contemporary Accounts from World War II* (Scholarly Resources, 1996). They are also the co-authors of 20 articles and reviews on women and World War II, including " 'To the Rescue of the Crops': The Women's Land Army of World War II," which appeared in *Prologue: Quarterly of the National Archives* and for which they were awarded the 1994 James Madison Prize by the Society for History in the Federal Government.

Leisa D. Meyer

Leisa Meyer is assistant professor of history at The College of William and Mary. While pursuing her B.A. degree from the University of Colorado–Boulder and her master's and doctoral work at the University of Wisconsin–Madison, she focused on women's social history, the history of sexuality, and the historical role of women in the military services. She was the recipient of four teaching awards and fellowships and grants. Professor Meyer acquired applied knowledge of women's military history as a U.S. Air Force Academy cadet in 1979–80. She has been active in presenting papers; writing book reviews, articles, and other publications; and serving in professional organizations. Dr. Meyer's first book, *Creating G.I. Jane: The Women's Army Corps During World War II*, will be published by Columbia University Press in October 1996.

Constance J. Moore

Maj. Constance J. Moore is Army Nurse Corps historian at the U.S. Center of Military History in Washington, DC. She holds an undergraduate degree in history from Iowa State University and B.S. and M.S. degrees in nursing from Seattle University and San Jose State University, respectively. Major Moore has broad experience in both nursing and teaching. Since 1986 she has been certified as a psychiatric/mental health nurse by the American Nurses' Association. While stationed at posts around the country and in Korea, she received decorations and commendations for her teaching and professional work, including the Nursing Supervisor of the Year Award at Fort Ord, CA. Major Moore has been active in publishing and presenting works on nursing history, research, and practice. Her master's thesis, entitled "Oral History Reflections of Army Nurse Corps Vietnam Veterans: Managing the Demanding Experience of War," reflects her work as an oral historian.

Bettie J. Morden

Col. Bettie Morden, U.S. Army (ret.), enlisted in the WAAC in 1942 and spent 38 months on active duty, primarily at WAC training centers. During a total of 33 years of active duty, she served in various command capacities in the United States and overseas as Deputy Director of the Women's Army Corps and as WAC historian at the U.S. Army Center of Military History in Washington, DC. Among her major military decorations is the Distinguished Service Medal. Colonel Morden has an M.A. degree in English from Columbia University. In addition to writing historical articles for service journals, Colonel Morden is the author of *The Women's Army Corps, 1945-1978*, which was published in 1990 by the Army Center of Military History and the Government Printing Office. She has served as president of the Women's Army Corps Foundation since 1973 and in 1994 became a member of the education committee of the Women In Military Service For America Memorial Foundation.

Jennifer Nelson

Jennifer Nelson is an archivist with the Cartographic and Architectural Branch at the National Archives at College Park. She has previously held positions in the Center for Electronic Records, the Textual Projects Branch, and the Motion Picture, Sound, and Video Branch. Ms. Nelson holds a B.A. degree in American studies from Occidental College and an M.A. degree in American civilization from The George Washington University. Her book reviews, published in the *Journal of American Studies*, have assessed works interpreting the culture of masculinity in the American Army of World War I and "reading" American photographs for cultural meaning.

Mary Harrington Nelson

Mary Harrington Nelson was a Navy nurse on duty at the Naval Hospital in Cañacao, Cavite, Philippine Islands, when World War II began. She had been there since February 1941, after tours of duty in San Diego and Mare Island, CA. She was a graduate of St. Joseph's Mercy Hospital School of Nursing in Sioux City, IA, and had worked in hospitals in Iowa and South Dakota before receiving her appointment to the Navy Nurse Corps in 1937. After the fall of the Philippines in January 1942, the Japanese moved the Navy nurses to the internment camp of Santo Tomas; there they cared for civilian patients until May 1943, when they were moved to Los Baños to set up a hospital for a new internment camp. When the camp was liberated by the American forces in February 1945, it held over 2,000 internees. The Navy nurses were awarded the Bronze Star and the Unit Citation with star for their work while prisoners of war. Lieutenant Harrington returned to the United States and in April 1945 married Page Nelson, a civilian Treasury Department employee whom she had met in the Los Baños camp. She resigned from the Navy in November 1945 when the Nurse Corps was downsizing and encouraging married nurses to return to civilian life. For many years Mrs. Nelson did volunteer nursing. She and Mr. Nelson have four children and six grandchildren.

Cynthia Neverdon-Morton

Cynthia Neverdon-Morton is a history professor at Coppin State College in Baltimore. Her experience in discovering and relating the contributions of African Americans—especially women—to the history of this nation has been extensive. Professor Neverdon-Morton earned her bachelor's and master's degrees in American history at Morgan State University and her doctorate in recent American history from Howard University. She has taught at both the secondary and college levels, developing teaching modules for larger use, serving in administrative capacities, and acting as historical consultant, coordinator, or project director for the development of historical and educational products. She has also served as historian for the Army's Aberdeen Proving Ground Ordnance Center and School and as HBCU Fellow with the Department of

Defense's 50th Anniversary of World War II Commemoration Committee. Dr. Neverdon-Morton has received multiple fellowships and grants for research and related travel (including Fulbright and NEH) and numerous honors for her work. She has been invited to take part in professional conferences and events both inside and outside government and in academic and community-service settings to discuss the many facets of the historical black experience. Dr. Neverdon-Morton has published numerous book reviews, book chapters, journal articles, a monographic study, and a book entitled *Afro-American Women of the South and the Advancement Race, 1895–1925*. She is a dedicated member and officer of many professional and community organizations.

Paula Nassen Poulos

Paula Nassen Poulos served as director of the conference, "A Woman's War Too: U.S. Women in the Military in World War II," and as editor of this volume of proceedings. As an education specialist in the National Archives Office of Public Programs, she develops educational materials and publications based on archival documents for a variety of audiences and conducts a wide range of courses on primary source research. She earned her Ph.D. degree in classics from The Ohio State University. Her teaching, research, and professional presentations focused on ancient Greek language, literature, and manuscripts. In conjunction with the National Archives' "Birth of Democracy" exhibition, she developed a symposium and public lecture series that highlighted aspects of ancient Greek democracy and served as academic consultant for the nationally syndicated issue of *The Mini Page* "Greek Democracy and Us." Dr. Poulos held previous positions on the tenured faculty of The University of Tennessee's Department of Classics and the general faculty of the University of Virginia's division of special programs. She serves on the policy board of the National History Education Network.

Mary T. Sarnecky

Col. Mary Sarnecky served as nursing history consultant to the Surgeon General of the Army and adjunct assistant professor of medical history at the Uniformed Services University of the Health Sciences in Bethesda, MD. She was also a nurse researcher at Walter Reed Army Medical Center in Washington, DC. Her nursing, supervisory, research, and teaching service has been recognized through the years with both research grants and awards and decorations. Colonel Sarnecky earned her master of nursing degree at the University of South Carolina and a doctor of nursing science degree from the University of San Diego. She has published articles in service and nursing journals on the history and science of nursing and the Army Nurse Corps. She is active in professional organizations. Her presentations to nursing, medical science, and U.S. Army groups have been extensive. Colonel Sarnecky retired from the Army Nurse Corps in June 1996 and is completing a history of the Army Nurse Corps, which will be published by the University of Pennsylvania Press in 1997.

Kenneth D. Schlessinger

Kenneth Schlessinger is an archivist with the Archives II Reference Branch at the National Archives at College Park. He has previously held positions in the Military Reference Branch and the Records Declassification Division of the National Archives. He holds a B.A. degree from Case Western Reserve University and has pursued graduate work at Georgetown University. Mr. Schlessinger is a member of the Society for Military History and the Mid-Atlantic Regional Archives Conference.

Janet Sims-Wood

Janet Sims-Wood is the assistant chief librarian for reference/reader services at the Moorland-Spingarn Research Center, Howard University. Her research interests encompass oral history, military history, and bibliographic research in African-American women's history. Included among her publications are six book-length bibliographies, newspaper articles, book chapters, and journal articles. She has also produced several slide presentations on African-American women. Dr. Sims-Wood is a founding associate editor of *Sage: A Scholarly Journal on Black Women* and founder of Afro Resources, Inc., which published the 1993 World War II Black WAC calendar. She received her doctorate in women's studies from the Union Institute upon completing an oral history dissertation funded by an NEH fellowship on black Wacs who served during World War II. Dr. Sims-Wood has acted as consultant to Carlson Publishing Company's *Black Women in America* series and to such special grant projects as the three-volume series *Voices of Triumph*, for Time/Life Books, and WETA's public broadcasting program on Marian Anderson. As an oral historian, she has interviewed World War II veterans for the D.C. Special Arts.

David C. Smith

David C. Smith is Bird and Bird Professor of History at the University of Maine. Together with Dr. Judy Barrett Litoff, Professor Smith has devoted the last decade to locating and collecting the letters written by U.S. women, both military and civilian, during World War II. Their accumulated manuscript holdings consist of 30,000 wartime letters and constitute the largest collection of its kind in the world. A microfilm edition of these letters, to be published by Scholarly Resources, Inc., is in preparation. Dr. Smith and Dr. Litoff are the co-authors of four books on Women and World War II: *We're In This War, Too: World War II Letters from American Women in Uniform* (Oxford, 1994); *Since You Went Away: World War II Letters from American Women on the Home Front* (Oxford, 1991; paperback ed., University Press of Kansas, 1995); *Dear Boys: World War II Letters from a Woman Back Home* (University Press of Mississippi, 1991); and *Miss You: The World War II Letters of Barbara Wooddall Taylor and Charles E. Taylor* (University of Georgia Press, 1990). They are co-editors of *American Women in a World at War: Contemporary Accounts from World War II* (Scholarly Resources, 1996). They are also the co-authors of 20 articles and reviews on women and World War II, including " 'To the Rescue of the Crops': The Women's Land Army of World War II," which appeared in *Prologue: Quarterly of the National Archives* and for which they were awarded the 1994 James Madison Prize by the Society for History in the Federal Government.

Eleanor H. Stoddard

Eleanor Stoddard's career has spanned both the public and private sector. During World War II she worked in the Office of Price Administration and the Army Quartermaster General. She later moved into journalism, advertising, public relations, and public policy research. Between 1965 and 1983, Ms. Stoddard gathered data on U.S. science funding for the National Science Foundation and produced reports for decision makers. Upon retirement, she took a course in oral history at the University of Maryland. Inspired by her first interview with a former Wac, she conducted oral history interviews with 35 World War II military women in almost all of the services, including military nurses, and two with Red Cross recreation workers. Her interviews are on file in the archives of California State University, Long Beach. Four oral histories have been published in *MINERVA: Quarterly Report on Women and the Military*. Ms. Stoddard is a graduate of Vassar College.

Mary V. Stremlow

Col. Mary Stremlow, USMCR (ret.), is Deputy Director of the New York State Division of Veterans' Affairs. Her responsibilities include planning, supervising, and coordinating the state's veterans service program as well as identifying and addressing issues of concern to New York's women veterans. The New York State Assembly named her Woman Veteran of the Year in 1994. After graduating from the State University College at Buffalo, she was commissioned in the U.S. Marine Corps and served on active duty as a commissary officer, platoon commander, battalion S-3, and battalion executive officer. As a reservist, she commanded the corps's mobilization station in Buffalo. Colonel Stremlow was awarded the Legion of Merit upon retirement in 1985. Among her publications are *The History of Women Marines, 1946-1977*; *Coping with Sexism in the Military*, intended for young women considering a career in the armed services; and *Free a Marine to Fight: Women Marines in World War II*, a Pamphlet History in the Marines in World War II Commemorative Series. She has also taught in Buffalo public schools and worked for Bethlehem Steel and at the LTV Aerospace and Defense Company, Sierra Research Division. Colonel Stremlow is on the board of directors of the Marine Corps Historical Foundation and the Buffalo Naval and Servicemen's Park. She serves as vice-president for the Sea Services of the Reserve Officers Association Department of New York and as a member of veterans' advocacy organizations.

Sheila E. Widnall

Sheila Widnall is Secretary of the Air Force and the first woman to head a branch of the U.S. Armed Forces. Appointed in 1993, she is responsible for recruiting, training, and retaining highly qualified service personnel; research and development; and other activities prescribed by the President and Secretary of Defense. In previous positions with the Air Force, she served on the USAF Academy Board of Visitors and on advisory committees to the Military Airlift Command and Wright-Patterson Air Force Base. Dr. Widnall received her doctor of science degree from the Massachusetts Institute of Technology. She was the first alumna appointed to the faculty of the school of engineering and the first woman to serve as chair of the 900-member faculty. During her 28 years at MIT as professor of aeronautics and astronautics and associate provost, she gained recognition for advancements in aerospace research and development, engineering education, and the expansion of roles for women and minorities in the fields of science and engineering. Dr. Widnall is internationally known for her work in fluid dynamics, specifically in the areas of aircraft turbulence and spiraling airflows, or vortices, created by helicopters. She has written more than 70 publications. Among her many impressive awards and honors is the prestigious *Young Man of the Year Award* bestowed by the American Institute of Aeronautics and Astronautics. Dr. Widnall has served on boards, panels, and committees in industry, government, and academia.

Barry L. Zerby

Barry Zerby is an archivist with the Archives II Reference Branch at the National Archives at College Park. He has previously held positions in the Military Reference Branch and the Records Declassification Division. Mr. Zerby holds a B.A. degree from Muhlenberg College. He is a member of the Mid-Atlantic Regional Archives Conference and the Naval Institute.

INDEX